# ASHOKA

*in Ancient India*

# ASHOKA
## in Ancient India

NAYANJOT LAHIRI

HARVARD UNIVERSITY PRESS

Cambridge, Massachusetts

London, England

2015

First published in India by Permanent Black, 2015

First Harvard University Press edition, 2015

First Printing

*Library of Congress Cataloging-in-Publication Data*

Lahiri, Nayanjot.
Ashoka in ancient India / Nayanjot Lahiri.
pages cm
Includes bibliographical references and index.
ISBN 978-0-674-05777-7 (cloth : alk. paper)
1. Asoka, King of Magadha, active 259 B.C.    2. India—Kings and rulers—Biography.
3. India—History—Maurya dynasty, ca. 322 B.C.–ca. 185 B.C.
I. Title.
DS451.5.L35 2015
934′.045092—dc23
[B]

*for*

RUKUN

As works of the imagination, the historian's work
and the novelist's work do not differ.
Where they do differ is that the historian's picture
is meant to be true.

**R.G. Collingwood,**
*The Historical Imagination* **(1935)**

# Contents

# Illustrations

*Items in italics denote colour pictures*

# Maps

# Acknowledgements

THIS BOOK ORIGINATED IN THE STRANGEST OF CIRcumstances. An email arrived from Sharmila Sen of Harvard University Press, inviting me to consider doing a single-volume biography of Ashoka which, as she put it, should be 'geared for a general, educated audience without sacrificing scholarship.' This was in the summer of 2009, during a phase in my life when I was steeped in administrative work at the University of Delhi. I had never met Sharmila, nor corresponded with her, and she is probably not even aware that her invitation became a lifeline of sorts, pulling me out of the fatigue of executive duties and endless files. While it took a couple of years before I could immerse myself in the fieldwork around the landscapes where this book took shape, I owe a great deal to Sharmila for writing to me and taking her chances. Over the years our conversations, and the unending supply of books on antiquity sent by her, have proved invaluable.

A number of friends and colleagues have supported this work in various ways. While he was vice chancellor of the University of Delhi, Deepak Pental gave me a powerful official position in his administration which provided a ringside view of how authority is exercised. That experience—notwithstanding the fact that Professor Pental had an entirely different end in mind—has played an important role in shaping my understanding of political authority in ancient India. Ramachandra Guha sent comments and insights on the initial proposal and has supported it ever since with great enthusiasm. Ratna Raman's companionship and formidable knowledge of all things culinary made fieldwork enormously pleasant in Andhra Pradesh, Karnataka, and Uttar Pradesh. I am also grateful to Devika Rangachari, Dilip Chakrabarti, Jairam Ramesh, Rakesh Tiwari, Vivek Suneja, and Upinder Singh for reading and critiquing parts of the manuscript. Ella Datta's advice on acquiring images was tremendously helpful. Kesavan Veluthat and Shalini Shah in Delhi and Parimal Rupani in Junagadh provided some important references, and Suryanarayana Nanda guided me through the inscriptions of Ashoka. I must also acknowledge the two anonymous reviewers who read the manuscript for Permanent Black and Harvard University Press with great care and insight. Some of their suggestions have improved the narrative in many ways.

At the various places where I pursued this research, I owe a profound debt to many institutions and people, especially the officers of the Archaeological Survey of India: in Junagadh, Rasik Bhatt, J.P. Bhatt, M. Sutaria, and K.C. Nauriyal; in Nepal, Hari D. Rai; in Karnataka and Andhra, S.V.P. Hallakati and Srinivas; in Uttar Pradesh, Subhash Yadav; in Madhya Pradesh, S.B. Ota; in Delhi, V.N. Prabhakar, the staff of the Archaeological Survey of India library, especially Satpal Singh, and Dr Narendra Kumar at the Central Library of the University of Delhi.

Because of the disappearance of high editorial skills in book publishing nowadays, Rukun Advani is already the subject of folklore among the discerning. The reason, in my experience, has to do with his breadth of knowledge and the surgical skill with which he transforms scripts when he relates well to them and their authors. His imagination and precision have made doing books with him the most intensely enjoyable experience of my professional life, and this book has been no different. His interest in the sound and music of prose as part of the art of writing well has also sustained me in numerous ways. For adding lightness to the often ponderous pen of a professional archaeologist, and much else, this book is dedicated to him.

At a purely personal level my greatest debt is to Kishore Lahiri for a lifetime of encouragement and support. This book is dedicated to the three children in our lives—our daughter-in-law Vrinda; our son Karan; and, of course, Soufflé—who are more precious to us than they can ever imagine. Vrinda and Karan's enormous affection and interest have enriched me and my work in myriad wonderful ways, and the unconditional love of Soufflé, our dog, is a constant source of joy in my life.

\* \* \*

The following illustrations are reproduced with thanks by permission from the following sources: Fig. 3.1 and Fig. 8.1, copyright Archaeological Survey of India (ASI), is from Marshall (1951), reprinted by permission of the ASI. The sculptural motifs in chapter opening pages and section separations are from Poonacha (2013); Fig. 10.9 from Patna Museum (Patna); Fig. 10.5 from Hari D. Rai (Lumbini); Fig. 12.1 from the Delhi Art Gallery (New Delhi); Fig. 12.2 from the National Gallery of Modern Art (New Delhi); Fig. Epilogue 3 from ITC Limited (New Delhi). Maps 1, 2, and 3 are drawn by Rashid Lone (University of Delhi).

# Prelude

THERE IS NOTHING SPECIALLY STRIKING ABOUT THE cluster of rocks which crowns the edge of a low hilly ridge near the village of Erragudi in the Andhra region of India. From a distance the cluster appears unremarkable, while the ridge on which it sits is somewhat bare, rising out of a patchwork of cultivated fields and sparsely dotted with vegetation. The rocks on it are not imposing, standing a mere thirty metres or so above the plains. It is what one sees on the rocks at close quarters that makes them spectacular.

Cascading down the rocks is a dramatic waterfall of words. More than a hundred lines in characters of the ancient Brahmi script are imprinted across several of the boulders (Fig. Prelude 2). Large portions of this ancient scrawl are even now exceedingly clear, the characters boldly etched across the rock faces. Some segments have deteriorated, while a few of the lines have been defaced by modern graffiti. Yet not even the English and Telugu scribbles of contemporary visitors to this hillock can diminish the overwhelming impression of messages from antiquity created by the profusion of these ancient words. This copious transcription on rocks is part of a royal enunciation. The words and phrases that comprise it were composed by and inscribed at the instructions of Ashoka ('the sorrowless one'), the third emperor of the dynasty of the Mauryas—and the subject of this book.

Fig. Prelude 1: Erragudi rocks as they appear from the surrounding fields

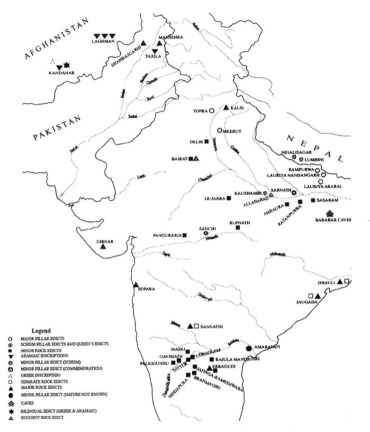

Map 1: Distribution of the Epigraphs of Ashoka

Some 2200 years ago this political figure made himself visible through the words that he caused to be inscribed at Erragudi as well as at scores of other places across India and beyond.

Ashoka's inscriptions represent a kind of historical daybreak, ending a long phase of faceless rulers. In approximately 600 BCE, kings emerged out of the realms of tradition to set up and rule over several kingdoms stretching from the highlands of the north-west frontier to the lowlands of the Ganges, and southwards across the Vindhya mountains till the Godavari river on the Deccan plateau. There were powerful and not-so-powerful kings, aggrandizing rulers who were aspirants to the appellation 'chief king of all kings', and powerful confederate clans.[1] Over a relatively short period of time—roughly coinciding with the domination of Athens in the classical period—a large part of this profusion of political entities was absorbed into a single imperial realm. Centred in Magadha, which was based in the middle Gangetic plains of Bihar, a succession of kings ruled over this empire straddling large parts of India. The first of these imperial houses was that of the Nandas. They were followed by the Mauryas. From the fourth century BCE till the advent of Ashoka (*c.* 269/268 BCE), there were said to have been eleven such imperial monarchs,[2] nine in the Nanda dynasty, followed by the two Maurya kings who preceded Ashoka: Chandragupta, founder of the dynasty (Ashoka's grandfather, who overthrew the Nandas), followed by Bindusara, Ashoka's father.

But though king succeeded king and one century followed another, the only evidence of those times are versions of them—some accurate, others fanciful, and practically never contemporary—that have survived. These remaining records of those times are the *Puranas*, certain Buddhist and Jaina texts, and histories of a sort by people who are referred to as 'classical authors'—mainly literate companions in Alexander's entourage—as also the famous Megasthenes who visited the court of Chandragupta. These sources provide us with nearly all the information that we now have of India's rulers and states in that antique time. The rulers themselves failed to speak to their subjects, and therefore to us. Many of their names, and of their principalities, are known: Janaka of Videha, Pasenadi of Kosala, the Magadha monarch Bimbisara, and Pradyota of Avanti are some. But how such kings defined their domains and powers, how they appeared to their subjects, what they and their queens donated, and what kind of worship prevailed in their courts—these remain hidden because no royal epigraphs or labelled sculptures, no coins carrying royal portraiture or the names of kings and queens, not even palaces or communications emanating from such places and people, have endured.

It is this pervasive absence of royal voices that makes Ashoka stand out as an irresistible historical subject. There are other reasons as well for the interest in him. In relation to his predecessors, he was the first Indian king to rule over an empire embracing much of India and its western borderlands, from Afghanistan to Orissa and towards the south as far as Karnataka. In relation to the rulers who followed him, it was his example which influenced thought—philosophical, religious, cultural—in Asia more profoundly than that of any other political figure of antiquity. The appeal of Ashoka as a model of rulership, even in his own lifetime, is clear from the way in which the Lankan king Devanampiya Tissa (*c.* 247–207 BCE) is said to have established the Buddhist faith in Lanka. This happened after Ashoka sent him gifts which were used for his second coronation, and a message encouraging him to take refuge in the Buddha.[3] Ashoka's influence, much after his time, is unmistakable because he became an icon among Buddhist rulers, 'the great precedent and model of some of the emergent polities of South and Southeast Asia.'[4] In China, for instance, his shaping influence became discernible from the directions taken by several rulers. Emperor Wu of the Liang dynasty (502–49 CE) is an example of a ruler who tried to emulate Ashoka by erecting stupas and forbidding the consumption of alcohol and meat; the Chinese empress Wu Zetian (623/625–705 CE), at least initially, followed suit by projecting herself as a wheel-turning monarch or 'chakravartin', an image of Buddhist kingship closely associated with Ashoka.[5] H.G. Wells had this in mind when, in his massive bestseller of the 1920s, *The Outline of History*, he said that amidst

> the tens of thousands of names of monarchs that crowd the columns of history, their majesties and graciousnesses, and serenities and royal highnesses and the like, the name of Ashoka shines, and shines almost alone, a star. From the Volga to Japan, his name is still honoured. China, Tibet, and even India, though it has left his doctrine, preserve the tradition of his greatness. More living men cherish his memory today than ever heard the names of Constantine or Charlemagne.[6]

But, above all, Ashoka stands out because his story is, to a considerable extent, preserved in his own words. This was nicely articulated by Jawaharlal Nehru in his *The Discovery of India* when he said that in their magnificent language Ashoka's edicts spoke to him of a 'a man who though, an emperor, was greater than any king or emperor.'[7] Nehru, like Ashoka, was for many years the unquestioned ruler of an Indian territory roughly the same size; more important, he followed Ashoka in being his own 'sutradhar' (narrator).

Ashoka naturally also figures in many ancient chronicles, even if not in those by his contemporaries. He appears in writings that were put together several centuries after his reign, ranging from the Sanskrit text *Ashokavadana* (*c.* second century CE) to the Sri Lankan Pali chronicles like the *Dipavamsa* (*c.* fourth century CE) and the *Mahavamsa* (*c.* fifth century CE). These will figure at different points in this story of Ashoka because such writings shape our understanding of his early years as prince and monarch, even as we bear in mind that their reliability as sources of biographical information is uncorroborated by anything written during or even close to his own time. The reliability of historical detail in such texts, though, can be assessed by juxtaposing them with what can be reconstructed about those times through archaeological evidence. This is perhaps one of the defining differences between monarchs of very ancient times on the one hand, and those of medieval and later times on the other. Of Akbar and some of the other major Mughals, for instance, we arrive at a picture via works by their contemporaries. And at least three of the close collaborators of Sultan Saladin (1137/38–1193 CE)—the iconic Muslim ruler whose name is associated with the Crusades (especially with the recapture of Jerusalem from European Crusaders in 1187 CE)—penned accounts of his life and reign, each providing direct testimony of the ruler.[8] Not so Ashoka, whose persona can be seen in chronicles written some four centuries after his death. These show us how a variety of texts chose to understand Ashoka's life and times; but the details within such accounts have to be looked at with a sceptical eye, in part because they may have been purposive, or shaped by the ideological predispositions of commissioning patrons; in part because they are frequently coloured by the individual preconceptions and assumptions of their authors; and in part because when reading them it often becomes difficult to separate the historical Ashoka from the idealized literary portrait of a Buddhist monarch. An element of discrimination can be introduced by using archaeology to assess the reliability of parts of the legends and literature surrounding the Mauryan emperor. But, on the whole, given the limitations, it is clearly not possible to write up Ashoka's life in a way that meets modern biographical criteria. Fortunately, Ashoka does not have to be written about only in this way. We can understand his kingship and his personality, his empire and its neighbours, because he himself, fairly early in his kingly career, chose to speak.

The communicator *par excellence* of ancient India, Ashoka spent a great deal of time thinking through and having messages about his conception of morality engraved on stone for public consumption. Other Asian rulers also communicated through inscriptions, notably the Achaemenid kings of Iran (550–330 BCE). However, unlike Ashoka's, their public inscriptions devote much space and superlatives to how foes were killed off and conquered.[9]

There is, of course, great communicative diversity in different societies and time periods, and kingly epigraphs carved on stone represent one method. Naturally, however, much of the communication in the first millennium BCE was really not through writing but through talk and speech. Rhetoric in ancient Greece, with its emphasis on logical argument, reasoned debate, and emotive persuasion was in this mode. Such communication between rulers and the ruled was far more direct and audience-centred than in classical China and early India, where the aim was to explicate what were believed to be self-evident truths.[10] The contrast can be made even clearer in other ways: in literary representations before *c.* 450 BCE, kings, nobles, and leaders in the Graeco-Roman world aimed to shape actions through words. So, for instance, in the *Iliad*, Nestor's 'argument sweeter than honey' is what convinces Patroclus to fight Hector, and later histories support this and other similar images of the power of rhetoric.[11] To break the rhetorical spell cast by a one-way address, most of the Socratic dialogues recorded by Plato introduce an interruptive dialectical method which makes speakers stop, repeat themselves, and explain what they mean. For such thinkers, written material—which by its very nature is a closed and one-way discourse—was the antithesis of 'the give-and-take' that formed the basis of public discourse and dialogue.[12]

In ancient China speech was the primary medium for the exchange of ideas, and effective speech was thought a valid and vital instrument of government.[13] In fact, an early work called the *Book of History* (which took proper form in the sixth century BCE) was primarily concerned with speech and speech-making. Unlike Greece, however, the focus in China was not on individual excellence but on the authority of a venerated past.[14] The kind of person who found favour with the Chinese was not one who spoke to attract attention to himself by being different but who manifested through his personality the sagacity to conform to the social norm. Even in the philosophy of Confucius (*c.* 530–479 BCE), with its focus on the self-purification of individuals, the aim was to create a society in which harmony would prevail 'because propriety and loyalty would be practised by the rulers and the people.'[15]

As in China, the oral tradition in India is massive and long, people in both these old cultures showing much greater faith in speech than written communication.[16] The cultural ethos within which debate and discussion took place was rarely individual-centred. Debates were usually communal and group oriented, and in India regulated and restricted along caste lines. Within the major religious traditions, as for example among Vedic priests and Buddhist monks, writing was not used for preserving knowledge until many centuries after their respective religious texts had been composed. In the Vedic tradition, the power of the word, and the dissemination of knowledge to restricted groups through recitation and repetition, depended entirely upon oral transmission.[17] Gautama Buddha (*c.* 540–480 BCE), who consciously chose to speak across caste lines, also did so through conversations and sermons, not via writing.[18] Even after the texts associated with him were written down, the importance of hearing about the Buddha's life and teachings remained pre-eminent and shines through in constant invocations, such as 'Thus have I heard' and 'when he had thus spoken'.[19] Political culture in the time of the Buddha—at least

wherever it finds mention in the texts that describe those times—
also emphasized orality. Meetings in assemblies were constantly
highlighted by the Buddha in his description of the clans that made
up the Vajjian confederacy of North India (*c.* sixth century BCE).
Their vigorous debates were oral interactions that never came to
be recorded. Listening rather than reading was also the hallmark of
political training among princes, as we learn from the *Arthashastra*,
a text whose core was almost certainly composed around the
time of Ashoka's grandfather, Chandragupta. The prince, the text
prescribes, should engage in 'listening to Itihasa', and he should
'listen repeatedly to things not learnt'.[20] The king was meant, too,
to 'hear' about all matters connected with the people, the emphasis
being on the ruler engaging with them in the assembly hall of his
royal capital, not in and around the places where the populace
resided. Royal communiqués on matters concerning morality or
welfare schemes or patterns of kingly conduct are absent from
such ruler–ruled interactions. From whichever angle we examine
the character of public communication in India before the time of
Ashoka, we find it was largely through some form of oral discourse.
The emperor's edicts, thus, were a milestone inasmuch as this type
of public communication in written form began with him.

The style of the new communication was also highly individual-
istic. In his stone messages we encounter Ashoka speaking about
the several watersheds of his royal life, and through his words we
witness how he re-created his own path while trying to remould the
lives of people in his empire (as also of those beyond its borders).
Candour and emotion, death and decimation, honest admissions
and imperious orders are all to be found in the Ashokan edicts. Since
his messages were not inscribed all at once but over many years, it
becomes possible to examine Ashoka's persona not as that of a static
sovereign but as an evolving emperor of uncommon ambition.

Equally, through these missives on stone Ashoka chose to reach
out to his people in, most unusually, the places where they lived and
worshipped. By doing so, he literally carved out a subcontinental
presence for himself. This is evident to anyone who has followed
his trail. One encounters him on rocks and pillars in all kinds of

places that formed part of his empire, right across India, Nepal, Pakistan, and Afghanistan. This is because the emperor chose to disseminate his messages by ensuring that his administration sent out multiple copies of them. That he wanted to be heard in the same way in Afghanistan and in Andhra, in Karnataka and in Kalinga, also means that Ashoka's version of his life and deeds is the one that was likely to have been the best known, certainly during his own lifetime. There is no example, in fact, of an ancient ruler whose voice, in the course of his own life, resonated in such a unique way across South Asia and beyond, articulating the shifting contours of his imperial vision and aspirations. As I said, this is not the only version of his life available to scholars, nor does it permit a complete reconstruction of his life. However, it has the great merit of being what was composed during his rulership, and on his orders.

The past comes down to us preserved in objects and words. The challenge lies in trying to tease out Ashoka's story by listening to the emperor's own voice even while paying attention to the many stories that emerge in archaeology about the lives and times of his more ordinary contemporaries. By Ashoka's own account, his wide dominions had a large and diverse population, from city residents and members of religious sects to ordinary rural folk, forest dwellers, and fisher people. Archaeology allows us to peep into the places where such ordinary folk lived, to find out what food they ate, to imagine their ideas about rulers and religion, to travel with them as they journeyed forth, and to appreciate the remarkable paintings that they sometimes made on the very waysides where the emperor's voice could be heard.[21] Such sights and subjects will be explored as we try to understand the India of Ashoka's time, above all because such archaeological glimpses offer a reality check on Ashoka's own prescriptions and proscriptions.

Modern India—as indeed modern Sri Lanka, Tibet, Nepal, and Myanmar—continues to be interested in Ashoka as the Buddhist king of later traditions rather than the all-too-human emperor of his own time. Notwithstanding the great deal that has been written about him, I will try to show that a 'biography' of Ashoka cannot really be disentangled from the legends and perceptions, Buddhist hagiography, and the many validations and valorizations of later times surrounding him. This difficulty is not specific to Ashoka; it is precisely the package of problems that scholars grappling with other ancient lives have faced. Biographers of Alexander the Great (c. 356–323 BCE) have, for example, drawn attention to the contradictory and non-contemporary character of narrative accounts of his life and career, all of which were composed many hundred years after his death. While such writings relied on a wide range of earlier works, none of those originals have actually survived except in highly fragmentary form, which has resulted in a lack of agreement among modern scholars about their reliability. Again, for a ruler whose public image was so important to him, it is ironic that the bulk of the surviving images of Alexander are later Hellenistic or Roman 'copies'. Even the two coins on which he is reliably represented were issued not by him but by his successors with the idea of deploying his power and charisma to elevate their own political standing.[22] These are among the reasons, as the archaeologist John Cherry put it, 'why there can really be no such thing as "the historical Alexander"'.[23]

And so is it with the story of Cleopatra (or Cleopatra VII), the extraordinary queen who ruled over Egypt (51–30 BCE) and who, like Alexander, has continued to fascinate the contemporary public imagination.[24] Notwithstanding the spate of 'biographies' written of her, no version of the events of her life and reign was penned in her own time, nor is there a detailed family background available which might have helped explain many aspects of her life. The name of Cleopatra's mother, for instance, is not known, and Cleopatra's own birth is unrecorded. That she was probably born in 70/69 BCE was calculated on the basis of her death in 30 BCE, and the fact that she was apparently 39 years old when she died. Even this calculation is based on the description of her life in Plutarch's *Life of Antony*, the most complete account of her career from the ancient world. However, Plutarch was writing in the first–second century CE, so his can hardly be considered a contemporary account.[25] As one of Cleopatra's most recent biographers puts it, 'we cannot hope to hear Cleopatra's true voice, and are forced to see her through secondary

eyes; eyes already coloured by other people's propaganda, prejudi-
ces and assumptions.'[26]

If therefore biographies of the kind that are written about
medieval and modern figures cannot be written of comparable
kings and queens of antiquity, however 'great' they may have been, it
makes the case of a Mauryan emperor less peculiar and much more
like those other ancient lives. Recovering Ashoka's life and times
from what has morphed into legend is an exercise in providing him
with contextual flesh, and teasing out his individual psychology
and personality to the extent possible from what was composed on
his orders as well as from what is archaeologically knowable about
the lifeways of the more ordinary people of his time. By peering
over the palisades of a Mauryan city, by journeying along the roads
that were used by travellers in those times, by studying the art and
artefacts made and used by his people, we can imagine the world
of Ashoka and understand the character and the challenges of the
times in which the life of this emperor unfolded.

This book, thus, is more in the nature of a chronicle around a
royal life. It deals with how Ashoka lived and how he ruled, and,
above all, what he thought and how he disseminated his ideas. I
salvage his persona as much as credibility permits. And my salvage
operation is based as much on what he himself articulated as on
what came to be preserved in the form of archaeological relics that
remain of the environment which shaped his life and times.

Why another *Ashoka*?[27]

Partly because Ashoka has fascinated generations of writers
and scholars. The fascination stems in some ways from the fact
that we are drawn to leaders and public figures whose ideas and
actions have influenced the lives of large populations. Ancient
India shows several powerful rulers, but they have not captivated
the minds of modern writers in the way that Ashoka has. A conquering king like Samudragupta (*c.* 350–370 CE), for instance,
combined aggrandizement on a subcontinental scale with a
personal predilection for music and poetry. The formidable queen
of Kashmir, Didda (*c.* tenth century CE), exercised political power
for close to fifty years, first behind the scenes and then overtly; in

the process she overshadowed every male ruler of that region. Yet
neither Samudragupta nor Didda has lured modern historians
with a biographical bent.[28] This may well be because the sources
are thought inadequate, a view borne out by a contrasting example,
that of Harshavardhana of Thaneshwar and Kanauj (606–648 CE),
whose biography, the *Harshacarita*, was composed in his own lifetime. Harshavardhana is known to have authored dramas and
epigraphs, and his court was visited and described in all its richness
by the Chinese pilgrim Xuanzang. The sources for writing about
him are therefore, relatively speaking, richer, resulting in a variety
of biographical and regnal studies.[29] On balance, though, there is
much truth in Ramachandra Guha's view that 'the art of biography remains underdeveloped in South Asia.'[30] Perhaps the only
scholar of ancient India whose books represent an exception to this
perspective is the historian-politician Radhakumud Mookerji, who
wrote voluminously and valuably on ancient kings, most notably
books on Chandragupta Maurya, Ashoka, and Harshavardhana.

Considering the general dearth of biographical interest in ancient India's royal *dramatis personae*, how may one explain the
popularity of Ashoka? In large part this is because of his own
keenness to appear to posterity as neither recondite nor imperious
but instead as a flesh-and-blood emperor guided less by power than
by compassion. Among rulers Ashoka is so exceptional in being
upfront about sharing his grief that it is difficult not to empathize
with him. An ancient sovereign who took responsibility for a politically reprehensible action, he seems at times less a political figure
than a strikingly self-reflective individual. The contrast with the
archetypically self-serving politician is so stark and rare that Ashoka
arouses in historians a knee-jerk admiration virtually unseen in
South Asia until the appearance of Mahatma Gandhi.[31]

Gandhi is also relevant for another reason. Indian nationalist
leaders and thinkers who fought the Raj under him and forged
the structure of an independent nation sought to image Ashoka
as their political fountainhead. India's long lineage of tolerance
and non-violence was seen as stretching back to the Buddha and,
from the perspective of the nationalist imagination, the temptation

to assume the mantle of Ashoka as a model of humane rulership was strong.[32] Tagore made this connection when he noted that 'countless great kingdoms of countless great monarchs have suffered devastation and have been razed to dust, but the glorious emergence of the power of benevolence in Asoka has become our proud asset, and is breathing strength into us.'[33] Gandhi's belief in non-violence, whether consciously or not, derived in part from the Ashokan worldview, and consequently breathed new life into a nearly forgotten political value system that Ashoka had inaugurated. The affinity that Nehru felt for Ashoka, movingly articulated in *The Discovery of India*, bears this out. On the verge of building a modern state in the shadow of Gandhi, it was natural for Nehru to identify with Ashoka.[34] Later, he invoked Ashoka on crucial public occasions—most notably when a resolution about India's flag was moved in 1947. This made explicit the association of modern Indian democracy with an Ashokan emblem, the Sarnath pillar capitol. When moving the resolution in the Constituent Assembly, Nehru said the presence of the wheel, the Ashoka chakra, made him feel 'exceedingly happy that in this sense indirectly we have associated with this flag of ours not only this emblem but in a sense the name of Asoka, one of the most magnificent names not only in India's history but in world history.'[35] With such rhetorical appropriations of antiquity are modern national identities forged and communities imagined, and it could be argued that Ashoka was the ace in Nehru's pack.

Adding to the charm and excitement of Ashoka was the dramatic way in which he had emerged out of unexpected discoveries and decipherments. Military men, antiquarians, and archaeologists had chanced upon epigraphs in an unknown writing on rocks and pillars in various parts of India in the early decades of the nineteenth century, a discovery saga which has been well told in various works on the evolution of Indian archaeology, most recently in Charles Allen's narrative history of the discovery of Ashoka.[36] Facsimiles of the objects and writings unearthed—from pillars in North India to rocks in Orissa and Gujarat—found their way to the Asiatic Society of Bengal. The meetings and publications of the

Society provided an unusually fertile environment for innovative speculation, with scholars constantly exchanging notes on, for instance, how they had deciphered the Brahmi letters of various epigraphs from Samudragupta's Allahabad pillar inscription, to the Karle cave inscriptions. The Eureka moment came in 1837 when James Prinsep, a brilliant secretary of the Asiatic Society, building on earlier pools of epigraphic knowledge, very quickly uncovered the key to the extinct Mauryan Brahmi script. Prinsep unlocked Ashoka; his deciphering of the script made it possible to read the inscriptions. All this and more has been superbly told by Charles Allen.

Allen's focus on the *British* discovery of Ashoka does run a small danger, namely the possible inference that this ruler of ancient India was pretty much a forgotten entity until Raj antiquarians and archaeologists exhumed him. While Allen is right in showing us the concatenation of chance archaeological discoveries that gave us the Ashoka we see today, it is worth stressing that there was a continuous textual tradition, from Kashmir down to Sri Lanka, in which Ashoka featured.[37] Historical memory in relation to virtually all rulers and dynasties was far more the preserve of textual traditions than of folk knowledge and popular belief. So, before his epigraphs were deciphered, Ashoka was known mainly to a fairly restricted group of traditional scholars and pundits in India and Buddhist communities across Asia. The fact that Ashoka was not common knowledge is not to say that he was largely unknown, unless one qualifies this with the truism that but for Orientalist endeavours virtually all of ancient India, as we have it today, would have remained unknown. The extent to which the British and other explorers and scholars fleshed Ashoka out moved the emperor from his hiding place in sometimes esoteric Brahmanical knowledge and hagiographical Buddhist texts, making him a far more generally familiar figure.

The earliest compilation to historicize Ashoka via his epigraphs was Alexander Cunningham's *Inscriptions of Asoka*.[38] Cunningham, founding father and first Director General of the Archaeological Survey of India, assembled the available epigraphs into the first volume of the *Corpus Inscriptionum Indicarum*. This epigraphic series aimed to make accessible all the inscriptions of ancient India. Cunningham did a great service to historical knowledge in seeing that a whole volume ought to be devoted to the Ashokan inscriptions (and a few others) that had, till then, been discovered. What added strength to Cunningham's compilation was that the archaeological dimensions of Ashokan sites—which, in many instances, he and his assistants had themselves explored—brought alive the landscapes over which Ashoka had inscribed his words. What may seem surprising from our perspective today—when we know that many of the edicts were inscribed on large rocks in Karnataka and Andhra—is that none of the emperor's southern epigraphs featured in that volume: those would be discovered a little later.[39]

Not all the nineteenth-century discoverers and decipherers, it is necessary to remember, were Europeans. One figure who was discovering Ashokan edicts in Maharashtra and Rajasthan around the same time that Cunningham and his assistants were scouring the countryside was the Indian archaeologist Bhagwanlal Indraji. His work is much less recognized than Cunningham's because the bulk of his early writings was in Gujarati.[40] In a letter of 1872 he reported his discovery of an Ashokan edict at Bairat: 'On the southern side of Virat is a hillock with ancient Buddhist ruins. Near the ruins once stood an engraved stone inscription of Ashoka, which at present lies in the Asiatic Society Museum in Calcutta. While I was on the northern side of Virat, I discovered a new inscription at the foothill. The inscription is broken, yet much of its portion is in a readable condition.'[41] Copies were made of this epigraph, but since his letter containing the details of his discovery was published in Gujarati in *Saurashtra Darpan*, he got no credit for it. Instead, A.C.L. Carlleyle, an assistant of Cunningham who arrived there soon after, came to be considered its discoverer. The conditions of power at the time of such discoveries, the inequality in equations between well-placed British officers and their subordinates, the superior abilities of Raj officials to articulate, communicate, and disseminate news—in short the conditions within which this knowledge was produced and circulated—are likely to have submerged or rendered invisible many a 'native informant' such as Bhagwanlal Indraji. This may seem a bit like raising the old query much beloved of Indian labour historians—did British supervising engineers build the Indian railways or were they built by Indian labour? The consensus presently being that all such achievement was both unequal and collaborative, the only sensible answer to such a question now is that the necessity of moving beyond it greatly exceeds its worth.

All the Ashokan epigraphs were not discovered in the nineteenth century. Engravings of the emperor have newly appeared through the twentieth century, from Afghanistan to Andhra.[42] The discoverers have been a diverse lot, from a gold prospector who chanced upon Ashoka's Maski inscription in Karnataka in 1915 to the guru of a math in Gavimath (also in Karnataka) who, in 1931, communicated the existence of what is today called the Gavimath edict. The discovery of an Ashokan edict was made at Ratanpurwa in Bihar as recently as 2009. The road to Ashoka is so paved with good epigraphs which keep popping out of the earth at irregular intervals that there is no reason to think of Ratanpurwa as the last step in this very rocky path.[43] Various texts and Buddhist works in which Mauryan rulers figure became widely available from the middle of the nineteenth century: the testimony of the Sri Lankan Pali chronicles, the *Dipavamsa* and the *Mahavamsa*, were central to the identification of Devanampiya Piyadassi as Ashoka. But it is perhaps the sheer volume of sporadically appearing epigraphic messages that has ensured the continuing scholarly interest in Ashoka.

Certainly, this was the assessment of the colonial scholar-civil servant Vincent Smith when he wrote *Asoka—The Buddhist Emperor of India*.[44] As the first modern biography of the emperor, this book strove to tell a historical story strongly on the basis of the emperor's words. Its core was devoted to the history and chronology of Ashoka, the extent of his empire, the way in which it was administered, the monuments that Ashoka built, and the epigraphs. Smith also provided translations of and subheadings to each of the edicts. So, for instance, the Thirteenth or Kalinga Rock Edict, where the war and Ashoka's repentance were described, was given the title 'True Conquest'. Textual traditions, those of Sri Lanka and India, too found a place even in Smith's book, though the author made his opinion of them clear at the outset. They were, he said, 'of no historical value, and should be treated simply as edifying romances.'[45] He was of the firm conviction that no king East or West could match Ashoka, the only ruler to combine in himself the duties of a monk and a monarch. Coming from Vincent Smith, an administrator of imperial inclinations and views, such unambiguous approval was a refreshing surprise: most of Smith's writings were known for their sweeping generalization that the stimulus of all ancient Indian high culture lay in the West.[46] Realizing that the obvious comparison would be with the Roman emperor Constantine, Smith quickly dismissed it for the reason that Constantine's patronage of Christianity was 'an act of tardy and politic submission to a force already irresistible, than the willing devotion of an enthusiastic believer.' Ashoka, on the other hand, transformed the creed of a local sect which had 'captured his heart and intellect' into a world religion.[47]

Smith's book set the tone for many subsequent works on Ashoka in the sense that epigraphic sources became the inevitable and desirable guide when depicting him. The emphasis tended to depend upon the scholar, the various aspects of his life and times emerging with variations. The *Ashoka* of Devadatta Ramakrishna Bhandarkar, Carmichael Professor of Ancient Indian History and Culture in Calcutta University, appeared two decades after Smith's book and relied on Ashoka's epigraphs and monuments for a history of the ruler, who was described as 'the royal missionary'.[48] Much more space was devoted to the nature of Ashoka's engagement with Buddhism and the morality that he advocated over his paternalistic conception of kingship.[49] 'Ashoka's place in history'—a phrase much used by historians in the first half of the twentieth century— was the subject of a whole chapter, with Bhandarkar believing that Ashoka was second only to the Buddha in the history of the sect. The emperor's exuberance may by its excess have disturbed the balance between the material and the spiritual in ancient India, but Bhandarkar's recognition of this flaw did not allow him to upset the balance of his overall admiration. Radhakumud Mookerji's *Asoka* was in the same mould, with chapters on history, administration, and monuments.[50] The bulk of his volume was devoted to the texts—to translation and annotation of the inscriptions.

Of the early works on Ashoka there are good reasons for seeing Beni Madhab Barua's *Asoka and his Inscriptions* (1946) as diverging in many ways from the books by Smith and Barua's older Bengali contemporaries. Barua used a wider panorama of sources and strove to structure a different kind of account around Ashoka. His use of epigraphs was extensive, though he invariably attempted to also weave textual references into them. Importantly, and perhaps for the first time, the *Arthashastra* now came to be carefully mined for understanding the Mauryan state. Different facets of the same phenomenon were juxtaposed in the narrative: imperial and provincial administration, Ashoka's personal and public life, rajadharma and upasaka dharma in relation to its more universal Ashokan form. Barua's assessment of Ashoka's 'place in history' could, for all this, have been written by either Smith or Bhandarkar: 'Asoka did for the religion of Buddha what Darius the Great or Xerxes had done for that of the Avesta and St Paul did for that of Christ. He indeed raised Buddhism from the position of a local faith to the status of a world religion.'[51]

Fifteen years after Barua, Romila Thapar's assessment of Ashoka, based on her PhD thesis, was published as *Asoka and the Decline of the Mauryas*.[52] This study, which has since enjoyed wide popularity, was both similar to and different from the many books that preceded it. Though the sections dealing with Ashoka's early life, accession, chronology, internal administration, and socio-economic activity were written broadly in the spirit of her Indian predecessors, what gave her work a different flavour was that it sought to more carefully contextualize Ashoka in his time. So, for instance, his involvement in Buddhism was seen in the background of the 'unusually lively interest' that his father and grandfather displayed in eclectic ideas, those that came with the Greeks who travelled to their courts, as also via the religions anchored around the Ganga—Jainism and the Ajivika teachings.[53] Similarly, while dhamma was recognized as having been nurtured by Ashoka, it was simultaneously highlighted as being the king's novel solution to what he recognized as the problems of binding a multicultural society: 'To any intelligent statesman of the period it must have been evident that some kind of binding factor was necessary in order to keep the empire intact . . . The policy of *Dhamma* with its emphasis on social responsibility was intended to provide this binding factor.'[54] Equally, her work showed his policy of dhamma as evolving over his long reign which, towards the end, was seen as being marred by an overconfidence in his own achievement.[55] Examined closely, the book shows Ashoka as anchored in the circumstances and responding to the challenges of his time, but the persona that emerges from this conceptualization is all the same exceptional. A king who 'stressed the conscious application of humanitarianism in social behaviour, thus appealing not to the narrower religious instincts, but to a far wider and immediate feeling of social responsibility' is certainly singular and different from every other ruler of ancient India.[56] The argument is that the exception grows out of the norm and takes shape as exemplary form.

The modern scholarly fascination with Ashoka and the changing contours of research on him are evident in many other writings but my intention is not to explore them in all their nuances. An excellent guide to the range and richness of Ashokan studies can be found in Harry Falk's bibliography, *Asokan Sites and Artefacts*, which contains nearly 1800 entries.[57] All the big names of ancient Indian studies figure there—James Prinsep, Georg Buhler, Emile Senart, Radhakumud Mookerji, Romila Thapar, Dines Chandra Sircar, P.H.L. Eggermont, Kenneth Roy Norman, Awadh Kishore Narain, Patrick Olivelle, and Dilip Kumar Chakrabarti, to name a few. The bibliography lists hundreds of books and articles about Ashoka's epigraphs, several of which contain their texts and translations; others are expositions on various elements of the scripts and languages used, as well as on similarities and variations in the different versions of the inscriptions.

Writings on other aspects of Ashoka are no less impressive and include accounts of the art and architectural features of his various monuments; the diverse archaeology and historical geography of Ashokan sites; the emperor's ideas on public ethics, spiritual victory, the rights of living beings, human and animal; the image of Ashoka in the literature of Asia; comparisons between the edicts and texts like the *Bhagavadgita* and the *Indica* of Megasthenes; the personality of Ashoka; the fascinating story of the discovery of the epigraphs and of the emperor in them; and so much else.

Having read a fair range of these writings, I am inclined to put myself in the shoes of my readers to ask once again: Why another book on Ashoka? What makes this one different from the others?

*Ashoka in Ancient India* is a historical study of the life and times of the emperor through his epigraphs, through the archaeology and traditions in and around the places where these were put up, and through an imaginative construction of how people in ancient India are likely to have understood these messages. The historical narrative in this book is not organized around the themes that many books on Ashoka are: the emperor's early life and later history, his empire and administration, the social and economic conditions of Mauryan India, Ashoka's policy of dhamma and his proclivity for constructing monuments, the emperor's place in the larger scheme of ancient India. Instead, mine is a narrative account of Ashoka in which a clear path that follows the trajectory of his life cuts through the jungle of legends and traditions, the epigraphs and monuments, and the archaeological facts and detail that surround him. Its narrative form will, I hope, also make it attractive to readers who enjoy digs into the past.[58]

As I began writing this book I found myself facing two dilemmas. First, notwithstanding the many accounts of Ashoka's life, I realized that the crafting of such a history is limited by the restrictions of sources, for crucial phases in the individual life which forms the subject of the narrative do not figure in accounts contemporary with him. The historical life of Ashoka only began when he started speaking through his epigraphs, a little after *c.* 260 BCE, this being much after he captured the throne at Pataliputra. This meant that to reconstruct his early life as a prince a different narrative strategy was required. What I therefore chose to do was use the archaeological resonances of ancient life that can be mined out of the many landscapes in India associated with Ashoka's princely years. This is one of the biggest problems with his early life: context and conjecture have to serve as compensatory mechanisms. To put it another way, in order to compensate the lack of textual detail I have used archaeology extensively to evoke the times in which Ashoka lived.

Second—and this perhaps seems clearer in retrospect than when I was researching the book—the narrative treatment of Ashoka's life needed to be extended to his ideas as they developed over the long years of his reign. Despite the fact that Ashoka has been an extraordinarily rich subject of study, his shifting mental horizons, as expressed in the public arena of his epigraphs, remain insufficiently studied. The Ashoka of the relatively short First Rock Edict, as I saw it, was an impatient confessor of his metamorphosis as a Buddhist. Several years later, as he spoke at greater length in messages engraved on other rocks and pillars, he appeared an altogether different kind of speaker. So, seeing his ideas unfold over time is crucial to this story of Ashoka, especially since much of it concerns his trajectory as a communicator. His changing ideas as expressed in his edicts, I might add, make him appear as a real human being changing over time. I attempt to delineate his intellectual evolution through a chronological teasing out of his thoughts and emotions from the texts in which he chooses to speak of his life and calling.

Finally, the Ashoka that I write of is very much a product of the places in which he engraved his messages. This explains why this book is called *Ashoka in Ancient India*. The title points to the fact that the archaeological and locational dimensions of specific places are crucial to my understanding of the messages and their author. My journey of discovery took me to many of Ashoka's edicts and monuments: outside India to the terai region of Nepal, within the country to Bihar, Gujarat, Maharashtra, Karnataka, Andhra Pradesh, Haryana, Uttar Pradesh, Uttarakhand, and Odisha. Scrambling across rocks and up steep inclines, walking through forests of unforgettable grandeur and beauty, stumbling upon his epigraphs in the middle of modern colonies and museums, getting tantalizing glimpses of relict structures and vanished waterbodies in the vicinity of the places where the words of the emperor can still be seen, all these gave me a first-hand feel of what generations of archaeologists had found. Such landscapes figure in monographs on Ashoka, but usually in separate sections or chapters dedicated to archaeological sites and monuments. Here, I have woven the places and landscapes into a narrative of the contexts in which Ashoka's life was lived. Juxtaposing his royal messages with the contextual flesh of surrounding landscapes has enabled me to highlight the ways in which the messages themselves were shaped, influenced, enhanced, and modified.

All of this—the epigraphs, the archaeology, the life—are part of the enormous outpouring of writings on an unforgettable monarch. Yet I think my weave is different. The carpet I will lay out blends the landmarks of life and landscapes to give another picture of the life and times of Ashoka in ancient India.

# 1

# An Apocryphal Early Life

WE DON'T KNOW EXACTLY WHEN ASHOKA WAS BORN. That he was born sometime in the cusp of the fourth and third century BCE (*c.* 304 BCE) is certain, but the particular day, month, and year is not known. Very few ancient writers share our modern obsession with recording such events with calendrical exactness, and certainly Ashoka's scribes cannot be counted in this category. Date precision in relation to an individual life came into existence much after Ashoka's time, usually when a court chronicler penned the biography of a ruler-patron. Harshavardhana, who ruled from Kanauj in North India nearly 900 years after Ashoka, was one such king whose court poet, Bana, made him the central character in a historical story woven out of the actual events of his reign. There, the month of Harsha's conception, along with his date of birth, were recorded, as also the fact that he was born just after 'the twilight time'.[1] Such precision grows commoner in medieval India, when accounts authorized by powerful emperors come frequently to be composed during their own lifetime. Akbar commissioned his court historian, Abu'l Fazl, to write what became the *Akbar Nama*, whose eponymous hero is recorded as having been born in Sindh, complete with all manner of extraordinary phenomena that heralded his arrival in the sixteenth century, including a strange light perceptible on the brows of his mother when she was pregnant with him.[2]

Ancient India's royal biographical tradition begins several centuries after Ashoka, which is why we merely know that his father Bindusara ruled from roughly 297 till 273 BCE, and that his grandfather Chandragupta's regnal dates are probably 321–297 BCE. The likely year of Ashoka's birth is surmised by working backwards from the time when he was anointed emperor, for which we have a reasonably accurate date. This accuracy for his ascension is because his years as emperor have been synchronized with the reigns of contemporary rulers in Asia and beyond: their dates are fairly certain, and several of them are mentioned by name in Ashoka's inscriptions, including Antiochus II Theos of the Seleucid kingdom, Ptolemy II Philadelphus of Egypt, Antigonus II Gonatas of Macedon, Magas of Cyrene, and Alexander of Epirus (or Corinth).[3] These kings and the context in which they are alluded to in Ashoka's epigraphs will be elaborated later; for the present it suffices that arriving at an accurate chronology for Ashoka has involved looking at overlaps in the chronology of these kings and the inscriptions in which they figure.

The emperor's consecration is likely to have taken place around 269/268 BCE.[4] As with several other kings in ancient India whose lives were described in regnal years, Ashoka anchored the various happenings in his reign in relation to the year of his consecration.[5] He is, in fact, the earliest known monarch of ancient India to have recorded events from the time when he was anointed. Many rulers, for centuries afterwards, such as the Satavahanas of western India, the Palas in the east, and the Cholas in peninsular India, would continue with this practice of recording events in relation to the time elapsed since the consecration of the king in question.[6] But there were other monarchs who, by the first century BCE, had begun to indicate events in terms of a more continuous era, where the continuity was reckoned in relation to the reign of a given king by his successors (and which could continue even after that dynasty had ceased to exist).[7] Inscriptions of the time of the Gupta line of rulers were frequently in this format: the Sarnath epigraph is dated to the Gupta year 154 ('a century of years increased by fifty-four'), this being the time of Kumaragupta II, with the year possibly suggesting that the era originated with the first 'Maharajadhiraja' of the dynasty, Chandragupta I.[8] Many rulers in their epigraphs provide dates wholly in relation to the starting year of their reign, with the additional provision of a second date which measures time over a relatively longer duration, often calculated according to a continuous political era. So, had Ashoka used a system of reckoning in this form, both regnal and dynastic, the time that elapsed between the accession of his grandfather Chandragupta and Ashoka's own consecration may well have been precisely known.

Ashoka's 'dates' figure in the astonishing number of his imperial texts that were inscribed on stone, rock faces, and pillars. On them the emperor offered all kinds of information, ranging from what was cooked in the royal kitchen to his distaste for inane social ceremonies. The epigraphs are frequently long, and the insights that they provide about his later life, his aspirations, and those of his administration and his subjects, are often communications in the first person: the emperor is addressing us. This in part is what has raised expectations among historians of this stoneware yielding something about Ashoka's early life. These expectations have been dashed. There is not even passing mention of any milestones relating to Ashoka's princely years; he does not speak of his ancestors, nor even of his own parents.[9] Epigraphs in later centuries are known to have expansively described the lineages of rulers who had had royal messages recorded. Even the lineages of previous and present queen-consorts sometimes appear, alongside details of victories in battle, which are often attributed by the kings to the gods and goddesses that they worshipped. Such inscriptions occasionally mention the life of the royal protagonist before he became king. This is so in the first century BCE Hathigumpha epigraph of Kharavela, the ruler of Kalinga who led successful campaigns against Magadha, Anga, and the Tamil region. There, an entire verse is devoted to the prince's training and learning: 'for fifteen years, with a body ruddy and handsome were played youthsome sports; after that (by him who) had mastered (royal) correspondence, currency, finance, civil and religious laws (and) who had become well-versed in all (branches) of learning, for nine years (the office of) Yuvaraja (heir apparent) was administered.'[10]

Ashoka's reticence over his personal affairs is stark. This, as we shall see, may well be on account of events specific to his early life, as also because by the time the epigraphs were composed he had possibly developed an aversion for social ceremonies performed on occasions—he specifies these—such as the birth of a son, or the marriage of an offspring.[11] There is also the fact that at the time he began the practice of inscribing edicts on stone surfaces, Ashoka had no traditional template before him. He does not appear to follow the provisions of the manual of statecraft, the *Arthashastra*, which tells the scribe that when the commands of the king are set down there should be 'a courteous mention of the country, the sovereignty, the family and the name' of the king.[12] Or else, perhaps deliberately, he chose not to follow the prescribed format. Instead of mentioning his family and genealogy—of immense interest to us but not it seems to him—he records only what was of central importance to him. His official consecration ceremony (or 'abhisheka') seems to have been important to him, suggesting that the wielding of power and the consequent ability to mould a population were what mattered. Events in the life of a *monarch*, and not those prior to his becoming a ruler, were significant. Where he was taking himself and his people mattered; where he came from did not.

If Ashoka did not care to create his own version of the events of his princely life, there is no independent contemporary account of it either. We hear of his early life only in legends so separated from his time—by hundreds of years—that it seems a primary necessity in any biographical account to discount their historical value. These are all texts that *create* stories about Ashoka's birth and early years, and in doing so show something of how he came to be represented after his death. What makes these stories useful despite the concoction is that they frequently include plausible historical detail about Ashokan times. Using the threads that make up the tapestry of such legends, one may at least begin to understand the contexts and circumstances in which the man was born.

The strongest thread to emerge from the lore is that Ashoka's 'coming' as emperor of India was predicted. It was first predicted during one of Ashoka's own earlier lives. The 'prophet' who foretold it all was an ascetic. This is unsurprising: ancient India, much like modern India, was awash in holy men claiming clairvoyance. But this specific sage was not your average run-of-the-mill soothsayer: he was the greatest of all ancient ascetics, Gautama Buddha himself.[13] While the Buddha lived much of his life in the sixth century BCE whereas Ashoka, as the third emperor of the Maurya dynasty, belonged to the third, within sacred biographies of the Buddhist tradition chronological fluidity appears to have been fairly common.[14] Within this textual mode biographies, especially those depicting the Buddha, characteristically recount a past life before moving into a later rebirth or rebirths, or moving from the present to the past. In the instance at hand, a Buddhist emperor is incorporated into this tradition, making Ashoka a prediction subsequent to the Buddha. His coming, by being foretold by the Buddha himself, conjoins the two, making them seem inseparable from each other. Such insertion via legend of an earlier life of the king allows the introduction of a standard motif used in the ancient world—predisposing an audience to feel awed at the arrival of a regal saviour long awaited. Jesus was foretold, the Buddha was foretold, Moses was foretold. In those times it almost seems that if you hadn't been foretold you were not likely to be a sufficiently important religious figure or kingly personage. The telling of the story of the Buddha's prophecy about Ashoka's future arrival is an instance of adroit religious narration.

The story is first told in the *Ashokavadana*, which is a Sanskrit version of the life of Ashoka (in the form of a legend) written in the second century CE.[15] 'Avadana' means a noteworthy deed that shows the ways in which the actions of one's existence are linked with those of former or future lives.[16] In this class of literature, as is evident from the *Ashokavadana*, the former and the 'real' lives of the 'greats' within Buddhism are frequently connected in order to milk various morals from the narrative. This is very much in the tradition of Buddhist sacred biographies, where the same sort of incident happens again and again under changed circumstances and different conditions,[17] the repetition serving as the narrative trope that induces the religious feeling of an approaching marvel— a variety of The Chronicle of a Birth Foretold.

The person of the Buddha is, in this tradition, instrumental in every story where glimmerings of future greatness are first revealed.[18] Here, the Buddha is shown as having encountered an earlier avatara of Ashoka in the city of Rajagriha. Ashoka was, when thus encountered, a young boy, Jaya by name, who lived in this city, Rajagriha, which the sage had entered seeking alms. Walking along Rajagriha's main thoroughfare, the Buddha saw two young boys playing in the dirt. One of them, Jaya, on seeing the Buddha, decided to place a handful of dirt in his begging bowl. Typically, in such a story, the act of offering is accompanied by the formulation of a wish or statement of intent about the merit to be gained by the act. Jaya's statement is straightforward enough. By the good merit he might earn, he said, 'I would become king and, after placing the earth under a single umbrella of sovereignty, I would pay homage to the blessed Buddha.' Children usually have more modest aspirations but Jaya was no ordinary child. The Buddha certainly believed so, as also that Jaya had the character and the resolve to achieve what he wanted. As he predicted, 'the desired fruit would be obtained because of his field of merit.' He therefore received the 'proffered dirt', and thus 'the seed of merit that was to ripen into Ashoka's kingship was planted.' Soon thereafter the Buddha predicted to his disciple Ananda that a hundred years after his death 'that boy will become a king named Ashoka in the city of Pataliputra. He will be a righteous dharmaraja, a chakravartin who rules over one of the four continents, and he will distribute my relics far and wide and build the eighty-four thousand dharmarajikas.'[19]

Legends, in order to sound plausible, create credible contexts for the stories they recount. This legend certainly got the historical trajectory of the capitals of Magadha right. In the time of the Buddha, the centre of Magadhan royal authority was indeed Rajagriha, while by the third century BCE, when Ashoka became emperor, it had long ceased to be so. By then, Pataliputra had become the capital city.

In the next chapter, what we know of the precincts of Pataliputra and its visible remains will be elucidated. Here, it is enough to say that the veracity of such historical details surely endows an authenticity to the text's description of those centuries. This cannot be said about all aspects of the text, as, for instance, its sense of chronology. The statement that Ashoka lived about a hundred years after the death of the Buddha is incorrect even in terms of the text's own pronouncement that eleven generations of kings separated Bimbisara, who was the king of Magadha in the time of the Buddha, from Ashoka. Apparently, 'one hundred years' was only a way of suggesting that the era of Ashoka was much after the time of the Buddha.[20]

But what about the story itself? For those readers who are interested in the telling of a good story, the Avadana account may leave them feeling shortchanged. This is because the future of Ashoka is foretold very early in the tale. Generally speaking, in the crafting of a biography, even while it is assumed that the reader is aware of the broad contours of the life of the personage who forms its subject, the story is told in a way that ensures there is anticipation, suspense, and drama. In this ancient saga around a historical life it is these elements which are in danger of being compromised— because of the prophecy. Very early on, this prophecy is made and an important intention in the narrative that follows is to show how it will be fulfilled.

But did the ancients see the pronouncing of a prophecy in the way that we do? Prophecy, as a narrative technique, was employed by the epic poets in Greece. There, such prophecies, by anticipating what would befall the protagonist, apparently ensured that those following the narration did so with heightened interest. The episodes connected with the return and vengeance of the Greek hero Odysseus in the *Odyssey* are an example of this, for through prophecies readers see in advance 'the doom that awaits the suitors at the hands of Penelope's much tried lord' much before it comes to pass.[21] Sophocles' play *Oedipus Rex* follows fundamentally the same principle: it is the chronicle of a doom not only foretold, but foretold very early on. The point such narratives seem to drive home is that 'plot' is more important than 'story', if by story we mean asking the question 'what happens next?' and if by 'plot' we want to know 'in what way did this happen?' So, it may well be that in some ancient literary cultures, rather than taking away the suspense, prophecy is considered as having aroused and maintained it. Possibly, this in part explains the ancient legend around Ashoka where the prediction by the Buddha gave the story a sense of unity. It ensured that the attention of readers and listeners was never diverted from the unfolding of the main plot even as the trials and tribulations of the hero, and those whose lives he touched, were fleshed out.

Predictions about Ashoka's 'coming' recur on two occasions in the narrative, though the predictors are different. The text has travelled some distance by then, into the arena of action involving the future emperor's real life (in contradistinction to his previous life). Now, the prophecy is first repeated when a beautiful young woman, who in the near future will become his mother, enters the narrative. We will call the woman simply his 'mother' because her true name eludes us. She is known by various names elsewhere, sometimes as Subhadrangi, also as Dharma, at times Durdhara.[22] Buddhist texts do not think it necessary to give her a stable name. Where she comes from, her native place, is not usually mentioned in the ancient texts, though in this respect the *Ashokavadana* is an exception because it does specify her birthplace: it describes her as the beautiful daughter of a Brahman from Champa.[23] If so, the maternal origins of Ashoka lie in an ancient city of some fame, an urban settlement not at too great a distance from Pataliputra. Like the Magadhan capital, Champa was in its day an imposingly forti-fied city surrounded by a moat, not far from the Ganga.[24] Its ruins still grace a high square plateau that can be seen on the outskirts of modern Bhagalpur in Bihar.[25]

But coming back to the reiteration of the original prediction: as the story goes, Champa's citizen, this daughter of a Brahman, came to marry a king, the Maurya emperor Bindusara, because such an event had been foretold to her father. Once more, the coming is presaged, this time by an anonymous someone or some people connected with the future king's mother. This too is a narrative archetype common in Indian religious and hagiographical texts as much as in Middle Eastern and European, the classic example being Mary's dream in which the Angel Gabriel tells her she will bear a king, the future Jesus. An instance of a trope where ambitious kinsmen of a prince's mother find special mention exists also in the *Arthashastra*. Possibly for this reason they are seen as posing a threat to the king by being in league with the princes.[26]

Unlike the prophecy by the Buddha, where the persona of the predictor endows his words with a religious aura, the diviners in this episode happen to be anonymous. Neither their names nor their social station are mentioned. They are merely people who inform the Brahman that his daughter will be betrothed to a king. Simultaneously, they prophesy the destiny of the sons she will bear, one of whom, according to the soothsayers, will become the emperor. As the passage puts it: 'The fortune tellers predicted she would marry a king and bear two jewel-like sons: one would become a cakravartin ruling over one of the four continents, the other would wander forth and fulfil his religious vows.'[27]

The story goes that the Brahman, excited by what he had been told, took his daughter to Pataliputra and offered her in marriage to the emperor Bindusara. Here again, the political circumstances of the third century BCE are accurately invoked in that the Brahman is shown as taking his daughter to the pre-eminent city of India, the political capital from where the Maurya king ruled. Unlike in earlier ages of multiple kingdoms and republics competing with each other, in the era in which Ashoka was born, as we have noted, large parts of the subcontinent had been brought within the political ambit of a sprawling empire whose monarch resided in Pataliputra. Certainly, for anyone with ambitions of greatness, it was logical, as in the case of the Champa Brahman, to be heading to that royal capital.

Meanwhile, the emperor was not 'waiting' for this girl from Champa to arrive in his court. By this time Bindusara had a substantial harem and is also said to have had an heir apparent, a son by the name of Susima. So, the Brahman's beautiful daughter was not Bindusara's only consort, nor in the usual order of things would the son that she was eventually to bear be considered the rightful heir to the throne.

Producing a son, in her case, seems to have required patience and guile. Because of her beauty, the concubines in Bindusara's court prevented her from getting physically close to the emperor for they feared that if he made love to her he would no longer pay them any attention. She was, instead, taught by them to be an excellent barber. Little did they know that she, being determined to fulfil her 'destiny', would wield her razor in a way that would ensure she seduced her ruler-husband. Apparently, as she began to groom the king's beard and hair, she did it with such skill that he began to relax completely and fall asleep. Since her grooming gave him so much pleasure, Bindusara decided to grant her a wish. It was then that she told him that she wanted him to pleasure her, make love to her. No ordinary man, Bindusara hesitated over her propositioning because of caste rules. He belonged to the Kshatriya (warrior) caste and he imagined that she, from the evidence of her skills, had been born into a lowly barber's family. When he learnt that she was the daughter of a Brahman, and moreover of a Brahman who had given her to him as his wife, he promptly made her his chief wife and fulfilled her wish. Bindusara must have had many wives and some of them, this story suggests, were forgotten as soon as he married them. But in any case, having discovered that his barber was intended as his wife, and having installed her in that capacity, Bindusara made up for lost time. There was much dalliance and mutual enjoyment which resulted in her becoming pregnant and giving birth to Ashoka.

The same legend which describes how the Brahman girl from Champa fulfilled what had been prophesied also recounts that, when her son was born, it was she who named him. Apparently, when the infant's birth was being celebrated she was asked what his name should be, and since she replied that she had no sorrow, the child was given the name Ashoka (a-shoka: 'without sorrow').[28] She seems to have continued to remain fascinated with this name because subsequently, when a second son was born to her, this younger brother of Ashoka was named Vitashoka. This was because, as the legend puts it, when he was born, all 'sorrow ceased' ('vigate shoke').[29]

Moving on now to the second occasion where Ashoka's future, figuratively speaking, was reconfirmed, this happened some years later, by which time he was a young prince. Again, it is his mother who is prominent as a protagonist in this story, now along with a wandering Ajivika ascetic. The Ajivika link with Ashoka's mother, it will be later evident, also appears in a different form in another legend around his birth. Among the cast of characters who knew about Ashoka's 'coming', the mother and an Ajivika are common to both the stories.

Unlike the anonymous soothsayers of Champa, this Ajivika mendicant was not a faceless entity. He is introduced to us as Pingalavatsajiva, a religious man who was requested by none other than Bindusara to examine his sons. This was because the ascetic had the gift of scrutiny, in this case the power to recognize who would rule best after Bindusara's death. Initially, Ashoka was unwilling to be examined, for his father is said to have disliked him. The reason for this, in the text, has to do with Ashoka's unattractive appearance—his skin was rough and unpleasant to the touch. However, his mother advised Ashoka not to resist being examined. Eventually, when he, along with various other princes, was subjected to the sage's gaze, it became evident to the Ajivika that Ashoka must succeed Bindusara. Yet although Pingalavatsajiva realized this, he thought it prudent not to pronounce his choice immediately, for he knew the ruler-father did not like Ashoka. So, without mentioning his name to Bindusara, he made the prediction that the 'one who had the best mount, seat, drink, vessel and food' would become the emperor. Ashoka later told his mother: 'The back of an elephant was my mount, the earth was my seat, my vessel was made of clay, boiled rice with curds was my food, and water was my drink; therefore, I know I shall be king.'[30] In much the same way that Jaya's persona had earlier passed the Buddha's scrutiny and been recognized as destined for future greatness, the suitability of the now-adult prince as Bindusara's heir is linked in the story with his personal qualities. Pingalavatsajiva is said to have met Ashoka's mother and told her that Ashoka would succeed Bindusara. Upon her advice the Ajivika left the kingdom lest he be forced by the king to give an answer which might endanger him. When Bindusara died, Pingalavatsajiva, it is said, returned to Magadha.

It was normal for a queen who had been made aware of her son's destiny, but whose progeny did not include the eldest male child of her husband, to have kept the knowledge to herself. In large polygamous royal households there were other queens who harboured similar 'kingly' ambitions for their sons: everyone familiar with the Valmiki *Ramayana* will recall the several wives of Dasharatha, king of Ayodhya, one of whom, Kekayi, machinates for her own sons against those of her co-wives and thereby sets the whole epic in motion. In terms of the present narrative, the queen keeping matters secret was also necessary because Bindusara's eldest son, Susima, who was expected to succeed his father, was very much around, as perhaps was Susima's watchful mother. And there was, above all, the emperor himself who actively disliked Ashoka and would not have taken kindly to such a prediction.

Let us, though, for a moment, stay with the sage who—following unknown to himself in the footsteps of the Buddha—reconfirmed Ashoka's destiny. Why does a sage of the Ajivika order figure as the one who makes this prediction? And who were these ascetics?

A 'vanished Indian religion' is how the doctrine of the Ajivikas was described by A.L. Basham, the pre-eminent authority on this sect, and he says 'vanished' because the religion, unlike other faiths with ancient roots, has no modern adherents.[31] This extinct sect's founder was a religious leader called Makkhali Goshala who lived in the sixth century BCE. It was a time when unorthodox doctrines flourished within a wider climate of religious ferment across North India. Like his contemporaries, Mahavira and the Buddha, Makkhali Goshala has been described as a charismatic preacher and leader. He is known to have created a sect around his beliefs, whose central tenet was an all-embracing doctrine of predestination, one in which human effort had no place.[32] Such rigid determinism was rare among Indian thinkers and preachers in the milieu in which Goshala and his followers flourished. The Ajivikas must certainly have closely interacted with other religious groups. Their relations with the followers of the Buddha were ambivalent, marked by both rivalry and friendship. For one, the Buddha was supposed to have apparently believed that 'in the ninety-one *kalpas* of his previous births', apart from one Ajivika no others had been reborn in heaven.[33] Buddhist monks are also shown as having greatly disliked being mistaken for Ajivikas. This happened, for instance, when they were robbed of their robes and, on entering the city of Sravasti naked, had the citizens wondering who these 'handsome naked Ajvikas' were.[34] At the same time, relations between them were frequently depicted as cordial, as for example when an Ajivika became the carrier of the news to a group of Buddhist monks that their teacher had attained 'parinirvana' (upon his death) in Kushinara. In this instance the Ajivika was shown holding a flower, the flower of the coral tree or 'mandarava', which he knew to be one that only grew in the world of gods or paradise, and which fell to earth only when a great and auspicious event had taken place.[35] As for relations between Ajivikas and Jainas, there is a similar play of cordiality and tension. The Jaina tradition alludes to the early friendship and association of Makkhali Goshala and Vardhamana Mahavira, the twenty-fourth Jaina 'tirthankara' (teacher of the path of liberation). Matters between the two sects, though, became much less cordial following a couple of conversions of Ajivikas to the Jaina faith.[36]

That all these sects were looking to expand their following and were thus competing for converts and adherents will have been an important reason for the rivalries among them. Another reason may well have been the competition for royal patronage. Like the Buddha and his followers, Makkhali Goshala was a name known in the royal circles of Magadha. During the Buddha's lifetime, we learn that ministers in the court of Ajatashatru, the king of Magadha, suggested the names of six teachers, one of whom was Goshala, as having the capacity to resolve the king's doubts. So, along with various other sects, the kings of Magadha were patrons of the Ajivikas as far back as the sixth century BCE. Later, such ascetics are shown exercising considerable influence in the court of the Maurya dynasty. This is obvious from the ease with which they move in and out of royal company in the varying versions of the story that link Ashoka's mother with an Ajivika.

Let us look at the prediction itself. Actually, the prophecy about Ashoka's future as told by the Ajivika unfolds varyingly, depending upon the text. One version—the one which has been recounted—

takes the prediction back to the time when Ashoka was a young man. Another version presents the prince's future as having been accurately predicted, again before he was born, by a religious personage who happened to be an Ajivika. When his mother was pregnant with him, her cravings for all kinds of unusual and odd things had apparently become a matter of concern for Bindusara. In this legend, the king first sought the assistance of the Brahmans in his court.[37] How many Brahmans he sought out is unknown, but they evidently failed to comprehend the queen's cravings. Eventually, it was Janasana, an Ajivika known to frequent the queen's family, who understood them and pronounced the political destiny of the unborn child as the future ruler of Jambudvipa. As a geographical term, Jambudvipa is sometimes used for an island, and at other times for the territory extending from the Himalayas in the north to the sea in the south.[38] We shall later see, by the time of Ashoka, as his own epigraphs underline, Jambudvipa meant the vast land that the emperor ruled. What is striking is that in this tale too the figure of an Ajivika ascetic is deployed to drive home the point that Ashoka was destined to be emperor of India.

Why an Ajivika acted as the augur and not, for instance, a Buddhist or a Jaina or even a Brahman sage, needs to be unravelled. Actually, a significant insight into this is offered by something we know about Ashoka from his own epigraphs: he actively patronized this sect after he ascended the throne of Pataliputra.[39] The caves that he donated to the Ajivikas at Barabar near Gaya are marked by his donative epigraphs. These elaborate caves and the king's carvings there will be examined at length later; here, it is worth pointing out that these were no ordinary caves but were created, through a substantial outlay of money and men, by hollowing out granitic outcrops.[40] Like the pillars that the emperor set up in various parts of his empire, their interiors were mirror polished, giving them uniquely glittering walls. The reasons for Ashoka making such a generous donation to the Ajivikas remain unknown but the memory of the emperor's patronage of this sect must certainly have survived him. So, for later composers of legends, endowing an Ajivika figure with the power of prophecy probably gave credibility to the legends.

The other noticeable element about these tales is that they are all retrospective predictions made several centuries after Ashoka occupied the Mauryan throne. The version of his early life in which the Buddha prophesied his future, and in which the soothsayers in Champa and the Ajivika Pingalavatsa in Pataliputra figure, is earlier and forms part—as we saw—of the *Ashokavadana*. There are several layers of tradition in the text, some of which possibly go back to the late centuries BCE.[41] In its present form, though, the *Ashokavadana* was, as noted, composed in or after the second century CE, which makes its prediction some four centuries after the time of Ashoka. A variety of related prophecies pop up at its very beginning, when the Buddha predicts the future birth of a Buddha-like figure. One hundred years after his death, he says at this point, a son will be born to a perfumer in Mathura who will carry forward his own work.[42] Prediction, then, whether of the birth of a future Buddha or a Buddhist king, is a specific narrative device that was culturally common when speaking of the 'coming' of figures important to the Buddhist tradition.

The second version worth noting is from the *Vamshatthapakasini*, a commentary on the *Mahavamsa,* the Sri Lankan Buddhist chronicle which was written 800 years or so after the *Ashokavadana* and more than 1200 after the death of Ashoka—i.e. in the ninth or tenth century CE. In the main text, the *Mahavamsa*, dated to the fifth century CE, one encounters soothsayers making predictions about royal children on various occasions. The ancestor of the first king of Indian descent, named Vijaya, is shown as the son of a king who was said to have been born of the union of a woman and a lion. This woman was a princess whom the soothsayers had prophesied as soon to be united with the 'king of beasts'.[43] Elsewhere in the text we are told that when Brahmans skilled in sacred texts saw the only daughter of a later king, Panduvasudeva, they foretold her son as slaying his uncles for the sake of the throne.[44] The *Vamshatthapa-kasini*, in predicting the destiny of Ashoka, follows the forms and conventions of the chronicle on which it is a commentary. In inserting the figure of Ashoka in this cycle of prediction, with an Ajivika foretelling the future (all of which is missing in the *Mahavamsa*), it could represent the incorporation of the Ashoka legend of the Northern Buddhist tradition.

Forms and conventions apart, are there any other reasons for the 'coming' of an emperor to have been predicted in this way? And are there other kinds of events that are prophesied in this way, or other historical figures whose destinies are similarly prefigured in ancient India?

By the time Ashoka was born, prophecies and prognostications—if one goes by allusions to 'events' that either would transpire or transpired as a consequence of particular signs—had long become acceptable practice, an incorporation of superstition into the dominant belief systems by which everyday life was lived. Future events, auspicious or otherwise, could be indicated by the cries of certain kinds of birds—as the oldest Indian text, the *Rig Veda*, indicates.[45] Birds also figure as omens in another text of the same genre, the *Atharva Veda*, in which something fallen from the mouth of a black bird was considered ominous because that kind of bird was supposed to be the mouth of Nirrti, goddess of death and corruption.[46] The disturbing or disruptive behaviour of birds and animals appears in all kinds of early literature, from the *Mahabharata* where a category of ascetics depicted are those who understand the cries of birds and monkeys, to the *Parantapa Jataka* in which the Bodhisattva (the future Buddha) learns to understand the meanings of animal cries while studying at the city of Taxila.[47] In other instances the signs to be 'read' depend upon the constellation of planets. A boy, for instance, believed to have been born on an inauspicious astrological constellation might himself die or bring about the death of his father or his mother.[48]

The power of such planetary conjunctions, as indicators of future fortune and misfortune, is also central to the great Sanskrit epics of ancient India. In the *Ramayana*, when Ravana is getting the better of Rama in battle, the planets are blamed: 'Mercury stood covering the Rohini nakshastra which is presided over by Prajapati and which is the favourite of the moon and thereby indicated evil fortune to people.'[49] The *Mahabharata* is crowded with similar prophecies. An instance is the vivid description of future destruction in the Bhishma-parva, the forthcoming apocalypse being read from astrological indications: here a white celestial body stood 'traversing Citra nakshatra', indicating the destruction of the clan of the Kurus, while when 'a very frightful comet stands covering Pushya-nakshastra' it meant that terrible evil would visit both the armies in conflict.[50] Such examples suppose that knowledge about the future, even though usually hidden, can be secured by understanding specific signs. The phenomenon of prediction and divination, in fact, is part of all kinds of ancient literature and one only has to think of Joseph in the Old Testament using a cup for divination, or of the Chinese work *I Ching*, the Confucian classic on divination, to realize that this phenomenon was not confined to India.[51] Much later, West Asia's Qu'ranic stories about Biblical prophets allude to such practices, as when the Qu'ran recounts that the signal for the commencement of the Flood, for Noah, was a boiling furnace.[52]

The devices used for foretelling events in the world of ancient societies, one imagines, were those that were culturally acceptable there. In the ancient world of the Greek epics it was usual for the poet to leave the role of prophecy to his characters. So, in the fifteenth book of the *Iliad*, it was Zeus in conversation with Hera who prophesied various deaths when 'Achilles shall send Patroclus into battle, but that when Patroclus has slain many Trojan youths and Zeus' own son, Sarpedon, Hector in turn shall kill him; then Achilles in anger shall slay Hector and later the Achaeans with Athene's aid shall take the city of Ilium.'[53] This also underlines the fact that in epic tales, from Greece to India, prophesying war and violence was commonplace, and that through these the listeners and readers knew in advance who was going to be defeated, who killed. While in the Greek texts such predictions were articulated by seers, heroes, and other such characters, in the Indian epics it was more common to spell out what the stars foretold.

Diviners and soothsayers in ancient India were well versed in this lore and used their knowledge to become powerful. Presumably for this reason, such specialists were not always liked. In specific instances, ascetics were prohibited 'from desiring to secure alms by foretelling the results of portents (like earthquakes) or of bodily movements (such as the throbbing of the eye or arm) or by naksatravidya (astrology) or angavidya (palmistry) or by casuistry.'[54]

Such censure did not *always* apply to them, and evidently they were considered acceptable in the royal court of the Mauryas. The *Arthashastra* seems to suggest that the king should appoint as his chaplain (or 'purohita') not only someone whose family and character were exalted and who had thoroughly studied the Vedic texts, but also one who had trained 'in divine signs, in omens and in the science of politics and capable of counteracting divine and human calamities by means of Atharvan remedies.'[55]

By this time, predictions at the time of their birth about the brightness of their future career also formed part of the popular lore about great men. The future glory of the Buddha had been predicted in precisely this way. He was born as 'Siddhartha' in the latter part of the sixth century BCE and, the story goes, it was a sage who first declared at his birth that he would attain greatness. This sage was Asita, a Brahman who was also the teacher of the Buddha's father, Suddodhana. He is supposed to have developed psychic powers and would often spend the day in the world of the gods (the 'deva' world). On one such occasion he encountered the gods engaged in great rejoicing and learnt that Siddhartha Gautama, destined to become the Buddha, had been born.[56] Immediately, he went to Suddhodana's palace and asked to see the child. From the auspicious marks on the child's body he knew that the infant was 'no common clay' but would attain Bodhi ('enlightenment'). His encounter with the infant is described thus:

> He took him up; and when his gaze
> found marks and signs his lore knew well
> he lifted up his voice and cried:
> 'He has no peer! He's mankind's best!'[57]

This story occurs in an early collection of discourses called the *Sutta Nipata*, a work which is part of the Buddhist tradition compiled within a hundred years of the death of the Buddha. Versions of Asita's prophecy continued into Buddhist texts for many centuries. The *Lalitavistara*, a text of the first–second centuries CE, recounted two versions of Asita's prophecy, one in prose and another in verse, which, in their main details, differ but slightly from the earlier Pali version.[58] In all instances, though, as in the case of Ashoka's coming, these are retrospective predictions made by ascetics.

In the centuries that followed, such stories about rulers came to be told most specially when recounting the life of a king who was not the first-born male child of the king or not in the existing system of primogeniture the heir to the throne. In the seventh century CE Harshavardhana's court chronicler Bana, using elaborate poetic detail, recounts that when his mother Yashovati was pregnant with Harsha, her behaviour reflected the thoughts of the future sovereign she was carrying. This was evident, we are told, in the fact that instead of jewelled mirrors she preferred to see her reflection on the blade of a sword, and instead of the lute she found pleasure in hearing the bow's twang ('ill suited to a woman', Bana says).[59] At his birth, even though he was the second son, it was predicted by an astrologer, whose advice was sought by the king, that Harsha was born at a conjunction fit for the birth of a universal emperor.

The similarities in the later legend around Ashoka and the story of Harsha—neither of whom were the oldest sons of their fathers and thus not rightful heirs to the throne—is striking. In both instances we have odd signs connected with pregnant queens, as also a figure who had powerful insights into what such signs meant. This is, in brief, the characteristic narrative mode of a culture in which the sacred is regularly smuggled into the picture in the shape of a prophecy, the function of such prophecy being to bestow legitimacy on an ascension otherwise dubious.

Now it is time to travel to Pataliputra, the city of Ashoka's childhood and of his later years. Not everything about the period of this future emperor needs to be extracted from legitimizing lore constructed hundreds of years after his death. Unlike the emperor himself, the character and culture of Pataliputra can be reconstructed from clues that are contemporary with Mauryan times. Through them one may come closer to an understanding of Ashoka's early life. As for whether Ashoka's future was actually predicted in this court, we will never know. All we can safely say is that, in this time of the late centuries BCE in North India, such a prophecy would not have surprised anyone.

2

# Pataliputra and the Prince

In the hundredth year after the Nirvana of Tathagata, there was a king called Ashoka (O-shu-kia), who was the great-grandson of Bimbisara-raja. He changed his capital from Rajagriha to Patali (pura), and built an outside rampart to surround the old city. Since then many generations have passed and now there only remain the old foundation walls (*of the city*).[1]

THIS IS HOW THE HISTORY OF THE CREATION OF THE capital city of Pataliputra was described by Xuanzang, the famous Chinese pilgrim who came there in the seventh century CE, more than 800 years after the reign of Ashoka. Of the many Chinese Buddhists who came to India, Xuanzang was the traveller best remembered for the extensiveness of his forays across India, ranging from Kashmir and Punjab to Bihar, Assam, and the peninsula. Wherever he went, he recorded his observations on monasteries, ruined cities, stupas, the myths surrounding them, and a great deal else.

Xuanzang's account of Pataliputra is marked by most of these features. It is part observation and part amalgam of legends. Upon leaving Vaishali and crossing the Ganga, this restless and intrepid pilgrim reached Pataliputra. Located on the holy river's right bank, the city he said was one that had, many centuries earlier, been created there as the new capital of Magadha by Ashoka—no doubt he had been told this or gleaned it from existing legend. Contrary to what Xuanzang believed, however, Pataliputra's establishment as Magadha's capital did not have anything to do with Ashoka, and the Chinese pilgrim may have been confusing Bindusara with Bimbisara—the latter, at any rate, had no relationship of any kind with Ashoka.[2] By the time of Xuanzang's visit, his account suggests, Magadha's realm included towns which were well peopled, whereas the old city of Pataliputra was a somewhat unimpressive and decaying settlement, one that he characterized as 'having long been a wilderness' whose 'foundation walls had survived'.[3] By this Xuanzang probably meant that the ruins of earlier buildings were still visible within the city. He had encountered such ruins in many places across India before, but, exceptionally in the case of Pataliputra, the visible traces of stupas, pillars, old towers, and strange stones seemed to him to be closely associated with Ashoka.

The associations appear to match many of the legends that by then surrounded Ashoka, and Xuanzang is likely to have been familiar with their Chinese versions.[4] So, for instance, the early part of Ashoka's reign was recounted in them as being marked by much violence, since the emperor was known to have been a notoriously cruel tyrant at that point in his reign. Proof of his tyranny was an earth-prison or 'hell' which he had built, a place where all who entered 'were killed without any chance of self defence'. After his conversion to Buddhism, the 84,000 stupas that Ashoka is supposed to have raised throughout his empire over the relics of the Buddha are specially mentioned, the first of these being recorded as created just south of the prison in Pataliputra. By the time of Xuanzang, this stupa was in 'a leaning, ruinous condition', though its crowning segment of carved stone, with a balustrade around it, had survived.

Then there was a stone on which the Buddha had apparently walked, marked by the impression of both his feet, a sacred feature which the king had surrounded within an enclosure. Modern archaeologists read the Chinese traveller's description of these details with approval, Xuanzang having shown the sorts of precise measuring skills that are the staple of the discipline of archaeology: he mentions the dimensions of the sacred footprints (18 inches long and 6 inches broad), the circle signs embossed on them, and the manner in which fish and flowers fringed all ten toes. Not far from this stone, he noted a massive stone pillar with a mutilated inscription which, he said, recorded that 'Ashoka-raja with a firm principle of faith has thrice bestowed Jambudvipa as a religious offering on Buddha, the Dharma, and the assembly, and thrice he has redeemed it with his jewels and treasure; and this is the record thereof.'[5] Since no Ashokan pillar that we know has such an inscription on it, this was possibly a story circulating around the epigraph that Xuanzang gathered from local people.[6]

Legend in fact is more the staple of the narrative than measurable accuracy: in the way he describes it, Ashoka's imprint on Pataliputra's landscape was practically predetermined since the Buddha himself had prophesied it as a city of the future. This happened when the Buddha, on his last journey towards Kushinagara, looked back in farewell at Magadha, and, impressing his feet upon the stone on which he stood, said to his companion-disciple Ananda: 'a hundred years hence there shall be a King Asoka; he shall build here his capital and establish his court, and he shall protect the three treasures and command the genii.' If Ashoka's destiny as emperor of India had been predicted by the Buddha in the *Ashokavadana*, here the sage is invoked as having prophesied, and thereby obliquely blessed, the creation by Ashoka of his royal capital.

Why Xuanzang's account of Pataliputra portrayed it primarily as Ashoka's city may have to do with what the pilgrim imbibed from its local antiquarians and the derelict relics that the populace had, by then, come to associate with the legends around the Buddhist emperor. His familiarity with Chinese versions of many of these, written several centuries before his time, may well have predisposed him to seek confirmation of their *in situ* authenticity.[7] The real Pataliputra, though, was very different from the remembered city.

* * *

Pataliputra was, in a manner of speaking, the progeny of the Ganga, having been seeded at the topographical point where people and goods moved across the river and along its right bank. Like the river, the trajectory followed by the settlement was linear. Some time at the beginning of recorded history, around the sixth century BCE, 300 years or so before Ashoka was born, a settlement stood in the area which the sprawling city of Patna has now overtaken, a little after the confluence of the Son river with the Ganga. We know this because surviving traces of that first settlement contain the archetypal deluxe pottery of that time, the North Black Polished Ware—so called because a lot of this pottery is usually a shiny black and has been found in many parts of North India.[8] This early settlement was also the one where the Buddha, on his last journey from the state of Magadha, is said to have stayed. Pataligrama was what it was called then, suggesting its origins in a village ('grama'). There he apparently addressed his devotees in a council hall before crossing the Ganga towards Vaishali.[9]

While sojourning in its vicinity the Buddha is reported as having seen thousands of magical creatures haunting Pataligrama. This he interpreted as a sign that a fortress was being built. The intuition was confirmed by his disciple, Ananda, who told him that the chief ministers of Magadha—the capital of which was located further south, around Rajagriha—were building a fortress to better defend themselves against the Vajji state.

Unlike monarchical Magadha, the Vajjis were a republican political confederacy which dominated a region that stretched beyond the left bank of the Ganga, in the vicinity of Basarh. Seeing this construction as the influence of powerful 'fairies' who 'bend the hearts of the most powerful kings and ministers to build dwelling-places', the Buddha is believed to have made a prophecy about the future of Pataliputra to his disciple: 'And as far, Ananda, as Aryan people resort, as far as merchants travel, this will become the chief city, Patali-putta, a centre of the interchange of all kinds of wares. But three dangers will hang over Patali-putta, that of fire, that of water, and that of dissension among friends.'[10] The Buddha is, essentially, evoked in the early Buddhist literature for every event or occurrence that needs to be justified, as well as to legitimize him as the great foreseer; it seems thus that much before he began predicting the future greatness of Ashoka, he prophesied the subsequent pre-eminence of Pataliputra. This prophecy to Ananda is a leitmotif in accounts from the late centuries BCE till at least the time of Xuanzang. In the early texts, however, Ashoka is not credited with the creation of the capital; the Chinese pilgrim's account of the Buddha's prediction about Pataliputra is in this respect novel.

The Buddha's sojourn at and pronouncements about what soon became the pre-eminent city of ancient India point to two crucial factors in the evolution of Pataliputra. One is the role of traders and trade routes in sustaining the city as a crucial hub. This is not surprising, for farmers and fishing folk were familiar with the rivers in the vicinity of Pataliputra from a time well before the Buddha. The links and locales of third millennium BC sites like Maner on the Son river, some thirty-odd km west of Pataliputra, and Chirand on the northern bank of the Ganga, not far from where the Ghaghara river joined it, suggest this. Pataliputra's land arteries too, from the beginning, linked it to Rajagriha and the Chhotanagpur plateau on the one hand, and Gaya–Bodh Gaya and beyond on the other.

The other factor, about improving the defensive strength of Magadha, relates to a more specific sixth century BCE feature. It concerns the shift that was necessitated from hill-girt Rajagriha, the first capital of the state of Magadha, to Pataliputra in the Ganga plains (Figs 2.1 and 2.2). Capitals are known to have been shifted in many other regions, Delhi for example being a city where seven capital cities are said to have come up at different points in time. However, whether Delhi's cities, like Indraprastha and Shahjahanabad, hugged the banks of the Yamuna, or as in the case of Lal Kot and Tughlaqabad, were located in the rocky Aravalli hills, they were all within a few kilometres of each other. Pataliputra and Rajagriha, on the other hand, were not contiguous but separated by a considerable distance—more than a hundred kilometres—with the two cities occupying very different kinds of terrain. While the Ganga in the vicinity of Pataliputra is grand in its breadth and

Fig. 2.1: The hills of Rajagriha with a stupa in the foreground

beauty, this is perhaps the only natural feature in its favour. The area is monotonously flat and fairly swampy on its edges, fringed on one side by marshes created by the Punpun river. Rajagriha, by contrast, was girdled by magnificent hills that gave it a naturally defensive character. Additionally, extensive cyclopean fortress-like walls were built across the hills, as also all kinds of structures ranging from monastic retreats to royal residences.[11] And yet, as Magadha expanded and jostled for territorial supremacy over states that extended along and beyond the left bank of the Ganga, it became increasingly clear that it was impractical for the political hub of an expansionist state to be located there. From the interior hilly terrain of Rajagriha, it would not have been possible to adequately protect the state's exposed long flank along the river.

The transition towards the swampy plains began in the time of King Ajatashatru (493–462 BCE). He is credited with converting the settlement of Pataligrama into the fortified urban complex which came to be called Pataliputra. As noted, he did this so that it could serve as a base against the aggressive Vajji (or Lichchavi) republic. In later years the Gangetic plains were dominated—as were many other parts of India—by the Magadha-based Mauryas, but at this point in time there were several states in North India, the balance of power fluctuating and shifting between them, creating tensions in their relationships with each other. The Lichchavi confederacy was one of these many states. Militarily, it formed a powerful force defeated by Ajatashatru only after a protracted conflict that lasted sixteen years or more (c. 484-468 BCE). The creation of fortifications at Pataligrama was probably an important part of the strategy to protect Magadha's Gangetic flank against the aggressive Lichchavis. Some fifty years later, in the reign of Ajatashatru's successor Udayin, Pataliputra became Magadha's capital city.

So, within some decades of his death, Pataliputra, it would appear, had moved fast towards fulfilling the Buddha's prophecy. Of course, considering that the travels of the great sage and the truisms transmitted by him began to be recorded only after his death—by which time a walled city at Pataliputra already dominated the brow of the Ganga plains—it is also possible that the recording of his

Fig. 2.2: The Ganga river near Patna

prophecy was a retrospective insertion into folklore (of the kind that we encountered around Ashoka in the last chapter).

Whichever way we look at it, what makes this first description of the city so spot on is that it captures its essence. The lifeblood of the urban metropolis of Pataliputra, as we shall see, was the web of connections, political and commercial, that inextricably bound it to regions and people, near and far, making it a place whose history extended much beyond the city walls that enclosed it. It also underlines the fact that whatever became its purported past by the time it was visited by Buddhist pilgrims from China, the historical origins of this city and its consolidation as a political capital had nothing to do with the family or the line of kings to which Ashoka belonged.

\* \* \*

What did Pataliputra, which was an integral part of his early years, look like around the time Ashoka was born? In the late third

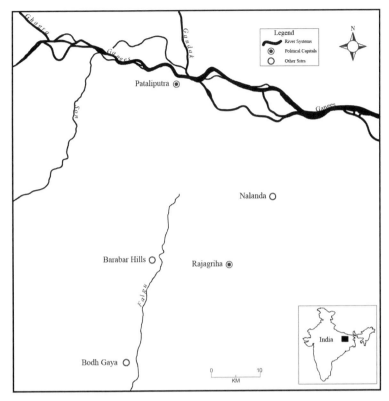

Map 2: Magadha's political capitals—Rajagriha and Pataliputra

century BCE, when Ashoka's grandfather Chandragupta was the reigning king, the famous Greek writer-traveller-diplomat Megasthenes spent some time in the city and left behind a vivid and, as confirmed by modern excavations, fairly accurate description of the dimensions and character of the city. So we can be reasonably certain that the city where Ashoka and his siblings spent their growing years was as described in the narrative of the Greek visitor.

What was Megasthenes doing in this part of India? Many Greek chroniclers and writers had been to India before him, the largest number having been part of the entourage of the Macedonian Alexander when he overran large parts of the north-west in the spring of 326 BCE. While the plains of Punjab figure prominently in their descriptions of Alexander's army as it sailed down rivers and marched across the Indus plains, they neither ventured further downstream nor south-east along the flow of the Ganga. Unlike his predecessors, Megasthenes did. He travelled much further and saw more of India, especially Gangetic India, than any foreigner before him. Starting off from Arachosia, he went across Punjab and the Gangetic plains to spend time at the court of 'Sandrakottos, king of the Indians', Sandrakottos being Greek for Chandragupta. Arachosia was located in the Helmand area of what is now south Afghanistan, and the region known by that name possibly stretched till the upper reaches of the Indus river. It was controlled by Sibyrtius, a satrap (governor) originally appointed by Alexander, and Megasthenes was part of this satrap's staff. He seems to have spent some time in Arachosia, but if he had any thoughts about that province he does not share them with us, nor says anything of note about the places that he saw or the people he met there. We do not even know for certain who he represented at the court of Chandragupta, though it is likely that he travelled at the Macedonian satrap's behest.[12] That he should have arrived from Arachosia is not surprising, for Chandragupta himself, after he had conquered the Nanda kingdom and ascended the throne at Pataliputra, is known to have had territorial designs on the Indus plains and beyond. Whether the region bordering that river had been annexed by Chandragupta by the time Megasthenes visited Pataliputra is a matter of some controversy.[13] The fact that he visited Chandragupta's capital city and left an eyewitness account of it, however, is universally acknowledged,[14] despite the original text in which he penned his account having been swallowed up by the sands of time.

The *Indica* is what that lost account by Megasthenes is called; the book has come down to us from fragments and quotations in the works of later classical writers. Doubts about several of these fragments have been raised time and again, it being sometimes unclear whether the writers were paraphrasing Megasthenes direct or using an intermediary.[15] The observations recorded are not always consistent, partly because Megasthenes was prone to speculative grandeur and wanted to say something about *all* of India, both what he knew to be true and what he didn't. He pronounced, for instance, that the women of the 'Pandaian' land bore children when they were 6 years of age, and described a race of men 'among the nomadic Indians who instead of nostrils have merely orifices' and whose legs are contorted like snakes.[16] Yet even those justifiably doubtful of absolute veracity in the account of such a fanciful observer are certain that he had the unprecedented advantage of having seen Pataliputra, and that the fragments in which the description of that city occurs were definitely penned by Megasthenes himself.

Of Indian cities in general he says, 'the number is so great that it cannot be stated with precision'; several, made of brick and mud, stood on 'lofty eminences', while others were built of wood and hugged the banks of rivers or the sea coast.[17] Of these, he only provides an expansive account of 'Palimbothra', the Greek name for Pataliputra, the greatest city in India, in part because of its close connection with the ruling Maurya, for 'the king, in addition to his family name, must adopt the surname of Palibothros, as Sandrakottos, for instance, did.' Whether Chandragupta's name was in fact given suffixed grandeur by his capital city is uncertain, but clearly, even as he built a vast empire, this was the city which formed the core and base of his imperium and of that of the Mauryan monarchs who followed him.

'Sandrakottos' plays second fiddle to Pataliputra in what survives of the Megasthenes account. It was a city that occupied a long strip of land where the Ganga and the Son (called Erranoboas by Megasthenes) met, 'a city eighty stadia [*c.* 14 km] in length and fifteen [*c.* 2.5 km] in breadth. It is of the shape of a parallellogram and is girded by a wooden wall, pierced with loopholes for the discharge of arrows. It has a ditch in front for defence and for receiving the sewage of the city.'[18] The description makes the city long and narrow.[19] One calculation suggests this would mean a city that covered some 4500 hectares.[20] What archaeology has revealed of its size does not exactly compare with the calculations above, but the spread of its ancient ruins does make it clear that the city was a very large one.

It is not easy to get archaeological precision on the size of the urban metropolis as it stood during Mauryan times since the houses and palaces, the streets and markets, the pillars and sculptures, and so much else of Pataliputra lies buried under some twenty-two centuries of strata below modern Patna. So, how have archaeologists managed to arrive at a rough calculation of its size? This has been possible because wooden ramparts of the sort described by Megasthenes have been detected in various areas of the city. They have not been unearthed in a continuous line, but even so, by plotting on a map wherever these were found, a conjectural sense of size can be obtained.[21] One calculation is that the area enclosed by the timber ramparts would have been around 2200 hectares; another assessment computes the fortified city as much smaller, between 1200 and 1300 hectares. Either way, as the archaeologist F.R. Allchin put it, 'even if the more modest figures are anywhere near correct, Pataliputra would have been far larger than any other South Asian city of its day, and on this score alone would certainly qualify for the title of Metropolis.'[22] Ashoka would later travel to other cities in the course of his duties as a prince, and when doing so is likely to have noticed that many of these too had massive ramparts and overlooked rivers. But they will have seemed Lilliputian compared to his ancestral city. Two locations that figure prominently in Ashoka's early years are Vidisha and Taxila. The ramparts of Vidisha enclosed around 240 hectares, while the Mauryan city at Taxila covered a mere 50 hectares. So, in terms of sheer scale, the urban landscape of Ashoka's early years was singular. The Pataliputra of his childhood was not just any walled city on the banks of a big river. It was by the standards of the time an enormous sprawl which, by comparison with other Indian urban centres and cities, was colossal.

This sprawling metropolis now formed the political core of a subcontinental empire which, with an emperor residing in it, possessed enormous authority. The king's palace in a city of these dimensions is likely to have been impressive, but Megasthenes does not describe it. The security arrangements of his residence, however, are: Shakespeare's 'uneasy lies the head that wears the crown' could have been said of Ashoka's forefathers instead of Henry IV, for Megasthenes tells us that the king was not meant to sleep in the daytime and by night had constantly to change his 'couch' because he had to safeguard himself against all the people plotting to kill him. For this reason his care was entrusted to women, Megasthenes says—the time lag between the Greeks and us leaving room for doubt about whether he was also being tongue-in-cheek when making the observation. But safety *was* a pressing concern; Ashoka's own grandfather had usurped the crown only a short few years earlier, and we know that some fifty years after Ashoka the crown was again snatched off the Mauryan brow by another usurper. So, every ruling dynast would have had as his first instinct the certainty of being the cynosure within a predatory, treacherous ambience, the daggers barely sheathed round every corner. The king, Megasthenes says, left his palace only on specific occasions: in times of war, when he judged cases in court, when he offered sacrifice, and when he went hunting. The rituals surrounding the hunt as the emperor left the palace are vividly captured in his account, not least because they are so extraordinary, the emperor being surrounded by an immediate ring of female security guards:

> Crowds of women surround him, and outside of this circle spearmen are ranged. The road is marked off with ropes, and it is death, for man and woman alike, to pass within the ropes. Men with drums and gongs lead the procession. The king hunts in the enclosures and shoots arrows from a platform. At his side stand two or three armed women. If he hunts in the open grounds he shoots from the back of an elephant. Of the women, some are in chariots, some on horses, and some even on elephants, and they are equipped with weapons of every kind, as if they were going on a campaign.[23]

In this matter the *Arthashastra* corroborates the *Indica*. It tells us of many women among the king's trusted helpers, from bow-bearing female guards when he rose in the morning to 'female slaves of proved integrity' who were supposed to 'do the work of bath-attendants, shampooers, bed-preparers, laundresses and garland-makers.'[24] In early sculptural representations too, as for instance at Bharhut in Central India, we find female attendants accompanying kings in procession. Ajatashatru is one of these kings and is shown sitting on his state elephant, with a woman attendant bearing the parasol behind him; the accompanying elephants are mounted by women mahouts.[25]

While all the anecdotes and allusions relating to the Mauryan royalty in the *Indica* contain no description of any of their residential quarters either, this may not have seemed a lack if the ruins of such establishments had survived. But nothing has remained. The archaeological evidence for a royal residence, and of the paraphernalia of streets and lanes and the secular and religious structures surrounding it, has been rendered insignificant by centuries of dust and over-building. Segments of structures and walls occasionally emerge in the course of modern construction, in localities such as Rajendranagar, where Mauryan terracottas were found when sewage lines were being laid; then in the Patna Dak bungalow area, which was demolished and replaced by a Kisan Bhawan, in the process exposing Mauryan pottery and numerous ring wells; and in the Patna Museum compound where Mauryan remains appeared in the course of digging for constructing a fountain.[26] But none of these appear to be royal buildings. This is disappointing to those interested in visualizing the world of royalty on the ground, especially since several medieval palace complexes, from those of the Vijayanagara rulers at Hampi to the Mughal palaces of Agra and Delhi, are well known and have survived. The residences and administrative blocks of ancient Indian city rulers have generally been more elusive. Even in the Mauryan city of Taxila, which has been extensively excavated, we see dwelling houses and structures along the streets and lanes, but the buildings of the elite tend to go missing; and this is true for other Mauryan cities as well.

An important reason for the problem in relation to Pataliputra is that much of what we know about it does not, in fact, come from the centre of the ancient city, where the palace was likely to be located, but from what has emerged of the edges and outskirts of the old town, where controlled excavations have been possible. Since fortifications were usually put up on a settlement's

boundaries, the remains of the wooden palisade which protected
Pataliputra have been revealed. This was an element of the urban
landscape vividly described by Megasthenes. Uprights of strong
timber that have been found in excavations in various parts of
present-day Patna make it clear that his description was, in this
case, based on what he actually saw. These defences were made
of two parallel rows of walls constituted by wooden posts about
4.5 m. high, paved with wooden sleepers, and covered above with
wooden planks. This was likely to have been a tunnel-like passage.
It was one that was covered with earth up to a certain height on
its exterior.[27] We also know that the city's drains, which discharged waste water outside the city, were made of wood. Such details
about drains and palisades are a consequence of numerous digs in
the area of Bulandibagh in Patna, a locality once dominated by a
fruit garden—thus allowing enough space to excavate.

Wood for defences and drains seems an odd choice of material
for the purposes at hand, but it was a carefully thought out choice.
The wood used, that of the sal tree, is unusually hard and possesses
the high survival capacity required in Pataliputra, which then had, as
Patna does today, a high level of subsoil water. In fact, in the 1926–7
excavations of Manoranjan Ghosh on behalf of the Archaeological Survey of India (ASI) at Bulandibagh, deep ponds of water had
to first be baled out before digging could begin.[28] The watery surroundings of Patna were known to cause waterlogging, which was
why wood was used for defences and drains. Interestingly, these
walls of wooden planks that have since turned up in numerous localities in Patna were not visible to the first archaeological explorers
of the city. J.D. Beglar's 1872–3 account categorically stated that in
modern Patna he failed to 'discover a single relic, or any traces of the
great edifices' that were supposed to have been built there. This he
explained with his hypothesis that the ancient city had been washed
away by the Ganga.[29] Beglar, an assistant to Alexander Cunningham, Director General of the ASI, did not in this instance display
the archaeological intuition of his superior, whose skill in discovering archaeological corroboration for literary descriptions
at ancient sites was legendary. A couple of decades later Laurence

Austin Waddell, a lieutenant colonel associated with the Indian Medical Service, who had a keen interest in the history of Buddhism and Patna, found substantial 'portions of the old wooden walls of the city described by Megasthenes.'[30] These regularly came to light when villagers dug wells: 'On striking these great beams standing erect so many feet below the surface the superstitious villagers, unable to account for the presence of the huge posts, usually abandon their attempted wells.'[31] Later, many more features of these intriguing structures were excavated by officers of the ASI. But by then the palisades had paled into the background as the remains of a large pillared hall of Mauryan times emerged out of the locality of Kumrahar.[32]

But coming back to Pataliputra's defences: whoever planned and built these extensive wooden structures evidently went to a great deal of trouble, for sal was not likely to have been available in any forest near the Ganga around Pataliputra. We do not even know where the forests from which the sal was procured were located. The popularity of the tree is suggested by evidence of the use of its wood in several other settlements discovered in this part of India, such as at Chirand and Senuwar, the contexts here greatly antedating its occurrence at Pataliputra.[33] But the real difference was in the scale of use: Pataliputra was the first city in the Magadha region to use this wood for such extensive urban infrastructure. The ancient town planners and builders seem to have known a thing or two, for the trouble they took to obtain and cart the wood was worth it: more than 2300 years later, long sections of their work remain intact.

How did Chandragupta's grandchildren view this vast wooden-walled city architecture? Did they climb up the watchtowers and move across the ramparts, spellbound by the view? Did they strike up conversations with soldiers patrolling the city? The day-to-day practicalities and pleasures of a Mauryan prince's life are not available from any of the sources, but it is a reasonable assumption that there must have been occasion for the children of the rulers to have moved around, to have ventured in and out of the city.

Tantalizing glimpses of a different kind relating to the urban culture of the city are seen in the antiquities that Mauryan citizens, royal and ordinary, will have been familiar with. Large free-standing dancing terracotta figures, unearthed from the locality of Bulandibagh, are thought to represent Mauryan court art.[34] The confident urbane sophistication of these female figures, with the edges of their skirts lifted, suggests dancers of the type that occasionally performed for palace people.[35] One of the dancers, her carefully combed hair in a cropped front fringe, carries a small drum ('damaru') in her raised hand. She also seems to have a heavy ring around each hand, the one on the right being pliant.

Another archaeological haul yielded a cache of twenty-one small soapstone discs. They were found packed together in a dried-up watercourse in the Murtaziganj locality.[36] Pieces of exquisite workmanship, with a great variety of fine detail, these miniature discs depict lotus flowers, nude female figures that are thought to be goddesses of fertility, and a profusion of birds and animals arranged in circles—parrots, peacocks, and geese; lions, stags, elephants, and horses; even an owl and a rhinoceros.[37] Why the discs were made and the purpose for which they were used are not clear, but they are carved with such exceptional skill that the supposition is they were meant to catch the eye of an elite clientele that probably used them in some sort of ritual. But the localities where such elites lived within the city have, like the royal palaces, not survived.

Having sufficiently rued the vanished structures of the Mauryan empire, let us look instead at an inestimable treasure that miraculously survived and has been found, namely the *Arthashastra* by Kautilya.[38] This is a text extensively used by practically everyone who writes on the Mauryas. Like the ramparts of Pataliputra, it remained hidden from scholarly gaze for many centuries: despite numerous allusions to it in later literature, as a material artefact the text was not in evidence.[39] The first manuscript appeared in 1904 when a pandit of Tanjore district handed over a set of 168 palm leaf folios in the Grantha script, along with the fragment of a Sanskrit commentary, to R. Shamasastry, librarian of the Mysore Governmental Oriental Library. Shamasastry soon realized that what he had acquired was the first available manuscript of the *Arthashastra*. This he went on to edit and publish, first in successive volumes of *Indian Antiquary* and eventually as a book.[40] While the manuscript was no more than a century or two old, Shamasastry recognized it as a copy of a much older text on ancient statecraft, one which could be dated to the time of the Mauryas. Several other manuscripts were later unearthed, some complete, others with a few folios missing, mainly in libraries in Travancore, Madras, and Cochin, with one version in North Gujarat.[41] These, along with commentaries on the *Arthashastra*, were used by R.P. Kangle, Professor of Sanskrit at Elphinstone College, Bombay, to prepare an excellent critical edition of the text, along with an English translation. This edition has been used by generations of scholars to come to grips with the treasure-house of insights and advice that the author of the *Arthashastra* offered to ambitious conquerors of the late centuries BCE.

Notwithstanding the fact that it is widely used for reconstructing Mauryan times, there are sharp differences about the date and authorship of the *Arthashastra*.[42] As with the Megasthenes *Indica*, experts differ over the usefulness of this work as a source in the conventional sense for conclusions about Mauryan material life and culture: unlike the *Indica*, the *Arthashastra* is a theoretical work which does not refer to specific events. The historian Patrick Olivelle has pointed out that there is a 'Kautilya recension' and a later 'Shastric redaction' in which the text's structure was imposed on the original treatise.[43] He also provides various arguments to suggest that the 'Kautilya recension' was put together much after the time of the Mauryas. However, the cultural data on the basis of which he has suggested this is flawed and some of that data actually underlines that the original recension was likely to be of Mauryan vintage.[44] On balance, it is reasonable to consider the core of this formidable manual of statecraft as being anchored in the late centuries BCE. Since it is focussed on the doings of imperial power, an incidental benefit is that it gives glimpses of palace life. Among its various subjects are regulations for the royal residence and its members. In the interstices of its hortatory pronouncements lies some of the context from the time when Ashoka was young.

The palace is described in the *Arthashastra* as standing to the north of the heart of the residential area of a fortified city.[45] The royal residence itself—if the text's prescriptions were to be followed, or conversely if they were based on some idealized form of actual practice—was made up of many halls. It stood within its own inner fortifications, comprising ramparts, a surrounding moat, and gates. The treatise designates specific places for a variety of people and activities: the royal family would have slept in quarters given to each member or group. The princes and princesses, for instance, were supposed to live in quarters outside the apartments for the royal women, including presumably their mothers. The king's chamber, on the other hand, was in the centre of the palace, at a distance from the family's quarters.

The provisions for making the king's living quarters impregnable and invulnerable are many and border on the paranoid:

> He should cause to be constructed a living chamber in the centre in accordance with the procedure laid down for the treasury, or a maze-house with concealed passages in walls and in its centre a living chamber, or an underground room with its opening covered by the wooden image of a deity in a nearby sanctuary and having many subterranean passages (and) above it a palace with a stair-case concealed in a wall or having an entrance and exit through a hollow pillar as a living chamber with the floor fixed to a mechanism (and thus) capable of sinking below, in order to counteract a calamity or when a calamity is apprehended.[46]

Did Ashoka's father Bindusara occupy this sort of chamber? Were his children allowed in, to be with him? If the prescriptions of Kautilya's manual were strictly followed, the children may well have been barred entry, for certainly the queens were strongly frowned upon as entrants to his majesty's living quarters. Instead, the recommendation was for the king to visit the inner apartments ('antaragriha') of the queen favoured on a particular day, though even this was meant to happen only after the host queen was 'cleared of suspicion by old women.' If Kautilya had had his way, all palace inmates would have lived forever segregated, more or less, each limited to his or her particular quarters, mingling only when strictly necessary.

So obsessed is Kautilya with security that his injunctions could have served as the rule book for a medieval nunnery. If he had also been allowed his way with plants and animal life, the royal home would have been insulated from many of these as well. Precaution being required against poison and serpents, only the shoots of plants such as the Ashvattha, as also 'Jivanti, Sveta, Muskaka and Pushpavandaka', were admissible. The fauna deemed worthy were those that apparently destroyed serpents, so 'letting loose peacocks, ichneumons and spotted deer' on the premises was a good idea. Similarly useful among bird life, 'the heron becomes frantic in the proximity of poison, the pheasant becomes faint, the intoxicated cuckoo dies, the eyes of the Cakora-partridge become discoloured.'[47]

In the quarters where Ashoka and his siblings spent their growing years, there might thus have been a plethora of restrictions. What of the provisions made by their emperor-father for their education? The number of Ashoka's siblings remains unknown, precision in such matters being difficult given the number of queens and concubines available to the king, the tendency not to count girl-children at all, and the possibility of some of the king's female entourage being impregnated by male courtiers whose progeny became indistinguishable from the king's. The tendency in many ancient Indian texts is therefore to offer a symbolic number indicating the virility and fertility of a regime: '101 sons' is often given as a stereotypical figure, which it is in one account pertaining to the Ashokan context, where this number of offspring are said to have been born of Bindusara's many wives.[48] The exaggeration shows in any case that many children in a polygamous royal establishment was the norm.

How they were educated remains unclear. The king himself was unlikely to have had much to do with their education since he did not see much of his family. His daily schedule as detailed in the *Arthashastra* suggests that his days and nights were divided into eight parts each. Time slots were allotted for looking into income and expenditure, the affairs of citizens and country people, military plans and a review of troops, consulting counsellors and dispatching secret agents, and even being blessed by a chief cook and astrologer, but no time was set aside for family and progeny. One imagines that the sixth part of the day, when he could 'engage in recreation at his pleasure',[49] refers to activities quite far removed from a devoted enlarging of the minds of children.

Proper arrangements were of course put in place within the palace for the education of princes. A general sense of their upbringing can be had from the section in the *Arthashastra* which sets out how princes were to be trained. Unlike Egypt, where we see Cleopatra employing a distinguished scholar of Damascus to educate her twins, Alexander Helios and Cleopatra Selene, in the court of the Mauryas the princesses were not thought worthy of an education.[50] No source says anything about Ashoka's sisters. Ashoka himself was likely to have been raised, like his male siblings, to be an effective leader and administrator. A prince's training ranged from the martial arts to more cerebral subjects. In his early childhood, probably at the age of 3, he would have been tonsured, and then instructed in writing and arithmetic. After his initiation ('upanayana'), he is likely to have had several tutors because he was expected to 'learn the three Vedas and philosophy from the learned, economics from the heads of departments (and) the science of politics from theoretical and practical exponents.'[51] The training was continuous, conducted daily. In the first part of the day the subject of study was how to use elephants, horses, chariots, and weapons; in the latter part the prince was expected to listen to what is described as 'itihasa'. This denotes 'history' in our time, but in Ashoka's it covered a range of knowledge about the world. A prince listening to 'itihasa' would have acquired narrative histories of the universe, economics, and the existing ideas about social functioning.[52]

One may reasonably assume that the range of able officials in the court of Bindusara included tutors designated for such work. A minister-in-charge of the princes was, we know, expected to live in the palace.[53] That Ashoka was well taught is evident from the fact that his inscriptions reflect a deep interest in and understanding of statecraft, philosophy, and ethics. His experiences and exploits in later life will have added to his personal and intellectual depth, but the propensity towards such expansion will have been nurtured by the princely instruction that first honed his character.

While this early training was meant to ensure that the ruler's sons were not lacking in discipline and mental development, all princes, disciplined and undisciplined alike, were thought to pose a danger to the king.[54] In one well-known analogy, princes are like crabs—creatures known to devour their begetters. It would seem from the existence of sayings such as this that the thought of regicide diluted the filial gaze in every sovereign of the ancient world.[55] Undisciplined sons, disaffected ones, those in disfavour, and those of evil intellect are described at length, as are the ways to neutralize them or otherwise do away with them. The provisions tended to vary according to the number of sons the king had. If his only son was disaffected, he was to be put in prison; if there were many sons, the recommendation was to send the disaffected one to the frontier or some other suitably distant region where he might in time be swallowed up forever.[56]

The palpable distrust that such provisions reveals was perfectly plausible since there was no shortage of kings who had either been killed off or dethroned by ungrateful or ambitious sons. Some three centuries before Ashoka a king of Magadha, Bimbisara, in about the sixth century BCE, was murdered by his son Ajatashatru—whom we met earlier as the builder of the fortifications at Pataligrama. Bimbisara's contemporary Pasenadi, monarch of the Kosala kingdom, fared little better. His royal insignia was handed over to his son Vidudabha by one of his own ministers, the son being then installed as king while the dispossessed father was deserted by practically everyone.

In the same breath that cautions kings against their sons, the manual offers survival techniques to princes out of favour. Disguise and seeking refuge with a neighbouring prince are very highly thought of; parricide is reserved as the last option in worst-case scenarios. The odd thing in this vicious terrain of royal sagas in which princes are ever ready to stab their fathers in the back is the tenacity of primogeniture. Blood, it seems, was always thicker than water. Kings guard themselves to the hilt against their own sons. But when the time comes, the son inherits.

Did Bindusara send Ashoka to different parts of his empire because he sensed a disaffected son? Ashoka apparently went to Taxila on his father's orders, but whether the emperor sent him there because he wanted to keep a contrary son at bay remains unclear. In any case, for us this seems a good moment to leave Pataliputra and see what Ashoka is likely to have encountered at Taxila if he did indeed go there.

Ashoka would have approached that very distant north-western city somewhat cautiously: it was really very far from Pataliputra, some 2000 km or so across a land, as we shall see, of large rivers and luxuriant forests. At that point in time, Taxila was also said to be a somewhat tense and turbulent place—exactly the sort of frontier location to which the discontented prince was, in Kautilya's opinion, supposed to be transferred.

# 3

# Mauryan Taxila

TAXILA IS THE NAME OF AN ANCIENT CITY AS WELL as the sobriquet of an archaeological site. When Taxila figures in the ambitions of eastern aggrandizers like the Maurya rulers based in Pataliputra, or in those of invaders from the West—the Persian Darius I and Alexander of Macedon, mainly—it is a single city that comes to mind. Its Sanskrit name, Takshashila, was first pared down to Taxila by the Greeks when they described it as the foremost city of Punjab, and presumably since the Greek version trips easier off the tongue than the Sanskrit—unlike the slightly absurd-sounding anglicization 'Sandrakottos' for Chandra-gupta—the abbreviation took root and was extended to describe the larger archaeological site of Taxila. The latter is actually an ensemble of several sites: three city sites, and the ruins of many Buddhist stupas and monasteries scattered across hills and spurs in the surrounding countryside, including knolls near the Tamra nala and the northern slopes of the ridges of Margala. Of these, it is the settlement of people that came to occupy what is known as the Bhir mound which is central to this story, since it was at the Mauryan city there that Ashoka is said to have arrived at the behest of his father.

No chronicle or record contemporaneous with Ashoka exists to tell us of his campaign to pacify Taxila. It is once again the second CE *Ashokavadana* which recounts his arrival there, as also the circumstances which drove him so far to the north-west frontiers of the kingdom. Taxila, the text tells us, was in the midst of a rebellion which Bindusara wanted his son to quell—bizarrely, says its translator John Strong, without weapons:

> Now it happened that the city of Takshashila rebelled against King Bindusara. He therefore sent Ashoka there, saying: 'Go, son, lay siege to the city of Takshashila.' He sent with him a fourfold army [consisting of cavalry, elephants, chariots, and infantry], but he denied it any arms. As Ashoka was about to leave Pataliputra, his servants informed him of this: 'Prince, we don't have any weapons of war; how and with what shall we do battle?'
>
> Ashoka declared: 'If my merit is such that I am to become king, may weapons of war appear before me!'
>
> And as soon as he had spoken these words, the earth opened up and deities brought forth weapons. Before long, he was on his way to Takshashila with his fourfold army of troops.[1]

Several interpretations seem possible. Given the tendency of this variety of hagiography to exaggerate and valorize its protagonist, sometimes to the point of deifying him, Bindusara's decision to send Ashoka to Taxila without the required means could simply denote an inadequacy of weapons rather than the absolute lack of them, the son's subsequent expeditionary success thereby becoming one of the many miracles associated with his glorious career. Alternatively, it could mean that Bindusara, who as we saw is supposed to have disliked this son of his, was engineering Ashoka's Taxila expedition to ensure a failure that would forever remove him from Magadha. It may be stretching it a bit to argue that the emperor had an accurate premonition about Ashoka not needing to resort to arms, but even this perspective on the affair is not unwarranted because, according to the text, though Ashoka arrived in Taxila at the head of an armed contingent, the swords remained in their scabbards: the citizenry, instead of offering resistance, came out of their city and on to its roads to welcome him, saying 'We did not want to rebel against the prince ... nor even against King Bindusara; but evil ministers came and oppressed us.'[2] This image of the prince in Taxila, armed yet not having to resort to arms, fits with the later textual representation of Ashoka who, as an 'iron-wheeled monarch' ('ayashcakravartin'), is supposed to have ruled Jambudvipa (India) with the threat rather than the actual use of the sword.[3] Whichever way you look at it, benevolence, compassion, and a benign attitude towards his fellow human beings seem to lie at the back of the assertion that Ashoka's Taxila campaign was non-violent from start to finish.

But did Prince Ashoka ever actually come to Taxila? He himself never says he did, but that is neither here nor there because we have seen how famously reticent he was about his early life. Whoever composed the *Ashokavadana*, though, may have known that the city bore many markers associated with Ashoka. For one, the most impressive Buddhist monument of Taxila was a stupa whose name, Dharmarajika, alludes to Ashoka. The nomenclature denotes a religious structure built by the Dharmaraja of the Buddhists, the emperor Ashoka. So, the *Ashokavadana*'s account of its protagonist's visit to a turbulent Taxila squares with the archaeological evidence. For another, the title by which Ashoka was known in his edicts which figure a little later in the book, was used in an Aramaic ins-cription that was found at Taxila on an octagonal pillar of white marble. The epigraph mentioned 'our lord Priyardarshi'.[4] That this 'Priyadarshi' was Ashoka is evident from the nature of the mes-sage which speaks of non-injury to creatures and obedience to the aged.[5] In other words, Buddhists and others familiar with Taxila who may have read or listened to this nugget about Ashoka's early life are not likely to have doubted its veracity.

It is not as clear how the scribe who put together this legend of Ashoka's life would have visualized the city itself. Travellers fre-quently went to Taxila, a flourishing urban centre in the early cen-turies CE, and they may have carried back impressions of its big buildings and broad streets. But by then it was no longer situated where Ashoka had been: it stood in a different location, at Sirkap, towards the northern side of the valley, occupying a small but well-defined plateau there. The *Ashokavadana* contains nothing enlight-ening for those curious about this old city, nor about how it would have appeared to Ashoka, nor why its citizens had rebelled against his father. But this is because the work is purposive and agenda driven: it is mostly a hagiographical and not a historical work. It is written to buttress Buddhism by highlighting the fact of a great monarch transformed by its tenets.

Modern readers are more fortunate than their ancient counterparts in that, because of the extensiveness of its ruins, they can imagine what ancient Taxila was like. This emerged from the long and detailed excavations conducted by the ASI under John Marshall for two decades or so from 1913. The ruins so patiently unearthed over long years still stand, testimony of the historical settlement which Ashoka apparently beheld as a young man.[6] The archaeological record of Taxila, it needs to be said, is very different from the narrative of the *Ashokavadana*. Dated imperial and official inscriptions, which can shore up the plausibility of events mentioned in ancient sources, are rare in India, as they are in large parts of the ancient world.[7] So an episode such as the arrival of an armed Mauryan prince and his party at Taxila has left no material trace at all and is basically unconnected with what has been identified by the excavations, namely the building and rebuilding of houses and streets, the changing stratigraphic features, and some events that may have influenced those changes. This makes it possible to describe the kind of city that Taxila was, and the quality of life of its citizens in Ashokan times.

\* \* \*

To reach Taxila the prince of Pataliputra would have traversed an enormous distance, nearly 2000 km, that being roughly the distance between present-day Patna and Punjab. The journey will have been across a vast crescent of alluvium created by the Ganga and its tributaries in the east and the Indus and smaller rivers that joined its flow towards the west. In the third century BCE, there will have been some open grassland and stretches cleared for cultivation, but large parts of the tracts were thickly forested. References in ancient texts like the *Mahabharata*, as also pollen records and charred wood specimens from sites in the upper Gangetic plains, suggest this.[8] These forests did not, however, deter either travel or trade.

A grand arc of communication existed across this northern axis, humming with people and products, and was called the Uttara-patha (northern road). Originating in the regions beyond Taxila and sweeping across the Indus and Gangetic plains, the Uttarapatha went much beyond Pataliputra, to the port town of Tamralipti on the eastern coast.[9] Traders, pedlars, caravan leaders, religious men, and princes commonly figure as travellers on this route; and, as we saw, Megasthenes too had journeyed over this stretch. Much before him, residents of Magadha are known to have travelled the long way to Taxila. In a story set in the time of the Buddha, a resident of the Magadhan capital Rajagriha, Jivaka by name, went to train under a renowned physician at Taxila,[10] returning to his home town after a studentship that lasted as long as seven years.

While texts make the Uttarapatha visible through such jour-neys, archaeological sites have yielded raw materials that were conveyed along the same route. Beyond Taxila, from Afghanistan, lapis lazuli, for instance, appears to have been in demand in the cities across this axis, from Rairh in Rajasthan to Sravasti and Rajghat in the middle Gangetic plains.[11] Many other exotic stones and metals, from tin to silver, came into northern India from Afghanistan. For Bindusara this was an important reason for ensuring peace in Taxila and friendship with its citizens. The settlement had become vital as a hub for traders and merchants from Central Asia on their journey into the heartland of Gangetic India.

Some decades before Ashoka's putative journey Chandragupta had pacified the Punjab and incorporated it into his empire, this being necessary to consolidate Magadhan supremacy further up towards the Hindukush mountains. If Taxila, the premier city of this frontier region of the Mauryan empire, was restive, the impact on overall stability within the geopolitical orbit could be disastrous.[12] Quelling turbulence there was additionally crucial because this was a very prosperous region. It was, in fact, reputed to be part of one of the richest provinces in the ancient East from a time preceding Alexander's arrival in 326 BCE: the twentieth satrapy of the Achaemenid empire in the sixth century BCE had been described by Herodotus as the richest in the Persian empire.[13] The king of Taxila capitulated to Alexander, who is said to have sacrificed there as well as held 'a competition in athletics and horsemanship'.[14] Subsequently, Alexander marched eastward to attack Porus, leaving behind at Taxila—as he did in various other conquered cities—a garrison of Macedonians and mercenaries under a commander. The mercenaries murdered their commander, but they too did not last long. Towards the end of the fourth century BCE Taxila was again subjugated, this time by Chandragupta.

Martial conquests such as those by Alexander and Chandragupta, as by other heroic men of the past, have been endowed with celebrity status because military success and the building of vast empires—which from a saner perspective might justifiably be thought of as male megalomania of the most revolting form—have come to be accepted as 'wonderful' and 'great'. Looked at from a more Ashokan lens, i.e. a moral common sense based on humanity, compassion, and fellow feeling, these men of drive and ambition slaughtered thousands of soldiers, divested Taxila of its independent political status, and ruined the lives of the city's residents and their families. The *Ashokavadana*'s account of a restive populace, resentful of the Mauryan ministers who oppressed them, if historically true, makes eminent sense. And Ashoka is likely to have been a relieved man if indeed its citizens, contrary to his expectations, welcomed rather than resisted him.

What did Taxila look like when it welcomed him? Literary accounts are unsatisfactorily silent about this. John Marshall, who devoted twenty-two years of his working life to excavating Taxila, writes of the curiosity of the Greeks accompanying Alexander when they saw the city's shaven-headed and long-haired ascetics, whom they encountered practising austerities. The Westerners endeavoured to understand Indian gymnosophy and related philosophical directions and were amazed by social habits such as offering the dead to vultures. But these observers, Marshall laments, had nothing to say 'about the appearance of the city, the houses of the people, or the countless other things that an archaeologist wants to know concerning material culture.'[15] Consequently we know nothing either about the city's governance by Mauryan officials which the Taxilans were supposedly rebelling against.

Luckily there is a welter of ruins—walls and wells, shops and squares, and much else—from which the lives of the citizenry can be reconstructed. Leading a contingent of men and animals, Ashoka will have sighted Taxila from a distance, standing as it did on a plateau which rose between 18 and 21 metres above the surrounding plains. The royal party will have seen a crowded congeries of structures covering virtually the whole of the Bhir plateau, which measures some 1097 metres north to south and around 668 metres east to west, as does the city atop it.[16] Size-wise Taxila was far smaller than some of the other great cities of Ashoka's time, but not many were located on a natural promontory visible from a distance. Taxila, Ashoka may well have thought, was in this respect a little like Champa—the place from where Ashoka's mother possibly hailed—in ancient Bihar, a very old town on a tableland, seen before it is reached, and not far from Pataliputra.

As the army reached Taxila's immediate surroundings the variable elevations that made up the skyline of the city would have become visible. Its flat-roofed houses were likely to have been of varying heights, the surface of the plateau being uneven and the rubble of earlier construction lying buried under them.[17] The houses were plastered with clay, this clay-clad appearance of the city being much the same as when the first settlement was established there in the sixth century BCE. That earliest settlement was substantially smaller than the cities that grew over it, but its structures would have looked the same because the walls of its buildings had across the centuries been evenly and thickly coated with a mixture of mud plaster and straw.[18]

Beyond that remarkable homogeneity given by mud plaster, the character of the house walls and public buildings had changed. These were now of stone, made from locally available varieties of a hard limestone found in the neighbouring foothills and the very soft lime kanjur available all over the plains.[19] Whereas the constructions of earlier settlements at Taxila were generally of a rough and loose rubble masonry, the blocks of buildings that made up the Mauryan city were neat and compact. The archaeological strata here span several centuries, going back to the fifth century BCE, if not earlier (this being designated strata IV), and continuing till the invasion of the Bactrian Greeks in the second century BCE (represented by the first or uppermost stratum). The Mauryan was the second stratum, and the walls of buildings of this period showed more careful and clean ways of construction. The stone walls, though, would not have been visible to the royal visitor because the practice of cladding them externally and internally with plaster seems to have persisted despite the improved building materials. The city's appearance will have struck Ashoka as starkly different from that of most of the cities seen on the way to Taxila: cities like Kaushambi and Hastinapur were brick-built since they stood on alluvial expanses bereft of stone.

Usually, the impression given by a city depends upon the harmony between the geometry of its streets and lanes with the residential and public structures that border them. Entering Taxila, the main street will have impressed the party from Pataliputra. Because of its width, averaging some 7 metres and its more or less straight alignment, 'First Street' is what it was fittingly called by its excavator. [20] Visitors in the third century BCE who used this street were travelling over an artery that had been Taxila's main thoroughfare since the time of its first settlement. We know this because there is no debris of collapsed or demolished structures of earlier strata underneath, of the kind usually encountered under blocks of houses that line roads. Instead, there is 'only a deep accumulation of small boulders and river pebbles that had been used to pave the street or had been dumped there from time to time when it became necessary to raise the level.'[21]

How visitors and city residents experienced the main street would have depended upon the season. This is because Taxila lacked a drainage system. While there may have been surface drains— such surviving remains have been found in the Fourth Street and

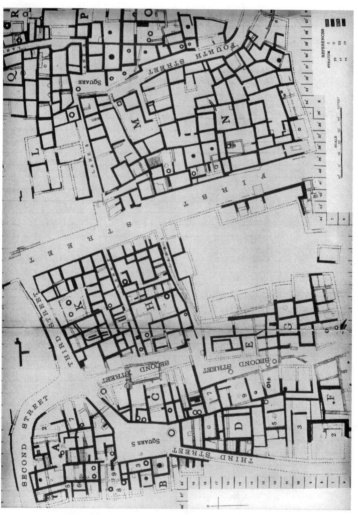

Fig. 3.1: The city plan of Mauryan Taxila on the Bhir mound

in Lane 1—they do not connect with a main drain of the type which would have carried rain water out of the city.[22] So, for all practical purposes, the impressive main street functioned both as a communication axis and wet-weather watercourse. Ashoka would not have enjoyed parading his troops through slushy water flowing down First Street had his arrival been during the monsoon, especially as the flow during downpours was more in the nature of an inundation on account of water from the higher lanes augmenting its own.

Taxila's geometry presents another contrast with the quality of planning that went into creating the system of drainage at Pataliputra, where we have already seen an impressive network of underground wooden drains. Taxila was also very different from the first cities of the north-west, such as Harappa and Mohenjodaro, that flourished in the third millennium BCE. Comparisons between cities separated by more than two millennia are not specially useful, but for the historian of archaeology it is difficult not to think of India's first cities in connection with Taxila since Marshall, who presided over the discovery of those first cities, also excavated Taxila. His report on Mohenjodaro describes streets that, like Taxila's First Street, run remarkably straight and most of them, he showed, had burnt-brick drains associated with them.[23]

Moving beyond the orderly if somewhat muddy First Street, the plan shows a city full of oddly aligned winding streets and lanes. It is unlikely that the royal visitor and his entourage undertook a tour of these, but since archaeological details about them help recreate the ambience of movement and habitation, it is worth going beyond what is likely to have been seen. Much narrower than the main street, these side streets and lanes are an odd combination of straight and winding segments.[24] The Second Street, for instance, begins on a somewhat straight alignment that, less than halfway through the city, moves by several feet towards the west, and again after intersecting the Third Street lurches in a wide curve towards the east. As for the lanes, 'they were narrower still, no more in fact than passages between the houses in which two persons would often find it difficult to walk abreast.'[25] A few of these narrow alleys appear to have been meant only for the private use of the houses that flanked them. This was the case with Lane 2 which, towards its western end, was cordoned off by a cross-wall.[26] This meant that people who wanted to cut across from First Street to Second Street could not use Lane 2, which connected them. Instead, they would either have to follow Lane 1 or move north and turn left, on Third Street. So, Lane 2 in effect became a kind of private alleyway.

What makes this mishmash surprising is that the elegant main street had been the city's thoroughfare from earliest times. Practically all the other streets and lanes, the awfully asymmetrical ones, were created later, during the late fourth and early third centuries BCE.[27] One would have expected the later development to have emulated the proportionate and urban good sense of the earlier rather than fallen short of them, so the disfigurations of Taxila's bylanes have disappointed many a modern scholar of those times, especially as images of cities in Mauryan times commonly suggest a reasonable degree of planning. So, for instance, the ideal urban layout as described in the *Arthashastra* is of a city space demarcated by six roads, three running from east to west and three from north to south; this is what anyone familiar with the literature of those times would broadly expect to hold generally true. The reality of Mauryan urban spaces, Taxila reveals, was far less regimented. Whatever the prescriptive vision, circumstances on the ground in those times, as mostly in contemporary urban India, were likely to be of greater significance in how the city and its streets were shaped.

In fact, the question in relation to Taxila that needs to be answered is this: if the city administrators had, as seems evident, undertaken a programme of public works and practically created a new communication network from scratch, why did they configure the streets to run in such an irregular way? The answer is unclear, but my guess, on the basis of what is known from below the streets and lanes, is that the city administration had to clear structures in the areas through which the roads were to be laid. Possibly, their clearance campaign was resisted by citizens whose lives were affected by the restructuring. It seems reasonable to think of some house owners, shopkeepers, and commercial proprietors willing to allow their properties to be acquired, and of others unwilling to allow their land and homes being cut for the sake of straight streets. The city planners at Taxila may have agreed in theory with Kautilya but found it prudent in practice to let the topography of subsidiary streets and lanes be determined by the availability of land rather than by a drawing board gridiron. The streets that resulted from this compromise are winding and haphazard, but they do seem to represent a citizen-friendly solution.

Realizing that the streets were inconveniently aligned for the pack animals that used them for the transport of goods, the planners took some care to ensure that the corners of houses in the streets were protected. This was done by constructing wheel-guards in the shape of stone pillars set up in corners. The pillars usually rose only a little less than a metre above the ground, with another half metre buried below ground. Also, even though the streets and lanes were usually narrow, there were substantial open squares at different points, a feature created to relieve the congestion in the narrow pathways. These squares were scattered all across the city, providing some breathing space amidst cramped and narrow lanes. The presence of a stone bench in the south-west corner of one of these squares, known as Square S, around or before the beginning of the Mauryan occupation also suggests that these were meant to be used by the populace. From such street furniture it is possible to imagine ancient Taxilans shooting the breeze in their city squares.

Except that the breeze they shot may have been rather smelly. The squares seem also to have served as public areas where large garbage bins, built of stone rubble, were located. One of these, on the east side of Square S, known by the bones and broken pottery that were excavated out of it, leaves little doubt that it was used by houses in its neighbourhood for refuse disposal.[28] These public garbage bins will have required a class of sweepers and refuse collectors, well-to-do citizens in the ancient world not being famous for personally disposing off their own household garbage, and certainly never in the subcontinent's caste-ordered social system. There would also have had to be a system in place to clean out those bins and prevent garbage overflows on to streets and squares.

Notwithstanding such a system, solid refuse was sometimes dumped into soak-wells meant for liquid refuse. This seems to have been the case with a soak-well situated in a square at the intersection of Lane 3 and Lane 4 in the eastern part of the city.[29] It was filled with a large quantity of pottery vessels, as many as 164 of them, choking the whole shaft of the well.[30] The dumped vessels may have contained household kitchen waste, or else they had outlived their utility and were just chucked. That they were thrown in such large numbers into a well meant for liquid waste suggests that the subcontinent's famed contemporary incompetence in the sphere of public hygiene and civic-mindedness goes quite a long way back. Of course, it is possible that when distant dignitaries and their emissaries came visiting, the city's municipality was galvanized into cleanliness. Ashoka would naturally never have experienced first-hand the normal state of insanitation in Taxila.

Was royalty expected to pay obeisance at the temple at Taxila, the most prominent public space in the city? The city brimmed with deities. Goddesses outnumbered gods. Miniature goddesses of clay outnumbered gods. Many of these were for domestic worship in homes, but also seem to have formed part of the paraphernalia of public worship at least in this most conspicuous area within the city, where the presence of an early temple is clear.

This place of worship is in the western part of the city and comprises two blocks with a narrow lane running between them. In the larger block, which is to the north, are two open courtyards, a large pillared hall on the western side of one of the courtyards, and some thirty rooms.[31] The rooms were dwelt in and the inhabitants are likely to have been the temple priests. The debris in this block yielded a number of terracotta reliefs, with a male and female deity standing side by side, so there seems little doubt about this having been a shrine. Marshall sums it all up:

> The position which it occupies alongside the street suggests ... that it served rather as a shrine of some sort, and if this was so the house attached to it may well have been occupied by the priests and their attendants or disciples. This seems more likely because in the debris of this building, as well as among the ruins on the farther side of the lane to the west, were found a large number of terracotta reliefs representing

a male and female deity standing side by side and holding hands. Such stamped reliefs were made to be sold or presented to worshippers at a shrine and to be kept by them as mementos or talismans, just as figurines of *devas* or *devis* are made and sold today in shops outside many an Indian temple. In this case it seems highly probable that the structure referred to on the opposite side of the lane was just such a shop, and this would explain why many of these plaques are found in it. If I am right in drawing this inference, then the Pillared Hall acquires an added interest as being the earliest Hindu shrine, by several centuries, of which any remains have come down to us.[32]

The room, designated B4, close to the pillared hall was dominated by a large square tank-like construction which, Marshall believed, could either have been an ablution tank or a fire pit. Either way, it is a facility found within Hindu shrines; neither has been found in early Buddhist and Jaina places of worship.

What of the deities found here, and do they provide clues to the religion of their worshippers? The commonest ritual objects found are votive plaques showing a male and female figure standing side by side.[33] The turbaned male, with necklace and earrings and wearing a dhoti, holds the side of his shawl with his right hand. The female, with ear pendants and a necklace as also a long veil on either side of her head, rests her left hand on her hip. Similar plaques and the terracotta matrix from which these were moulded were found together in a shop opposite the pillared hall. Their presence there indicates a shop-cum-manufactory which possibly supplied all manner of deities—a votive relief shows a standing female deity holding a bird in her left hand;[34] another is a pot-bellied squatting dwarf (called 'kumbanda') with bulging eyes and a wrinkled face. The establishment could produce grotesque standing figures too, the mould for such a shape having been found. The wrinkled face is evident, but the pot belly characteristic of such figures is in this instance missing.[35]

Usually, such votive plaques were procured by devotees and offered up at the temple, possibly part of a promise for the fulfilment of vows linked with recovery from illness, success in business, and so on, this kind of worship being common in Indian shrines from earliest times till now. Ashoka could conceivably have been here and made offerings, his conversion to Buddhism being an event associated with his later years. As with a great deal else here, while the temple remains clearly etched, the historical characters who came to it, prominent outsiders or resident citizens, remain unknown.

* * *

Where did important visitors, such as visiting royalty, stay when they came to Taxila? From their proportions and facilities, none of the blocks excavated appear to be palatial. An affluent resident of the city may have played host. With their many small rooms built around large courtyards and their frontages marked by shops or nearly blank façades, these house blocks will have seemed prominent to Ashoka the moment he encountered the city. Many Mauryan settlements have been excavated, but few of them have as extensive a collection of surviving walls and foundations. Taxila is much smaller than many of its contemporaries, but its ruins allow the reconstruction of house patterns missing elsewhere.

Taxilan houses tended to give the city's streets a distinctive aesthetic. Several houses had shops in front, but many were fronted by uninspiring and largely blank walls relieved only by narrow window slits on the ground floor. Wide windows, the norm today, do not show up in the domestic architecture of that period; it was the courtyard inside the house which was crucial for natural light and ventilation. Most Taxilan houses are organized around such courtyards. A good sense of the sizes and plans of residences appears in Marshall's description of a house within a well-to-do quarter of the city:

> The average ground area of this class of house runs to about 3,600 ft., of which some 700 ft. were taken up by open courts, leaving some 2,900 ft. for rooms. Assuming that there were two storeys (and there were certainly not less), this would give a room space of 5,800 sq. ft. in all. On the ground-floor, the rooms, which numbered some fifteen to twenty, were small—rarely covering more than 150 sq. ft. each, and

often not more than half that area. It must be remembered, however, that among the wealthier classes many of the lower rooms would probably be occupied by slaves and dependants, and for this reason they were smaller than the upstairs rooms where the family would live . . . As a rule, this type of well-to-do house was provided with two courts, one of which, it may be assumed, was more private than the other, but both courts were usually so placed that easy access to them could be obtained from the street or lane, and through them to the various rooms which gave off from them or from passages connected with them.[36]

These were houses whose room floors were either of beaten earth or 'bajri' (a coarse sandy aggregate) rammed with mud. Earth also covered the roofs of these houses.

Many of these Taxilan abodes of the third century BCE had been built over earlier habitations going back some two hundred years and more. Instead of removing the remains of collapsed and destroyed roofs, walls, and floors, the common practice seems to have been to level them and build new rooms and courtyards over them. Under Mauryan period houses, facilities that had existed in houses of a greater antiquity have been found simply buried intact. One of the affluent homes, called House K, had a drain under two of its rooms, while in another room two large storage jars lay beneath the floor.[37]

Since the old debris, made up of stones, pottery, and other kinds of rubbish, was unlikely to have been an easy matrix to dig into, residents usually chose to keep the foundations of the new structures relatively shallow. This was an easy enough way of rebuilding. The problem was that it failed to provide the necessary stability to the new structures. Cracks and crumbling plaster must have been quite common, alerting the citizenry to structural weaknesses in their dwellings. To provide additional support, wooden pillars were then erected inside the rooms. Such pillars have not survived but their existence has been surmised from the several shafts (filled with rubble) that have been identified; on these, heavy limestone blocks were placed to provide a firm base for the pillars. One house which required such support was House H, where the roofs of rooms are thus propped up. The remains of a circular pillar stand in the middle of a room, while another room shows the remnants of a square pillar.

The use of English letters as designations—'House K', 'House H', etc.—can seem odd, but it is common practice when the names and identities of the residents are unknown. Firmer names tend to be given when a building's resident or purpose is clear. In the ancient town of Bhita near Allahabad, south of its High Street, a Mauryan establishment is described by the excavator as 'House of the Guild' because of the presence of a Mauryan seal-die inscribed with a legend mentioning a guild ('Sahijitiye nigamasa').[38] Even where no such inscribed objects have been recovered, inferences have been made on the basis of the particular types of objects and structures found. The 'priest house' at Daimabad in mid-first millennium BCE Maharashtra is known to have contained fire altars of various shapes; in the phase following, houses like those of the lime maker, the potter, and the bead maker were similarly identified.[39] The occupations of those in Taxilan houses have not been ascertained with this degree of assurance.

But it is possible to reconstruct the uses to which some of the rooms in Taxila's houses were put. There are bathrooms and kitchens, and in chamber 15 of House K one can imagine clothes and utensils getting cleaned and hung: a soak-well and the remains of some rough stone flooring, as also large water jars found close by, support the inference. Soak-wells are basically vertical pits. In Taxila these were either stone-lined, or constructed of earthenware rings, or of large earthenware storage jars set up one above the other with holes in their bottoms to allow percolation. These were not for drawing water but were maintained in every house for sewage and waste household water. Logically, the rooms in which they were located were either kitchens or bathrooms or privies. In several such rooms the soak-wells are found in pairs, close to each other, and the 'explanation of this may be that when one well was full, it was closed in and a new one opened alongside. Or it may be that they were intended to be used alternately, one being left to dry while the other was in use.'[40] Soak-wells were also placed in courtyards, so washing and scouring happened there as well. The usual wells, though, used for drawing water, are missing from the city. There was a functional reason for this. The height of the Bhir plateau made it impractical to dig wells. They would have had to be very deep to reach the ground water. Instead, people got their water from the Tamra nala, a rivulet which flowed outside the city.

Where a row of chambers fronted the houses it is assumed they served as shops, positioned as they were along public pathways. House H has a row facing the First Street and another adjacent to Lane 1.[41] Living rooms and bedrooms are more difficult to identify. The rooms to the front are described as living rooms because they were positioned towards the street. Tiny rooms, Marshall felt, could not either serve as living or sleeping rooms because they were too small. His assumptions are not based on anything other than the positioning and size of the rooms.

Can we identify the people, *en masse*, who occupied these blocks? How, for instance, do we recognize the administrators of the city and their official areas of work? This is not easy since there are neither names nor dates for those who occupied public office—neither in inscriptions nor texts. Their presence can in some instances be inferred in a general way from the paraphernalia of administration, such as seals and coins. Seals, though, were used by all kinds of people, for example to authenticate quality by manufacturers and traders, and as a marker of kingship. Taxilan seals are of various types but they never bear names or designations; they are etched with a variety of symbols. Hypothetically, if the same symbols were found on the coins of the Mauryan era, it would suggest the seals were used by administrators—a congruence absent here. It is likely that the seals were primarily commercial in function.

One would expect at least a few of the public buildings to be different in appearance from the dwelling units. But none, with the exception of shops that front streets and lanes, differ from each other, the unvarying look being that of a series of house blocks. Some of these may have housed administrative staff: the complex of rooms centring around Block A, suggested the archaeologist

Ahmad Hasan Dani—he reinterpreted the data that Marshall had excavated—was not a domestic unit. Located at the crossing of two streets, Second Street and Third Street, which 'cross each other just in front of this building', the building, Dani believes, 'served some special purpose'.[42] The frontage on the eastern side, adjacent to the Second Street, is semi-octagonal, with a ring of rooms on its inner side. The arrangement of these rooms, as also the square rooms on the western side, he says, shows an administrative purpose. The weakness of the inference, as in Marshall's interpretation of rooms being used for 'sleeping' and 'living', lies in the fact that it is entirely extrapolated from the alignment of the rooms and not based on paraphernalia associated with city administration.

The paraphernalia of commerce, though, is more visible than that of administration. We have seen that the seals were likely to have formed part of the repertoire of merchants and traders. Made out of copper, glass, clay, and stone, the Taxilan seals are either pyramidical or scaraboid. The pyramidical shape was very popular at this time, being used not only for seals but also for delicate carnelian and agate pendants. Such seals are considered typically Mauryan and were usually very small. Why they were engraved with human figures remains unknown. In one instance, the presence of a staff, a circle, and the 'nandipada' (bull's hoof) to the left of a standing man suggests that it could well represent a deity,[43] the bull being much worshipped in ancient India. The nandipada symbol also occurs on a terracotta sealing—the stamp being the impression made by the seal.[44] This sealing has the figure of a humped bull on both sides with the nandipada symbol above the hump. Yet another pyramidical seal, made of copper, has engraved on its base a 'lotus-tree of life', a symbol much used on early Buddhist monuments.[45]

The scaraboid seals, on the other hand, are thought to be of Western workmanship. So called because their shapes resemble the scarabaeid beetle, these were fairly popular in Persia. Their workmanship in Taxila is sometimes described as Greek—as, for instance, in the case of a black agate scaraboid with a lion's back, and a chalcedony specimen with two winged animals, a horse and a bull, engraved on it side by side.[46] At the same time, some of these engravings appear to be Indian in inspiration. Above the scarab with the lion's back is engraved a nandipada. This symbol is unlikely to be of Greek or Persian inspiration. Similarly, the bull, notwithstanding its wings, is typically Indian, not Persian. The scaraboid seals are in fact curiously reminiscent of seals in the Indus civilization of the third millennium BCE, some of which were shaped in ways similar to those in the Persian Gulf and Mesopotamia, even as the designs and script characters on them were typically Indian. Square and rectangular Indus seals in Mohenjodaro were, we know, embossed with Mesopotamian designs. The interconnections of trade between Taxila and the West are what the engravings on the scaraboid seals evoke, the hot money being on their use by merchants for transactions relating to West Asia and beyond.

Since the seals were not found clustered in one part of Taxila, it seems unlikely that there was a specific merchant's quarter in the city. The same seems true for people practising other crafts. Craftspeople are occasionally visible here and there: a crucible with a pointed bottom lined thickly with burnt sandy clay, a precious metal polisher, and a chalcedony burnisher of the type used for polishing small gold and silver articles—all these evoke the presence of metal craftspeople.[47] They are not limited to any particular sector of the city.

How much of Taxila's character and commerce, its citizens and the caretakers of the city, was visible to Ashoka is unknown. But this was a city that impressed him because many years later, as the Mauryan monarch, he is said to have built a magnificent structure in Taxila. This was outside the city, on the rocky spurs and knolls that lay to the east of the Bhir, where he created a new kind of religious establishment. The worship in this new structure was qualitatively different from that carried out via rituals connected with the deities of the city and its temple. Known as the Dharmarajika, this was a Buddhist stupa whose Mauryan fabric has vanished but whose religious character was in line with Ashoka's. What kind of religious devotion this Dharmarajika evoked among the people of Taxila, who lived within walking distance of it, we cannot know for sure. My own view is that the various goddesses of the Taxilans, and the old rituals around them, were likely to have had more religious power and meaning for the citizens than the grand stupa made at the instance of their emperor.

The emperor's connection with Taxila ends at this point—his stupa there points us in the direction of Buddhism, and towards the time when he had gone beyond being a prince pushed to a frontier.

# 4

# Affairs of the Heart and State

IN ANCIENT NARRATIONS OF ASHOKA'S LIFE, ROMANTIC passion appears for the first time when the Pataliputra prince is sent to Malwa in Central India. Tellings of this intersect with him falling in love with a young woman who is known in the ancient Sri Lankan textual tradition as a Buddhist.

Her name was Devi and the romance began in the city of Vidisha, where her father was a prominent merchant. Soon enough, Ashoka married Devi and moved on to Ujjayini. Ordinarily, romantic love is a popular theme in ancient India's epics as well as in numerous plays that revolve around the romances of princes and kings in royal courts and cities, sometimes the same story being told and retold across many centuries.[1] The famous love story of King Dushyanta and Shakuntala in the *Mahabharata* is one of these and became the theme of Kalidasa's (*c.* fourth–fifth centuries CE) play *Abhijanashakuntala*, which brings love to life in the way that the best drama does. Unluckily, this variety of interest cannot be discerned in the Buddhist literary sources. Their purposes being religious rather than literary, description of the dynamics of a future Buddhist king's romantic relationship is fairly peripheral to the templates of their narratives. Ashoka's whirlwind courtship of Devi are fleeting and passionless despite, it seems, this relationship being life-changing.

Fig. 4.1: Ujjayini's ancient mounds with the Sipra river in the background

Before getting to that courtship, what seems of interest are the circumstances which brought the prince to Vidisha. This happened when Ashoka journeyed to administer Avanti in the heartland of India, travelling across the black soil of the Malwa region, 'rough, and trampled by the feet of cattle'.[2]

Ashoka was dispatched to Avanti as viceroy by Bindusara. Unlike his brief Taxila sojourn, he is depicted as having spent some ten years at Avanti while headquartered at Ujjayini, the political and administrative centre of the province, a city described as the 'Greenwich of India' since the longitudinal prime meridian was reckoned by Hindu astronomers from this city.[3] If so, he would have arrived there roughly around 282 BCE, some ten years before his father Bindusara died. By the time Ashoka got there, it was an urban centre of respectable antiquity, having flourished along the Sipra river for 300 years or more before it became the Magadhan prince's place of functioning. Fortifications of mud were first erected around Ujjayini in the seventh century BCE, and in about the sixth century BCE the state of Avanti, whose capital Ujjayini was, became a powerful independent kingdom.[4]

The territorial ambitions of this state extended beyond Central India into the Gangetic north. Pradyota, the ruler of Avanti, was a contemporary of Bimbisara, king of Magadha (and father of Ajatashatru, fortifier of Pataliputra). The Avanti-based Pradyota is known to have had designs on Magadha and, in one tradition, attacked Rajagriha, the Magadha capital during Bimbisara's lifetime. Apparently it was out of fear of an aggrandizing Pradyota that, later, Ajatashatru strengthened Rajagriha's defences. Subsequently, one of Pradyota's successors conquered the North Indian kingdom of Vatsa, after which a prince of Ujjayini ruled from its capital, Kaushambi. So, the practice of princes administering distant provinces of large states seems to have been fairly common much before Ashoka.

Avanti, though, could not sustain hegemony over Vatsa and, over time, ceased to be an independent kingdom. When this happened is not known, but by the time Bindusara took over the reins of empire the Magadha-based Maurya state assuredly exercised control over it. The emperor's decision to dispatch Ashoka as its viceroy suggests that the Malwa-centred Avanti province, on account of its wealth and links with various parts of India, was strategic for political and commercial reasons.

A trail of sorts can be discerned as Ashoka travelled on his father's orders from Pataliputra to Malwa.

\* \* \*

Ancient India's royalty travelled in style: that is what sculptural representations of large royal processions of chariots and elephants suggest. Some of the earliest such reliefs can be seen at Bharhut in Central India of the second century BCE, where historical kings figure. Prasenajit of Kosala, for instance, is shown on a chariot drawn by four richly caparisoned horses with attendants and riders, while Ajatashatru of Magadha is depicted sitting on a state elephant with the others accompanying the leader controlled by female mahouts.[5] Like military expeditions, the itineraries of travelling kings were presumably planned well in advance, with calculated halts on the way in villages, towns, and forests.[6] The forethought that went into these expeditions was crucial because, to facilitate the movement of sovereigns and armies, travel tracks had to be made suitable for such retinues. It is for this reason that Bharata, younger brother of Rama of the *Ramayana*, is said to have first organized technical people and labourers to construct the road to Chitrakuta on which he would travel when trying to persuade Rama to return and assume the throne at Ayodhya. The arrangements in that instance were so elaborate—with topographers, guides, surveyors, masons, carpenters, diggers, and even tree planters involved in the expedition—that the trade routes scholar Moti Chandra was reminded of modern sappers and miners who level the ground, chop trees, repair roads, and construct new ones.[7]

Ashoka as newly appointed viceroy is likely to have undertaken his march to Malwa in a similar style, even if his accompanying

entourage, by virtue of his being viceroy and not king, may well
have been smaller than those depicted on ancient sculptural reliefs
and described in epic tales.

If Ashoka began his journey from Pataliputra, the track he
followed was well trodden, forming part of the long traverse of
a network of routes known collectively as Dakshinapatha, or the
southern route. It was along the Dakshinapatha that Jivaka, the
physician of Rajagriha who trained in Taxila, went to the court of
Pradyota, the king of Ujjayini, at the king's request, to cure him
of jaundice.[8] Among the more frequent travellers were traders in
caravans ('sartha') carrying goods from the regions south of the
central highlands. Ranging from the Deccan and peninsular India
to the western and eastern coasts, these found large markets for their
wares in the cities of Gangetic India. The *Arthashastra* describes the
Dakshinapatha as preferable to other routes, singling out conch-
shells, diamonds, rubies, pearls, and gold as plentiful along this
route.[9] Along with this trade, mendicants moved from North India
to the Deccan and back, a movement reflected in the story of the
Brahman sage Bavari of Sravasti, who went along the southern route
and settled down on the banks of the Godavari. On learning that
the prince of the Sakyas, the Buddha, had become a mendicant, he
sent sixteen of his disciples to Rajagriha, the old capital of Magadha,
to meet the great sage.[10]

Regions along this route are also sometimes depicted as being
different from those in the North. Avanti, for instance, is shown in
the literature as different in its practices and customs from places in
the Gangetic plains. It is described as the land where people attach
great importance to bathing, and where 'sheep-skins, goat-skins,
and deer-skins were used as coverlets.'[11] Ashoka will have noted
such differences as he travelled towards Ujjayini.

Considering that Pataliputra and Ujjayini were separated by
nearly a thousand kilometres, a splendid retinue of elephants and
chariots is not likely to have accompanied the armed contingent
and provision-laden carts required for the expedition too far. The
ceremonials were probably only heraldry at the beginning and
conclusion of expeditions, in the manner of 'triumphs' allowed by
Romans to their great generals, such as Pompey and Julius Caesar,

a couple of centuries later. Many more centuries later, in the time of the Mughal emperors, on the best-maintained royal road from Agra to Lahore, the average daily distance covered by caravans was a little over 30 km. Thus, in Mauryan times, on a far more difficult traverse from the Gangetic heartland into Central India, 30 km would have been a steep distance to aim for as the daily average. If we allow 25 km per day, Ashoka's journey to the viceregal region will have taken him 40 days. The variability and difficulty of tracks and terrain encountered on the way make this an optimistic estimate.

While within cities like Ujjayini, where Ashoka was headed, all-weather roads were constructed with a veneer of gravel over a clay soling, long-distance alignments in this part of the region were generally levelled tracks whose width is likely to have depended upon the terrain and on what was considered sufficient to facilitate movement.[12] In the hilly areas—comprising part of the terrain in Ashoka's traverse across Central India—were narrow passageways created by cutting through rocky areas. Ashoka is unlikely to have begun the trek before the monsoon months because travel over this time was specially difficult. The Damoh area in Central India, for instance, which falls along his route, could not have been crossed with wheeled conveyances between July and October, its soil being black loam which became soggy to the point of stickiness after the first rains. Whatever the weather, the pragmatic option would have been pack animals and carts, not elephants. We also know from the accounts of later travellers that one of the major problems was to harmonize different modes of transport. Oxen and elephants move at a different pace. Jean Deloche, the historian of early transport and communication in India, provides a seventeenth-century travel account highlighting the trouble with heterogeneous groupings:

> Camels, pack oxen and oxen harnessed to the heavy carts of Hindusthan did not proceed at the same rate. When, in addition, it was necessary to adapt to the pace of light equipages of some wealthy patron travelling with swift elephants, only deplorable contretemps could result. To give a vivid example, we relate here the experience of Peter Mundy, who in 1633 had been charged to conduct the last caravan of the season,

consisting of 268 camels and 109 carts, from Agra to Surat. Underway Mundy encountered the new governor of Gujarat, Baqir Khan, who was journeying to his residency along with his entourage, and asked to accompany him in the hope that he would thus avoid payment of local taxes and thereby reduce the transport expenses. The decision proved to be imprudent and costly. The troubles soon began. It was impossible for Mundy's caravan to keep pace with the fast rhythm of the official escort. At Khamva, a sand-storm broke, followed by profuse rains; the camels were thus delayed and reached the next stage one day after the carts. Fortunately, the governor had halted because of the rain, and together they continued onwards to Bayana. Two miles before arriving at that destination, one cart wrecked and another became stuck in the river; it was impossible to extricate it and the men had to carry the bales of indigo on their shoulders.[13]

There is every reason to imagine that the travails of terrain and weather that large convoys, such as the one described by Mundy, were part of the pattern of travel of the Ujjayini-bound royal party in the first quarter of the third century BCE.

The route that Ashoka and his retinue took, having long ceased to exist, remains unknown, but we can try and visualize it by exploring the villages and towns of his time that existed along its alignments, as also the itineraries of ancient traders and travellers. The general sweep is clear enough: moving south-west from the middle Gangetic plains, the Kaimurs, which form the eastern scarp of the Vindhyan highlands, will have been ascended. By Himalayan standards these mountains are molehills, the highest point in the entire 1000 km long Vindhyan range being only about 1100 metres. But any forty-day journey at the head of a large travelling contingent more than 2000 years ago will have seemed Himalayan, even to a cosseted emperor in his tent.

Moving from the middle Gangetic plains, the Kaimurs would have been ascended, and here Sasaram's location will have been crucial for the prince's travelling procession to move further west towards the Rewa plateau.[14] From Rewa, the Damoh and Sagar areas would have been traversed to Vidisha, and then onwards towards Ujjayini. Each of the important nodes in this broad alignment, incidentally, was linked in multiple ways and could be accessed through various routes. The research of the archaeologist Dilip Chakrabarti, who made it his professional vocation to travel along ancient routes, highlights this. So, for instance, if Ashoka began his journey from Pataliputra and was headed towards the Kaimur hills on the eastern edge of the Vindhyas, the most direct route would have been along the valley of the Son river. The presence of Deo Markandeya, a site flourishing in Mauryan times and even before, shows that there would have been relatively little problem for ancient travellers who followed this alignment.[15] The other alignment from Pataliputra followed the Bodh-Gaya and Gaya line in order to gain access to the Kaimur hills, but there again two routes existed between Rajagriha and Gaya: one via the Barabar caves and another via Kurkihar.[16] Practically all these were ancient places of habitation and repute, and therefore it is impossible to decide which of these old historic alignments Ashoka will have chosen to follow. We can only be pretty certain he travelled on one of them.

He will have passed through captivating country. Anyone with even holidaying knowledge of the Central Indian hilly climes and the Malwa plateau will vouch for the beauty of the land. Masses of jungle terrain and incredible cliffs teeming with rock shelters are interspersed with long vistas of impressive undulating plateau areas and riverine plains. The Rewa jungles were in the nineteenth century often dense, full of trees like sal, tendu, saj, and khair, and were teeming with wildlife—tigers, leopards, bear, antelope, and chinkara deer.[17] Large parts of this territory must have been sparsely inhabited, but even so, some settlements and sites would have been found along the way. So, from Rewa towards the Jabalpur area the Magadhan entourage may well have chanced upon Rupnath and Kakrehta. Considering that at Rupnath there are springs full of water issuing from the rocks, the entourage may even have camped there and, if so, it may be one of the reasons why, many years later, Ashoka had a set of his royal edicts inscribed at this spot. But Kakrehta, only a kilometre from Rupnath, could also have been a stopover. Situated near the Suhar rivulet, a tributary of the Hiran river, historic pottery (North Black Polished Ware, among other types) of the Mauryan era was excavated out of its ancient mound, whose remains also show that the settlement had stood there for hundreds of years before the time of Ashoka.[18] As the prince moved across the central highlands, he will have noticed how starkly different his native land was from the mighty Ganga and its near monotonous alluvial plains, and from the Vindhyan rocks and the villages and towns that nestled so frequently at the foot of scarps or on isolated hills.

Not all the areas that fall on Ashoka's hypothetical travel itinerary have yielded ancient remains. Damoh and Sagar are among the areas where the ruins of early settlements have been remarkably elusive, while later mid-first millennium CE architectural remains and the coins of the Gupta dynasty are widespread.[19] Future exploration may yield an older or later past, but this sparsely inhabited stretch will almost certainly have felt Ashoka's footprints, or those of the animal on which he was mounted. Within a day or more after crossing Sagar, the prince's party will have encountered the fortified city of Airikina, which falls in the area of the present-day town of Eran. Located some 75 km from Sagar, Airikina is also about equidistant from Vidisha. It was built to ensure protection on three sides by a bend in the Bina river.[20] A mud rampart secured the unprotected side. The rampart was substantial, more than 45 metres wide and with a moat around it.

Ashoka could have halted here and partaken of the city's hospitality. Airikina possessed the means to provide him and his entourage the chance to recoup in somewhat more comfortable surroundings than the jungles of Sagar and Damoh. Shortly afterwards, he would have moved towards the part of Malwa on which stood the city of Vidisha. Lying about 250 km east of Ujjayini, Vidisha will have been Ashoka's last city stop before the last leg of his long expedition.

Its accessibility and distance from Pataliputra make Vidisha interesting on a journey's map. But more interesting are the romantic associations that it evokes, and these are central to any story of the life of Ashoka.

This story, of Prince Ashoka and Devi is, like many other romantic liaisons of antiquity, an account of unsatisfactory brevity. She

Fig. 4.2: The Malwa plateau's hills and forests as they appear near Bhimbetka

was the daughter of a prominent city merchant in Vidisha, this we know, but she is otherwise an elusive figure. Nothing is known of her early life or upbringing or even about her persona before she encountered Ashoka, except that she was, like most future queens, extraordinarily pretty before becoming one. As we saw in the story around Bindusara and the Brahman girl from Champa (later Ashoka's mother), royal men have the habit of noticing female commoners only when they are arrestingly beautiful. Bindusara's son seems to have been in his father's mould. And, naturally, the texts would have us believe it was love at first sight.

Also in line with the template, it is less the state of the heart than the reproductive outcome of this affair of the heart which is central to the story. The *Dipavamsa* puts it blandly: 'the daughter of a Setthi (or merchant), known by the name of Devi, having cohabited with him, gave birth to a most noble son.'[21] A later account is positively loquacious by comparison: Ashoka, it says, 'made her his wife; and she was (afterwards) with child by him and bore in Ujjeni a beautiful boy, Mahinda, and when two years had passed (she bore) a daughter, Samghamita.'[22] Either way, this is the defining incident recounted in relation to Ashoka's life in Avanti, an instantaneous falling in love even before reaching his destination Ujjayini, and the birth of two children to the couple in the course of his obviously long sojourn there.

While historians agree with these aspects of the story, there has been enormous disagreement about other threads. One strange spat—at least that is how it appears to those who engage with the ideas of investigators much after they are played out—concerns the legal status of this relationship, and whether Ashoka did or did not marry Devi. The historian Romila Thapar, in her book titled *Asoka and the Decline of the Mauryas*, is certain that Devi was 'not legally married' to Ashoka since, among other things, there is no reference to a marriage in the *Dipavamsa*.[23] Given the brevity of the evidence, this is not surprising. In fact, such sources don't describe a great deal else that we know to have transpired in the life of Ashoka.[24] The disagreement has also been fuelled by differing interpretations of the word *samvasa* in the Sri Lankan chronicles. The word was initially translated in a way that suggested sexual relations outside marriage, but is supposed to mean co-residence, presumably within a conjugal relationship.[25] And then there is the odd argument that the absence of a 'legal' marriage could be the reason why, after Ashoka's consecration, Devi did not become his chief queen ('since she would have been debarred from performing the duties of the chief queen').[26] Given that this prince showed himself self-willed in going against the tradition of primogeniture by which most princes ascended the throne—he snatched the throne of Magadha at his father's death—it seems to me more likely that Devi was the wife of Ashoka, declared or undeclared, and that the children she bore him, as will become evident, grew into people who were an integral part of his public life.

How authentic is the testimony of the texts which give a glimpse of Ashoka's love for a Vidisha woman, their marital residence in Ujjayini for many years, and the birth of two children to them? This interlude figures in the Sri Lankan tradition and in it the purpose of the retelling is to provide a synoptic account till the time when Ashoka's son and daughter from Devi went to Sri Lanka. The Sri Lankan scholar Ananda Guruge believes there 'was a special reason why the Sri Lankan Pali sources should have taken special care to preserve the memory of this particular phase in the life of Ashoka. It was on his way to Ujjain that Ashoka enjoyed the hospitality of the guild-chief Deva of Vedisa, met his daughter Vedisadevi and married her. The royal missionary Thera Mahinda who introduced Buddhism to Sri Lanka, and his sister Theri Sanghamitta, who brought the sacred Bodhi-tree, were both born of this relationship.'[27] It remains possible to test the veracity of this retelling by looking at them from the perspective of other allusions. That Ashoka was sent to Ujjayini seems authentic since his own edicts as emperor refer to the presence of a prince or 'kumara' at Ujjayini. A royal prince heading the administration there seems to have been normal practice, so the likelihood is that Ashoka, like his son later, administered Avanti from the city of Ujjayini.[28] A geographical logic in the textual references is also pertinent: Ashoka is shown as meeting Devi at Vidisha, and Vidisha falls on the way to Ujjayini from Pataliputra. Its description as a town ('nagaram') is a characterization of the settlement that matches what we know it to have been in Mauryan times, an urban centre of commercial repute probably integral to the larger Mauryan scheme of administration in Malwa. Vidisha's remains show a strong pre-Mauryan core going back to the mesolithic period, followed by a long phase when it was occupied by people who used stone and copper.[29] The first historic phase of occupation there is substantial and goes back to *c.* 500 BC, to a time before the Mauryas. Its prosperity continued into and beyond Ashoka's time. So, Ashoka's halt there looks very plausible, and his interaction with citizens of substantial means such as Devi's father, a man of commerce ('setthi'), even more so because an important function of the viceroy was to collect revenue. Traders and merchants were important in this scheme of things since they contributed significantly to the coffers of the Mauryan state.

A point about Ashoka's personality also seems worth considering in this context. By the time he was sent to Ujjayini he was a young man of some experience, a prince who had possibly travelled to Taxila and other parts of his father's empire. If later textual recountings of incidents relating to his life had wanted to conjure up a story around the sowing of his wild oats rather than a regular marriage, they did not have to wait till he reached Vidisha. And, in any case, why Vidisha in particular? If the idea was to show him in a romance rather than a relationship more sober, the story could well have been woven around places that figure earlier or later in his life: Pataliputra, the city of his childhood, or Ujjayini, where he was headed. The fleeting and somewhat incidental way in which Vidisha appears renders the accounts of it as the locale for the beginning of Ashoka's relationship with Devi all the more believable.

The same circumstantial logic has to be applied in order to understand whether Devi was a Buddhist. The places associated with her have strong Buddhist connections. Vidisha is universally recognized as the pivot of the monuments of Sanchi. Marshall's opinion was that 'from first to last, the story of Sanchi was intimately bound up with the fortunes of the great city in whose shadow

Fig. 4.3: Ujjayini's Kanipura stupa which is associated with Devi

its sangharama grew and flourished and on whose wealth it was mainly dependent for its support.'[30] Again, local traditions link the largest stupa at Ujjayini, the city where Devi is said to have resided, as one that was built for her. The Kanipura stupa, made of large Mauryan bricks at a height of more than 10 metres, is on the north-eastern outskirts of present-day Ujjain. It is locally known as the Vaishya Tekri ('Vaishya caste's mound') since Devi was the daughter of a merchant, this being a characteristically Vaishya occupation.

Beyond the Buddhist associations, the way in which Devi is described in the Pali texts suggests she followed this relatively new faith. Unlike Ashoka, or even her own children, there is no men-tion at all of her having *converted* to it. In fact, her portrayal in the *Mahavamsa*, where she is shown—much after the time period that forms the focus of this chapter—as leading her son Mahinda, by then a monk ('thera'), 'up to the lovely vihara Vedisagiri', suggests that she was already a Buddhist and strongly associated with that vihara. Because this was on a hill, the conjecture is that the monastery where the mother chose to take her monk-son and his companions was Sanchi. This happened, of course, much after

Ashoka's early years, but the incident is worth looking at here in order to make the point that if she was a Buddhist in her later years without there being any allusion to her *conversion* to that religion, then she is likely to have been a Buddhist when she first met Ashoka. Her children—the son Mahinda, and daughter Sanghamitra—are described as having chosen to 'receive the Pabbaja ordination', i.e. a ceremony for what can be translated as 'leaving the world'. This was the initial step before ordination into the monastic order.[31]

That said, the fact that Ashoka had loved and lived with a woman who is remembered by history as a Buddhist does not seem immediately to have influenced the trajectory of his life. On the contrary, his long sojourn at Ujjayini would come to an end in circumstances which would, almost certainly, have been disapproved of by devout Buddhists.

* * *

Some ten years after Ashoka became viceroy in Ujjayini his emperor-father fell critically ill in Pataliputra. Grave ill health in a monarch usually has serious political ramifications, and in this case the king was quite old. The prevailing sense will have been that he would be dead before long. It is thus not fortuitous that his father's failing health became the reason for Ashoka ending his residence in Malwa and returning to Pataliputra, where his bloody assumption of the Mauryan throne would happen. As before, we must depend on later traditions in which this turn of events figures amidst a fascinating if somewhat unverifiable maze of memories and stories.

There are various versions of how these events came to pass. The *Mahavamsa* records the accession of Ashoka with characteristic brevity, merely mentioning that upon Bindusara's illness he came back to Pataliputra: here 'he made himself master of the city, after his father's death, he caused his eldest brother to be slain and took on himself the sovereignty in the splendid city.'[32] There are other ways in which this right royal fratricide is remembered in the Sri Lankan texts, where Ashoka is described as having killed many more brothers in his bid to capture the throne of Magadha. The *Dipavamsa* says a hundred brothers were so killed.[33] Figures such as this, as we have seen, are a common stereotype, merely a way of saying that many brothers were killed, not just one, as the *Mahavamsa* would have us believe. Killing off his brothers may well have allowed Ashoka to rule, but it is possible that protracted fratricidal battles had first to be waged, for the *Dipavamsa* suggests a gap of four years between that bloody assumption and Ashoka's formal consecration as emperor.[34]

A far more gory and viscera-filled tale is told of Ashoka's accession in the *Ashokavadana*, where certain kingmakers, rather than Ashoka, are ministers and key figures in the court of Bindusara. The decision to ensure that Bindusara's eldest son would not succeed him is traced back in this text to a slight that the king's prime minister suffered at the hands of Susima, the heir apparent. It seems the prince slapped the bald head of the minister in jest. The minister, however, was not amused and formed a coalition hostile to the 'jester'. The turn of events is described:

> 'Today he slaps me with his hand,' the minister reflected, 'when he becomes king he'll let fall his sword! I had better take action now to ensure that he does not inherit the throne.'
>
> He therefore sought to alienate five hundred ministers from Susima, saying to them: 'It has been predicted that Ashoka will become chakravartin ruler over one of the four continents. When the time comes, let us place him on the throne.'[35]

Soon after this, the people of Taxila again rose in rebellion. This time, instead of Ashoka, Susima was sent by the king to quell it. Almost immediately thereafter, Bindusara is said to have fallen seriously ill. He recalled Susima, intending to consecrate him as his successor, and ordered that Ashoka be sent to Taxila in his place. But the coalition of ministers pretended that Ashoka was ill. On his deathbed, in fact, they urged Bindusara to instal Ashoka as his successor for the moment and replace him with Susima upon the latter's return.

This, however, made the king furious.

Ashoka, therefore, declared: 'If the throne is rightfully mine, let the gods crown me with the royal diadem!' And instantly the gods did so. When King Bindusara saw this, he vomited blood and passed away.[36]

Ashoka was finally consecrated in 269/268 BCE when apparently he was 'alone continuing his race'.[37] The *Ashokavadana* supports the idea that Ashoka's ascent to the Mauryan throne followed the hot and bloody contest: Susima is said to have been roasted alive when he returned to Pataliputra. It seems 'he fell into a ditch' that happened to have been filled earlier with the live coals of acacia wood. Famed for his compassion as a Buddhist, Ashoka seems to have done a fair amount over his years as an aspiring monarch to require a long life of contrition and contemplation.

But for us to stretch his Buddhist inclinations to cover the sins of his youth would need Ashoka to have expressed his own thoughts on the matter, make some sort of admission, or allude to feelings of guilt about the manner in which he assumed the throne. Is there anything in his edicts which can make us believe that the later textual accounts of his accession are based on hard self-confessional evidence? To make sense of all this, it is necessary to go back to Ashoka's reticence over his early life and lineage, to his silence about being the son and grandson of earlier Mauryan rulers. It is tempting to speculate that one reason for his silence was because he became emperor by violating the tradition of primogeniture, specially as his father had wanted his first-born son to succeed him. In such circumstances, it would have been logical for Ashoka to draw a curtain over his early life and say as little as possible about it. In fact, given what we can glean of his probable misdeeds from texts that are in fact intent on showing his beatitude, Ashoka's silence on these years of his life is deafening. Unless in the future some scintillating new discovery comes along to piece together this puzzle— of why a man so explicit and articulate about his reigning years chose to be so taciturn about his early life, it is extremely unlikely that we will know for sure the scale and details of the carnage that Ashoka is believed to have wrought to succeed to his father's throne.

5

# The End and the Beginning

Ashoka's 'struggle for succession ended in or around 269 BCE when he was consecrated as ruler of the realm carved out by his grandfather and consolidated by his father. The usurper prince took over the throne that he was not meant to inherit, and the large subcontinental empire that came with it, but beyond this his early years as emperor remain an enigma. As before, plausible speculation must serve instead of an empirically strong and convincing narrative because there are neither eyewitness accounts nor any that survive from the years proximate with his own lifetime. As for Ashoka's own testimony, just as he remained silent about his early life and the bloody aftermath of his bid for the Mauryan throne, so he chose not to speak about the initial years of his reign.

Ashoka's early years as emperor came to be recalled in literary texts some centuries later. Those recollections tend to be one-dimensional, as we shall see, ranging from those that see him as an intemperate and violent ruler to others where his persona is that of a searcher for truth. We have no means of telling if these accounts are based on things that Ashoka actually did or are merely retrospective projections of their composers' predilections. My assumption, though, is that some do contain grains of truth. This is suggested by the circumstantial evidence around which allegorical tales of physical violence or spiritual passion were created.

One set of narrations, forming part of what is known as the Northern tradition—the staple for constructing some of the contours of the life of Ashoka as prince—portrayed the early years of his reign as a kind of continuation of his manner of succession, where he settled matters to his own satisfaction, as he had settled the question of succession, with violence.

Ashoka's assumption of the throne is in the *Ashokavadana* immediately followed by an orgy of state-sponsored terror. A chapter title 'Chandashoka', which can be translated as 'Ashoka the fierce', graphically spells out the new king's cruelty and killings.[1] The first episode of his reign discussed in some detail concerns various ministers who were put to death by him. The clique from Bindusara's time which had helped Ashoka become king had now apparently begun treating him with contempt. To test their loyalty Ashoka ordered that they chop down every flowering and fruiting tree while preserving those that were thorny. On the face of it, the order seems absurd (quite apart from the taxonomic stupidity: trees that have thorns often bear flowers and fruit). But, as Tennyson might have put it, this was a bad case of 'Theirs not to make reply,/ Theirs not to reason why,/ Theirs but to do and die': the criterion for establishing loyalty to this monarch rested not on questioning the king's command, however absurd it sounded, but in just blindly obeying it. His ministers were not loyal enough, for, despite being repeated three times, the order was not carried out. Consequently, Ashoka is said to have personally cut off the heads of 'five hundred' of them.

The story is reminiscent of the secret tests that the *Arthashastra* prescribed for kings to test the integrity or lack of it in ministers. Such officials were to be instigated through secret agents to go against the king. This was done by the agents suggesting to them that the king was impious, and that they should 'set up another pious (king), either a claimant from his own family or a prince in disfavour or a member of the (royal) family or a person who is the one support of the kingdom or a neighbouring prince or a forest chieftain or a person suddenly risen to power.'[2] If the instigation was repulsed, the minister was said to be loyal. To judge from the statecraft prescribed for rulers in Mauryan times, this aspect of the *Ashokavadana*'s image of Ashoka appears to hark back to the political tradition of the *Arthashastra*.

The carnage did not end with the decapitated ministers. Many more came to be killed, and now the victims were women who formed part of Ashoka's harem.[3] Again, there was mass slaughter, revenge for having slighted the emperor. It all began in springtime as a consequence of a stroll by the emperor in a park on the eastern side of Pataliputra. While strolling there with his harem and enjoying trees fruiting or in bloom, the king came across a beautiful flowering Ashoka tree—'my namesake', as he put it. The sighting put him in a good mood and he is said to have become 'very affectionate' towards his concubines, no doubt a euphemism for the pleasures of the royal bed. Here it seems that the young women of his harem did not sufficiently enjoy caressing his body, which was rough-skinned. And so, after he fell asleep, 'they, out of spite, chopped all the flowers and branches off the Ashoka tree.' On learning of this the king is said to have burned alive five hundred of these women as revenge for their dismembering his beautiful Ashoka tree. (The number 500 seems a favourite in this text, as 100 and 101 are in others.)

At this point, alarmed by the scale of the killings that Ashoka was personally carrying out, his prime minister is said to have made him appoint a royal executioner who could be delegated the task of future mass extermination, leaving the king unsullied. A suitable candidate was found in a Magadhan village, a weaver boy called Girika who, on account of his ferocity and sadistic tendencies, had the suffix 'fierce' attached to his name. 'Girika the Fierce'— or Chandagirika—is said to have crowed about his prowess to the king's men when they asked him if he felt up to the task of being Ashoka's executioner: the boy exclaimed that he 'could execute the whole of Jambudvipa.' This seems to have got him the job, for we next hear that at his request the king built a jail in Pataliputra, one that people called 'the beautiful gaol' because 'it was lovely from the outside' while 'inside it was actually a very frightful place.' Chandagirika enjoyed full sway in these quarters, revelling in the infliction of all kinds of torture on prisoners, and, when the king allowed, ensuring they never emerged alive.[4]

Sadistic cruelty is virtually a literary trope in Buddhist hagiography, the objective being to show radical and fundamental transformation in temperament and personality consequent upon conversion. Because Ashoka would soon be shown as the ideal Buddhist ruler in the *Ashokavadana*, episodes of extreme cruelty were almost required insertions. The moral change in the king would stand out so much better against an exceptionally brutish background in which he was shown cold-bloodedly killing off even his immediate circle of ministers and concubines. This image of Ashoka is not confined to the Northern tradition; it figures in the Sri Lankan tradition as well. The *Mahavamsa* briefly alludes to it when noting that Chandashoka was so called in ancient times because of his evil deeds; later, through his pious acts, he came to be known as Dhammashoka.[5]

It is possible, of course, that these representations of a merciless monarch were a redeployment of elements that formed part of the accepted remembrance of Ashoka's earlier years of violence-filled usurpation. Cruelty could not have been far during the early period of Ashoka's rule because it is almost certain that he got rid of his older half-brother, and possibly several others who had supported the rightful heir. And this may not have been just a palace revolution: the resistance to his kingly ambitions was likely to have extended beyond the royal family. Who resisted him and how remain unknown. If the records of the Sri Lankan Buddhist tradition are relied upon, it took some four years after his bid for the throne for him to be finally consecrated. This was around 269 BCE, some four years after the death of Bindusara. The interregnum can only really be explained as the context of sustained opposition. And if he consolidated his position ruthlessly, there was bound to have been collateral damage.

Given that Ashoka succeeded to the throne in a manner that was never planned or anticipated by his father, and in bloody circumstances, his consecration could not but have left him acutely aware of the problems that would likely beset his monarchy. Ensuring the loyalty of administrators would in such circumstances have been imperative. It is, then, a fair guess that the *Ashokavadana* embroidered an elaborate story around the motif of loyalty to the king, of punishment by death in the face of disobedience or vindictiveness against him. It resonated completely with what was known about the early exigencies of his rule.

\* \* \*

If the Northern Buddhist tradition produced an exaggerated portrait of a fiercely cruel Ashoka in the years after his assumption of kingship, it was an entirely different image, that of a restlessly enquiring emperor, which was woven into the tale that the Sri Lankan texts told about his early reign. The purpose of their telling was to highlight the notion that Ashoka's quest for a worthy spiritual preceptor was what led him to Buddhism, not because he had any inherent predilection for the faith. He might, after all, have chosen the other newly risen faith, Jainism, which was so fiercely opposed to harming all forms of life that its tenets in favour of non-violence were fanatic. A king in search of a faith advocating compassion could well, in normal circumstances, have looked more favourably upon the worldview of Mahavira than on that of the Buddha. To account for Ashoka's preference for Buddhism over every other competing form of religious compassion thus seemed to require the attractions of a wise man, someone sage-like whose charisma swayed the emperor in the direction he chose. So we learn that the recently consecrated king 'unceasingly . . . searched after virtuous, clever men', and for such men he was willing to give up his kingdom—all that he had inherited and conquered. Considering that Devi was an important part of his life and happened to be a Buddhist it is somewhat strange that the Pali chronicles do not write of her playing a pivotal role in Ashoka's conversion. Possibly, a male protagonist as the crucial character in making him a Buddhist was more in line with the thinking of the times. Ashoka's importance in converting the Sri Lankan king Devanampiya Tissa is matched by that of his son Mahinda who carried, in a manner of speaking, the Buddhist faith to Sri Lanka. Women in such narratives, and not just in India, are mostly the 'helpmeets' of dominant males.

Coming back to the emperor's quest, the most elaborate telling of the story occurs in the *Dipavamsa*. The search began shortly after he became ruler, this being mentioned in a matter of fact way in relation to his son Mahinda, a crucial figure for the Sri Lankan tradition because of his mission to establish Buddhism there. The text notes that Mahinda was 10 years old when 'his father put his brothers to death', and he was 'anointed king in Mahinda's fourteenth year'. For three years Ashoka is said to have honoured people who are described as 'Pasandas'. This is likely to be an umbrella term for a variety of religious orders since many are mentioned in the narrative—Pasandas who proceeded from the Sassata and Uccheda doctrines, Niganthas, Acelakas, Brahmans, Titthiyas, other ascetics, and sectarians.[6] They were invited to the palace, and great gifts were bestowed on them in the hope that they could answer a question the king posed to them. Disappointingly, none of them could answer his question. What this question was the text passes over in silence, but it was apparently 'an exceedingly difficult question'. In this way the Pasandas were 'annihilated' and the sectarians 'defeated'.

The search ended when Ashoka came upon a Buddhist Bhikshu called Nigrodha looking for alms on a Pataliputra road, 'a handsome young man of tranquil appearance, who walks along the road like an elephant, fearless and endowed with the ornament of tranquility.'[7] This virtuous monk's disposition and fearlessness, as much as his preaching, were responsible for Ashoka becoming a lay disciple of the Buddha. In a wonderful reply to the king's plea asking that he teach him the faith that he had learnt, Nigrodha offers a sermon on earnestness: 'Earnestness is the way to immortality', he tells Ashoka, 'indifference is the way to death; the earnest do not die, the indifferent are like the dead.' Ashoka is said to have made an offering of four lakhs of silver and eight daily portions of rice to Nigrodha. Thereafter, according to this tradition, promoting and propagating Buddhism became the hallmark of his reign. As we shall see later, it also became the connecting narrative thread which ensured that the faith reached Lanka, where the text that tells this story was composed.

As with the fierce Ashoka of the *Ashokavadana*, we have no direct evidence that the emperor's initial years of rule were dominated by a spiritual quest. Considering that it took him some years to consolidate his position and be consecrated, such a quest appears unlikely. But a revealing series of inscriptions—the first that Ashoka caused to be inscribed—give us the emperor speaking in the first person about what Nigrodha preached to him. The sermon concerned the importance of 'zeal'—which Ashoka is said to have realized a year or more after he had visited the Buddhist Sangha. His zealousness, the fruit of it, and the possibility that his example would be more generally followed are spelt out in those first epigraphs. It could therefore be that the sermon on earnestness that the *Dipavamsa* speaks of was derived from Ashoka's own rendering of his transformation.

Perhaps such posthumous stories contain elements that are within the realm of possibility, or perhaps they do not. The verifiable truth is that Ashoka's transformation had little to do with his quest for a spiritual preceptor; in fact, it had very little to do with spiritual matters at all. I say this with some confidence because it is through the emperor himself, in words that he himself formulated, that we learn of his metamorphosis being the consequence of activities which fell squarely within the realm of certain very material matters of state. It was a common kingly pursuit which became the starting point for Ashoka's radically different rule and life.

What matters of state was the ruler expected to oversee? If the *Arthashastra* is to be believed, the range was formidable. The countryside had to be settled ('by bringing in people from foreign lands or by shifting the overflow from his own country') and irrigation works built.[8] On the frontiers, fortresses for frontier chiefs had to be set up. Work in mines and factories, and trade in ports and via trade routes, had to be supported, revenue from such areas being central to state requirements. The king had to protect his subjects by the wielding of danda (coercion), 'For the Rod, used after full consideration, endows the subjects with spiritual good, material well-being and pleasures of the senses.' And the social order had to be preserved, presumably in conformity with the system of varnas and ashramas.[9] The key to the king's success was his power over the treasury and the army, so he needed time to focus on these as well.[10]

Of all these, most relevant at this point is that the king was meant to be a 'vijigishu' or would-be conqueror with, we are told, an ambition to own the whole world. Conquest and empire-building, or in other words the extension and exercise of a monarch's power within and beyond his realm, are quintessential within the state ideology outlined by this manual of politics. Naturally, such activity was bound up with every state's relations with all other states, contiguous and outlying. So, the would-be conqueror contemplating the expansion of his dominion had to overcome an impossible number of states in his quest for suzerainty, a fact of life discovered by megalomaniac conquerors such as Alexander and later the Roman Caesars. These other states are frequently denied an autonomous existence in contemporary narratives and primary sources by being defined wholly in relation to their territorial position *vis-à-vis* the would-be conqueror and his superordinate state.

Why were war and conquest so important? The bottom line appears to have been economic and strategic necessity: if you don't exercise power, you will find others exercising it over you. So the king was only properly a king if he had the ambition to conquer and extend his sway over the universe. There was no escaping the need to augment the economy of his state to the detriment of other states and powers: 'he should follow that policy by resorting to which he may be able to see, "By resorting to this, I shall be able to promote my own undertakings concerning forts, water-works, trade-routes, settling on waste land, mines, material forests and elephant forests, and to injure these undertakings of the enemy."'[11]

In his early years, it is a virtual certainty that Ashoka was very much within the mould of the *Arthashastra* ideal of kingship. Because of his conquering ambitions he, who till this point in time seems remote to the point of invisibility, becomes historical and real. A major military expedition, the first event of his reign that he chooses to mention, is now led by him and recorded for posterity. The territory that Ashoka had his eye on was Kalinga, a state on the eastern seaboard of India in what now forms part of modern Orissa and Andhra Pradesh. This desire to bring Kalinga within his fold became manifest in approximately 260 BCE, when Ashoka led a large army marching from the heartland of Gangetic India towards the east.

This is a good place to go beyond our protagonist's ambitions and examine war and territorial aggrandizement in a somewhat larger perspective. Take the specific time of Ashoka's march around 260 BCE: it happened a little after Rome began its extended conflict against Carthage in the first of the three Punic wars which, all told, lasted more than a hundred years (264–146 BC). At the juncture that Ashoka made up his mind to conquer Kalinga, imperial quests and the enlargement of dominion over territories sometimes far distant had become common in many parts of the ancient world. Some three hundred years before Ashoka the army of the Persian empire, with its centre in what is now modern Iran, had crossed into Europe and stamped its authority across regions that stretched from Turkey in the west to north-west India in the east.[12] Persia was the first world superpower of its time. About two centuries later the Persian model inspired Alexander's successful emulation. Starting from his small kingdom of Macedon near Athens he crushed revolts in several Greek cities before leading an expeditionary force that annexed kingdoms in Africa and Asia extending from Egypt to Persia, and eventually defeating eastern adversaries as far away as Punjab.[13]

Alexander died in his thirties and upon his death this vast empire, which at the best of times was difficult to effectively hold, quickly broke up into smaller realms. In Egypt the satrap appointed there by Alexander became the founder of a new dynasty. The fourteen kings of this dynasty, all bearing the name Ptolemy, ruled Egypt for almost three centuries. By the time of Ashoka's consecration the early Ptolemies had ensured that Egypt was the principal naval power of the eastern Mediterranean. In those parts of Asia which lay to the east and north-east of India, similar kinds of consolidation would soon commence. Some fifteen years after Ashoka's Kalinga march, King Zheng, later the first emperor of the Qin dynasty, came to power, and by 221 BC, after conquering rival states, presided over the unification of China around a centralized bureaucratic monarchy.[14]

Given all these conflicts and rivalries, it is hardly surprising that a considerable part of the history of the ancient world is of battles, wars, and conquest. Homer in about the eighth century BCE relating incidents around the conflict between the Greeks and the Trojans, and Herodotus in the fifth century BCE writing of the expanding Achaemenid empire, are probably the best-known chroniclers of ancient conquest, Homer more literary and Herodotus more gossipily historical. Why wars were thought necessary at all is a larger question which strikes one immediately and forcefully, but we dismiss it out of hand as foolish because of many of the things outlined in treatises such as the *Arthashastra*—that power must lie in the hands of powerful and capable men at the apex of armies, that the sustenance of dominion requires the expansion of power via these men and their armies because the alternative is loss of dominion and enslavement. Beyond this arena of competitive imperialism as necessary to survival lie other causes, such as the predominantly male desire to acquire goods and land, food and women. In the 'Warring States' period of China in the fifth and fourth centuries BCE we see that controlling territory became crucial to the consolidation of political domination, while in the 1400s the 'Flower Wars' of the Aztecs aimed to seize people required as sacrificial victims for the gods.[15] Over much of ancient history, territorial expansion also ensured enormous economic benefit. The acquisitions of the Assyrian king Ashurnasirpal II (*c.* ninth century BC) are an example. Even among his smaller campaigns, the booty included 40 chariots with men and horses, 460 horses,

120 pounds of silver, 120 pounds of gold, 6000 pounds of lead, 18,000 pounds of iron, 1000 vessels of copper, 2000 heads of cattle, 5000 sheep, 15,000 slaves, and the defeated ruler's sister.[16]

How much of this *weltanschauung* formed part of the mental horizons of Ashoka cannot be specifically known, but conquerors and kings from the West were very much part of political happenings in South Asia at the time his own grandfather captured power. So the possibility of this emperor having been influenced by the world beyond South Asia is very far from being remote. Plutarch, in his biographical history of Alexander, says Chandragupta, when a mere lad, saw Alexander in person. When he began to rule from Pataliputra, embassies from the Western powers came to his court; later, in Bindusara's years as sovereign, they were there again. A charming story told about him and Antiochus I of Syria highlights this: the Indian monarch asked for sweet wine, dried figs, and a sophist, to which Antiochus's reply was that while figs and wine would be sent, it was forbidden by law to sell a sophist![17]

The expedition to Kalinga was preceded by massive arrangements, from ascertaining the strength of the enemy's forces to understanding the terrain through which the army would move to working out the logistics of the whole operation to deciding on the season best suited to such an operation. In a territory as hot as Kalinga was for most of the year, winter was considered the best time to begin. This would also ensure optimal use of animals like the elephants which were an integral part of the army.[18] We do not have Ashoka's version of the size and character of the fighting force that he led. But if our knowledge of his grandfather Chandragupta's force is extrapolated to assess the grandson's, Ashoka's army had combat units of archers, foot guards armed with spears, combat commanders, horses, and large numbers of elephants under the control of mahouts.[19] Weaponry and war paraphernalia—maces, catapults, spears, swords, bows and arrows, giant stone catapulting machines—were likely to have been transported in bullock trains, which would also have carried provisions for the soldiers and animals. Imperial armies moved slowly, and given the size of the contingent and terrain the daily distance covered by Ashoka's army is unlikely to have exceeded an average of around twenty km. Pataliputra to Kalinga is a distance of some 900 km, so even just getting the army to the target ground would have taken five or six weeks.

How the army reached Kalinga has been variously imagined. Was the battlefield approached along a route that hugged the right bank of the Ganga through Bengal to Midnapur, from where the Mahanadi delta of Orissa is easily approached? This had been for centuries a pilgrim path well trodden by the devout making their way to the shrine of Jagannatha in the coastal town of Puri. Or did the army cross Chhattisgarh to reach the Ganjam–Srikakulam coastal belt on the southern edge of the ancient state, this having been the line of movement of the later Samudragupta (c. 328–78 CE, another emperor from Pataliputra) to Kalinga, which he invaded as he marched to conquer the southern regions? The size and strength of the defending forces that Ashoka's army encountered is very much in the realm of speculation. The description of its brutal decimation suggests it was considerable in size. If there is one thing vividly described, it is the scale of slaughter, death, and deportation resulting from the war. The epigraph which records the carnage says:

> One hundred and fifty thousand in number were the men who were deported thence, one hundred thousand in number were those who were slain there, and many times as many those who died.[20]

Many who perished had fought for the Kalinga ruler; others rather more ordinary and outside the arena of war were badly affected too, innocent civilians whose lives, described as principled and virtuous, were violently interrupted by the bloodbath. The epigraph speaks of these hapless victims as well and deplores the collateral damage:

> (To) the Brahmanas or Sramanas, or other sects or householders, who are living there, (and) among whom the following are practised: obedience to those who receive high pay, obedience to mother and father, obedience to elders, proper courtesy to friends, acquaintances, companions and relatives, to slaves and servants, (and) firm devotion—

to these then happen injury or slaughter or deportation of (their) beloved ones.

Or, if there are then incurring misfortune the friends, acquaintances, companions and relatives of those whose affection (for the latter) is undiminished, although they are (themselves) well provided for, this (misfortune) as well becomes an injury to those (persons themselves).

This is shared by all men and is considered deplorable . . .

Therefore even the hundredth part or the thousandth part of all those people who were slain, who died, and who were deported at that time in Kalinga, (would) now be considered very deplorable . . .[21]

This is only part of a longer account graphically capturing the pain and repentance of Ashoka in his hour of victory, and we will return to it later. For the present, what makes the story unusual is that it is the only surviving contemporary narrative description of the catastrophe. Such narratives are scarcely known to have endured from ancient times down to ours. As we saw, the original works of those who accompanied and recorded Alexander's campaign in India have disappeared. As against this, the narrative of the killing fields of Kalinga was composed within a few years of the battle and can still be read in the script and language in which it was first composed.

Why did Ashoka choose to immortalize the gory details of war? The victorious king tells a tale of death and decimation entirely against himself, damning his actions in the very hour of what every conquering general of that period in history, regardless of country, context, and culture, would have proclaimed as a triumph. This is not just rare, it is astonishing enough to seem bewildering. A long litany of kings after Ashoka got their military accomplishments eulogized in dramatic verse and prose. Kharavela of Kalinga (c. first century BCE), even while recording donations to the Jaina community, describes at length how various contemporary rulers—the Rathikas and Bhojakas, the Yavana king Dimi(ta) and the king of Magadha Bahasatimita—were forced into submission by him.[22] In much the same way, Rudradaman's second century CE account of the repair of a dam in Junagadh simultaneously sketches in some detail all the various territories, ranging from Sindhu-Sauvira to Saurashtra and Aparanta, that he valorously gained.[23] Ashoka's utter uniqueness is that the one and only account that he caused to be recorded of a successful war is one in which the conventions of state propaganda are turned on their head. The triumph is recorded as a disaster. Defeat is snatched from the jaws of victory. A chronicle of imperial misfortune is concocted in defiance of the established practice *of all preceding time.* The emperor weeps when he ought to swagger. This reversal of the most hoary narrative tradition of conquest is now so well known that we hardly see it any longer for what in essence it was, and remains: a staggering reversal of the very conception of kingship. The compassionate and caring king is born and proclaims himself, as H.G. Wells recognized, for the first time in world history. Ashoka's amazing contrition also signals the beginning of a different phase of his rule, a phase in which the historian enters the comfort zones of hard evidence.

And hard evidence never got harder. For Ashoka had it all carved on stone.

# 6

# The Emperor's Voice

PLUNGING ASHOKA INTO AN EMOTIONAL CRISIS, THE
result of the Kalinga war radically redirected the entire
subsequent life and career of the grieving conqueror. The
personal upheaval was also, inadvertently perhaps, a powerful and
new political idea: by replacing subjugation with compassion as the
most fundamental principle of monarchy, it introduced the earliest
glimmerings of a rule of law in which ordinary folk and the citizenry,
rather than only the powerful elites and royalty, were consequential.
If one were for a moment to visualize the scenario symbolically, as
a single image, it could take the shape of Ashoka calling for a copy
of the *Arthashastra* and setting it on fire in full public view. A new
perception of kingly calling emerged out of this victory-as-defeat,
one which Ashoka touched upon some years later when describing how he discharged his royal responsibilities and duties over
this part of his reign. Central in his narrative in the aftermath of
securing territorial supremacy was the contrast between his conduct
and that of earlier kings. Ashoka's self-understanding and how he
chose to arrange his narrative of kingship are therefore crucial to
any account of his reign.

It was a little after 260 BCE when Ashoka sent out a communiqué
to his administrators in various parts of India—from the edge of

the Yamuna flood plain in North India to the castellated hills of Karnataka in the South.[1] To distinguish it from the more expansive later edicts on rocks that are known as his 'major rock edicts', this communiqué has been classified among his minor rock edicts.[2] Actually, when Ashoka decided to disseminate his words in this way he did not (or possibly could not) bring himself to publicly remember the traumatic watershed of his career. Rather, it was a related personal experience in the slipstream of the Kalinga war that he shared, one which he hoped would inspire his people. So, I shall go back a little in time to Ashoka's first articulation of his metamorphosis, and through that remembrance explore how he sought to galvanize others along the same path.

The reception of any message, and most certainly a royal one, has a great deal to do with circumstances around its articulation. How was Ashoka's voice likely to have been understood by those who heard and read his words? As there are no references or reactions to Ashoka's edicts in any class of India's ancient literature of the first millennium BCE, our reconstruction has to be rooted in historical conjecture. Much of the Brahmanical literature of the late centuries BCE deals with subjects like codes of conduct, paraphernalia pertaining to rituals, norms of social behaviour, and the law. As such, events like the composition of kingly communiqués and citizens' reactions to them were never going to find mention. Nor were the Buddhist texts of the time in any way primarily concerned with kings who patronized Buddhism. They were preoccupied with the Buddha's discourses, his previous births, and the do's and dont's for monks and nuns. No account by any ambassador from a neighbouring kingdom of that era has turned up. If an *Indica* had been written around Ashoka's reign, containing information of the kind Megasthenes recorded about Chandragupta, public reactions to the emperor's messages may well have featured.

All the same, some glimpses can be arrived at by juxtaposing the message with the cultural landscape—by looking at the various places across his empire where the words were inscribed, at the cultural patterns in those places as captured in the material evidence that has survived, and at what the emperor's sudden visibility in that world may have entailed. Exploring what has appeared in the archaeological record should at the very least enable one to imagine the perspective of the subjects of the Mauryan state facing this novel way of looking at them.

\* \* \*

Communicating with provincial officials lay at the heart of the political system in ancient India. The provinces were, as we have seen—when noting Ashoka's movements to Taxila in the northwest, Malwa in the south, and Kalinga in the east—spread out over thousands of kilometres. Ashoka had inherited an empire extending from Afghanistan to Karnataka and from Gujarat to Bengal. Administering an entity of this size required regularly touching base with provinces, these being frequently governed by princes of the royal family. Having served as viceroy at Ujjayini himself, Ashoka seems to have maintained the practice of delegating close male kin to run the provincial bulwarks of his empire. Directions and orders were frequently given to these local functionaries through edicts. Their centrality can be gauged from the fact that directives for both peace and war appear within them. The decrees also include commands by the king concerning punishment and favour, gifts and exemptions, authorizations for issuing orders and carrying out certain required works.[3] The *Arthashastra* considered it necessary for such communiqués to be written with clarity and prescribes the employment of literate scribes with a beautiful hand who 'should listen with an attentive mind to the command of the king and set it down in writing.'[4]

The importance of royal communications as an anchor of imperial administration is in inverse proportion to what has remained of them: no messages of any kind prior to the time of Ashoka have survived. The usual materials used for writing were palm leaf, birch-bark (or 'bhurjapatra', *Betula utilis*), cotton cloth, and possibly wooden boards. These are mentioned in several textual sources and, being all highly perishable, specimens have never shown up.[5]

Except just once. This sole exception relates to the settlement of Sringaverapura near the banks of the Ganga, where wood charcoal of bhurjapatra was recovered in an archaeological context of the early first millennium BCE. This suggests a long familiarity with the tree whose bark, in the form of thin papery layers which were peeled off in broad horizontal rolls, was used for writing.[6] Remnants of bhurjapatra have only survived at this one site, and this paradoxically only because the wood got burnt.

As with generations of rulers before him, it is likely that some of Ashoka's official communications would have been recorded on the product of such bark and leaf. The major post-Kalinga revolution in communication was that the emperor ordered several of his promulgations to be inscribed on stone and in public places. These stone edicts have survived remarkably well: found some 2200 years after they were carved, several appear in much the state they were when created. The survival of an ancient document in the shape and place where it was originally inscribed is in itself unusual. What makes it even more so is that, in Ashoka's time, it was relatively rare. Alexander of Macedon, as we saw, went to great lengths to ensure he was remembered, even appointing an official historian for the purpose. This notwithstanding, the available narrative accounts about Alexander date to more than 300 years after him.[7]

Glimpses of rescripts that Ashoka first sent out to his provinces and which were inscribed on his instructions can still be seen at a large number of their original locations because the messages were engraved on immovable rocks and boulders. There is much variety in the kinds of surface upon which they were inscribed. Some are on flattish horizontal rock faces, as at Rajula Mandagiri in the Kurnool district in Andhra, and near Srinivaspuri in New Delhi.[8] Others, such as those at Maski and Nittur in Karnataka, are engraved on vertical surfaces. The rocks are sometimes easily accessible, as at Bairat in the Jaipur district of Rajasthan, where the boulder is at the foot of a hillside; and in the case of the rock face on which the Erragudi edict in the Anantapur district of Andhra Pradesh is engraved. Some are more difficult of access, such as the inscribed

Fig. 6.1: The Rajula Mandagiri edict is engraved on the flat rock in the foreground, in front of the tree dominating a waterbody, with a temple behind it

Fig. 6.2:  Worn-out section of the Rajula Mandagiri edict

slab at Sasaram, which is located on top of the hill in the Rohtas district of Bihar; and the one at Palkigundu in the Koppal district of Karnataka, which crowns a high and fairly inaccessible ridge, can only be reached after negotiating a very steep elevation. The reasons for inscribing rocks in places that appear today to be rather remote from ancient habitations will be explored; for the moment it is the act of engraving messages on such surfaces that gives us pause.

The medium that came to be used for inscribing royal epigraphs in early India depended upon the message and the audience addressed. Two demi-official epigraphs of Mauryan times, one from Mahasthangarh in Bangladesh and the other from Sohgaura in Uttar Pradesh, recorded instructions for the distribution of grain during drought and famine.[9] The commands were intended for 'mahamatras', a category of administrators associated specifically with urban centres, and were inscribed on plaques. More common are donative epigraphs of the type which were engraved into what was being dedicated. King Kharavela in Orissa in the first century BCE recorded the dedication of residences to Jaina monks in the Hathigumpha rocks—the caves themselves constituting the donation. He also used his dedication to indulge in much

Fig. 6.3: Palkigundu canopy rock—the edict is on a ledge beneath the canopy

Fig. 6.4: View of the surrounding area from the edict rock at Palkigundu

chest-thumping, graphically describing how he defeated and terri-
fied many contemporary rulers into submission.[10] The early edicts
of Ashoka were addressed to his administrators too, but were
not meant only for them, the messages being more democratically
motivated for communication to his subjects in general. For this
reason it seems logical to assume that the Mauryan officials engraved the emperor's words on rocks located in areas that were
frequented or commonly accessed at the time.

The epigraphs were all in the Brahmi script, while the language
itself was an amalgam of the dialects of Prakrit. Brahmi and Prakrit
were what the administrative functionaries would have been familiar with.[11] Prakrit, though, was not likely to have been the language spoken in regions like Karnataka and Andhra, where there is
a profusion of such inscriptions. So, when these messages were
transmitted to the people in such regions, for the meaning of the
message to be intelligible it would have had to be translated into the
local language.

How did the process of disseminating such messages, from the
time when they were dispatched to when they came to be inscribed, unfold? In trying to answer this it is necessary to remember
a second innovation. Each message that Ashoka sent out to his
administrators in the scattered parts of his empire *was in a form
more or less identical.* In the modern world, where the print
revolution has made it possible to place the same text in the hands
of large numbers of people within a very short space of time, the
novelty of Ashoka's innovation may not be immediately obvious.
What has to be kept in mind is that in ancient India, where the
technology for multiple reproduction did not exist, the state could
not reach out and express its desires and directives in the way it does
now. So, the emperor's decision to get multiple copies of his message
prepared and sent to various provinces was an attempt at text-based
mass communication, a kind of force multiplier which ensured that
the message had a massive reach. Usually, when we think of culture
in ancient India as text-created, formalized religious iconography
comes to mind—images that depict textual narratives. Here, by
contrast, a ruler attempts to create an image of himself via the

words of his message, his attempt being to convey the *same* image of himself in every part of his empire. In this reaching out it was of special importance to him that his subjects hear the singularity and sameness of his voice across the land that he ruled.

The messages will have been composed on the orders of the emperor, at points in time when he was possibly on tour, first written out on materials which have since perished. They were then dispatched to various administrative centres. In each instance, it was likely that the message was sent to a prince who was the viceroy of the province and who, in turn, readdressed it and conveyed it to officials in his territory for onward dissemination. We know this because in one instance, where three versions of an edict are found within a few kilometres of each other, the subsidiary instructions and greetings from the provincial head have also been inscribed. These three form a cluster in the Chitradurga district of Karnataka, at Brahmagiri, Siddapura, and Jatinga-Rameshwara.[12] All of them note that the prince, described as 'aryaputra'—a designation suggesting that the man addressed was Ashoka's own son—and officials, called mahamatras, from Suvarnagiri (the capital of the southern province of the empire) wished the mahamatras at Isila good health. After this initial greeting, the message is much the same as elsewhere. Transcribing the address by the dispatcher to the recipient was obviously a mistake made when the edicts were finally engraved from the common exemplar sent to all three places. However, thanks to this ancient error, we have a rare glimpse into the mode of transmission of the message: we know that the emperor sent it to the provincial governor who, in turn, forwarded it for transcription at different locations within the province he governed.[13]

The provincial functionaries and engravers who were most materially responsible for transmitting Ashoka's messages are shadowy figures. One exception is a character who signed off those three texts in Karnataka. Presumably, he was the 'lipikara' or writer-clerk who prepared the exemplar from which the rock engravings were made. The scribe's name was Capada, this being mentioned in all three edicts—which of course does not necessarily mean he was the engraver.[14] The engraver was more likely to have been a literate worksmith; even more likely, several worksmiths, for though the three texts were inscribed within a few kilometres of each other, the engraving hands are different, indicating more than one engraver.[15] Instead of Brahmi—the script used in the main part of the edict—Capada chose to use Kharoshthi for his own signature. Kharoshthi was frequently used in the area of Gandhara, around the upper Indus and Swat valleys in contemporary north Pakistan, bordering Afghanistan. Capada may have used Kharoshthi for signing off to show his dexterity with scripts, as also perhaps to signal that he either hailed from or was in some way linked with north-west India. The local engraver inscribed his signature along with the emperor's message and so immortalized his name. Of the many writer-clerks likely to have been employed in the administration, he remains the only one we know by name.

While other clerks and engravers are not visible in the same way, sometimes the style of engraving attracts our attention to the particularity of their skill. One such scribe was the engraver of the Erragudi edict in Andhra. When inscribing Ashoka's message there, he made part of it bidirectional. This segment is boustrophedonic, a form of writing often found in the remains of ancient Greece in which the lines, rather than following one direction, turn right to left and left to right.[16] Was this unnamed scribe using the rock surface to suggest that he was familiar with other writing systems? Kharoshthi was the only regional script written from right to left, so was the engraver indicating his possession of a more cosmopolitan knowledge of scripts? And why did he give up writing in this way after a few lines? The rest of the text, in fact, was rather haphazardly put down on the remaining space, with no concession to readability at all.[17] There is no clear answer to why he engraved the message in this way. What can certainly be said is that every official who expected to read or translate this engraving would, instead of marvelling at the engraver's skill, have roundly cursed the fellow for his rotten cursive. Boustrophedon is not exactly easy on the eye at the best of times.

Apart from such epigraphic quirks, which occasionally bring alive engravers and writers, some changes were made at the level of the locality so that the identity of the emperor sending out the message was easily apprehended. The emperor himself evidently imagined that his subjects would recognize him by his titles alone. 'Devanampiya' (dear to the gods) or 'Devanampiya Piyadasi' (dear to the gods and one who looks affectionately or amiably) was how the emperor was alluded to in the bulk of these edicts. In some provinces, though, the administrators in charge of propagating his message added the king's name to it. At places like Maski in Karnataka and at Gujjara in Central India, this king is mentioned by name as 'Ashoka' and 'Ashoka raja', respectively. In all likelihood the local administrator believed that the people hearing or reading the words needed clarity on the identity of Devanampiya.

The quality and the quirks of writers and engravers, and what was inadvertently or consciously added to the epigraphic text by local officials, represent only one part of the story. How were the words set down on rock communicated to the people of the locality? This was done by a specially designated official through a public reading in which those who had congregated at the place of inscription were required to listen. So, even if Ashoka's message was inscribed, its dissemination was oral.[18] That orality was central to this spectacle is evident from the proclamatory 'Devanampiya speaks thus', a phrase frequently encountered. It draws attention to the fact that what had been written had first been spoken, and that the speaker, being the emperor, had to be carefully listened to. Living in faraway Pataliputra, the monarch was compensating for his absence in most of his empire by speaking to his subjects via intermediaries who were standing in for him via reading out his utterances. The interplay of orality and textuality also raises the question of whether the message was read as it appeared on the rock, or from a copy that the reader-communicator fished out of from the folds of his clothes or his bag. In the case of a site like Maski, the edict was inscribed in a fairly compact way and could be read fairly easily. This was not at all so everywhere. At Siddapura, for instance, it would have been impossible for the official to position himself in the very restricted space that separated the engraved rock from an overhanging boulder. So, in such places, a written exemplar was almost certainly used.

Fig. 6.5: The Maski edict, relatively legible and easy to read by people standing near it

Fig. 6.6: Siddapura edict, cramped by the ledge above it

Considering how important it was for the emperor to communicate with his subjects, did local administrators appoint officials with rhetorical skills for the readings? Were there many such officials who could both read well and recite powerfully? Considering the oral culture of early India, it is very possible that even if this was a novel experience for Mauryan functionaries they would have attempted to render a public discourse by the emperor in a style similar to that deployed by poets addressing an audience of listeners. The difference between an oral performance by a poet-entertainer and a functionary carrying out the orders of the ruler would have lain mainly in the content—a political rather than literary agenda—with the manner of the address being perhaps similar, if more declamatory and officious in tone.

\* \* \*

What did Ashoka want to convey in his very first rock edict? This earliest communication has survived in the very form in which it was put down in the third century BCE at Rupnath, and a full English translation of it gives a good idea of how the emperor set about the business for which he is best known. Other versions of this message will figure subsequently, but the Rupnath edict gives a good sense of what Ashoka thought worthy of recounting and communicating to his subjects: not matters of state, but the state of his mind. He has become a Buddhist. His metamorphosis needs to be understood and emulated. So it is the process and the consequences of his conversion that he highlights.

> Devanampiya speaks thus.
> Two and a half years and somewhat more (have passed) since I am openly a Shakya.
> But (I had) not been very zealous.
> But a year and somewhat more (has passed) since I have visited the Samgha and have been very zealous.
> Those gods who during that time had been unmingled (with men) in Jambudvipa, have now been made (by me) mingled (with them).

For this is the fruit of zeal.

And this cannot be reached by (persons) of high rank (alone), (but) even a lowly (person) is able to attain even the great heaven if he is zealous.

And for the following purpose has (this) proclamation been issued, (that) both the lowly and the exalted may be zealous, and (that) even (my) borderers may know (it), (and) that this same zeal may be of long duration.

For, this matter will (be made by me to) progress, and will (be made to) progress considerably; it will (be made to) progress to at least one and a half.

And cause ye matter to be engraved on rocks where an occasion presents itself.

And (wherever) there are stone pillars here, it must be caused to be engraved on stone pillars.

And according to the letter of this (proclamation) (You) must dispatch (an officer) everywhere, as far as your district (extends).

(This) proclamation was issued by (me) on tour.

256 (nights) (had then been) spent on tour.[19]

This first edict of Ashoka is also among his shortest. It is not part of a set of several edicts, as are those inscribed in later years. The personal glimpse of the emperor's inner life is linked to a range of pronouncements about his mission. The message is partly confessional, presenting his self-realization and organizing it in terms of a chronological pattern of development. The text was dispatched by a ruler in the midst of a long tour, it having been surmised that the presence of the number 256 in all versions of this message indicates the number of days (or nights) that Ashoka had been away from the royal capital, Pataliputra. The 'date' also shows that all of these were dispatched more or less simultaneously.[20]

Perhaps because it captures an important moment in the life of Ashoka from the time he converted to Buddhism, the brevity and crowding are understandable. They betray an impatience in wanting to share what the metamorphosis meant for him as a ruler, and therefore ought to mean for his empire at large. There were good political reasons as well for sharing the information, inasmuch as it made it simpler to expect his subjects to try and emulate him if they understood the context within which his transformation had happened. Let us try and understand the information and instructions contained in this imperial message and see how they are interlinked.

Ashoka made grassroots contact with his people only after he became a Buddhist, there being no epigraphs showing this kind of intent for his pre-Buddhist phase. He appeared as a charged-up Buddhist ruler across a large part of his empire in the North (Bairat, Delhi, Ahraura, Ratanpurwa, and Sasaram), in the heartland of Central India (Gujjara and Rupnath), and in the Deccan where, in fact, the most frequent articulation of his persona as a royal Buddhist convert came to be set down—this message being engraved in ten separate places there.[21] Reading it would have left no one in doubt that the emperor was now an ardent advocate of Buddhism. He declared at the outset that he had become a Sakya, meaning a Buddhist (after the Buddha's well-known title 'Sakyamuni'). Elsewhere, in some versions of this message, he described himself as a lay follower ('upasake') of the Buddhist faith.

Ashoka had become a lay worshipper, he stated, some two and a half years earlier, although his initial formal adherence to the new faith was not enough, in his assessment, to make him sufficiently zealous. This seems to mean that Ashoka did not at first feel great interest in the morality and faith of the religion. It may also mean that, as with other laypersons, a great deal within Buddhist discourses and 'laws' had not been communicated to him. From an oft-recounted story about Anathapindaka, the rich banker who generously set up the Jetavana monastery at Sravasti for the Buddha, we learn that this kind of reticence with laypersons was fairly common. During an illness, Anathapindaka called Sariputra, the Buddha's disciple, who, when comforting him, expounded a sermon on a subject that the ill banker was not aware of—disgust towards sense-objects, we are told. At the end of it the banker was in tears and told Sariputra that while he had revered the Buddha a long time, this was the first time he had heard such a religious discourse. Sariputra is said to have told him that such expositions were not explained to the laity but only to the religious order.[22]

The same hesitation to expound a powerful doctrine immediately upon the king's conversion may have been considered desirable, the assumption probably being that a graduated process was in the longer term more effective towards ensuring future zeal by letting the convert himself arrive at the conviction that he was now truly set on the path to nirvana.

Instrumental in making Ashoka a zealous Buddhist, he revealed, was his association with the Sangha, the Buddhist mendicant order, a year and a half after he became a lay follower.[23] Such congregations of monks and nuns were by the third century BC known to exist in many parts of India. Precisely which branch of the Sangha enchanted him is not known, but Mahabodhi is a definite possibility since we learn from a later Ashokan epigraph that the emperor visited it in the tenth year of his consecration, a year which can be inferred to coincide with the time when he became fervent. The other possibility is that his constant interaction with monasteries in and around Pataliputra caused him to feel more deeply about his new religion. There is no way for us to know anything on this matter with certainty, nor what exactly transpired between Ashoka and the Sangha. That he became closely associated with it is all that he tells us, and this simply underlines that he was now seriously imbibing the teachings of the Buddha. What he learnt of the doctrines is likely to have been what had by then been established for the instruction of laypeople and fresh converts. The instructions included discourses of all kinds, especially those concerned with 'giving, morality and heaven: the first emphasized the advantages of renunciation, the second revealed the harm, vanity and defilement of desires; the third mellowed, liberated, exalted and appeased the mind of the listener.'[24] Various texts that contained the teachings and discourses of the Buddha will also have been inhaled and digested, since some years later the emperor confidently offered advice to the Buddhist Sangha as well as to the laity on the texts that they should listen to and reflect upon.

For the Sangha, the conversion of the region's most powerful man to a religion which the state had hitherto largely regarded as a philosophy of dissent against the Brahmanical faith was a coup of unimaginable magnitude. The confidence of monks proselytizing and encouraging the expansion and reach of the relatively new faith will have acquired an altogether new dimension. The closest parallel to this in the West is perhaps the Roman emperor Constantine in the third century CE, whose espousal of the relatively new religion of Christianity—coincidentally, as with Ashoka, roughly 300 years after the birth of the religion—has sometimes been described as a transition of the imperial state into the sacred state. In fact, a detailed comparative study of Ashoka and Constantine—a subject too large for present purposes—could yield fascinating insights into the character and consequences of massively influential monarchical conversions in the ancient world. At any rate, Constantine in Christian ecclesiastical history has the same position of absolute assurance that Ashoka has in the Sangha's versions of key moments in the trajectory of their faith.

Whatever the quality and length of Ashoka's interaction with the Sangha, his message confirms what resulted from it. His new-found ardour was now demonstrated in two main ways. First, he drew attention to the eight months or so that he had spent touring—leading to the surmise that he issued this first edict while on tour. Second, whereas in preceding times humans and gods had not mingled, now in Jambudvipa—Ashoka's name for his empire—the king took credit for making their intermingling possible. This was a way of saying that by creating a shared moral universe for his people with their gods, their emperor had made Jambudvipa a land of greater morality.

In asserting this Ashoka used a motif that occurs in Buddhist literature, one that he must have picked up during his interaction with the Sangha. John Strong, an important scholar of Buddhism, maintains that implicit in this first edict was the idea of a 'double utopia' in which gods and humans mingled either on earth or later in heaven, and that this commingling carried the resonance of what the Buddha himself is said to have created—as recounted in certain texts.[25] Whether the notion was picked up by Ashoka from such texts, or whether this was plucked out by the Buddhist tradition from Ashoka's words, Strong points out, is not easy to answer. What seems likely though is that Ashoka used an idea well understood by people familiar with the faith of the Buddha. If they had not understood what the commingling of gods and humans implied, he would have taken some pains to explain what he meant, as he did with so much else.

The emperor also communicated the possibility of this morality being open and available to all those who followed his example, from the most humble to those who occupied high rank. In emphasizing the possibility of equal access he was quite evidently following the Buddha himself in positioning a new moral universe fundamentally different from the stratified hierarchy of the Brahmanical order. Within the social and cultural milieu of the first millennium BC, it was social differentiation that was usually emphasized: the four varnas—Brahmans, Kshatriyas, Vaishyas, and Shudras—were posited as possessing different innate characteristics and differential access to a variety of social goods, from occupation to justice. This was a relatively absolutist system of reservations. The reservations were supposedly ordained by a primeval divinity, and therefore inviolable. The individual acting against, or against the grain of, his status was thus supposedly disobeying a sacred ordinance—an ordinance which had of course been created, perfected, and imposed by the powerful upon the lowly, and largely internalized both by the lowly and by society at large. Such 'internalization' within Hindu society, i.e. the willing consent to their own subjugation by the subjugated, has been widely exposed by modern interpretation and analysis as among the world's most effective hegemonies precisely because of its incredibly effective deployment of gods and goddesses within great literary stories that were accorded the status of religious texts. The creation of this social and cultural universe of supposedly sacred acts, examples, and orders from heavenly beings who descend into the world of men—partly in order to reinforce the tenets of the varna system—has been so powerful that its hold in the subcontinent, notwithstanding Ashoka and Ambedkar, has never been seriously undermined from the time when the Vedas were composed down to the present. The Buddha and his best-known disciple Ashoka seem to have recognized that in order to combat and counter a system of brainwashing as powerful as Brahmanical Hinduism required the use, for different ends, of some of the same story-telling techniques. This basically meant ensuring that the Buddhist message, while asserting a socially inclusive view—both the lowly and the exalted could occupy the same moral plane by following a zealous path and achieve heaven ('svaga') equally—was not delivered in ways that were out of line with notions of the sacred that had been internalized by caste Hindus. In other words, the commingling of gods with ordinary people was a motif that Ashoka saw the value of for the spread of a dissenting faith within an old culture: to that extent, it was new wine being made more heady by being poured out of an old and recognizable bottle.

The same initial message also shows purposive variety: Ashoka suggests that, his own subjects apart, people on the borders learn about what has moved him in this new direction. So, from the time when he began publicly communicating through edicts, he presents himself as a ruler not merely providing an example to his own existing subjects, but equally to potential converts beyond the limits of his empire. The message, in fact, strongly underlines the emperor's self-proclaimed mission to pursue the promotion of moral zeal amongst all his subjects, whose continuous progress he will ensure by enlarging his imperial reach. There was nothing tentative about this mission. Instead, as Ashoka put it, the mission 'will (be made to) progress considerably'. Thus, instructions were given on how he wanted it disseminated. These were fairly precise and required that the proclamation be sent everywhere, to the extremities of the district boundaries of the administrators to whom the instructions were addressed; and that in each district the message be engraved on rocks as also on stone pillars wherever these had been erected. By ensuring that his voice was cast in stone, Ashoka made sure that this part of his life was set out as exemplary in exactly the way that he wanted.

Presenting his life in this way was central to Ashoka's mission-ary intent. This was now life-history as model and prototype, the sole example for the populace to follow. The new hegemonic enterprise shines through his first edict as much as in those that follow. What is less evident but appears in retrospect implicit is that he was interpreting his own life and behaviour in a way that would have reminded knowledgeable observers of crucial incidents within an earlier historical life. As one ponders over the constituent elements of this edict, one cannot escape the strong feeling that there is in the emperor's autobiographical vignette some echo of Siddhartha Gautama, the man who became the Buddha in the sixth century BCE.[26] Siddhartha's decision to renounce worldly life, his later biographers underlined, was related to a personal trauma. Ashoka does not mention the Kalinga war and his post-war crisis in his first edict, but we cannot escape reading even this pithy tablet in the light of one of the most famous nuggets of ancient history, namely the transformative impact of the Kalinga war on the conqueror. Again, while the Buddha moved from being the head of his household to a wandering life in search of truth, the king's traditional calling as head of his 'household', the state, changes to a moral mission. Like the wandering Buddha, who taught as he travelled, the converted Buddhist king embarks on his mission by touring his empire. His inclusive moral path is patently the Buddha's. Above all, just as the Buddha never failed to reveal personal experience as the basis of his teachings, Ashoka's life and his new kingly calling are inextricably combined. The Buddha acquired disciples; Ashoka's disciples were in a sense his entire administrative apparatus. Was Ashoka indeed framing his life and message to evoke some elements of the Buddha? This possibility, apparent enough to us, may have been made known, or made more explicit, to those unfamiliar with the correspondences by those disseminating Ashoka's message.

The one thing we know for certain about Ashoka's first message is that its wording and meaning was, for the average person, unlike anything that had in the past formed the day-to-day reality of royal rule. While kingship had a distinguished antiquity in large parts of Ashoka's empire, going back in fact many centuries prior to Mauryan rule, a king was not prone to confiding the life-changing episodes of his career to his people. As warrior and protector of his realm and subjects, as also a supreme arbitrator of their disputes, he was meant to project himself as powerful, not spiritual. The people may have had to be forgiven if they were confused by a king who, instead of proclaiming his strength via grandiloquent titles, alluded to himself humbly as 'beloved of the gods'. The very thought of such a man being their ruler will have run contrary to normal thought processes within the populace, which, on the odd occasion that it thought of him at all, perhaps only feared him as a kind of god at the apex of a tax-extracting administration backed up by an army, the dread lord who might some day rain down on them with his soldiers for reasons unanticipated. The power and persona of such rulers was mediated on the ground by various administrative functionaries. Villagers and townspeople would normally have been familiar only with local functionaries, not with the monarch. Now, through this novel intervention, the ruler had brought himself within the direct ambit of their world. The situation will have seemed bewildering, the imperial initiative without precedent.

\* \* \*

The vast bulk of Ashoka's subjects, not being mobile or itinerant, are only likely to have been familiar with at most one of his edicts, the one located closest to them—it being understood, of course, that very many are likely not to have been familiar with any. Those who encountered the first minor rock edict will have been left in no doubt that the message of the emperor was Buddhist-inspired because of the specificity with which the connection is made at the outset. In his compilation *Asokan Sites and Artefacts* the scholar Harry Falk puts this succinctly: 'reduced to its essence it seems to propose that everyone become a Buddhist layman, develop zeal and thus mingle with the gods.'[27] However, in some of his other edicts the message is less specifically Buddhist and more broad based. This is so in Minor Rock Edict II which, along with the first edict, is found in many places in the Karnataka–Andhra region.

While elucidating in this edict what he wanted his subjects to observe as part of the morality that he was propagating, the earlier clarity of connection with Buddhist virtue is missing. Rather, the listing suggests a sort of universal morality that no religious faith in India was likely to have any quarrel with. The broad-based nature of its ethic seems one that would have appealed to all sections of the populace. The key elements of its Brahmagiri version are:

> Obedience must be rendered to mother and father, likewise to elders; firmness (of compassion) must be shown towards animals; the truth must be spoken; these same moral virtues must be practised.
> In the same way the pupil must show reverence to the master, and one must behave in a suitable manner towards relatives.
> This is an ancient rule, and this conduces to long life.[28]

These various virtues have a universal rather than specifically Buddhist resonance. In reiterating them Ashoka also invokes ancient law or tradition ('porana pakiti') and does not take credit, as he did in his first message, for initiating a mission. The other striking thing about it, says the historian Patrick Olivelle, is that this enumeration is marked by a 'silence on social vices or crimes, such as theft, murder, adultery, and other sexual offenses' which were matters of major concern to the state.[29] Possibly, Ashoka considered his mission 'to be something far more personal and "religious"— the development of character, virtue, and spiritual growth—than abiding by civil and criminal law.'[30] It must at the same time be kept in mind that if the emperor was merely reminding people in a general way about the path of morality as defined by age-old tradition, it may have been because the generality of the message was at the time of its transmission supplemented or accompanied by further instructions pertaining to the specific area where it had been sent. So, this may well have been the way in which this message was understood in the Chitradurga area of Karnataka, where the cluster of three sites mentioned earlier—Jatinga-Rameshwara, Siddapura, and Brahmagiri—bears practically this same message in this very form. But the brevity and consequent generality seems to have been because the engravers omitted all reference to

Ashoka's administrative instructions which had originally accompanied his message. What makes this second message seem rather too broad based and humane is those absent instructions. On the rocks of Erragudi and Rajula-Mandagiri, as also at Nittur, stern orders accompanied the message. Whether Ashoka's orders were meant to be inscribed or propagated orally has been debated, but once inscribed could be imperious and authoritative;[31] in fact they were very considerably at variance with the softly focused universal virtues.

The message in the latter places bristles with directions. The emperor expected that the governor 'should pass orders in the words of the Beloved of the Gods' and that his mahamatras pass orders about the necessity of obeying the morality expounded by him to the 'rajukka'.[32] The mahamatras were officials based in cities, while in the country areas the crucial administrative functionaries were the rajukkas.[33] They, in turn would 'order' the people of the countryside, as well as a class of officials called 'rashtrikas'— governors of parts of a district. Additionally, the orders were expected by the emperor to be passed on to elephant-riders, scribes, charioteers, and Brahman teachers. Pupils too had to be instructed in accordance with ancient tradition or 'porana pakiti'. Ancient tradition figured on more than one occasion in the instructions, with Ashoka dwelling constantly on it, even ordering that all propagation be in line with it ('this should be propagated in the proper manner among pupils in accordance with what is ancient usage'). This implies the emperor's belief that traditional values and usage, which comprised 'porana pakiti', had been forgotten. From first to last, the manner in which the decree was drafted would have explicitly reminded those who read it that they had no choice in the matter of following ancient tradition, the last line firmly decreeing, 'thus orders the Beloved of the Gods'.

The inclusion of the emperor's orders, or conversely the act of editing them out, shows how a more or less identical message can acquire varied meanings when inscribed in different locations. It is a reasonable assumption that this second message which, in the cluster in Chitradurga, would have been viewed as loosely moral and rooted in tradition, would in other places, sandwiched between stern imperial orders, have been seen and possibly resented as authoritarian. So, while Ashoka may well have seen his mission as being personal and moral, the end result of his constant invocation of Buddhism in the form of orders to and by administrative officials may have been considered by many as an extension into their sacred space of the laws of the land.

* * *

If the emperor's first message and its resonance across large parts of India depended on specifically how his words came to be engraved at each particular location, the encounters of his mission with the cultures and practices of people in varying terrains will also have differed considerably. Of the large number of texts that have survived of this message, none were found located at or near the large cities of the Mauryan realm. Pataliputra, Vidisha, Ujjayini, and Taxila are among those that have figured in Ashoka's life, and which we know already as being commercially and politically important. There were many others cities as well, such as Sopara, Sannathi, Malhar, Kaushambi, and Champa, to name a few that were fairly prosperous: the material evidence of archaeology and documentary sources suggest this. However, these urban agglomerations were not the spots chosen for inscriptions. Ashoka's earliest message was engraved mainly in the hills, in rock shelters, and on prominent rocks in the vicinity of locally significant places. Whether he wanted his words to be engraved in such places and not in the premier cities of his empire, he doesn't tell us. So, let us turn to the places he chose, or which happened to be chosen by his officials, to try and see why such places were picked.

Maski in Karnataka is one of these. Maski is the modern name, after a village there which either got its name from or gave its name to the Maski nullah, a tributary of the Tungabhadra river that flows nearby. In the third century BCE, not far from present-day

Maski, was a settlement in the south-east of the hill now known as Durgada Gudda, that being the most conspicuous hill alignment to be found here. The settlement today is only recognizable from large quantities of potsherds that litter the soil where cultivated fields of cotton and sunflower now stand. But a few thousand years ago, in the time of Ashoka, a copper- and iron-using culture flourished at the spot.

From finds that emerged out of excavations conducted at Maski in 1954, we learn how some of the subjects of the Mauryan emperor lived in this part of Karnataka. This was a sedentary agricultural society which reared cattle and goats.[34] While the houses have not survived, we know that timber was used in their building since post holes—in which originally were wooden poles that have decayed without a trace—have been seen and these must have supported the frame for thatched roofs. The habitations have more or less disappeared, but the burial practices of these people have survived a little. That the burials and habitation were contemporaneous is evident from the fact that there is an identity in the kind of pottery found in both deposits. Several of the burials were within the habitation area itself. Lots of bright-coloured black and red pots and jars, iron objects such as arrowheads, lances and knife-blades, and animal bones were buried with the dead. Undressed granite menhirs were also found here, and this is one reason why these people in Maski have been given the appellation 'megalithic-building people'. The monoliths, though, were not associated with funerary deposits, so what exactly they signified remains unknown. There is also uncertainty about what the uses to which some of the objects were put, as for instance certain mysterious-looking spheroidal stone balls. In the opinion of the excavator, these could have been sling-stones, or 'bolas', for killing fast-moving game. They could also well have been playthings since two of them were buried with a child, placed near its feet. Perhaps dear to the child, they 'were placed along with the dead body as part of the funeral furnishings.'[35] Other favourite toys of the children of Maski have also been found in such graves. One of these, placed in a grave pit with a child's body, is a painted disc that resembles a hopscotch diagram.

Maski's structurally unprepossessing settlement pattern can give the mistaken impression that this was an isolated interior village. Scholars who know the area's history point to the presence of all kinds of artefacts and inscriptions here which capture its links with other regions in the subcontinent and beyond. An early hint of this, in all likelihood before the time of Ashoka, is a terracotta cylinder seal engraved with a man driving an elephant. While the elephant is characteristically Indian, the man's 'radiating' headdress and the contours of his mouth, as also the seal's cylindrical shape, suggest strong affinities with Mesopotamia.[36] Such cylinder seals were known to occur more frequently in the third millennium cities of the Indus civilization further north, at places like Mohenjodaro and Chanhudaro. Did a merchant trading goods between Mesopotamia and India visit this region? If yes, what was the trader looking for in the Maski region? Gold may well have been one such resource which, as we shall see, has been found here.

The region also had a strategic significance. More than a thousand years after Ashoka, among a bunch of inscriptions that either referred to Maski (called 'Mosangi', 'Musangi', or 'Mosage') as the chief town of the administrative region or as a political capital, is an eleventh century CE epigraph which alludes to it as a battlefield. In the list of conquests of the Tamil king Rajendra Chola I, which ranged from Sri Lanka and Kerala to Orissa and Bengal, is the vanquishing of Jayasimha, identified with the Chalukya king Jaya-simha II, who was described as being put to flight at Musangi.[37] Even though Jayasimha's base was at Kalyani, while Rajendra Chola came from the deep south, the fact that the invading Chola king defeated the Karnataka-based Chalukya in the vicinity of Maski is a pointer to its critical location.

We can glimpse similar subcontinental links in the time of the iron-using society of the region. The inhabitants used beads that may have originated from areas very far from ancient Karnataka. Beads in several kinds of raw materials, ranging from those made of carnelian and garnet to terracotta and paste, have been found here. Lapis lazuli, shell, and coral are also in evidence: the lapis was probably of Afghan origin, while shell and coral in this interior area would have travelled along routes that linked it with the western coast. The raw materials would have come in with commercial people of all kinds: traveller-traders from the north-west carrying lapis with them, and people from this belt travelling there and returning with saleable goods. The material yields of trade add to our image of the intersection between these regions at huge distances from each other. This intersection, as we saw, was evident from the presence of scribes in Karnataka–Andhra accomplished in Kharoshthi and employed by the Mauryan provincial administration.

There was one precious resource here that traders and rulers coming to Maski would have dearly sought: gold. The region was rich in gold deposits. Known to geologists as the main Maski band of the Dharwar series, a number of old gold workings here underline the fact that these deposits were exploited in premodern times. Old workings have been found near Maski, and many in areas not too far beyond. Two gold objects of the first millennium BCE found at the site make it seem most likely that the auriferous veins here were mined in very ancient times.[38] The chance discovery of the Ashokan edict at Maski was in fact the result of the prospecting for gold in 1915 by a gold-mining engineer of the nizam's dominions, C. Beadon, in that area. One may even imagine that Ashoka's provincial capital in this region, known as Survarnagiri ('golden mountain'), may have been so named because of its control and regulation of gold, with Maski as a base for prospecting and mining.

The sense that the reference points of this settlement extended much beyond its immediate environment is reinforced by different kinds of graffiti marks on some of the pottery, from the habitation area as well as from burials. There were some nineteen types of marks, either scratched or incised, including trident-like marks, bows, carelessly incised crosses, V-like incision marks, and one resembling an arrowhead. These form part of a marking system that has left its signature at several places in South India and Sri Lanka. Those who have carefully studied the contexts in which these were found believe this graffiti is a kind of precursor of a writing system, with places like Vallam (near Thanjavur) and

Mangudi (south-west of Madurai) yielding sequences where the initial phase reveals only graffiti, followed by one where the graffiti combines with the Brahmi script, and eventually the Brahmi script appearing to the exclusion of earlier forms.[39] In other places, as at Kodumanal near Erode, Brahmi inscriptions on pottery show graffiti marks incised at the end.[40] Either way, graffiti seems to have been used to convey messages in a way that script signs did in more sophisticated forms.

The meanings encoded in the Maski graffiti marks remain unknown, and no potsherds with Brahmi inscriptions have been found here. Yet there is every possibility that by the third century BCE some people in Maski were familiar with the Brahmi script signs, which they may well have seen on the cultural equipment of contemporary groups further south and west. So, even if this was the first time that the king had made his presence felt in this form in the neighbourhood of their settlement, such inhabitants would have recognized the script in which his message was engraved.

The area possesses many gneissic hills and outcrops; the provincial officials responsible for engraving Ashoka's message chose the largest and most conspicuous of these hills, in whose shadow Maski stood. Unlike many other sites in Karnataka where both the first and second minor edicts were set into rock faces, here only the first message of the emperor, Minor Rock Edict I, was found engraved. But instead of a rock face near the settlement, the message was inscribed some distance away, on its western face, making it invisible to the local population. Importantly, it was not even visible to those who passed that part of the Durgada Gudda ridge. This is because Ashoka's message was written inconspicuously, on an interior-facing outcrop of a rock shelter with a massive ledge above it. It was not as if other rocky outcrops were not available. Much nearer the settlement area and beyond it were more accessible rock faces than this one, which is rather too thoroughly tucked inside a cavern on the slope of Durgada Gudda.

So why was this particular rock face chosen for the edict? One possibility is that the local officials entrusted with the task wanted the emperor's message to survive for as long as possible, and the protection offered by the overhanging ledge made them glance favourably at the location. Simultaneously, this was a location conducive to community rituals and local festivals. Such conjecture can only be affirmed or rejected via excavations in and around the rocks of the large cavern. But certainly it made sense to engrave a message within a place ritually visited: what appears an idiosyncratic location may not have been so then. That said, considering that the area for people to gather in by the edict is limited, the audience at any point in time was unlikely to have been a large one.

Maski folk who came to the outcrop could hardly have failed to ask local officials about the emperor. The name 'Ashoka', inscribed at Maski, would through constant use have become familiar. The declamatory use of a first-person voice revealed that he was a Buddhist, a religion which would have been perceived to have a new and powerful backer. People thousands of kilometres away from their emperor in Pataliputra would at the very least have been curious about what he was saying to them in this dramatic and unexpected way, by inserting himself into their landscape. For a community with connections in the large subcontinental world, the imperial presence in this form may even have been considered an honour specially bestowed to the area. The assurance of an egalitarian moral universe may have struck an emotional chord: the most humble cultivator at Maski was being told that he was not inconsequential and could exalt himself merely by following in the king's footsteps.

These are some possibilities. It is also possible that the notion of a mingling of gods and humans sounded alien to the populace. The Buddhist faith was not a part of the local sacred landscape, nor did anything in the king's message show awareness of Maski's ancient religious practices. The message on the rock had been parachuted into their midst, and his expectation that they move in a direction simply because he had personally chosen it could have seemed foreign and unconvincing. During Ashoka's lifetime and subsequently, Maski reveals no change in its faith. There are several bruisings on the rocks here—circles, fish symbols, and much else—

but nothing remotely resembling Buddhist symbols. No Buddhist stupas were ever constructed here during or after the third century BCE, such as those which came up in other areas associated with Ashoka. The greatest likelihood is therefore that, as before, Maski's community continued to believe in the deities that had traditionally protected them in life and death. The emperor's strange message was read, heard, and ignored.

\* \* \*

The great man's wishes were engraved into only one area of the Maski locality; in other places there seems a greater anxiety to ensure dissemination, for the same message is inscribed at more than one place within the same locality. The Chitradurga cluster of Ashokan epigraphs at Brahmagiri, Siddapura, and Jatinga-Rameshwara is a dramatic instance of this anxiety. Many stunning rocky landscapes can be encountered across large tracts in this part of Karnataka, so an abundance of locations was available. But these three epigraphs, instead of being spread out, are within a radius of five km. Siddapura was a little over a kilometre west of Brahmagiri while Jatinga-Rameshwara was less than five km north-west of it. These spots seem interlinked because of intervisibility. Siddapura looked towards Brahmagiri. From Brahmagiri, Siddapura and Jatinga-Rameshwara were both visible. From the panoramic hilltop of Jatinga-Rameshwara, in turn, these rocky locations in the neighbourhood where the emperor's message was inscribed could be seen. It is entirely possible that the combination of locational visibility and a more or less identical royal epigraph at all three locations ensured that they came to be seen as interconnected.

Let us look at these landscapes a little more closely. Brahmagiri is the name of a hill of granitic outcrops where, close to the base alignment that looks towards the Jatinga-Rameshwara hill, lies the boulder where a composite message combining the two early edicts of Ashoka was set down. The message had been sent here

Fig. 6.7: Brahmagiri enclosure with Siddapura rocks in the fields and Jatinga-Rameshwara hill in the background

Fig. 6.8: Brahmagiri edict

from Suvarnagiri, the provincial capital. Suvarnagiri was the base of a prince whose name we do not know but who was possibly Ashoka's son. It was 'at the word of the aryaputra' (prince) and of the mahamatras of Suvarnagiri that the message was sent to the mahamatras of Isila ('they must be wished good health', the message said). Brahmagiri was thus where ancient Isila was situated. And since administrative officials of the rank of mahamatras were attached to it, it was likely to have been an urban centre.

Has Isila been identified on the ground? In 1940 the archaeologist M.H. Krishna believed he had searched out ancient Isila a little ahead of the edict-bearing rock, and the place was so described by a later excavator of Brahmagiri:

> The northern slopes of Brahmagiri, largely covered by a tumbled mass of granite boulders, bear extensive signs of ancient occupation in the form of pot-sherds, fragmentary walls and remains of small terraced platforms roughly revetted with dry-stone walling. It is to be presumed that two thousand years ago more earth remained amongst the boulders than at the present day, and that much evidence of this part of Isila has been washed away. But at all times the main area of occupation must have lain, as surface-remains and excavation combine to indicate, along the gentle slope which forms the transition from the hill to the plain. Here a long strip some 200 yards in width is a mass of occupation-earth and sherds. Beyond it, the fringe of the plain itself, to a depth of 500 yards or more and a length of about a mile, forms what must have been an almost continuous belt of megalithic structures, mostly cist-tombs. Many of these have been removed by agriculturists, but some hundreds still survive in intermittent patches.[41]

Reading this description it is apparent that, like Maski, this was marked by habitational debris packed with plenty of potsherds, and with a cemetery area of multiple burials alongside megalithic structures. The royal rescript was meant for this iron-using culture marked by multiple megaliths.[42] As at Maski, the inscribed rock is not at the habitation site but towards its periphery. This would thus have been a place that Isila's inhabitants regularly passed and possibly visited, especially since behind this rock water was available through a seasonal watercourse.[43] A couple of millennia later, washing this boulder (then known as 'akshara gundu', or letter rock) with water was believed to endow it with usable medicinal virtues, which leads logically to the supposition that the superstition may have persisted down to the later period from a time after the Mauryan. What has also survived some distance south-east of the Brahmagiri boulder, up the hill, is a small apsidal structure made of bricks. The ruins revealed a structure made of large bricks (1'5" x 9" x 3–3½") which were thought to be indicative of a fairly early time, although no evidence which would help provide a secure date was found.[44] If this was indeed a Buddhist chaitya or temple, as is surmised, it would mean that the imprint of Buddhism at Brahmagiri went beyond the Buddhist-inspired message of the monarch.

Moving ahead of Brahmagiri, the question arises why Isila's administration decided to get the very same edict inscribed on a rocky knoll just a kilometre or so distant. This falls within the modern limit of Siddapura village and so is known as Ashoka's Siddapura edict. But in the third century BCE the town community of Isila would have been the target audience for the message—the same citizen body that will have imbibed the Brahmagiri message. The oddness of this near duplication cannot be missed, nor the mystery of why such proximity seemed desirable in a context where boulders of a sufficient size for engravings were not remotely in short supply. Here, in the middle of cultivated land is a horizontal ledge in the rocky outcrop which was used for the engraving. A large boulder hangs over the ledge and seems almost to have squeezed the space between it and the inscribed surface. Interestingly, this part of the knoll faces the Brahmagiri hill and not Jatinga-Rameshwara. Was the Siddapura slab's orientation merely functional, in that it was perhaps the best surface available for putting down a message running into twenty-two lines, even if the restricted space above it made the business of reading it difficult? Alternatively, were the Brahmagiri and Siddapura rocks places where local festivities or rituals had been established and which the administration hoped could be redeployed for the new message? Were the emperor's edicts actually seen regularly, as they were in the nineteenth century, only because local cattle-keepers and goatherds used shady overhanging rocky eaves as protection against the hot summer sun? At the point in time when Ashoka's inscription was discovered, Siddapura's low hilly landscape bore a name that suggested such links. It was called 'Yenamana timmayyana gundlu', or 'the buffalo-herd Timmayya's rocks'.[45] Which of these is the best explanation, and whether other deductions lurk are matters for unending speculation because, as at Maski, no specific archaeological pointers can guide enquiry. But there is every reason to imagine that all who came to Siddapura—devotees, shepherds, local children, lovers in search of privacy—could not have failed to note a Buddhist emperor's presence looming larger than life in their lived landscape.

If at Brahmagiri and Siddapura the edicts were inscribed around the base areas of the rocky ridge, at Jatinga-Rameshwara, the third point in this cluster, they happened to be located on a high hill some distance from the surrounding town and villages. Some similarities link the Jatinga-Rameshwara edict with the other two locations. As there, the writing is cut into a slanting horizontal rock face and has a large boulder overhanging it. It is likely that the same group of officials located the appropriate rocks here, for at all three places they considered horizontal faces best suited to their purpose. At Maski a more vertical face had been used, as also at Udegolam and Nittur. So, within each province the local officials seem to have had their own clear preferences when it came to deciding on an appropriate rock face to write on.

Coming back to Jatinga-Rameshwara: what makes it most dramatic is that the engravers, instead of using the base or an easily accessible part of the hill, carved his message on the summit. The hike to the hilltop, made relatively easy today by some 700 steps, must in Ashokan days have been steep and strenuous. The character of the landscape of this hilltop location in the third century BCE remains unknown from the range of religious associations presently visible there. The highest part of this spectacular rocky eminence, a little beyond the horizontal surface where the edicts were inscribed, we know to be a spot soaked in the mythology of the Ramayana story. It is known as 'Jatayu sthana' because it is here that the injured bird is believed by many to have fallen, even as Jatayu tried to rescue Sita. In the part of the rocky eminence that lies above and behind the edict-bearing rock lies a pond whose surrounding rock surface is marked by the impressions of human feet. Among these are a pair described as 'Sita pada' (the feet of Sita). There is nothing, though, that can help track such beliefs back to the time of the Mauryan emperor. The hilltop became famous over time as a pilgrimage spot called Balgoti Tirtha, a place of pilgrimage for devotees of the god Shiva under the name Rameshwara. Like Ashoka, many of the powerful royal patrons of this 'tirtha' inscribed their messages on rock surfaces and boulders. But that happened more than a millennium later.

In short, though we do not know what brought people to this hilltop in Mauryan times, the simple truth remains that no state functionaries would have taken the trouble to carve an important royal message at a place no one visited. My hunch is that the sheer physical grandeur of the Jatinga-Rameshwara hill, dominating everything in the landscape around it, was likely to have had a symbolic spiritual dominance in the lived world of ancient communities within this area. Such communities climbed the hill on specific ceremonial occasions. The pre-existence of sacredness associated with a hilltop explains its reuse. The edicts, in turn, transformed the place. Jatinga-Rameshwara was probably a local or at best provincial religious spot. Ashoka's message made it part of a web of places connected to each other by the imprimatur of an emperor who ruled from the Himalayas to the hills of Karnataka and beyond.

How did people who trudged here to pay obeisance to their own deities respond to the Buddhist message? There will have been many kinds of responses, from rapt interest to scarcely concealed indifference. However, by contrast with the Brahmagiri rock—which even in the modern era was seen as endowed with special properties—Jatinga-Rameshwara's ancient spiritual mission was rendered quotidian over time. At the time that the Ashokan edict rock was discovered in the late nineteenth century, it had become the favourite spot of bangle-sellers hawking their wares to pilgrims. The rock was called 'balegara-gundu', or bangle-sellers' rock; various holes were punched into it for posts that supported a tent erected by them at the annual fair.[46] An ancient sacred space later marked by an emperor's new-found spirituality now supported a more mundane and entirely material quest.

\* \* \*

If unprepossessing iron-using communities with remarkable grave-building traditions dominated the places in Karnataka where Ashoka's early edicts were inscribed, an entirely different repertoire of associations existed around the king's message at Panguraria in Central India.

A forested hilly tract with a range of rock shelters is how one might describe the landscape of Panguraria. It is a place with rock paintings done very many centuries before Ashoka even as it carries a strong resonance of his Buddhism. The prehistoric paintings show animals, including monkeys, and hunters. They are in the same line of rock shelters, halfway up a hill, in which Ashoka's message is engraved. Spread across the hillside are a large number of stupas made of dressed stones, some with platforms, the diameters ranging from 2 to 76 metres. Alongside are monastic cells within rubble enclosures. A stunning architectural remnant from Panguraria is a stone umbrella and an umbrella shaft that supported it, which may well be Mauryan. Engraved on the shaft is an inscription which records that the umbrella is the gift of 'bhikshuni' (nun) Sagharakhita; it was caused to be made by Pusa, Dhamarakhita, and Araha, the 'amtevasinis' of Koramika.[47] 'Amtevasinis' literally means those living on the border, although it was usually used to describe pupils.

This juxtaposition of painted rock shelters and Buddhist remains is a very widespread feature of large parts of Central India. Not far from Panguraria is Talpura, where again rock shelters show prehistoric and historic paintings, while above stand two stone stupas on a large platform. The famous Buddhist centre of Sanchi, whose great stupa built by Ashoka we will discuss later, stands on a hill where a line of rock shelters can still be seen along an old road leading to Vidisha. The shelters bear prehistoric and historic representations—animals, men, an antler mask, horse and elephant riders. The pre-existing sacredness of these places from prehistoric time suggests a continuity into historic time of a new variant of the same basic religious impulse, the shape now being Buddhism. Monastic groups, adherents of the later faith, sometimes chose to inhabit these shelters in unconscious or deliberate acknowledgement of some sort of emotional kinship with those who had gone before.

This would have been true for Panguraria as much as for other such spots. What makes Panguraria both different and distinctive is that it is the only place within this region where Ashoka's rescript was recorded on the stone walls of a rock shelter.[48] Known as the Saru-Maru cave (or 'gufa'), the edict-bearing shelter lies in the Rehti reserved forest, in the midst of jungle foliage and spectacular scenic views of the surrounding landscape. An uneven back wall within the shelter shows the writing. Part of the rock seems to have been found unsuitable by the engraver. So he set down the epigraph in two parts, three lines of writing in the first part and five lines in the second.[49]

There is a further distinction: Ashoka directly addresses the local governor, a Kumara called Samva.[50] Such direct communication is not evident at Maski, Brahmagiri, or any other Ashokan location at this point in time. All who read or heard the Panguraria message, as we do today, would have learnt that the governor was the recipient of a message from the king himself. The governor's title, 'kumara', meant he was a scion of the royal family though not a son of the king—as was the 'aryaputra' in Karnataka.

The place from where the king sent his message is also provided, for the first time. Ashoka is communicating with Kumara Samva 'from his march to the Upunita-vihara in Manema-desha'. Upunita-vihara was a Buddhist monastery, though it has not been identified on the ground; nor has the territorial unit referred to as Manema-desha. Even so, that the emperor was journeying to

Fig. 6.9: Ashoka's edict in a rock shelter at Panguraria

Fig. 6.10: View of the countryside around the Panguraria rock shelter

reach a vihara offers a precious hint about some of the places that he was heading for during his long tour of 256 nights (or days). This then prompts us to wonder about the reactions of resident Buddhist monks and nuns in such viharas to the royal visitor and his entourage. The man appearing on the horizon will have been perceived as the first monarch to be touring his kingdom not to consolidate it materially but to extend it spiritually. His extraordinariness will have seemed to many to border on the peculiar.

On receiving this communiqué from the king, we imagine Kumara Samva arranging to get it inscribed in a place where Buddhists were already resident. The governor himself will have been headquartered in one of the cities of the region. If it was in the vicinity of Panguraria, either Nandner or Ninnore, both commercial centres, could well have been his capital.[51] It is logical to suppose that he was in touch with the Buddhist monks of his territory; he may even have encountered many wandering the nearby towns and settlements, begging for food in the traditional way prescribed by the Buddha.

One suggestion is that the Panguraria complex may well have been the very Upunita-vihara mentioned in the rescript, which 'the king was asking the royal governor to visit', we are told, 'in anticipation of the promulgation' of his message there.[52] Whatever the ancient name of the present site of Panguraria, it was by then already a Buddhist sanctuary. This means that the intended audience, unlike many other audiences, for the emperor's inscription was a monastic community already in existence at this location. Ashoka's edict here is similar to those at Maski and Rupnath, but the fact that the intended audience here was Buddhist will have resulted in a different kind of reception for it.

The resident monks and nuns will, one assumes, have felt greatly reassured about the rightness of the path they had chosen, considering their afflictions worth the while now that this same path was being trodden by the emperor himself. The mendicants here, as in the other viharas that Ashoka will have visited, may nonetheless have been surprised by the import of his message. Kings as conquerors of the lands of other rulers, or as builders of political capitals, were commonly encountered within stories that circulated in the third century BCE of the time of the Sakyamuni. Here, however, was a king proclaiming he was one of them. What next? Might he decide to join them and live among them? The tenor of these new proclamations might well have made the discerning feel there was no saying what might happen in the future.

7

# Extending the Arc of
# Communication to Afghanistan

WHILE OFFICIALS AND SCRIBES WERE ETCHING THE emperor's messages in the various parts of India, a royal communiqué was promulgated beyond the subcontinent around 259 BCE. The timing of the proclamation, around the tenth year after Ashoka's coronation, makes it broadly contemporaneous with the others that we have just waded through. Unlike those messages, though, this one was in Afghanistan, in the vicinity of Kandahar.

Why did Ashoka get an edict engraved in a region as remote from Pataliputra as Afghanistan, and how may we visualize the desire for making his presence felt there? Speaking historically, Ashoka's imprint in this territory should not surprise us as the region had become part of the Mauryan realm since the time of Chandragupta, when large parts of it were seceded to him by Seleucus. Geographically speaking, however, its remoteness within a generally harsh terrain and climate make it an odd choice for an edict. But then strategically speaking the largely mountainous character of the province had resulted in it being seldom secluded at key points of exit and entry, the Khyber and Kurram passes being much used for access from the south and east, and the Caspian route from Herat towards the north. Mainly for this reason, many millennia before the appearance of Ashoka, specific points in Afghanistan had become a zone of cultural interfaces and trading connections of all kinds.

Ancient artefacts strikingly evocative of links with the West and the East, from Greece and Iran to the heartland of Gangetic India, have turned up from sites in the region.[1] Agricultural settlements had for long existed here, in what have been described as the 'toothpaste squeezes' of rivers and tributaries.[2] These are found in a fairly large stretch, in the area of the Amu Darya river in the north, and in the southern mountains and foothills. The fourth millennium BCE saw the appearance of pottery in an extensive series of mounds at Mundigak near Kandahar, sharing clear parallels with ceramics from sites in Baluchistan. Those, in turn, occasionally had motifs that appear to be of Iranian inspiration.[3] All this is perfectly logical since an important route to Baluchistan from Iran passed through Kandahar. The ceramic parallels also show that, to begin with, Afghanistan's relationship with Baluchistan was far more crucial while with the more distant regions to the west, the cultural interaction was limited.[4] Later, in the third millennium BCE, the material culture of this area shows parallels with that seen in Iranian sites of the same timespan. Shahr-i Sokhta in Iran manufactured alabaster vessels which reached Mundigak.[5] As for northern Afghanistan, in the third millennium BCE a Bronze Age commercial outpost, exclusively marked by antiquities and artefacts of Harappan tradition, was flourishing at Shortughai near the Kokcha river.[6] Shortughai perhaps represents the earliest Indian diaspora community settled far from its land of origin while maintaining strong links with it. Harappan settlers came here for its rich resources, ranging from metal ores to the deep blue lapis lazuli stone of Badakshan. Lapis was fashioned into beads worn in Harappan settlements stretching from Punjab to Gujarat.

With the advent of the early historical period the political imprint of rulers with an appetite for vast tracts of territory swims into view, these being conquerors who brought Afghanistan within the ambit of their empires. In the sixth century BCE, when the Achaemenids from Iran made central-south Afghanistan a

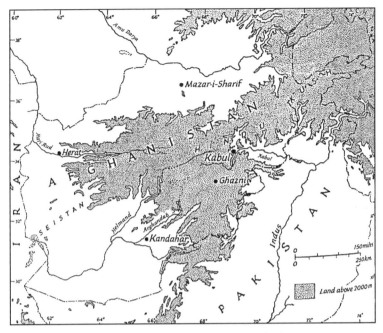

Map 3: Afghanistan in relation to Iran and Pakistan

province of their realm, Kandahar became their main bastion. From that point in time, very likely, the Aramaic language, steeped in local Iranian terms, came to be used in the administration here. The province where Kandahar stood came to be known as Arachosia and was considered an important political prize, having been fought over by a loyalist of Darius I of Persia against a rebel pretender to the Achaemenid throne.[7] Later it was overrun by Alexander in 330 BCE, a consequence of his defeating Darius III in 331 BCE. The Macedonian conqueror, now the ruler of the satrapies of the Achaemenids, placed new administrators in position to hold his conquests.[8] He is known to have appointed a Greek governor at Arachosia who was provided with a military arm consisting of some 4000 infantry and 600 horsemen. Kandahar, rechristened Alexandropolis, remained the capital of the province.

By the late fourth century BCE Arachosia was part of the Mauryan state. Following Alexander's death, Seleucus I Nicator emerged as king of Syria and parts of western Asia but he failed to hold on to south-east Afghanistan and the Indus area, being forced to make peace with Chandragupta Maurya. Through a diplomatic detente the Seleucid king ceded Gandhara, Arachosia, and Paropamisadae (the ancient Greek name for the south-eastern part of present-day Afghanistan). In return he received 500 elephants and a female relative of Seleucus (for a matrimonial alliance). Paul Kosmin, historian of the Seleucid empire, believes that this was a mutually beneficial exchange: 'Geopolitically, Seleucus abandoned territories he could never securely hold in favour of peace and security in the east.'[9] As for Chandragupta, he 'gained unchallenged expansion into India's northwest corridor. His gift of elephants may have alleviated the burden of fodder and the return march!'[10] What Arachosia was called in Mauryan times remains unknown, but a people called Kambojas are mentioned in sources of that era as locally resident. From the geopolitical perspective these territorial acquisitions meant that the Mauryan monarch's powerful pan-Indian empire now had unfettered access across this part of Asia.

Ashoka's communications were one element of this larger lineage of interconnections that left a mark on Afghanistan, a land whose fortunes had for long been tied to those of political overlords located thousands of kilometres distant. The great trade and military routes in this part of Asia passed through its territory, so the populace was no doubt habituated to the comings and goings of kings and conquerors.[11] All the same, like populaces around other edict sites, it may well have cogitated and scratched its head for a long time when first confronting Ashoka's epigraphic scrawls in the vicinity. While here we look at the first of Ashoka's epigraphs in Afghanistan, some years later several more were put down in that remote region, a couple of them in Kandahar itself.[12] Two others were in the valley of Laghman in eastern Afghanistan, carved into *in situ* stones on ridges known as Sultan Baba and Sam Baba, two km distant from each other.[13] A third, also from the Laghman region, was on a stone tablet found in Pul-i-Darunta.[14] The population of the localities in which these were inscribed may have become accustomed to being accosted by their sovereign as an epigraphic presence in their midst.

It was in south Afghanistan that the emperor first addressed his north-western subjects, on the outskirts of Kandahar. The city lies in a region sandwiched between mountains and a sandy area appropriately called Registan to its south.[15] The plain on which it stands is between the Arghandab and Tarnak rivers and commands the road going through the Tarnak valley by Ghazni to Kabul. Towards the south another route skirts Registan to Quetta and the Bolan pass, from where the Indus plains could be accessed.[16] The ancient city lay west of the modern one, about four km from it. The ruins of this old Kandahar, while eroded and robbed in most places, reveal a massive citadel in the midst of an imposing walled enclosure with a series of superimposed defences.[17] Covering several thousand square metres and rising some 35 metres above the ground, the citadel was an entirely man-made elevation, built on bedrock. Very possibly it was the location of the city's administrative centre.[18]

Sometime after 260 BCE, those resident in Kandahar (as also those who visited it) would have noticed unusual activity around an easterly facing rocky outcrop which was part of the Kaitul massif, a natural stronghold. They were sure to have noticed it because it lay close to the road to Girishk and Herat, a track frequently used by travellers and traders. They will have spotted the preparation of a trapezoidal panel which was inset into the rock and smoothened with great care. The involvement of the local government would have been apparent from the presence of officials co-ordinating the preparation of the panel on which, soon enough, a few hundred words appeared. Ancient bystanders, like us today, may have wondered why the state functionaries had chosen this particular rock for those words. Was it, like many other places where the emperor's epigraphs had been inscribed, part of a sacred vicinity or near an ancient shrine? Perhaps. The attractions of engraving royal messages into rock here may have been considerable, given the availability of carvable rock. Many centuries later the Cehel Zina of the first Mughal Babur, commemorating his battle against the city in the early sixteenth century, was cut into the same mountains that protect old Kandahar.[19] Ashoka's engraving was conceivably

visible and known to later wayfarers on this trail, though it is
likely that Babur's engravers, encountering it, would not have made
head or tail of what their predecessors were getting at.

In the third century BCE, what would have drawn residents and
visitors to this chipping and grinding will have been the fact that
the emperor's message was in two familiar languages. The other
messages that we waded through, which were sent out around
the same time as this one, were a fairly similar broadcast, being
also in the same language and script. This first Afghan rescript of
Ashoka, on the other hand, used neither the Brahmi script nor
the Prakrit vocabulary of the carvings we saw earlier. Greek
and Aramaic were served instead, the Greek featuring above
the Aramaic, keeping two readerships in mind. An example of
such bilingualism is the medieval stone tablet discovered in the
foundations of a monastery near the Gauri-Kedara temple at
Bhubaneswar in Orissa. The tablet was inscribed in Oriya and
Tamil because it recorded a transaction between a debtor, a man
of Tamil descent associated with the monastery, and a creditor, a
moneyed Oriya.[20] Many centuries before this, in large parts of
Asia and beyond, epigraphic records in more than one language
had become a fairly familiar sight. With the Achaemenids,
in fact, multilingual inscriptions became almost the rule, the
earliest and best-known example being the monumental epigraph on a limestone cliff on Mount Behistun in the Kerman-
shah province of western Iran. Here, Darius I (Darius 'the Great')
of the sixth century BCE had a trilingual epigraph inscribed in old
Persian, Elamite, and Babylonian. Later, such inscriptions were
engraved further west, such as for example those of the reign of
Artaxerxes III (425–338 BCE), the eleventh emperor of the Achaemenid empire. These are at Sardis and Xanthos in Turkey. Literary references to such inscriptions also abound, and, if Herodotus
is to believed, stelae with inscriptions in cuneiform and Greek were
set up at the site of the Darius bridge around the Bosphorus.[21]
Clearly, this template enjoyed wide currency in the regions west
of Afghanistan and beyond much before it was deployed for the
Ashokan message at Kandahar.

The use of Greek alongside Aramaic by a Pataliputra-based emperor shows us that at least part of his audience was Greek-speaking. That Kandahar had such speakers is also known from a Greek inscription found at old Kandahar, recovered a few hundred yards from Ashoka's bilingual rock edict and inscribed on a statue base. It mentions a Greek-speaking citizen who describes himself as the 'son of Aristonax, one of Alexandria's citizens'.[22] Thus, the first citizen of that city known to history was a Greek. The partially surviving epigraph suggests that he dedicated what may have been the statue of a 'beast' to what is called a 'temenos' of Alexander. A temenos was likely to have been a kind of sanctuary or area dedicated to a Greek deity, which means that not only did this city have Greek inhabitants, it also had structures associated with Greek life.[23] There were Greek settlers in other parts of Afghanistan as well, as at Ai Khanoum in Bactria, a Hellenic city that flourished from times somewhat later than those of Alexander.

Before the arrival of Greek, Achaemenian Aramaic, the language of official communications in the Persian empire, was in use here. In the second half of the first millennium BCE, Aramaic had become the most widely used script across the ancient Near East, from Assyria to north-west India, as well as in Egypt and Asia Minor, because this was what officialdom used.[24] Presumably, it was introduced by the Achaemenids into their satrapies in Afghanistan and the Indus valley, roughly from Arachosia to Gandhara. The empire collapsed but Aramaic continued. This explains why the Mauryan emperor used it for transmitting his message. Incidentally, it is from Aramaic that the Kharoshthi form of writing, widely used in north-west India, evolved: Ashoka later used it for another set of messages there. Everywhere else, in the subcontinental mainland, as we have seen, the Mauryan empire's administrators used Prakrit via the Brahmi script. While many different languages will have been spoken across the area, the Mauryan administration had earlier stuck uniformly to Prakrit, the assumption having been that there were enough bilingually fluent people around to translate Prakrit into the locally common tongues. Now, for the first time, and deviating from the practice followed in the rest of the empire, an Ashokan message was composed in two 'foreign' languages, one from Persia and the other from Europe.

The Kandahar situation is not, however, as singular as it seems. Ashoka's edicts were inscribed in languages used here in governmental memoranda. It was a pragmatic decision. If the administrators of large parts of India conducted official business in Prakrit, in this part of Afghanistan the familiarity was with Greek and Aramaic. By using these the administration was ensuring trouble-free dissemination by factoring in the nature of bilingualism here. Greek and Aramaic apart, other languages and dialects are likely to have been spoken in the region, though what these might have been we don't know because they were not used by the local administration—at least not on surviving rocks or anything that has come down to us from that period. Such antique speech forms are likely to have persisted beyond the conquests and inflows of the West. The persistence does not necessarily mean the existence here of separable population clusters—Greeks and Persians, Magadha migrants and indigenous groups. All it means is that while two of the main languages and scripts were used by the administration, people in general continued to speak in earlier autochthonous tongues. This regional linguistic situation was being kept in mind by those who carved the inscriptions.

The form and content were also qualitatively different. Unlike the royal Buddhist convert of mainland India who took pains to explain his spiritual evolution, in Kandahar we see a remarkably self-assured emperor who has already converted others to his path. This message is not about his metamorphosis, it is a supremely confident summary of the sovereign's spiritual success:

Ten years (of reign, or since the consecration) having been completed, king Piodasses (Piyadassi) made known (the doctrine of) Piety to men; and from this moment he has made men more pious, and everything thrives throughout the whole world. And the king abstains from (killing) living beings, and other men and those who (are) huntsmen and fishermen of the king have desisted from hunting. And if some (were) intemperate, they have ceased from their intemperance as was in their power; and obedient to their father and mother and to the elders, in opposition to the past also in the future, by so acting on every occasion, they will live better and more happily.[25]

This rescript was issued around the time of the edicts we have seen earlier. The differences between it and those are several: in his Kandahar message he relates no personal experience nor gives other reasons for propagating his doctrine of piety. He does not appear as a converted Buddhist. The confessional mode is omitted, as are the earlier moral expectations from administrators and subjects. The message is closer to being an announcement outlining the advent of a new era of general spiritual success following the tenth year of the king's consecration. In its tone it is similar to panegyrics extolling the successes of ancient conquerors, except, again, in the nature of the victory. The conquest proclaimed is now a promotion of piety which has enabled his subjects to live 'better and more happily.'

What of the character and quality of the language in this bilingual inscription—does it capture what constituted Ashoka's piety? One commentator, Paul Bernard, remarks on the excellence and contemporary nature of the Greek language which, as he puts it, does not give the appearance of having languished 'in exile, barbarized by misuse'. The vocabulary suggests an absence of hybridization and dilution with local accents and usages. It is—

> a language full of vitality, aware of contemporary usage, skilled in the handling of the literary language, familiar with the terms used by philosophers and sophists, as well as those found in the vocabulary of politics, able to find the closest equivalents to specifically Indian concepts such as *eusebeia* for the notion of *dhamma, diatribe* which means 'school of philosophy' in Greek for *pasamda*, the Indian term for religious sect, and *enkrateia*, the Greek expression for self-control, which applies to the restraint which the emperor's subjects must practice among themselves.[26]

Clearly, the scribe's skills in Greek were fairly advanced. The Greek edict does not seem like a translation of general statements unspecific to locality either. On the contrary, care seems to have been taken to adapt the ruler's voice to a form locally appropriate and comprehensible. Mortimer Wheeler had such elements of Greek culture in mind when remarking that at Kandahar 'we need then no longer to hesitate to accept a full-blown "Alexandria" upon the side of Old Kandahar. This was no mere tired vestige of a passing army. It was a balanced Greek city with its writers, its philosophers, its teachers, no less than its executives and its growing environment of Hellenized "natives"'.[27]

Setting aside the encomia for a moment and looking at possible problems in the wording, it would seem that in the third century BCE the precise terminology required in Greek for Buddhist concepts will have involved something of a wrestle because of the lack of exact equivalents. The deployment here of the Greek 'eusebeia' or piety is an example. The intention is to introduce the idea of dhamma, but in fact the Greek word is something of a far cry from the Ashokan notion of dhamma.[28] Eusebeia apparently 'defines a respect or awe by humans towards the gods or other divine beings; it applies much less to interactions between mortals themselves.'[29] It also involves the idea of sacrifice, which in the Greek context meant killing animals. This would make it most contradictory to Ashoka's dhamma, ceasing to kill animals being central to the emperor's concerns. Moreover, rather than anything that relates to gods, dhamma is a moral order involving humans and their roles in that order. In the early edicts of Karnataka it occurs in association with the Buddhist virtues ('dhamma-guna') which were to be practised. So, what the north-western people of the empire made of eusebeia seems worth thinking about. The interpretive outcome of using a language to transmit a message culturally grounded elsewhere will have modified the meaning of the message, at points perhaps crucially enough to seriously puzzle people.

What of the other epigraph in Aramaic inscribed below the Greek? This too uses words more at home within a culture rooted in the West rather than in the subcontinent. The Aramaic is not an exact translation of the Greek but corresponds in its general character to that text inasmuch as Ashoka's spiritual success is the main thrust of it:

10 years [having] fallen [it] was made which [was that] our Lord Prydrs, the king, promoted Truth (*Qsyt'*). Since then evil has diminished for all men, and he has caused all hostile things to disappear, and joy has arisen throughout the whole earth. And moreover, there is this (?): for the feeding of our Lord, the king, little is killed; seeing this (?) all men have given up [killing animals], and those who caught fishes, those men have given up [doing it]; similarly, those who are without restraint (?) have ceased to be without restraint (?). And [there is] good obedience to one's mother and father and to the old people, as destiny has laid down on every one. And there is no judgment for all men [who are] pious. This has benefited all men and will continue to benefit.[30]

Line by line, the Aramaic phrases do not correspond with the Greek. The differences are worth highlighting. The king here 'promotes truth' ('qshyt' in Aramaic) while in the Greek he makes known his doctrine of 'piety'. Unlike the king who abstained from killing in the Greek inscription, here 'for the feeding of Our Lord the king, little is killed'. Presumably, this meant that hardly any animals were being slaughtered for the royal kitchen. This reduction apparently encouraged his subjects to give up the killing of animals—or so the epigraph says. The declaration's end—'And there is no Judgment for all pious men'—stands out because the Greek message does not include it. Overall, however, the Aramaic vocabulary seems able to get Ashoka's message without the possible interpretive difficulties of the Greek. The Persian cultural grounding of Aramaic seems more conducive to a translation of concepts from the heartland of Buddhism. The overt preoccupation of this edict with giving up the killing of animals, incidentally, continues to figure prominently in Ashoka's later Afghanistan epigraphs. The Aramaic Pul-i-Darunta stone inscription noted that no living being was to be 'fattened' with other living beings, while two other edicts, also in Aramaic, from Laghman speak about the king having dispersed and expelled from 'the prosperous (population) the lovers of . . . hunting of creatures and fishes.'[31]

But coming back to our Kandahar message: who exactly composed it and what decisions on its content were taken by the provincial administration rather than the emperor? Did an exemplar emanating from the king determine the matter or were the translators left largely free? These questions connect with how political authority was constituted in the separable parts of the Mauryan empire, the dominant issue studied by historians thus far being the extent or lack of an authoritative centralized administration. Evidence of varying kinds of authority exercised across different regions led Romila Thapar to describe the Mauryan administration 'as a relationship between three categories of control: between the metropolitan state, the core areas and the peripheral regions.'[32] Her definition is based on the history of the political formation, the nature of the administration, and the character of the economy. The metropolitan state was Magadha, a state with centralized bureaucratic control much before the Mauryas. The core areas were already states before they were conquered by the Mauryas, states like Gandhara and Avanti. On the other hand, the peripheral regions were areas of relative isolation with no antecedent histories of state formation, but possessing natural resources much valued by the Mauryas. These categories were not immutable and core areas could become independent kingdoms just as peripheral areas changed into core regions.[33]

That all administrations, ancient and modern, exercise power differently across large territories is only natural, given varying political requirements. The problem is that macro analyses using state power or economic might as their measure of all things tend to posit somewhat singular ground realities across diverse regions. From such perspectives, outlying regions come to be seen as passive providers for the metropolitan state, as also passive recipients of innovations emanating from a distant central authority. Historians employed by royalty in dominant centralizing states defined the distant regions that their masters conquered and controlled primarily in relation to the needs of the centre. Interpretations of the pre-Mughal, Mughal, and British colonial periods were also for long based on these somewhat reductive assumptions in which aspects of autonomy, subversion, and precolonial continuity in regions distant from the centre tended to be steamrolled out of existence. So also the ways in which core and periphery are described in works on ancient India which tend to overlook the

Fig. Prelude 2: Part of Ashoka's message on the rocks of Erragudi

Fig. 1.1: Ashoka and his queen on a second century CE panel of the Kanaganahalli stupa in Karnataka

Fig. 10.5: Worshipping monks in front of Lumbini's Ashokan pillar

Fig. 12.1: Tissarakshita, Queen of Ashoka (Abanindranath Tagore)

Fig. 12.2: Sanghamitra with the Bodhi tree (Nandlal Bose)

Fig. Epilogue 1: Depiction of Ashoka supported by his wives on the upper segment of gateway pillar at Sanchi

Fig. Epilogue 3: Sculpture of Ashoka at Kalinga by Meera Mukherjee

peripheries of empire as the homeland of real people with their own languages, cultural predilections, and continuing everyday traditions of spirituality as well as resistance to impositions from the world beyond. The central state's armed might was, besides, often exercised only sporadically, and sometimes restrictedly for revenue extraction, leaving many areas of activity open for local modification and variation. The fundamental point is that regions have their own local histories additional to the history of their subsumption or control by an external state, and in fact the most interesting or detailed history of a region can be more connected with aspects that make it autonomous rather than controlled. Karnataka, which Thapar sees as a periphery, seems not to have been peripheral in that broader sense; it was not remotely the passive recipient of cultural innovation from the Mauryan metropolis. How the king's message was received there seems to have depended on a variety of factors at the level of the locality, ranging from the character of communities to the nature of trade and commerce.

The same processes can be seen at work in Afghanistan. This was a frontier region at the edge of the Mauryan empire continuously open to influences from Greece, Iran, Central Asia, and India. Very possibly, it was through this part of his empire that several of the emissaries Ashoka would later send to sovereigns of the Hellenistic world passed.[34] Even at this point, the existence of a Greek sanctuary at Kandahar within a few yards of the emperor's edict underlines the presence of citizens who were familiar with and engaged in cult activities rooted in the classical world of the West. We have also seen that terminology locally introduced, such as eusebeia or 'piety' and qshyt or 'truth' in place of the Prakrit dhamma, exemplifies how inter-ethnic contacts resulting from those influences played a part in translating Ashoka, even if the tone and character could not have been an entirely local conception.[35] In other words, while Afghanistan marked the physical limit of the empire of Ashoka on the west, the cosmopolitan communities here were heirs to a multicultural heritage independent of the Mauryas, and one which, historically speaking, is not evoked in descriptions that see this region as peripheral.

It has been suggested that the Kandahar edict has less in common

with other minor rock edicts while showing a general concordance with another edict of Ashoka, Rock Edict IV, in which a
similar sense of prior ethical accomplishment is conveyed. The
concordance can only be general because Rock Edict IV is a far
more elaborate statement within which the obedience that is
exhorted in the Kandahar edict figures in only one of its senten-
ces. What further complicates the question of such a link is that
Rock Edict IV came into being two years after the one at Kandahar.
So, because of the chronology, not much is gained by trying to
locate the genealogy of the first Afghan edict in other royal rescripts.

It is better, perhaps, to seek an explanation for the qualitatively
distinct character of the Kandahar epigraph in a different set of
historical facts. One possibility is that the edict was specially composed for this part of his empire, which had formed part of the
territory of many earlier conquerors. Local administrators may
have felt that a confident and assured message was more appropriate here than one where the emperor's personal angst and
spiritual metamorphosis were spotlighted. These officials had a
familiarity with the world of Persia, where kings made triumphant
proclamations about their deeds and battles in elaborate detail.
So, composing a message which spelt out what Ashoka had achiev-
ed would be more in line with what monarchs in this part of Asia
generally disseminated. For this reason, there are elements in it
which have been described as similar to the great Behistun inscription of Darius in Iran, in which the facts narrated are counted
from the king's succession to the throne, with the king stating
that everything changed with his reign.[36] But Darius is shown as
victorious over his enemies and protected by a god (Ahuramazda).
Ashoka by contrast emphasizes personal humility and the ultimate
triumph of non-violence.

* * *

Afghani food has traditionally been rich in all kinds of carnivorous delights. A graphic description of this diet—including hunks of mutton, the head and feet of sheep, chicken, skewered meat, hot mutton stock soups, even dried meat—has been provided by a scholar of Afghan history and culture, Louis Dupree. Hunting game, particularly gazelle, markhor, ibex, quail, pigeon, and partridge, and eating fish were equally important to the average Afghan.[37] It would be nice to know even more about the range of food that ancient Afghanis ate, but the list of non-vegetarian delights is already sufficient to turn the stomachs of vegetarians, the evidence for the consumption of animal flesh being not exactly skeletal. In this kind of context, might there have been hoots of laughter at the efforts on behalf of vegetarianism from distant Pataliputra?

The bones of domesticated sheep, goats, possibly cattle, red deer, gazelles, and horses have turned up in neolithic contexts.[38] Later, at the major urban centre of Mundigak, some 55 km north of Kandahar, material from the second millennium BCE exposes species ranging from domesticated animals like the ass, the horse, and the dog, to wild fauna. Apart from the ibex, the lynx, and the gazelle, the bones include those of a raptor.[39] It is likely that later too, in the first millennium BCE, this dietary pattern was maintained. So, whatever the claims of administrators on the success of Ashoka's policy of non-violence towards living beings, it is difficult to believe that vegetarianism took off here. Epigraphic announcements were listened to, not necessarily followed. People continued to carry on with their lives as before.

In some ways the Ashokan message here is really much larger than anything that the emperor intended. Looking at it now we understand that what the king said did not always define or even considerably influence the tenor of daily life. The populace will have seen some of these particular exhortations as most peculiar, and therefore taken them with a large pinch of salt.

# 8

# An Expansive Imperial
# Articulation

ASHOKA'S MAIDEN EXCURSIONS IN PUBLIC COMMUNI-
cation were aimed at converting his audiences into
adherents. 'Rock of ages cleft for me/ Let me hide myself
in thee' says the singer in the popular eighteenth-century Christian
hymn, seeking refuge in Christ. 'Rock of ages cleft for me/ Let me
show myself in thee' would have been Ashoka's version, seeking
exposure for the Buddha. It is perhaps not generally recognized that
use of the autobiographical and confessional mode to propagate
religious views, familiar to us in the Christian tradition from the
time of the pioneering fourth century CE *Confessions of St Augus-
tine*, was anticipated by over six centuries through Ashoka's virtual
invention of the tradition, if not the genre, in the shape of his
edicts. The short earlier versions whetted his appetite for such
discourse. He seems to have grown ever more convinced that
governance involved not just ruling well and prescribing policy but
ensuring direct and affective communication with his subjects. So,
around 256 BCE, some three years after his first edicts, he went on
to elaborate and disseminate information on what appear to be
very novel modes of governance, as well as norms of public and
personal conduct. The contrast between this articulation and his
earlier messages lay not merely in the spectrum of ideas and sub-

jects outlined, nor only in the vivid combining of personal elements with political practice. It lay also in the length and elaborate nature of the new edicts, rendering them qualitatively different from the earlier short ones.

Ashoka's voice was first heard in edicts that ran from some six to twenty-two lines. 'Short' is a relative term, the relation being to the size of rescripts that came to be transcribed in the second campaign of epigraphs. As against the first articulation of the 'minor' edicts, we now encounter a series of messages, of more than a hundred lines covering, in several instances, multiple rock surfaces. By common consent these are known as Ashoka's major rock edicts, the word 'major' denoting the length and possibly the gravitas of the message. Collectively, the rendition appears like a finished and coherent anthology comprising fourteen edicts.

On the orders of the emperor, this set of edicts was transcribed in several places across India. At many of their locations they have survived well. The most extraordinary of these sites is Erragudi in Andhra, where we saw the first of Ashoka's minor epigraphs—which graces the most easily accessible of the Erragudi rocks, inscribed on the lowest of the boulders. Five further boulders marked by similar scrawls are clustered across the hill face, the most imposing of these forming a precipice some six metres or more above the lowest. Many of the boulders crowd the eastern slope, their surfaces marked by a riot of Brahmi characters, some still easily decipherable, others only faintly visible. The varying conditions of preservation apart, what strikes the observer is the plethora of words. Their sprawl is seen best on the topmost rock, generally described as Boulder A, which has two inscribed faces. In general, the boulders show the ancient letters unevenly: sometimes, seven lines of writing cover 2.5 x 0.5 metres, while on the same rock five lines also crowd into a space only 1 metre long. The same message is also known to cover several rocks—one of the edicts has twenty-nine lines on a single boulder (Boulder B), while the last seven lines are continued on another (Boulder C) which lies a few feet to its south.

Versions of the major edicts like the one at Erragudi appear on rocks at Girnar in Gujarat, at Shahbazgarhi and Mansehra in

Fig. 8.1: Part of the inscribed Kalsi rock in Uttarakhand as it appeared before a shed was built over it

Fig. 8.2: Stone slab of the Sannathi edict

north-west Pakistan, at Kandahar in Afghanistan, and at Kalsi in Uttarakhand. In two places within Orissa—Dhauli and Jaugada—there is a complete set of edicts, though some of what is found on them differs from that on the axis from Pakistan to Andhra. A few of the major edicts have not endured well: Sopara in Maharashtra has yielded fragments of a mere three edicts, while at Sannathi in Karnataka only four edicts have been found. Similarly at Kandahar, as we saw, a mere two edicts have survived on a single rectangular block of limestone. Interestingly, the edicts at all these places—Kandahar, Sopara, and Sannathi—are not inscribed into large *in situ* rocks but on dressed stone slabs. Unusually, in Sannathi, they cover both the front and back of the slabs, leading to the inference that the slab was vertically set up by the inscribers so that their inscriptions could be read. Ashoka's major rock edicts could sometimes be termed his major stone edicts.

What are these enunciations, what do they say about Ashoka, what can we surmise about their reception and audiences? First, however, let us look at the important events and career trajectory of the emperor as he presented them.

\* \* \*

Around 261/260 BCE Ashoka fought the first and possibly only large-scale war of his reign, at Kalinga. This is the only conquest he mentions here, and since no other territorial victory figures in any of his later edicts it can be presumed that this was his only major military battle.[1] The number displaced ('one hundred and fifty thousand'), killed ('one hundred thousand'), and dead as a consequence of the war ('many times as many those who died') make it clear that this was warfare on a very considerable scale,[2] even if one discounts the tendency to top up the headcount by offering epic figures rounded off to the nearest hundred thousand. The carnage also seems to have brought suffering indiscriminately upon all—Brahmans, Shramanas, other sects, households—many among them people who had actually practised the dhamma that Ashoka now espoused.[3] The future protocols for human relationship that would come to define the emperor's idea of dhamma— from obedience to parents to proper courtesy towards slaves and servants—were those that the king now saw as having been already lived by many whom he had slaughtered, dispossessed, and deported. He describes his victory as deplorable because of the blind uniformity with which he had inflicted misery, the ironic democracy of suffering he had created.

What he proceeded to do in the immediate aftermath of Kalinga is unknown. Certainly, he lost all appetite for conquering new territory and soon, he became a Buddhist. Within a couple of years, in the tenth year after his coronation, we see him on a pilgrimage to Mahabodhi, where the Buddha had attained enlightenment roughly 300 years earlier. This was the beginning of what Ashoka describes as the second part of his reign, a watershed in the conduct of his personal and political life.

He now undertook what were described as 'dharma yatras' instead of the usual royal 'vihara yatras'. Vihara yatras were marked by pleasures such as the hunt; Ashoka's yatras were mass contact programmes involving donations and guidance on dhamma: 'On these (tours) the following takes place, (viz.) visiting Shramanas and Brahmanas and making gifts (to them), visiting the aged and supporting (them) with gold, visiting the people of the country, instructing (them) in morality, and questioning (them) about morality, as suitable for this (occasion).'[4] It was this, Ashoka declared, which gave him supreme pleasure while those in the 'other part', meaning the earlier pleasures, were deemed inferior.

Can these yatras be described as tours? Vihara yatra and dhamma yatra have been generally understood as pleasure tours and dharma tours, respectively, travelling and journeying being their central features. The factor of enjoyment and hedonism in vihara yatras is also evident in descriptions other than Ashoka's. The scholar Manindra Mohan Bose points to the *Mahabharata*, in which a yatra, called the 'Ghosha yatra', of one of the epic villains, Duryodhana, is vividly described. The passage where permission is sought by this character of his father for the yatra reads: 'O monarch, this also is an excellent season for thy son to go ahunting'; and further: 'indeed, we desire very much to go on a hunting expedition and will avail of that opportunity for supervising the tale of our cattle.'[5] However, 'yatra' in ancient India also indicated festivals. Bose's view is that a dharma yatra should be understood as a festival, not a tour. This is academic quibbling over a term with no likelihood of a resolution: perhaps some of the tours were conducted with an air of festivity. The point in our context is that, whether festival or tour, it would have seen the king moving around his realm. This is what the edict suggests when it says he met people in the country ('janapada'). Ashoka was making himself accessible by being often on the move, meeting people of all kinds, donating money and gold, instructing them about the dhamma.

Within a couple of years after he began touring, around 257/256 BCE, the king vested enhanced spiritual responsibility in his officers. Specifically, the rajukkas and pradeshikas and other such local administrative officials were ordered, even while carrying out their routine duties, to undertake an inspection circuit every five years to preach the dhamma, the usual Ashokan favourites being enjoined—proper behaviour towards various classes of people and animal life, respect to be shown to parents and elders, liberality with friends as well as, importantly, to persons with differing religious inclinations. The injunction against slaughtering all living beings—presumably animals, birds, and fish—was naturally a strong recommendation in this idea of the moral life. Whereas Minor Rock Edict II had underlined the need for proper behaviour towards all as something that 'should' be done, or as an order of the emperor, here it was expected to be preached by his officials so as to earn his subjects personal merit.

> Meritorious is obedience to mother and father.
> Meritorious is liberality to friends, acquaintances and relatives and to Shramanas and Brahmanas.
> Meritorious is abstention from the slaughter of living beings.
> Meritorious is to spend little (and) to store little.[6]

The importance attached to such public instruction of morality resonates with the way that Buddhism had always tried to establish its doctrines, alongside the giving and donating expected of the laity.[7] Yet the conformity with established doctrinal practice does not explain everything: there is an interesting deviation. Shramanas were ascetic renunciants that included but were not limited to Buddhist monks. By alluding to Brahmanas and Shramanas in the same breath, Ashoka extends Buddhist ideas somewhat beyond their normal boundaries into a broader humanism. The espousal of moderation and thrift within the fold of meritorious conduct extends religious morality into administrative duty and state function. Crass materialism and conspicuous consumption are cautioned against, possibly as a veiled warning to affluent citizens who heard his message as also to sections of officialdom. Ashoka does not seem to censure the acquisition of wealth per se, the donation of riches to the deserving perhaps justifying the initial acquisition.

These actions on the ground were combined with a sweeping public assurance of the impact of such measures. In the twelfth year after his coronation the emperor issued a public rescript in which he decided to explain with graphic detail how the practice of dhamma that he had instituted had led to a social transformation within his kingdom. This was obviously a king not content with merely elucidating the nature of the social change required, he was also interested in ensuring they had been made to happen and would subsequently benefit posterity. The edicts emphasize both that there has been a break with the past and the intent to ensure a transformed future for those who will come.

The repeated mention of past times in relation to the present was intended to highlight this change. Earlier, 'for many hundreds of years, slaughter of lives, cruelty to living creatures, disrespect to relatives and disrespect to the Shramanas and Brahmanas increased.'[8] Now, what had increased 'to a degree as was not possible to achieve for many hundreds of years in the past' was 'abstention from the slaughter of life, absence of cruelty to living creatures, seemly behaviour to Shramanas and Brahmanas, obedience to mother and father (and) obedience to the aged.'[9] He intended to ensure that this continued after his time: 'the sons, grandsons and great-grandsons of king Priyadarshin, Beloved of the Gods, will promote this practice of Dharma till the time of universal destruction and, (themselves) abiding by Dharma and good conduct, will instruct (people) in Dharma.'[10]

In the epigraphs of later kings, this kind of proclamation would become formulaic and used to underscore the permanent nature of what was being enacted, whether the grant of land or the construction of a memorial pillar. Ashoka's epigraph is novel in being the first in a line of inscriptions that made such declarations. It must nonetheless have appeared formulaic to his listeners because third century BCE audiences, familiar with sons murdering royal fathers and brothers, may have been sceptical of any king, however well disposed, being able to ensure the continuity of his predilections as policy by his successors.

Were his subjects even vaguely convinced that a change of such magnitude had come to pass merely because their king said so? Governments in our time equipped with excellent communication systems and far more effective methods of coercion have not managed to successfully bring about social transformation simultaneously across the regions of India, so Ashoka's claim that he had does not seem credible. Their encounter with Mauryan officials charged with new responsibilities may have prompted the recognition within the populace of a ruler with exceptional drive and ambition who at least aimed, even if he did not succeed, at moral change. This may well have been Ashoka's intention. His Buddhist emphases and the outlining of differences from what had existed 'for many hundreds of years' was a statement of intent couched in the language of achievement. Departing from his minor rock edicts, the emperor now made no allusions to the value of age-old traditions, or what he had earlier called 'porana pakiti'.

In the following year, the thirteenth after his coronation, he introduced a major innovation in the institutional structure of his administration. The moral inspection tours aiding the spread of dhamma were now supplemented by the creation of a new class of very senior officials called dharma-mahamatras. The exposition on their functions is long and detailed and reveals a proactively interventionist administrative group spread across his dominions. Dharma-mahamatras were engaged everywhere 'among the adherents of Dharma (to determine) whether a person is (only) inclined towards Dharma or is (fully) established in Dharma or is (merely) given to charity.'[11] And who were the people within the domain of their work? Practically everyone, it seems: the edict specifies all religious sects, people dwelling on the empire's western borders (including the Yavanas, Kambojas, Gandharas and the Rastrika-paitryanikas), the servile class, the Aryas, the Brahmans and the ruling class, the destitute and the aged, even prisoners. The new officials were to cater to all kinds. With prisoners their work was very definite: they were to distribute money to those who had children, help in 'unfettering of those' who had committed crimes because of the instigation of others and help in getting aged prisoners released.[12] The larger-than-life presence of this class of officers is underlined by the fact that they were said to be engaged in Pataliputra and other towns, as also in the households of Ashoka's siblings and relatives. The impression is of a considerable administrative apparatus having been put in place to oversee the practice of morality in the public and private domains, including the king's own kin.

These were events for which Ashoka provided a series of chronological markers. They spanned from 261–260 BCE till 256–255 BCE, from the Kalinga war in his eighth year (261–260 BCE) to the various ways in which, from the tenth (259–258 BCE) till the thirteenth years (256–255 BCE), he altered the administrative focus towards the creation of a moral empire. There is good reason to believe that other events and innovations in statecraft were also introduced over these years. No specificities such as 'dates' are provided for these, their existence being inferred from their inclusion alongside the record of changes in officialdom.

Ashoka's territorial canvas for moral action also now enlarges. He appears to have added a new dimension to the terms of engagement of the Mauryan realm with the states bordering his empire and beyond, towards the north-west and across the deep south.

There was a range of such states and people: the Cholas, Pandyas, Satiyaputra, Tamraparni; there were the territories of the Yavana king Antiochus and chieftains neighbouring him. The basis for the existence of relations with foreign powers is in the *Arthashastra* a prelude to the monarch's expansion of his own realm through conquest. Ashoka's consideration in the matter overturned this Machiavellian thumb rule. The king's circle of influence in other kingdoms came to be based, or was showcased as being based, on welfare measures, specifically medical care and the nurture of living beings in distant realms, both human and animal. Two kinds of medical facility were established: hospitals, and facilities in which roots, fruit, and medicinal plants hitherto unavailable were imported and planted. Roads were laid and wells dug for 'enjoyment' by animals and humans. The compassionate and moral life now also becomes Mauryan foreign policy.

The monarch's immediate personal access to officials at all times is another policy carefully proclaimed:

> Formerly, in the ages gone by, there was no transaction of state-business and no reporting (of incidents to the king) at all hours.
>
> So I have made the following (arrangement).
>
> The reporters should report to me the affairs of the people at any time and place, whether I am engaged in eating (or) am in the harem (or) in the bed-chamber (or) on a promenade (or) in a carriage (or) on the march.
>
> And I am now attending to the people's affairs at all places.
>
> And, when I issue an order orally in connection with any donation or proclamation or when an emergent work presses itself upon the Mahamatras (and) in case there is, in connection with that matter, a controversy among (the Ministers of) the Council or an argumentation (in the Council in favour of a particular view), the fact must be reported to me immediately at any place and at any time.
>
> Thus have I ordered.[13]

The *Arthashastra* had stressed the importance of such accessibility too. The king was expected to be always active, hear urgent matters and never put them off, look into the affairs of all kinds of people and places: 'temple deities, hermitages, heretics, Brahmins learned in the Vedas, cattle and holy places, of minors, of the aged, the sick, the distressed and the helpless and of women, in this order, or, in accordance with the importance of the matter or its urgency.'[14] The manual prescribes designated areas for the king's public interactions. Unrestricted entrance was necessary for those wanting to see him in connection with their affairs, but it was in the assembly hall that such audiences were to be held. Like other areas in the palace where interactions and decisions relating to state matters were made, this hall was to be separated from the inner apartments, the fear of violence being a constant threat. Indeed, 'everyone (in the palace) should live in his own quarters and not move to the quarters of another.'[15]

None of these anxieties feature in Ashoka's account of his administrative innovations. The informality outlined is so complete that one is tempted to imagine the king's eating and love-making interrupted by people with problems rushing in and out of his private chambers. The reality is likely to have been far less colourful, the access to the emperor careful and limited. The change would nonetheless have been seen as a new political culture in which the common weal required 'exertion and prompt dispatch of business [. . .] Whatever effort I make is made in order that I may discharge the debt which I owe to all living beings, that I may make them happy in this world, and that they may attain heaven in the next world.' The expressions here are uncannily and ironically similar to the extolling of the energetic king in the *Arthashastra*:

> In the happiness of the subjects lies the happiness of the king and in what is beneficial to the subjects his own benefit. What is dear to himself is not beneficial to the king, but what is dear to the subjects is beneficial (to him).
>
> Therefore, being ever active, the king should carry out the management of material well-being. The root of material well-being is activity, of material disaster its reverse.[16]

Such similarities are the consequence of historical retrospection. How do we make sense of them in the context of the third century BCE? It is entirely possible that Ashoka had imbibed the *Arthashastra*, its core having been composed earlier and its author very possibly living in the time of Ashoka's grandfather, and therefore known at least by repute down the decades. A ruler based in Pataliputra was in fact very unlikely not to have been familiar with the work, at least as a body of ideas. In tracing the genealogy of Ashoka's welfare statism it would be fair to say that it had, in a variant form and with different ends in mind, been enunciated before his time.[17]

\* \* \*

The fourteen major edicts, all formulated and inscribed in the third century BCE, seem to resemble an anthology now because we look at them as a group authored by the same king. But the fact that the edict set's locations are hugely diverse also makes aspects of them specific to each, while the thousands of kilometres separating them simultaneously suggest an asynchronous history that could be said to sometimes complement and at other times contradict the general impression of similitude.

Their composition was individual: each decree was composed and issued before being inscribed. The edicts themselves make this evident when alluding to the years in which Ashoka chose to issue specific decrees. As the last date that figures is the thirteenth year of coronation, the edicts could only have been set down after that event, though whether they were composed and erected immediately after or a couple of years later is not clear. Why the emperor now chose to get earlier promulgations inscribed in other parts of his empire—to which, at the time of engraving, many more texts were added—is also unclear. He was probably anxious to show them as part of an interconnected whole, much like different chapters of the same story. A symmetry of official accountability through the realm seems another strong part of the desiderata.

Since he began to dispatch the pronouncements individually they were not, obviously, a complete compilation at any single point in time. In several instances the edicts were dispatched in batches, with the pattern of dispatch showing many variations.

We know this because of the pattern and placement of the writing, the Kalsi Rock Edict providing an instance. Kalsi is situated on the banks of the Yamuna river in Uttarakhand, at the junction of the plains and the hills, from where Hindu pilgrims are known to travel towards Yamunotri. Here, one part of a fine-grained rock was carefully polished. Onto it were carved the first nine edicts in very small letters. Below this set, however, the letters become thrice as large as on the upper part (constituting edicts 10 to 14). And then, realizing that the original surface was too small for such large letters, the remaining record came to be carved on the left side of the rock as well. It is unlikely that the same hand inscribed all the edicts, or that they were inscribed simultaneously. It also seems that while initially the engraving was carefully crafted, the last four edicts were done sloppily.

A staggered engraving process can be seen at Shahbazgarhi in the present-day Mardan district of Pakistan. Here, unlike at Kalsi, more than one rock was used. Unlike both Erragudi and Kalsi, the Kharoshthi script was preferred. The first eleven edicts are on the east face of a large mass of trap rock up a hill.[18] The next is engraved on a separate boulder towards the foot of the hill, and the final two edicts (13 and 14) are on the west face of the same big rock up the hill whose eastern face was first inscribed. This west face was not suited to chiselling.[19] Why the scribe chose it and ignored the many other available rock surfaces eludes us. But their variant pattern of engraving, as well as the different sizes of letters in the three sets, shows a process of accrual, a progression stretched out.

Some 200 km to the east, at Mansehra in Hazara district, the pattern mimics the Shahbazgarhi form. Kharoshthi, the script considered better suited to the area, is used again. On the highest boulder, a well-polished square was created at the surface and upon this the first eight edicts were inscribed in very small characters.[20] The scribe who wrote on the second rock, located a little below the first, used large letters to engrave the texts of three edicts (9 to 11) on the north face and one edict (12) on its south face. The third rock, now in a fallen state, carried the last two edicts.

Such was not always the case. Occasionally, the edicts were simultaneously engraved at one place. In the most spectacular of

Fig. 8.3: Rock edicts arranged in columns at Girnar

these, at Girnar in the Junagadh district of Gujarat, some thirty metres on the north-eastern face of a large granite boulder shows all fourteen edicts. The writing is uniform, arranged in neat columns. Each of the edicts appears to be divided from the other by straight lines. The various cartouches, carved into clear compartments, can still be clearly seen. It seems plausible that this was ordered to be written at a single point in time, when all fourteen texts were available. Since the composition of the edicts was more usually a staggered process, instances of inscriptional simultaneity would seem to suggest they were set down later. All the edict texts will have had to first be available in finished form to be set down together in a single engraving campaign.[21] So, Girnar is likely to have got its edicts after those at Shahbazgarhi and Kalsi, to which successive batches had been sent.

* * *

Erragudi is a good place to begin looking at this full anthology of edicts, its uniqueness being that it is the only site where both the early messages and the new ones are found together. At Kandahar there are two different Ashokan inscriptions as well, but not on the same set of rocks.[22]

When setting down the new message, the first modification made and one that his subjects at Erragudi would have noticed, was an addition to Ashoka's early title, 'Priyadarshin, Beloved of the Gods'. Now, for the first time, Ashoka was called a king. This king did not begin by recounting what he had instituted in the five-odd years since Kalinga, but with an enunciation of dhamma concerned primarily with protecting animals from mindless sacrificial ceremonies:

Here no living being should be slaughtered for sacrifice.
And also no festive gathering should be held.
For the Beloved of the Gods sees manifold evil in festive gatherings.
    There is (however) one kind of festive gathering, which is considered good by king Priyadarshin, Beloved of the Gods.[23]

Alongside this proscription is the intent to prohibit festive gatherings ('samajas') involving animal sacrifice. This was a departure from how Ashoka had enunciated his idea of morality a few years earlier: the first minor rock edict mentions kindness to living beings without outlining prohibitions. Now, 'restraint' orders were proclaimed near towns.[24] While the location of ancient settlement in the vicinity of Erragudi where this order would have been known remains unclear, elsewhere it was inscribed either near or at urban centres, at Girnar and Sannathi, for instance, which were provincial capitals. The Orissa edicts are at Dhauli, not far from a fortified town, and at Jaugada, within the ramparts of a fort. Although the exact location of the Sopara message is not known since only fragments of three edicts were found, we know that Sopara was a thriving port in western India. Towards the north-west, Shahbazgarhi and Mansehra were, as noted, strategically important on account of trade routes.[25] The populace in all such locations will have needed a lot of persuading to abstain from eating meat and organizing sacrificial ritual. From the abundance of bones in early historic sites spread over both North and South India, there is little doubt that animal flesh was in great demand,[26] with people of means probably also importing exotic livestock. The earliest of these, the Harappans of the third millennium BCE, relished catfish brought in from a coastal location several hundred kilometres distant. There is no reason to believe that the well to do two thousand years later did not crave similar delicacies.

In the Karnataka–Andhra belt, death rituals as evident from megaliths included animal parts in the burials alongside the human dead. Similarly, in ancient Hindu belief and practice, sacrifices of goats, oxen, rams, and horses commonly figure in offerings to the gods. The merit so obtained, one commentator points out, is extolled in the *Mahabharata*: 'animals killed in sacrifices to the accompaniment of Vedic mantras went to heaven and it [the epic] narrates the story of king Rantideva in whose sacrifices two thousand animals and cows were killed every day.'[27] Some scriptures frowned on or had misgivings about these. In the *Satapatha Brahmana* the eater of meat is said to be eaten in his next birth by the animal killed.[28] Regardless of these occasional scriptural impediments, the general picture is one of a populace not just carnivorous but eagerly so.

Ashoka could scarcely have been unaware that his dictum would spur resentment. This is possibly why the edict presents the proscription alongside an outline of altered culinary palace practice:

> Many hundred thousands of living beings were formerly slaughtered every day in the kitchen of king Priyadarshin, Beloved of the Gods, for the sake of curry.
>
> But now, when this record relating to Dharma is written, only three living creatures are killed (daily) for the sake of curry, two birds and one animal.
>
> Even this animal is not (slaughtered) regularly.
>
> These three living beings too shall not be killed in future.[29]

That the dhamma being propounded must be regarded as work in progress was an idea Ashoka sent out via other parts of the message. His successors—sons, grandsons, and 'the generations coming after them till the destruction of the world'—would continue his acts of merit, for 'whosoever among them will abandon even a part of it will do an act of demerit'.[30] This warning betrays anxiety at the spectre of impermanence: guilt over his own usurpation may have been some part of the anxiety since the expectation that his successors would respect a tradition he was establishing had been diluted by his own record. Hammering home the dhamma, literally as well as metaphorically, by casting it in stone seems in part at least to have been the consequence of some nervousness over whether 'his descendants may conform to it'.[31] Stating and re-stating that he wanted dhamma to continue as state policy beyond his reign betrays a deep insecurity at the obvious difficulties in ensuring continuity faced by all monarchs of the time, such continuity having been violated in other respects by his own actions as a prince.

Concern over continuity through time is complemented by the interest in dissemination through space. To provide his administration and subjects with a sense of the territorial length and breadth of the empire to which they belonged, and of the larger world of rulers that formed part of his sphere of interaction, will have been an important motive for the massive coverage Ashoka wanted. This was, in a sense, a message given out via the spread of a message—the sense being given of a huge empire. A panoramic vista of states in every direction beyond it is ultimately also a technique for communicating imperial strength, and obliquely thereby the power of the message and the requirements being spelt out. At Erragudi, for instance, people were likely to have known of political entities beyond their borders in the South, such as the Cholas and the Cheras. These realms had cultural and commercial contacts with North India from at least the fifth century BCE.[32] Kodumanal, presently in the Erode district of Tamil Nadu, was a flourishing centre complete with a gemstone industry. Beads in different stages of manufacture, discarded chips, raw material blocks, and a range of precious stones—sapphire, beryl, agate, carnelian, amethyst, lapis lazuli (probably from Badakshan), jasper, garnet, and soapstone—have been unearthed from habitations there. At Porunthal in the Amaravathi river valley of Tamil Nadu as well, beads of quartz, carnelian, and glass have been found in large quantities. The several hundred glass beads and a glass furnace found suggest production on a commercial scale.

An aspect of the present and the past juxtaposed in these inscriptions is the use of dramatic and effective rhetoric. In a passage redolent with metaphor, Ashoka suggests that the change could be charted through a transformation in sound: where war drums had once sounded the emperor was now ensuring the sounding of morality ('bherighoso aho dhammaghoso').[33] While in the past music had accompanied armed battles—the beating of the 'bheri' was a call to arms—there was now only the sound of dhamma being proclaimed. Rhythm and onomatopoeia were to be deployed to render the messages sonorous and effective. The enunciation in this set of edicts is marked by emphases placed at various points by the repetition of particular phrases. The message returns time and again to a contrast of past and present so that the effect of what Ashoka claimed as achievement was highlighted with each juxtaposition. The words 'Formerly, in the ages gone by', in particular, recur constantly for oratorical effect.

Among the more striking aspects of the major edicts is the emperor's perception of himself as a sovereign spiritual guardian with social responsibilities. The seventh edict includes an impassioned plea for the practice of religious tolerance. It is the emperor's wish, the edict says, that everywhere in his dominions all religious sects should live. Proto-secularism is a possible term for this desire, making the Ashokan link with the modern Indian state's constitutional commitment to such values entirely logical. Ashoka also speaks of how he imagined ordinary folk should conduct themselves. People, as he put it, were of 'diverse inclinations and diverse passions. They will perform either the whole or only a part of (their duty).'[34] His view was that being liberal was worthless without self-control, pure thoughts, gratitude, and solid devotion. It was a reiteration of what he had said in the same message earlier when distinguishing between a person fully established in dhamma from one merely charitable.[35] Religiosity was frequently expressed only through conscience-salving donations, and the emperor was making it known that he did not consider such giving sufficient.

His subjects would not have had a problem imbibing this part of his message. What is likely to have made them wary was the authoritarian tone with which he offered his opinion on how they ought and ought not to conduct their social rituals. An instance of this appears in the ninth edict, which expounds on the kinds of rites which Ashoka considered superficial and unsatisfactory: 'auspicious ceremony on the occasion of illness, the wedding of a son, the wedding of a daughter, (and) the birth of children . . . on such occasions, the women folk (in particular) perform many and diverse (kinds of) ceremony which is trivial and meaningless.'[36] The people were warned that such acts lacked all efficacy whereas those associated with dhamma produced results. And dhamma, he repeated, comprised 'proper courtesy to slaves and servants, reverence to elders, restraint in (one's dealings with) living beings, (and) liberality to the Shramanas and Brahmanas.'[37]

The recurrence of dhamma and its vital relevance are obsessive.

The core principles running through the edicts, of proper behaviour with parents, friends, and holy men, and giving up killing living beings ('prananam'), are continuously elucidated, the eleventh edict offering a variation on the same theme. The results of acting in line with dhamma mean happiness in this world and endless merit in the next. The king's subjects will have seen this frequent reaffirmation as a sermon in which the foundational message works as a leitmotif to underscore its significance.

The sermonizing monarch returns to proto-secularism in his twelfth edict, which has been generally seen as the supreme proclamation of tolerance for all religious and philosophical sects.[38] Its core feature is the belief that at the root of dhamma is a public culture in which every sect honours every other (they 'should learn and respect one another's Dharma'). And how is this to be practised?

> ... restraint in regard to speech, (which means) that there should be no extolment of one's own sect or disparagement of other sects on inappropriate occasions and that it should be moderate in every case even on appropriate occasions.
>
> On the contrary, other sects should be duly honoured in every way (on all occasions).
>
> If (a person) acted in this way, (he) not only promotes his own sect, but also benefits other sects.
>
> But if (a person) acts otherwise, (he) not only injures his own sect but also harms other sects.
>
> Truly, if (a person) extols his own sect and disparages other sects with a view to glorifying his own sect owing merely to his attachment (to it, he) injures his own sect very severely by acting in that way.
>
> Therefore concord is commendable.[39]

The tolerance defined here is not a passive virtue of cordial disregard of the Other but rather a positive effort at a concord recognized as mutually beneficial. This being an important priority, the king said he bestowed 'men of all religious communities with gifts and with honours of various kinds, ascetics or householders.' Such gifting and honouring were not done for themselves but to ensure the growth of dhamma among them which, as he put it, required amiable and respectful forms of public interaction among them.

This proclamation of a social philosophy and accompanying political programme at Erragudi and elsewhere is likely to have reassured local populations that the emperor's Buddhism was not in the end intrusive. His articulation of moral zeal bordering on authoritarianism in relation to customary practices is undercut or alleviated by this espousal of tolerance, this idealization of a public concord as the essence of dhamma. And, as in the other edicts, the emperor highlights how he intends his administration to realize this end. Apart from the dharma-mahamatras, mahamatras who superintended what are described as matters relating to women (probably of the royal household and harem), and officers in charge of the king's cattle and pastures, are said to have been roped in for such duties.

In the thirteenth edict the emperor is at his most poignant, finally finding the inner strength to speak about the life-changing episode at Kalinga. This is where he exposes the destructive consequences of his military victory and pronounces himself the chief villain of the carnage. It is here that he draws attention with great detail to the horror and repentance it aroused in him in order to convince his listeners about the importance of self-realization. The composer of the edict says the people of Kalinga ('Kalingya') were successfully conquered by the king in the eighth year following his coronation. The graphic accompanying details need not be repeated here. What is significant is how from that painful past Ashoka moves to the present, appealing to a group of his adversaries to follow his example. These were forest dwellers ('Atavi') who he hoped would repent, as he had, so that they would not be killed. Kalinga had been pacified by force and the Atavikas may well have been the next in line: '(It is hereby) explained (to them) that, in spite of his repentance, the Beloved of the Gods possesses power (enough to punish them for their crimes), so that they should turn (from evil ways) and would not be killed (for their crimes).'[40] The threat provides a glimpse, inadvertent perhaps, of the realities of ruling a large empire in which powerful groups had the capacity to undermine the ruling monarch's hegemonic effort. Ashoka was also implicitly outlining here the limits to his philosophy of tolerance: for all his pacific Buddhism, the resort to war and pacification was not ruled out. Groups in large forested tracts were found especially difficult to deal with by monarchs at this time. The *Arthashastra* is categorical that the Atavika, 'living in their own territory, are many in number and brave, fight openly, seize and ruin countries, having the same characteristics as a king.'[41] Ashoka's edict, threatening and cajoling this group, shows the persistence of powerful enemies within the ambit of empire. The message speaks of various kings and people beyond his frontiers and those within his territories:

> And such a conquest has been achieved by the Beloved of the Gods not only here (in his dominions) but also in the territories bordering (on his dominions), as far away as (at the distance of) six hundred yojanas, (where) the Yavana king named Antiyoka (is ruling and where), beyond (the kingdom of) the said Antiyoka, four other kings named Tulamaya, Antikeni, Maka and Alikasudara (are also ruling), (and) towards the south, where the Colas and Pandyas (are living), as far as Tamraparni.
>
> Likewise here in the dominions of His Majesty, (the Beloved of the Gods)—in (the countries of) the Yavanas and Kambojas, of the Nabhakas and Nabhapanktis, of the Bhoja-paitryanikas (i.e. hereditary or tribal Bhojas) and of the Andhras and Paulindas, everywhere (people) are conforming to the instructions in Dharma (imparted) by the Beloved of the Gods.
>
> Even where the envoys of the Beloved of the Gods have not penetrated, there too men have heard of the practices of the Dharma and the ordinances issued and the instructions in Dharma (imparted) by the Beloved of the Gods, (and) are conforming to Dharma (and) will continue to conform to it.[42]

The recitation of these names has a pattern to it. The kings and people mentioned either lived beyond the western borders of the Mauryan empire or across its southern rim as far as Sri Lanka. These were powerful independent rulers and polities and speaking about his conquest of them through dhamma was Ashoka's way of drawing attention to his sphere of influence.[43] We see a victorious king announcing his authority over other polities and rulers by unusually pacific means.[44] Some of them may well have been states over which an expanding Mauryan empire had territorial designs. Possibly, Mauryan envoys now deputed there would have had to explain Ashoka's change of heart. The hope may also have been expressed that these rulers abandon all thought of aggression, including against Ashoka's territory.[45]

The pattern seen above recurs with regard to people in Ashoka's own dominions: specifically mentioned are inhabitants of areas in the north-west, west, and towards the south. Among these were the Andhras: the populace at Erragudi may have seen this as a reference to them and, if so, one wonders if they agreed with their emperor's assessment that they were conforming to the morality that was now his mission. The Yavanas and other people who lived in the southern and north-western parts of the kingdom are similarly mentioned, possibly because Mauryan control over them was tenuous. That they are described not by an encompassing expression such as people ('jana') but in terms of their ethno-geographical identities means that Ashoka wanted to specify them as people who must, above all, conform to his dhamma. People in other parts of his empire are not mentioned because presumably they were known to have been or assumed to have been conforming in the required ways.

Such passages demonstrate an acknowledgement of the actual state of affairs within the Mauryan realm, the potential sources of instability. There is a similar acknowledgement now of what could realistically be expected by Ashoka of his successors. The 'dhamma-lipi' had been written so that his sons and grandsons would not think of fresh conquests. Yet, pragmatically accepting that conquest by his successors was very much in the realm of possibility, the emperor wished that they would be somewhat merciful in the event of victory in such warfare. 'In any victory they gained there should be mildness ("khamti") and light punishment ("lahudan-data")', which as one scholar puts it, would make such conquest 'unlike his own victory, with its terrible consequences, in Kalinga.'[46]

In the end the king sets forth the range of variations in his records, and the reasons for the range. Since his dominions were wide, he says he has ensured that a great deal was written down, and more would be written in future. A great deal, though was not written everywhere. If some of his records were expansive, others were concise, and still others of a medium form. For the long records, as in this case, one reason for their elaborate form is that 'there are (some topics which) have been repeated over and over again owing to their sweetness, so that people may act accordingly.'[47] On the other hand, their abridgement is in many instances deliberate because a particular place may have seemed unsuitable for the full record. In some, the king acknowledges, a poor scribe had put down an incomplete record. In any case, all types of records, we are told had not been placed in their complete form in all places.

Looking at this anthology as a whole and in relation to his first message, Ashoka will now have appeared to his subjects in a somewhat different way. While in his first message the emperor showed his conversion to Buddhism as instrumental in his political life, that connection is now no longer overt: the repentance over Kalinga is now central. In the minor edicts a broad-based morality rooted in tradition was disseminated. Now the emphasis changes into the necessity of transparent governance. The writ of state is not laid down, but the emperor takes trouble to elucidate the spiritual basis of his political interventions.

That this constitutes a unique political intervention is worth underlining. Empires make their presence felt in the archaeological record in various ways. Kings frequently and literally coined their presence over their dominion—for instance, the Indo-Greek rulers' coins bear their names in Greek, and on the obverse in Prakrit. Other empires sculpted their rulers in stone. The Kushana kings were particularly partial to this, the iconic image of the empire being the martial representation of a belted and booted King Kanishka, his hand on the hilt of his sword. Of yet others, the regal presence is made apparent through the use of seals inscribed with the names and administrative designations of a governing class: those of the Gupta dynasty mention police officers ('dandanayakas'), judges, and even a council of the 'heir apparent'.

These are not the methods by which Ashoka makes his political authority visible. There are no imperial portraits on coins or sculpture. Nor are there courtly structures where one might imagine the emperor living with his family and in the proximity of core commanders and ministers. Instead, the artifact indisputably Ashokan is the epigraph. His political reach is best visualized via these written objects, which mark out the Mauryan empire of his time. Many later kings would also appear as rulers through words they inscribed, but Ashoka is distinguishable from them because he so conspicuously shuns the standard regal template of boasting about material possession and territorial grandeur. He does not set down messages proclaiming battles won and empire augmented. He proclaims himself, instead, as a man of strong intellect seeking to convert subjects to his point of view instead of demanding their blind obedience. And he wants to convert them by inscribing his messages near the places where they live, where they worship, along pathways that travellers use and the hilltops overlooking them.

The success of these interventions on the ground is, of course, difficult to judge. But what is beyond dispute is the fact that Ashoka had through his major edicts advanced the notion of a fundamentally new kind of political and social community.

# 9

# The Message in the Landscape

TEXTUAL ANALYSIS OF ASHOKA'S ROCK EDICTS NEEDS supplementing with context. The conclusions arrived at by examining authorial voice, political-moral agenda, and intent in using specific concepts and terms have been on the assumption that the edicts comprise a single long anthology. Analysing them as texts, however, is not enough for understanding how they were read and understood in the places where they were purposefully inscribed. The situating of documents within public spaces and arenas requires to be understood as well since the message was made a visible aspect of social and sacred landscapes. The specific histories of some of these locations till the time of Ashoka actually help us in going beyond the textual similarities of the edicts to see their contextual particularities.

The edicts were, as noted, located in the suburbs of towns, on routes travelled by caravans and used by the itinerant. The Pataliputra king's anthology was not floating unnoticed at such points, it was anchored in places that conditioned perceptions of it and possibly altered the message. Such landscapes include features that influenced how political authority was perceived, so the interpretation of this narrative of political and spiritual power was bound to depend partly on the arena within which the document was seen. Ashoka's imprint remains vivid in many of those places, a signature combination of words on rocks that acquires a resonance both from the remarkable ruins of settlements and stupas as also local traces of Mauryan intervention. In short, historicizing the regions and towns and their suburbs in which the edicts were placed is necessary.

\* \* \*

At Girnar the message was, in its full form, beautifully and compactly laid out on the eastern side of a single large rock. This is located in the suburbs of Junagadh city in Gujarat. The hand that inscribed all fourteen edicts was likely to have been the same, the characters clearly and decisively cut, more or less uniform in size. The rock itself is spectacular and on ancient visitors its impact may have been as considerable as it is in our time. While no ancient description of it has survived, the response of a visitor in 1822 seems strikingly well worded:

> Let me describe what to the antiquary will appear the noblest monument of Saurashtra, a monument speaking in an unknown tongue of other times . . . The memorial in question, and evidently of some great conqueror is a huge hemispherical mass of dark granite, which, like a wart upon the body, has protruded through the crust of mother earth, without fissure or inequality, and which, by the aid of the 'iron pen,' has been converted into a book. The measurement of its arc is nearly ninety feet; its surface is divided into compartments or parallelograms, within which are inscriptions in the usual antique character. Two of these cartouches I had copied, by my old Guru, with the most scrupulous fidelity, and a portion of a third, where the characters varied . . . I may well call it a book; for the rock is covered with these characters, so uniform in execution, that we may safely pronounce all those of the most ancient class, which I designate the 'Pandu character,' to be the work of one man.[1]

The writer is Lieutenant-Colonel James Tod, famous Rajasthan annalist and army antiquarian of the East India Company. His

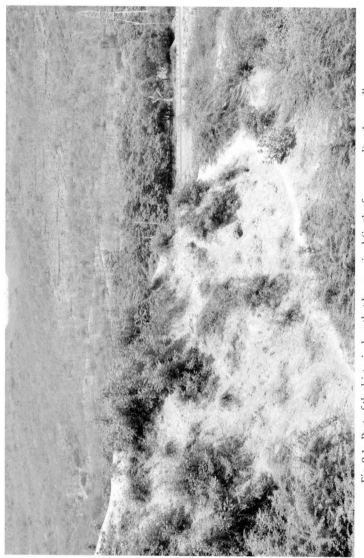

Fig. 9.1: Part of the historic dam that has survived (in the foreground) at Junagadh

reaction to Girnar was written before the Brahmi script had been deciphered. His account is arresting for the recognition that the edict is both monument and inscription, an ancient rock transformed to a monument by the writing on it.[2]

The way in which the Girnar edicts were inscribed on a single rock ensured that, at least theoretically, it would have been possible for an official placed on a specially created platform to be at eye level with the edicts and read them out to listeners below. The relatively compact manner of the layout made it possible. This was, as we saw, impossible at Erragudi, where the edicts were engraved across multiple boulders at different heights. A more important difference was that the Girnar rock stood—and was probably chosen for this reason—in the vicinity of an artificial lake, not far from the water's edge. Known as Sudarshana lake, this waterbody was created as a consequence of the construction of a dam during the time and on the instructions of Chandragupta Maurya. There is an archaeological configuration of structures and remnants in Junagadh which makes it possible to see Ashoka as part of a dynastic continuum to which he was adding.

Unravelling this configuration is possible on account of details available from subsequent historical records. The dam built in Chandragupta's time is mentioned as having been embellished in the time of Ashoka. The signature of these monarchs on the dam is not known from Mauryan records but was recorded in the Junagadh rock inscription of the king Rudradaman, more than 350 years after Chandragupta.[3] This tells us that Mauryan monarchs were part of the historically remembered landscape of Junagadh in the early centuries CE. Still, that this glimpse is offered some four centuries after the dam was built highlights the non-contemporary nature of the evidentiary threads used for re-creating the fabric of Junagadh's landscape in the time of Ashoka.

Considering the time lag, can this inscriptional reference be used for understanding state-building in Mauryan times?

The existence of the Rudradaman record makes it possible to speak of at least a quasi all-India state authority with a ground-level administrative presence in Junagadh. The epigraph tells us the

dam was constructed by Vaisya Pushyagupta, a provincial governor of Chandragupta.[4] The same record notes that conduits had
been added to it by the Yavana king Tushaspha, who governed the
province in the reign of Ashoka. Evidently, one of the emperor's
governors shared ethnic affiliations with the Yavana rulers on the
north-western borders of the kingdom. Perhaps more noteworthy
is that this system of governance, in the longer-term political
history of Saurashtra, is an aberration, for only when an all-India
state possessed enormous strength could it bring Saurashtra into
its administrative orbit.[5] So, for instance, though the Marathas collected tribute from this province, they were not powerful enough
to establish an administrative apparatus within it. Only when
Akbar conquered Saurashtra in the sixteenth century was Gujarat governed by officers appointed by the Mughal. Akbar was in
this respect the first ruler after Chandragupta to have properly
conquered Saurashtra—in the sense of also establishing his own
provincial administration there. Ashoka was evidently the legatee
of Chandragupta's spoils and administrative system.

If the political governors of Mauryan kings were based in the
region, what had made them choose Junagadh as their provincial
capital? This is hard to say for certain, but one reason will have been
the naturally defensive neighbourhood of Junagadh. The area was
forested and hill-girt, with the highest mountain in Gujarat, the
Gorakhnath summit, located at Girnar. The hilly areas of Kathia-
war district were relatively secure, causing many towns to come
up over the centuries, including Adityana, Mendarda, Talala, and
Visavadar.[6] Junagadh's access to the coast must have been another
important factor. The ocean is less than 80 km from here and from
Girnar a glimpse is sometimes possible of forests and low hills
that run in a continuous sweep to the sea. Tod, having ascended
the summit of the seven-peaked Girnar, marvelled at having seen
'the ocean lighted up by the sun's last rays, while silence ruled over
the remains of fading glory.'[7]

The provincial governor, in all likelihood, administered the entire territory from the Junagadh hills to the Arabian Sea. There
was a Mauryan settlement at Prabhas Patan, not far from the

temple site of Somnath, which means the Mauryas ruled a swathe from Girnar to the south-west coast of Saurashtra. Situated on the right bank of the Hiran river, Prabhas Patan was a port which regulated trade and traffic to and from the hinterland. If Junagadh's location was naturally secure because of the hills, Prabhas Patan was made secure by the creation of a fortified core. The time period contemporary with the Mauryas (Period IV which stretches from the fourth till the first century BCE) saw the creation of a stone citadel, with the wall marked by bastions at cardinal points.[8] The creation of this kind of town in Saurashtra continued well into modern times, with eighteenth-century urban centres here being primarily military fortresses.[9]

The other aspect of Junagadh which comes alive thanks to inscriptional allusions to the construction of a dam by the Mauryan state in the time of Chandragupta, and which continued to receive royal attention during the reign of Ashoka, is the availability of water. Presumably it was required for cultivation, as drinking water, and for the other usual purposes. So, was there a large town here? Where was it located? And why did the administration decide to build an embankment rather than, for instance, dig wells?

Where the Mauryan town was situated is not known. It could well have been in the area of the Chamunda locality of modern Junagadh, where the accumulation of habitation deposits in a mound-like formation is visible over the hillside in its vicinity, and on the outer edge of the fortifications in what is known as Uparkot. The present residents of Chamunda are known to find sculptural relics, pottery, stone artefacts, and even skeletons where they stay. This area is also not far from what must have been one edge of the lake that came to be formed behind the dam. Why a dam-like embankment was constructed here has to do with the suitability of a large bowl-like space that is naturally available in this hill-encircled basin, the only exit being the Sonarekha (sometimes called Suvarnarekha) river. Perhaps the creation of an embankment-dependent water management system may also have had something to do with the limitations of well technology in Mauryan times. It is unlikely that this technology was capable of plumbing the depths at which water was to be found, for in city areas and their environs water is usually found at a great depth. The elaborate historic 'vavas' or wells there, all constructions of the medieval centuries, go very deep. The Adi-Chadi Vava in Uparkot has a depth, from top to bottom, of some 41 metres. Such deep wells were unknown in Mauryan times. Taxila provides an example: the height of the Bhir plateau on which the city stood made it impractical to dig wells. The residents therefore got their water from the Tamra nala, a rivulet which flowed out-side the city area.[10] In Junagadh the Sonarekha river perhaps fulfill-ed a similar function.

Alongside, a state-sponsored embankment was built across the river. The likely locale of the lake and the remnants of the embankment were identified by Khan Bahadur Ardeseer Jamsedjee, the Naib Diwan of the princely state of Junagadh, in the nineteenth century.[11] He believed two dams had been constructed, one in the reign of Rudradaman and an earlier one in Chandragupta's. The Mauryan dam was older and smaller and he sought to identify it with the blocks of masonry in the bed of the Sonarekha river near the Dharagir gate of the city, in whose vicinity there were mounds. While the dam is no longer visible, the description given by Jam-sedjee suggests what it looked like in the nineteenth century:

> From the top of the mound on the right or north bank it was clear the blocks of masonry were remains of a dam that once lay across the river and stretched westward till it joined the easternmost spur of the Uparkot rocks. Surely this was the original Chandragupta dam of which we were in search. The length of the gap or breach in the dam is 36 yards. Of the mound that ran from the right bank of the Sonrekha to the Jogini spurs few traces remain. The height near the river bank is about thirty feet. The length of the embankment or west side of the river between the bed and the Citadel was 314 yards. Of this about 140 yards of masonry remain; 174 have been carried away for building. The breadth of the masonry varies from 43 to 53 yards.[12]

The lake that was created behind this embankment would have covered some 140 acres. Jamsedjee also attempted to identify the conduits or sluices that Rudradaman's inscription mentions as a feature of the renovations carried out by Ashoka. In the Dharagir garden he found labourers excavating huge blocks of stone which formed a pavement hollow in the centre, and which passed northwards from the bank of the lake. This had the appearance of being the remains of a conduit or canal. Clearly, keeping the bund in working order had been ensured by Ashoka's administration. The dam being in this area, one edge of the lake would have been in the vicinity of the Girnar rock.[13] Such a landscape, created, altered, and sustained by Ashoka and his predecessors, will have been seen and experienced as a symbol of the power of the dynasty in improving the lives of its citizens, possibly in a far more meaningful way than the edicts. The basic point is that Ashoka's voice in Girnar would have been seen as one element, albeit singular in content, of a broad constellation of Mauryan interventions, creating in their totality the groundwork of power within which state pronouncements were received and interpreted.

\* \* \*

While Girnar had an impressive lineage of connections with the Maurya monarchs, there was something that the emperor had spoken about earlier at various places from the outcrops of Andhra to the rocks beyond the Ganga which was missing in this much more magnificent setting. At Girnar the full set of major edicts had been engraved to create one long sermon. The overall impression here is of an emperor doubling as spiritual preacher, holding forth on matters at variance with local religious rites and practices. But the populace here was not privy to what the Erragudi people knew. There, via his minor rock edicts, Ashoka had specified that his metamorphosis had a Buddhist basis before he spoke at length about all kinds of other matters in the major rock edicts engraved there; at Girnar there is no evidence of his new religion in his edicts.

This lack of specification does not mean the local people would not have known about Ashoka's religious conversion. Traces that remain in the immediate hinterland of ancient Junagadh and Girnar point to the possibility that this was common knowledge which

Fig. 9.2: The Bhoria stupa in the Girnar forest, the massive cut created by nineteenth-century excavations still visible

probably did not need to take up precious rock space. In several parts of India the epigraphs had been positioned in the vicinity of early Buddhist monuments. At such spots there were early stupas and temples ('chaityas'). These were either known or likely to have been constructed with Ashoka's patronage. Knowledge of the king's conversion will surely have travelled out from such places.

Structural relics in the landscape of Junagadh which have an early association with Buddhism reinforce the idea. One such is the Bhoria stupa, also called the Lakha Medi stupa. Located in a state-protected forest known as the Girnar Reserve Sanctuary near the present-day Bhordevi temple complex, this is the most impressive early Buddhist structural relic of the area. Built on a rocky knoll some 7 km to the east of Junagadh city, it stands in a delightfully secluded valley which provides a magnificent view of both the rugged Girnar and the Datar hill, the highest mountain after Girnar. Excavated by J.M. Campbell in 1889, with the massive cutting left behind by him still clearly visible, the entire ground around it is strewn with bricks and brick fragments, as also many small mounds. The main stupa is made of solid brick in herringbone bond.[14] Inside, a stone coffer was found with a stone pot. Inside this pot were relic boxes of copper, silver, and gold, with semi-precious and precious stones—such as an aquamarine bead, a ruby, a sapphire, and an emerald—inside the last. There was also coaly grit and a 'relic' which 'had the appearance of a dried twig, though perhaps a trifle heavy . . . the fractured ends or sections, do not, however, show a woody texture.'[15] Various stone pieces including two heavy railing slabs and the remains of a stone umbrella were also found 'in the vertical axis of the mound', which probably means they were buried inside the stupa. Why were these buried inside the stupa, and were they part of a previous stupa that had been vandalized? Possibly.

Since the excavations did not yield either a coin or an inscription, it is difficult to precisely date the Bhoria stupa. That it may well have been built in the time of Ashoka, however, can be suggested on the basis of the fact that, like many Mauryan stupas, it is a solid brick structure. An example of a Mauryan brick stupa is the one at Vaishali in Bihar, where the Mauryan enlargement that came to encase the original mud stupa was done in burnt brick. Similarly, the Dharmarajika stupa at Sarnath is made of brick, surmounted by one or more umbrellas set within a square railing.

Was burnt brick used as a construction material in Gujarat in the late centuries BCE? The archaeologist Y.S. Rawat surveyed an early historic fort on the Taranga hill in north Gujarat and suggests it was used fairly early there.[16] The fortified settlement dated to the third century/second century BCE shows burnt-brick cons-truction over granite boulders. Like the bricks of the Bhoria stupa, these were fairly large. The use of brick is, culturally speaking, a significant aberration in Junagadh since this is an area where, from the early medieval period till today, stone is primarily used for construction, good quality stone being locally abundant. The tradition of brick building in Junagadh might have remained an enigma but for the fact that bricks were much used for Buddhist shrines in Ashokan times, and that the emperor had a strong pre-sence in Junagadh.

Ancient literature credits Ashoka with the construction of as many as 84,000 stupas over the relics of the Buddha, which he is supposed to have redistributed after exhuming them from earlier

Fig. 9.3: Copies of the copper, silver, and gold relic boxes found inside the Bhoria stupa (now in the Junagadh State Museum)

ones.[17] The exaggerated number apart, the Ashokan stamp on stupas in different parts of India is unmistakable. Within this programme of stupa construction and relic redistribution, it is unlikely that a provincial capital like Junagadh would have been bypassed, especially as the edicts were so majestically inscribed. If so, the Bhoria stupa can be the only site where such relics would have been interred in the Junagadh area. The relics that have been found inside the stupa also lend credence to this assumption.

In and around the hills of Girnar, structural complexes of which remnants survive also used large burnt bricks.[18] Their Mauryan ancestry thus seems likely. At Surajkund in the Girnar sanctuary there was a circular well cut into the natural rock, and another lined with bricks.[19] The bricks are large and of various sizes, some decorated with figure marks, a chaitya, and a conch. In another part of the forest, in the Hasnapur dam area and close to a local religious place called Jina Baba ki Samadhi, is a stupa site. This appears to have been made of a combination of large bricks and some stone. Incidentally, in the dam area too, which is now submerged, brick structural ruins exist and become visible, according to local people, when the water level in the dam drops. Thirty km from Junagadh, near the Ramnath forest checkpost, a large concentration of solid bricks and brickbats lies scattered. In the suburbs of Junagadh are sites marked by large bricks. One of these, near the Palasini river, is known as Hajam Chora, named after a hill where it is located. Towards the top of the hill are big blocks of dressed stones interspersed with large bricks and a number of earthen lamp ('diya') remains. Finally, there is Intawa, a Buddhist monastic site in the midst of a thick jungle on a hill above Bhavnath. Intawa was excavated in 1949 and yielded the foundations of monasteries, as also many artefacts ranging from water pots and coins to a rounded clay sealing which bore a legend that mentioned the seal as belonging to the Bhikshu sangha of the vihara of Maharaja Rudrasena.[20] This is likely to have been Rudrasena I (199–222 CE). Thanks to the clay sealing, this early historic site with burnt-brick architecture can be assigned a firm date.

Is there a pattern in this monumentality? The places marked by early historic bricks are dotted across a large landscape. While at

Hajam Chora the brick complex is within walking distance of the remnants of the Sudarshana lake, the Ramnath Mahadev mandir site is far from the Junagadh area. In fact, it cannot be visualized in any way as forming part of the circuit that sustained the ancient provincial centre here. The distribution of the other sites in the Girnar forest area, however, begins to make sense when it is juxtaposed with the topography of the hill zone. The forested tract does not have a great deal of flat land. There are four small valleys between the Girnar range and the surrounding hills which are in the vicinity of Bhavnath, Hasnapur, Surajkund, and Bhordevi. The traditional halting places of the famous Girnar pilgrim circuit (or 'parikrama'), which starts annually from November, are these very valleys. It is in the vicinity of these places that early historic brick ruins are found. Intawa is above Bhavnath and was a Buddhist monastic site. Surajkund, marked by a late centuries BCE well and other undetermined brick remains, may well be part of a Buddhist ruin. As for Jina Baba ki Samadhi and Bhordevi, both are marked by the remnants of Buddhist stupas.

Thus, much before its fame as a centre of Jaina and Hindu worship, Girnar appears to have been sacred to the Buddhists, and possibly the earliest circuit of worship in and around the Girnar was Buddhist. It is hard to be sure of Ashoka's role in the creation of this circuit. But as the emperor's provincial capital will have been the circuit's support centre and as the emperor himself was a Buddhist, the presence of brick in the early Buddhist monuments of the Girnar forest does seem to suggest that Ashoka ploughed resources into developing places of worship and shelter for the Buddhist monastic community there.

\* \* \*

My account of Ashoka's imprint in the environs of Junagadh has tried to show why the idea of a standard or more or less identical message inscribed across a wide area of the empire needs to be rethought. Local interpretation mediates reception and colours understanding at every point. The fixity of inscriptions carved on rock, combined with the roughly similar ideas conveyed regardless of location, tend to make us arrive at a singular meaning, a sense of the entire edict range being reducible to a narrow range of summary statements about a contrite emperor's endeavour to create a new ethos of citizenship within an ethically governed empire. To note common threads running through the edicts should not undermine the possibility of interpretive variation and plurality of meaning. Political authority and cultural hegemony vary across regions and mediate the reception of every statement and message. Comprehension in a particular way is also a consequence of the landscape and historical structuring in which the speech act happens. So, for example, it can hardly be denied that perceptions of Ashoka's guilt and repentance will have differed in Orissa, where the Kalinga war was fought, from perceptions of these at Erragudi and Girnar.

To continue with this theme of local interpretive difference, we could look at Sannathi in Karnataka, where the message was inscribed on a free-standing slab (or slabs) which bore edicts on both sides.[21] From what has survived, it is clear that two of the edicts inscribed here had earlier been found only at Dhauli and Jaugada in Orissa. So, whereas before the Sannathi discovery it was believed that this part of Ashoka's long rescript was meant for Kalinga alone, it is now evident that they were also intended for other places. The designations they bear, though, are the same as those in Orissa and are alluded to as Separate Rock Edicts 1 and 2. As in Orissa, the Kalinga Edict is omitted here, but unlike in Orissa the emperor's magnificent statement on tolerance in Rock Edict 12 is included. Among the other edicts, what has survived at Sannathi are Rock Edicts 12 and 14. The absence of the Kalinga Edict, the thirteenth in this anthology, means that it was deliberately dropped.

What explains the absence of Ashoka's account of Kalinga in Karnataka? During the late second and early third century BCE a part of the Bhima river valley, or 'greater Sannathi' as its excavators have called it, was marked by a strong Mauryan presence.[22] This was of an entirely different order from the preceding cultures at Sannathi. Habitation here goes back to the time of specialized hunter-gatherers who used microliths of all kinds. Their material equipment will have included other sorts of objects that have not survived. The site was then abandoned and later occupied by a black and red ware culture. This was an iron-using society and its pottery was of the kind usually associated with megaliths in Karnataka and beyond. The Mauryan occupation here overlay this horizon. With the advent of the Mauryas, a far richer material culture made its appearance, marked by the use of burnt bricks, North Black Polished Ware, polished stone pestles, shell bangles, beads of terracotta and semi-precious stones (jasper, carnelian, crystal, coral, lapis lazuli), coins and a disc stone bearing a typically Mauryan relief of standing goddesses flanked by palm trees and various animals.[23] A major moment in the life of any site is when a system of fortifications is constructed, indicating what is considered worthy of defence and consolidation, and at Sannathi the first phase of the fortifications—constructed by cutting a moat and heaping the earth to create walls—goes back to Mauryan times.

The Maurya advent seems to have coincided with prosperity of a kind not seen before, but that would not in itself suggest that this important town was established by Ashoka, or that he established it after conquering the region. The date of the urban centre cannot be precisely established, but that it existed in the time of Ashoka seems fairly certain—the presence of his edicts suggests this. Equally, the stupa of Kanaganahalli, situated very close to Sannathi, was first established in Mauryan times. This was in the form of an earthen mound, some 16 metres in diameter and rising to a height of a little over 7 metres. The Mauryan antiquities included a mutilated polished sandstone lion capital fragment on the west of the stupa, along with a single sherd of North Black Polished Ware. Ashoka, we have seen, established stupas marked by his various messages at many locations, and the first stupa here must have been built with his patronage.

On the question of Ashoka's conquest of Sannathi, the evidence is more tenuous. A great deal has been invested in the etymology of the name of the large 80-hectare habitational mound here, where the cultural levels just described were recovered. The mound bears the name of Ranamandala, suggesting it was a battlefield. K.P. Poonacha, who led the excavations of the Archaeological Survey of India, believes 'the place may be the historic battlefield or site wherein the Mauryas subjugated the local Satavahanas in a battle and included this territory in the Mauryan conquered *vijita*.'[24] This, of course, is not enough, especially since no part of the emperor's message has any reference to or remembrance of the conquest of Karnataka. What is certain, though, is that Ranamandala revealed artefacts and antiquities which appear to be Mauryan, ranging from NBP sherds to a circular medallion bearing reliefs of standing mother goddesses flanked by trees and animals. These belong to the same family as those found at Mauryan sites in North India.[25] Another suggestion has been that the reason why Kalinga was not mentioned is that Ashoka *did* conquer Karnataka. What transpired in the Karnataka conquest was not comparable to Kalinga, but because this was a recently annexed region the emperor was being circumspect in omitting mention of warfare at Sannathi. This theory would also explain the omission of the Kalinga edict.[26]

A major problem with the Sannathi edicts as compared to those in Kalinga is that the slab-bearing part of Ashoka's message was not found *in situ*. When it was discovered it formed the pedestal of the idol of Kalikamba in the Chandralamba temple. This means that while it is likely to have been around the early historic city at Sannathi, or possibly in the vicinity of the Kanaganahalli stupa, we cannot be sure where it originally stood. From the perspective of imagining what the ancient landscape looked like, Orissa is easier to speculate on since the rescripts are exactly where Ashoka had them engraved. Unlike the Sannathi slab, which bears only part of the message, the Orissa edicts are fairly complete. This makes it possible to offer an imaginative yet historically grounded account of how political exigencies resulted in a changed royal message.

\* \* \*

In Orissa the process is especially clear because the edicts there have survived much better. At Dhauli and Jaugada, significant chunks of Ashoka's longer message were not inscribed, three edicts being omitted: No. 11, which reiterated the emperor's idea of dhamma; No. 12, the magnificent statement on tolerance; and No. 13, which records the Kalinga conquest in ghastly detail. Two other edicts, described by historians as Separate Rock Edict 1 and Separate Rock Edict 2, exist here.[27]

Before discussing the nature of the message that these separate edicts recorded, it seems advisable again to examine their landscape. Kalinga being the ancient name for the eastern edge of India that straddles Orissa and part of Andhra, this was the scene of Ashoka's infamy and its omission here is thus logical: only a few years had elapsed and the emperor would not have wanted to rub salt in the wounds of the wounded. He also took his time getting his long message inscribed there at all: the engraving was undertaken only after the entire anthology was complete. The arrangement of the texts at one of these places, at Dhauli near Bhubaneshwar, reveals this fact. Two of the three columns here carry edicts 1 to 6 and 7 to 10 as also 14—this last edict would not have appeared here if the master set prepared at Pataliputra was not already complete. Below this set, within a border of straight lines, the two separate edicts were placed.[28]

The rocks of Dhauli form part of a hill which is in turn part of three ranges of parallel hills. These ranges are not far from the banks of the Daya river, some 7 km from Bhubaneshwar.[29] Here, an epigraph and monument combination was created. The rock had a large space specially created for the edicts, and a little above it was a terrace where, out of solid rock, an elephant was hewn, one of the finest specimens of early sculptural art.[30] Ashoka's epigraph refers to what this elephant represents: at the end of the Sixth Rock Edict is inscribed the appellation 'seto' or the 'white one', indicating that the elephant symbolizes the Buddha. It was as a white elephant that the Buddha was supposed to have entered the womb of his mother, Maya. This juxtaposition of a white elephant with an inscription lauding dhamma is intended to make the emperor's Buddhism abundantly clear.

The other site of Ashoka's message is Jaugada, much further south, near the Rushikulya river in Orissa's Ganjam district. Much before Ashoka, this area was inhabited first by people who used neolithic celts and black and red pottery, and then by iron-users who were fond of beads made of shell, bone, agate, carnelian, crystal, and quartz.[31] By the historical period it had become a township. In fact, Jaugada is perhaps the only site of Ashoka's major rock edicts within what must have been an extensive town surrounded by high walls. Both Jaugada and Dhauli are in the eastern coastal belt. Both are also adjacent to hilly jungle-covered regions—the Khurda area which forms part of the Chhotanagpur plateau in the case of Dhauli, and the rocky forested stretch from Bastar to Vizianagaram in the case of Jaugada.[32]

Can these places be identified with the towns that find mention in the epigraphs? The Dhauli inscription alludes to Tosali while Samapa is mentioned in the Jaugada epigraph. Jaugada was likely to have been located inside Samapa, the city mentioned in the Separate Edicts. The mahamatras of Samapa, who were the judicial officers ('nagalaviyohalakas') of the city, are specifically address-ed.[33] The inscribed rock was part of a group of outcrops located inside an old earthen square fort surrounded by a moat. On the other hand, identifying Tosali is more controversial. While it is mentioned in later inscriptions both as a region and as a place, here the mahamatras of Tosali were alluded to as the judicial officers of the city.[34] The location of the city has been a matter of some dispute, with the fortified early historic site of Sisupalgarh, which lies a short distance from Dhauli, being the most popular contender.[35] It has deep habitation deposits going back to pre-Mauryan times. On the other hand, the mound of Radhanagar in the Jajpur sector of Orissa also appears to have been an important early historic city, situated some 60 km to the north of Cuttack, on the right bank of the Keula river. Radhanagar was fortified, with wide (some 40 metres wide) ramparts and gateways. Its remains are broadly contemporary with those recovered from Sisupalgarh.[36] Either way, Dhauli could not have been located inside Tosali. However, if Tosali was indeed located at Sisupalgarh, Dhauli's rocks were in its immediate hinterland. This was a crucial hub in the Mauryan scheme of things in Kalinga. A prince was headquartered there, in the same way as at Suvarnagiri, Ujjayini, and Taxila. Many other segments of this eastern region were dotted with settlements, including Manamuda in the Boudh district which has yielded pottery with a close affinity to that of the Gangetic plains and Central India; and Asurgarh, a port town in Kalahandi district which was fortified and contemporary with Sisupalgarh.[37] However, only Tosali and Samapa find mention in Ashoka's epigraphs.

What of the place of the fateful battle? While it is likely that it was in the zone stretching from Jajpur to Ganjam, precisely where the Mauryan forces were actively resisted by the Kalingans remains unknown. Where one would like to locate the definitive military combat—whether near Bhubaneshwar and not far from Sisupalgarh and the Dhauli rocks, or much further south beyond Srikakulam—depends upon the route that one imagines Ashoka's forces used in their traverse from Pataliputra to Kalinga. One view is that the Mauryan troops took the same route that centuries later was followed by the Gupta king Samudragupta in his subcontinental campaign. Samudragupta is supposed to have arrived in Kalinga from Chhattisgarh.[38] Dilip Chakrabarti finds this an acceptable hypothesis because 'both these monarchs came from Pataliputra and both had Kalinga in their purview.'[39] The Gupta monarch's campaign, though, was qualitatively different from that of the Mauryan. Samudragupta was moving in a very determined fashion against the confederacy whose kingpin was the Pallava king of Kanchi. So, his line of movement across Dakshina Kosala and Ganjam-Srikakulam made eminent political sense. On the other hand, Ashoka's campaign was a far more circumscribed offensive, and for him, the Bhubaneshwar–Jajpur area was likely to have been strategically significant. The presence of urban centres like Sisupalgarh and Radhanagar, as also his edicts later engraved at Dhauli, suggest this. So, his army possibly took the Bengal–Orissa route, moving south-west from Midnapur. The location of Radhanagar makes sense in terms of this alignment, as do Dhauli and Sisupalgarh. If so, the decisive battle would have taken place in this part of Kalinga. Following a brutal pacification of the area, a strong

Mauryan provincial government must have been headquartered there. It was to the administrators of Kalinga that, as we shall see, Ashoka directly spoke in his separate edicts.

\* \* \*

How did Kalinga's landscape recast the message put there? Since the consequences of his actions haunted Ashoka, it seems likely that, years later, along with eleven of the original anthology that made up his major rock edicts, he caused two further edicts to be engraved there, both qualitatively different from the others.[40] In them the emperor, speaking in the first person, instructs the officials at Tosali and at Samapa, whom he specifically mentions as being occupied with many thousands of people, his object being to gain their affection. For the first time, he uses words that indicate a filial relationship with his people. The Second Separate Edict, which actually occurs before what is designated as the First, says:

> All men are my children.
>     As on behalf of (my own) children I desire that they may be provided by me with all welfare and happiness in this world and in the other world, even so is my desire for all men.[41]

This became a recurring motif: his officials were asked to fulfil their duties and inspire people 'in order that they may learn that the king is to them like a father, (that) he loves them as he loves himself, (and that) they are to the king like (his own children).'[42] Much the same can be seen in the First Separate Edict: 'just as for (my own) children I desire that they may be provided with all welfare and happiness in this world and in the other world so I desire for all men also.'[43]

In his exploration of ancient kingship B.G. Gokhale has suggested that this sentiment was rooted in the idea of early Buddhist kingship where political society was depicted as a family presided over by a morally elevated being in the image of the father.[44] However, if this was so, why were the officials in Kalinga being informed that the king treated all people as his own children—unlike, for instance, those who manned the administration in Gujarat and north-west India? Is it possible that, after its annexation, the newly conquered people were being treated harshly by Mauryan officials? Among a people so recently vanquished, could Ashoka have appeared in the avatara of a father figure? We can only guess that there was a degree of alienation in Kalinga, and Ashoka was therefore being discreetly reticent. Enveloping his rescript within an affective mould was one way of building bridges with them.

His 'unconquered borderers' ('amtanam avijita') in Separate Rock Edict 2 were also addressed in this intimate way.[45] Border people could be quite troublesome and those on the borders of the Mauryan empire certainly were. In addition to describing them as his children, the emperor used every temperate word at his disposal to convey to them that he was not an aggrandizing and brutal overlord but one who wanted their confidence. Simultaneously, he hoped to induce in them the practice of morality:

> It might occur to (my) unconquered borderers (to ask): 'What does the king desire with reference to us?
>
> This alone is my wish with reference to the borderers, (that) they may learn (that) the king desires this, (that) they may not be afraid of me, but may have confidence in me; (that) they may obtain only happiness from me, not misery; (that) they may learn this, (that) the king will forgive them what can be forgiven; that they may (be induced) by me (to) practice morality; (and that) they may attain (happiness) both (in) this world and (in) the other world.[46]

His image suffered from a trust deficit *vis-à-vis* those addressed: this is evident. Presumably, these borderers would have been privy to the ruthless way in which Ashoka had run over Kalinga and may have feared they were next in line. Ashoka is at pains to persuade them otherwise.

As for Ashoka's subjects in Kalinga, his main concern in Separate Rock Edict 1, what exactly was he asking his administration to do even as he addressed all and sundry as his progeny? If one pays heed to a strong hint in the edict, he was looking at ways of changing and improving an insensitive Mauryan administration in Kalinga. He alludes to this when he exhorts officials to pay attention to being even-handed in the administration of justice ('niti'), and to cultivate the right qualities necessary to the discharge of their duties:

> It happens in the administration (of justice) that a single person suffers either imprisonment or harsh treatment.
>
> In this case (an order) cancelling the imprisonment is obtained by him accidentally, while (many) other people continue to suffer.
>
> In this case you must strive to deal (with all of them) impartially.
>
> But if one fails to act (thus) on account of the following dispositions: envy, anger, cruelty, hurry, want of practice, laziness, (and) fatigue.
>
> (You) must strive for this, that these dispositions may not arise to you.
>
> And the root of all this is the absence of anger and the avoidance of hurry.
>
> He who is fatigued in the administration (of justice), will not rise; but one ought to move, to walk, and to advance. [47]

Ashoka seems very aware that all was not quiet on the eastern front. Looking for words to motivate his administration there, he was unequivocal about the dire consequences of failure: 'there will be neither attainment of heaven nor satisfaction of the king'. They would attain heaven and pay the king's debt by listening carefully.[48]

The idea of paying a debt had figured in the Sixth Edict, where Ashoka spoke of discharging the debt he owed to living beings.[49] Now, in this new articulation, it was the officials who by carrying out their duties would enable Ashoka to discharge this debt. A sense of solidarity between ruler and administration was being sought, and one imagines that this message was necessitated by problems specific to Kalinga.

In most places, Ashoka's engraved messages were read out by officials. This, in turn, entailed careful listening by the people gathered. For his 'unconquered borderers' and in Kalinga, the king practically ordered that these edicts be regularly read out. Separate Rock Edict 1 is pretty straightforward in telling his officials to get the job done: 'And this edict must be listened to (by all) on (every day of) the constellation Tishya. And it may be listened to even by a single (person) also on frequent (other) occasions between (the days of) Tishya. And if you act thus, you will be able to fulfil (this duty).'[50] Considering that the edict is primarily concerned with improving administration and justice delivery, a reading between the lines seems called for: the emperor seems to be saying he disapproves of the existing state of affairs and has given officials specific redressal instructions. Via repeated broadcasts heard at least three times a year (implied by reference to the Tishya constellation), some sort of accountability is being attempted. The line ensuing makes this apparent: 'in order that the judicial officers of the city may strive at all times (for this), (that) neither undeserved fettering nor undeserved harsh treatment are happening to (men).'[51]

He says, further, and specifically at this location, that a quinquennial scrutiny will be conducted by a mahamatra of suitable character, 'neither harsh nor fierce, [but] of gentle actions,'[52] to ascertain if judicial officers have been acting according to instructions. This promise of supervision was not restricted to Kalinga: other centres of provincial administration—Ujjayini and Takshashila are specifically named—were also instructed to send out mahamatras for the same purpose triennially. On account of this command it has been assumed that these separate edicts were not Kalinga-centric but intended for administrators in other parts of the empire as well.[53] This may well be so, and the Separate Edicts at Sannathi suggest it. All the same, at Kalinga the instruction will have carried a meaning more loaded by recent events and the remembrance of them.

Those parts of Ashoka's message that are found at Dhauli and Jaugada are neither about the preaching nor the practice of dhamma. They are centrally concerned with delivering better administration in a politically sensitive province. The emperor modifies the content and tenor of his message keeping in mind the situation on the ground.

At one level, it seems a truism to say that because reception within specific contexts mediates messages and colours interpretations, uniformity of meaning across landscapes is a myth. In the peculiar case of Ashoka's edicts, which despite being spread over thousands of kilometres tend very strongly to be seen as disseminating a single message, it has seemed worthwhile to me to scrutinize the truth content of this truism. The valorization of Ashoka by Buddhist historiography is understandable, yet it cannot be denied that the religious agenda driving such history has helped immensely to reinforce the idea that Ashoka's messages can be reduced to a singular sermon in defence of the faith. By contrast, because the ways in which political authority is inscribed in a landscape are necessarily varied, attentiveness to situational variety is necessary. Some regions are conquered by the sword and require healing; others need pacification; yet others may respond best if addressed in Greek and Aramaic. Landscape, in relation to Ashoka's edicts, is not a *tabula rasa* on which nothing other than contrition and a new moral agenda, bordering on missionary zeal, are written. Local history offers possibilities sometimes invisible.

As one anguished king pointed out to his companion in a very different context: 'There are more things in heaven and earth, Horatio/ Than are dreamt of in your philosophy.'

# 10

# Building Beliefs into Edifices

ASHOKA'S INITIATIVES AND ORDERS, MADE KNOWN across his empire through epigraphs addressed to his subjects, are only one of the constitutive elements of the emperor's authority. There are important others, of a qualitatively different order, which too left a material imprint. Among these are Ashoka's royal programmes for building, renovating, and modifying religious edifices. His epigraphs pertaining to these programmes are largely about religion, religious personages, and interventions regarding the practice of his new faith.

The range of such structures is as diverse as the places where they were constructed. Some are caves that the sovereign got excavated as abodes for ascetics. Others are spaces sedimented with Buddhist associations where Ashoka's stamp can be seen because he journeyed there as a pilgrim. He installed numerous pillars at places that had featured in some way in the life and death of the Buddha; others at places the Buddha could not have visited. Stupas too were built with Ashoka's patronage, sometimes over relics of the Sakyamuni that he is believed to have extracted out of older stupas. The stunning pillared hall in the Magadhan capital, which is likely to have been built in his time, may well carry the same religious associations.

The points in time of their construction remain uncertain in a significant number of instances. Unlike the edicts, the chronology of the edifices usually cannot be delineated with the same degree of accuracy. Among the epigraphs of the emperor which adorn several of these structures, only some bear dates in relation to the king's consecration, dates which would make it possible to clarify when they were built. Some carry no inscriptions. In such instances, the basis on which the structures are said to have either been built or expanded is either literary—the authors of ancient texts describing them as built by the emperor—or else include elements generally considered diagnostic for identifying Ashokan edifices, such as polished pillars and the specific sorts of bricks used. Archaeological cultures are usually identified by 'type fossils'. The archetypal objects of the Harappan civilization, for instance, range from long flint implements to rectangular and square inscribed seals. Similarly, pillars with the polish so typical of inscribed Ashokan pillars, as also religious structures made of bricks—which, in terms of size and fabric, resemble other structures built in this period and which have occasionally been found constructed on the same floors where the pillars stand—can be reliably identified as type fossils of Ashoka's phase.

These locales perhaps had fixed or flexible associations with the sacred which may have been the initial reason for Ashoka's journeys to and engagement with them, as for instance Lumbini, the Buddha's birthplace. His visits to them were, however, often transformative—personally, they may have made him more devout, but, more important, via the structures he built there he changed the existing configurations and gave them new meaning. Other patrons may have done this as well, but Ashoka's ability to influence sacred landscapes was much greater because massive monoliths and temples required large resources and labour. They also perhaps required, in many instances, reaching understanding with Buddhist monastic custodians. At some Buddhist sites Ashoka assumed the role of a religious instructor. As the powerhouse of belief in his day, 'both a monk and monarch at the same time',[1] he felt he was entitled to address the Buddhist Sangha on religious and doctrinal matters.

\* \* \*

Fig. 10.1: Hills around the Barabar caves, the Phalgu river in the background

In 257/256 BCE, the year that Ashoka issued his rescripts about the merit of proper courtesy and proper behaviour towards 'Shramanas and Brahmanas'—subsequently these appeared in the Third and Fourth Major Rock Edicts—he had caves excavated, these being incarnations, in a way, of his beliefs. Tolerance for all sects, the honouring of elders in all religious communities, and the desire that religious sects live across his dominions were thus supervised and ensured as material events. Appropriately, the four Barabar caves were not exclusively for Buddhists. One of them may have been Buddhist; at least two were given to the Ajivikas in the twelfth year after his coronation.

Barabar is the name of the highest hill among the rocky ridges that presently lie in the Jahanabad district of Bihar, some twenty-four km north of Gaya, and therefore only a day's journey from Pataliputra. A large part of the area around the hill, like the environs surrounding Pataliputra, comprised an expanse of cultivated plains. The monotony of these plains was broken by the dramatic Barabar alignment of granite, rising 'like rocks from the sea'.[2] Today, the Siddeshwarnath temple crowns one of the peaks. From here the hilly contours, rock exposures, water reservoirs, and the Phalgu river in the distance form a stunningly beautiful landscape, enough to evoke some envy for the ascetics who made this hill their abode in the third century BCE. Ascetics of the Ajivika order had, as we saw, prophesied glad tidings for Ashoka, so a disinterested distribution of caves to sundry sects may not have been the idyllic scenario painted sometimes by those desiring to boost the emperor's proto-secular credentials. This was all the same a major philanthropic act, the first instance of caves created on this scale in this part of the world, and very likely to have been widely recognized in Ashoka's own time.

There are four such caves. Three are located in a prominent whale-shaped natural outcrop,[3] the Lomasha Rishi cave and the Sudama cave being adjacent to each other. When these names came to be attached to the caves is unknown, they did not exist in Mauryan times. The Sudama cave was called 'Nigoha Kubha' or Banyan cave,[4] and is referred to thus in Ashoka's short donative epigraph there. The recessed entrance of the Sudama cave bears a

Fig. 10.2: Interior of the Sudama cave with a hut-like structure carved
into the rock

dedicatory inscription by 'Priyadarshin' dating to when he had been
anointed twelve years. A great deal of effort went into the creation
of this cave. It comprises two chambers, both of which were highly
polished, a rectangular outer one with a vaulted roof and an inner
chamber with a hemispherical ceiling circular in plan and imitating
a thatched hut. Like the Sudama cave, the adjacent Lomasha Rishi
cave was two-chambered. What made it different was a carved
architrave above the entrance on its exterior. In this, the central arch
shows a row of elephants in motion, moving towards a central stupa
from both sides. Immediately above this, in the middle arch, a kind
of lattice screen is made up of an intersecting circle design—the type
that is carved on the throne ('vajrasana') that Ashoka is supposed
to have given in honour of the Buddha at Mahabodhi. While this
cave does not carry an epigraph, the polished character of the outer
chamber and its general architecture leaves little doubt that this
too was excavated in the time of Ashoka. The third cave, known
as Vishwa Jhopri, is on another outcrop and, like the Sudama cave,
carries a donative record of Ashoka. This cave ('kubha') was for the
Ajivikas and is mentioned as being in the Khalatika mountain, the
name by which the Barabar hills were then known.[5]

The last of Ashoka's dedications is now known as Karna Chaupar. It was chiselled out of the outcrop within which the Lomasha Rishi and Sudama caves were created. Facing north, it is a one-chamber edifice with a vaulted roof. Polished to a high lustre, it is marked by a low rock-cut platform on the western end. However, this was created seven years after the others, i.e. nineteen years after Ashoka's coronation. The Ajivikas are not mentioned here. Instead, the king speaks in the first person to say that 'this cave in the very pleasant Kha(latika mountain) was given by me for (shelter during) the rainy season.'[6] It is possible that wandering mendicants in need of reliable shelter during the rainy season used this cave. There may also have been free-standing structures in Barabar since at places the stone foundations of walls peep out of the ground. Whether they were contemporaneous with the caves excavated on the orders of Ashoka remains uncertain. In any case, recipients of such a substantial royal donation had to be influential; so, had they approached the emperor in person? Or did Ashoka, along the lines of the rescripts issued around the same time—those highlighting the importance of respect to religious people—create these structures out of regard for such sentiments? On the whole, after the long hortatory epigraphs, the brevity of Ashoka's donative records at Barabar seems both striking and somewhat unsatisfactory.

Much more is known about the technology and design of construction of the Barabar caves which, like the writing of public edicts on rock surfaces, represented an innovation. With their inclining walls and invariably rounded roofs, they imitate the architecture of more humble wooden and bamboo dwellings. They appear to create in rock the form of habitations in which ascetics usually felt comfortable. Except that, unlike huts, these are rooms of high quality. The walls are plain but, because of the proportions of the rooms, have a highly developed aesthetic appearance which, in turn, is enhanced by the remarkable polish. The lustrous inner surfaces actually are mirror-like in their effect. These surfaces enhance every sound inside the caves and so, living in them, one imagines, presupposed perfect silence. It was this proclivity of the caves to echo so unusually that is the anti-spiritual centrepoint of E.M. Forster's *A Passage to India* (1924). Forster comments on aspects of the Marabar caves (a thinly disguised reference to Barabar), their lack of ornamentation and sculpture, a remarkable echo in them, the polished stone surface which captures light like an imprisoned spirit and yields colours and shadings that seem to reveal the life of granite. One of the characters, Mrs Moore, dies with the echo of the Marabar Caves in her head; another, Adela Quested, is misled by the echo, 'Ou-boom', in one of the caves into believing she has been molested. Ashoka could not in his wildest dreams have thought that his gift to the Ajivikas would, 2000 years later, result in a classic novel using these caves as the lynchpin of its plot.[7]

Is it possible to demonstrate the planning that went into the Ashokan excavation of these Ajivika abodes? While the caves are of varying dimensions, it has been suggested that they have all been made on a grid using integers of a unit of *circa* 85.5 cm.[8] This would mean that the size of the interiors was not random but based on a fixed measure. Further, the various steps by which this major building work was executed can be partially reconstructed on the basis of clues that the incomplete Lomasha Rishi cave has provided.[9] The fact that this cave's interior was only partially finished reveals that the orders of emperors, even those as powerful as Ashoka, were not always followed in letter and spirit. The messiness of the engravings of some of his edicts at Kalsi and Erragudi suggested this; in the Barabar caves it looks as if the administrators either did not inspect the caves or did not think it necessary to finish them to the required standard. Odd—because Kalsi and Erragudi are at a considerable distance from the Mauryan capital whereas the Khalatika hill is close to Pataliputra, making it easier for the emperor to catch recalcitrant building contractors by the neck. *Plus ça change, plus c'est la même chose.*

For those interested in the technology of their construction, the sloppiness is a blessing. Through the scooping, chiselling, and grinding marks still visible on the floor, ceiling, and walls of the Lomasha Rishi cave, the construction and finishing processes can be reconstructed in some detail. The first stage would have involved removing the rocks to produce a hollow cave. Initially, chunks of rock were removed with the help of short, heavy chisels along the required area of the cave. This was followed by rough chiselling to bring out the cave's overall outline. From the chisel marks it appears that the work progressed from bottom to top. The chisel edges were very sharp, ranging between 0.7 and 1.3 cm—the marks preserved inside the cave and outside it suggest this. After this, the dressing of the interior was done, now with a lighter chisel. Dressing involved making parallel straight grooves over a comparatively even surface. These can be seen on the floor and on the outer face of the hut inside the cave. The depth to which the grooves were cut seems to have been a consequence of keeping in mind the surface which was to be eventually polished.

The dressed stone was then treated by pecking and grinding. Pecking involves thinning the ridges left behind by chiselling so that some kind of flat surface is produced. The hewn surface, though, still remained rough. This was evened out by grinding—the surface was rubbed by using coarse sand, water, and a coarse-grained stone. This removed all marks: the pitted parts, the coarse texture, etc. The smoothened surface then had to be polished. Polishing was only a kind of grinding where the rubbing stone used was of a fine texture, just as the sand too was very fine grained. In these caves, the polishing actually produced a glistening surface because the rock had large mineral particles like feldspar and hornblende which have shining properties. These are the particles which reflect like brilliant mirrors to this day.

This summary of the several stages involved in creating caves in a granite hill points to a meticulous process and careful planning. Creating a set of edifices on this scale needed lavish outlays. The overall impression of such a construction programme is the trouble to which the emperor is prepared to put himself to for religious sects and cults. Mendicants and ascetics of some authority considered worthy of such abodes by the powerful Magadhan court will, in turn, have altered social perceptions of the worth and power of asceticism and mendicancy. The hollowing out of a hill is also a landscape taking a new sacral shape, a reconfiguration with consequences for posterity, a change in the historical trajectory of a region.

Were these caves benefaction intended only for the Ajivikas? Two of them, the Sudama and Vishwa Jhopri caves, certainly were. The Karna Chaupar cave, created as a shelter against rain, specifies

Fig 10.3: Lomasha Rishi cave architrave, with elephants moving towards a stupa

no sect as recipient and could have been for the Ajivikas or other mendicants. More challenging is the Lomasha Rishi cave. The architrave on its exterior has strong Buddhist overtones, so it may have been a dwelling for the desirably faithful. If so, it would suggest an Ashokan way of promoting harmony among religious cults, the sort proclaimed in his edicts. Inter-faith coexistence and rivalry were integral to this period of strife and competition for sectarian adherents, and relations between Ajivikas and Buddhists were, for instance, depicted in a variety of ways. In the Buddhist literature some Ajivikas are cruel and deceitful, others are shown in the company of Buddhists and, on occasion, fed by them.[10] The Jainas were thought to have had an early and close relationship with the Ajivikas, but there were tensions when several Ajivikas converted to Jainism.

One may speculate that the frieze on the Lomasha Rishi cave—with its elephants and stupa and lattice frame design resembling that on the Mahabodhi throne gifted by Ashoka—signifies a cave for Buddhists. In that case, at Barabar Ashoka was creating dwellings for Buddhists, Ajivikas, and sundry sects and ascetics simultaneously, the Buddhist connection with Barabar becoming significant at a later period. Many centuries after, the ancient name of Barabar, Khalatika, was inscribed on a stupa at Kanaganahalli in Karnataka: 'Galatiko pavato' or 'Khalatika parvata' is mentioned on a label inscription engraved on one of the upper drum slabs of the stupa.[11] So by then Khalatika had been integrated within Buddhist stories, elements of which are usually depicted on stupas. At Khalatika itself there are no early Buddhist stupas or chaityas, the decorative aspects of the Lomasha Rishi cave indicating the only possible connection with Buddhism. Secular abode-donations at single locations were not unknown. King Pandukabhaya, grandfather of Devanampiya Tissa (Ashoka's contemporary in Sri Lanka), was depicted in the Buddhist tradition as having built proximate hermitages for Nigranthas (possibly Jainas), Ajivikas, and Brahmanas.[12]

* * *

We are now at the phase when Ashoka's Buddhist persona becomes most visible. Though involved in many matters of state and governance, taxes and punishments and land grants were evidently not, within his perspective, matters to be recorded on stone. Subjects that have attracted the record-keeping of most emperors—such as provinces lagging in paying taxes, safety measures for state highways, and complaints of harassment and incompetence by the administration—if put down anywhere at all by Ashoka have not survived. They do occasionally appear, but only in relation to his larger moral agenda. On the other hand he projects the persona of a devout Buddhist in several of his epigraphs and through these it seems possible to chart both his progress as a convert and understand the scale of his influence over the monastic community.

Ashoka strove to portray his own illumination, in the tenth year after his consecration, as a consequence of his pilgrimage to the site of the Buddha's enlightenment at Mahabodhi. Unsurprisingly, the first temple at Mahabodhi is generally attributed to Ashoka. Whether its building coincided with or followed his visit is not clear. The large sandstone throne that today lies behind the present temple and in the shade of the Bodhi tree is also regarded as an Ashokan donation. The temple that he is thought to have set up lacked a roof, being in the form of an open pavilion supported by pillars. As with many other buildings attributed to the emperor's patronage, there are no Ashokan epigraphs on the pavilion of the kind at Barabar: the attribution is largely based on what we know from other sculptures. A century or so later a representation at the Buddhist stupa of Bharhut in Central India depicted a throne, with the trunk of the Bodhi tree behind, surrounded by an open-pillared pavilion. This was labelled in the Brahmi script: 'Bodhi tree of the blessed Sakya Muni', or 'Bhagavato Saka Munino Bodhi'.[13] Since the throne ('vajrasana') is so realistically depicted at Bharhut, it seems likely that the pavilion-like temple was also a faithful image. Which is why the art historian Ananda Coomaraswamy took this to be 'the representation of the one, asserted by tradition, very probably correctly, to have been erected by Asoka at Bodh Gaya.'[14] The tradition which remembered the temple as having been built by Ashoka figures in a fair number of texts. The *Divyavadana* refers to Ashoka having built a chaitya at Bodh Gaya as also at Lumbini, Sarnath, and Kushinagara.[15] Mahabodhi's seventh century CE Chinese visitor Xuanzang says Ashoka had surrounded the Bodhi tree with a nearly three metres high stone wall.[16] A Burmese record of repair of the eleventh century CE says that 'King Dhamma Asoka' built a temple on the spot where Buddha took a meal.[17] The throne itself is an enormous carved seat made up of two horizontal slabs. The lower one is highly polished while the upper has designs on all four sides of honeysuckle motifs; on one side, these alternate with those of geese. The carving is very similar to those on some Ashokan pillars (a further category of monumental sculpture). Considering the quality of the sculpture, the polish, and the massiveness of the throne, this was likely to have been a royal commemorative gift.

In the ensuing years the emperor provided vivid glimpses of other places of Buddhist sanctity by inscribing his presence at them. We meet him at Nigali Sagar (or Niglihawa) in the Nepal terai, some four years after his Sambodhi visit. This is in the Kapilavastu district and gets its name from a large artificial pool in its vicinity, the 'Nigali Sagar'. The focus on an epigraph here was a stupa dedicated to the Buddha Konakamana (or Kanakmuni): Ashoka expanded and rebuilt it in the fourteenth year after his consecration. Buddhists believed Konakamana to be twenty-third in the list of twenty-four Buddhas; many stories about him exist in Buddhist chronicles which resonate with leitmotifs from the Buddha's life—such as his early years being spent in palaces, the practising of austerities at the end of which the daughter of a Brahman gave him milk-rice, and his having attained enlightenment under a tree (an Udumbara tree).[18] The point is that by the third century BCE a cult around the previous Buddhas was geographically anchored, the Mauryan emperor's beneficence and building activity adding to their importance. The Nigali Sagar edifice that Ashoka enlarged can no longer be traced on the ground. However, for many centuries after his time, a stupa did grace the place associated with Konakamana and, as recorded in Chinese pilgrim accounts, long continued.[19]

The enlargement of the stupa of Konakamana is mentioned by Ashoka six years after he had it done, which is when he visited Nigali Sagar. The pilgrimage is datable to the twentieth year of his reign. By this time there was already in the Nepal terai a kind of pilgrim circuit around places associated with the Buddha. This expanded into the Gangetic plains and is possible to recognize from the emperor's edifices along the path of his pilgrimage. In that crucial twentieth year he paid obeisance at three sacred sites: Nigali Sagar, Gotihawa, and Lumbini, all fairly close to each other. The first two were native places connected with Buddhas who, within the cosmogony, antedated Gautama Buddha. Nigali Sagar was connected to Konakamana, Gotihawa to his immediate predecessor Kraku-chhanda, the twenty-second Buddha. Lumbini of course was reputed to be the garden where Maya had given birth to Siddhartha.

How did Ashoka get to these places? The entourage would have traversed the stretch from Pataliputra across the Ganga through north Bihar to the terai. This was then, as it is today, a 'sweep of rich agricultural plains': the archaeological sites there show it clearly.[20] The arterial alignment that linked Pataliputra with the area where Lumbini stood was dotted with early historic settlements and cities—from the Ganga bank opposite ancient Pataliputra, through Vaishali, Katragarh, and Balrajgarh to the terai area. Considering the marshes in the terai, travelling by elephant would have been a sensible option. Alongside, there would have been bullock carts carrying provisions, and an armed contingent. In the terai, during the nineteenth century, the cart tracks on which bullock carts travelled were so circuitous that they took double the direct distance to the destination. It may have been worse in Ashoka's day. Many streams will also have had to be crossed: rivers and rivulets such as the Banganga, Tilar, Jamuar, and Siswa.[21] People in the villages and towns on the route may have been made aware of the king's travel plans. The presence of advance parties would have ensured it while crosschecking the state of repair of roads, vetting the halting places along the way, ensuring provisions of animal fodder. Elaborate arrangements will have been put in place to receive the royal visitor at each point of his halt.

Over the days that Ashoka was in the terai (there is no knowing how long), arrangements would have had to be made in the towns he stayed in. It is possible that he halted briefly at the city of Tilaurakot near the eastern bank of the Banganga and not far from the places that he would visit. Whether this was then called Kapilavastu or was known by another another name we don't know.[22] The fortified site, though, was most impressive. Originally of mud, brick walls, protected by a deep ditch, were subsequently raised.[23] The terai bristled with habitation sites of all kinds and formed an important segment of the imperial domain, quite apart from being important to Buddhists. The local administration will have been on its toes in many of the locations.

Which of these pilgrim places did Ashoka visit? Lumbini first of all, perhaps, being already a hoary place of pilgrimage. What today lies inside the modern Maya Devi temple pre-dated Ashoka by centuries.[24] The Buddha's birthplace is represented as a square brick box-like platform on which is a longish sedimentary sandstone marker pinpointing what was believed to be the exact place of birth.[25] There would in Ashoka's day also have been a large brick platform near it. Did Ashoka think it too modest as a shrine given the Buddha's stature? Or was the emperor inscribing his presence in the place of his preceptor's birth as his most powerful patron? This question is relevant because Ashoka did not merely pay obeisance. He erected a pillar and erected a much larger temple-like edifice over the birthplace. The magnificent monolithic pillar was hewn out of sandstone. While only part of it has survived (nearly four metres below the ground and a little more than five metres above), when it was set up the pillar was likely to have been several metres taller, with an inverted lotus capital and an animal image on top. The remnants of the abacus and bell capital have survived, but not the crowning animal. Xuanzang, much impressed in the seventh century, reports seeing the column topped by a stone horse.

Many similar pillars were fashioned during Ashoka's reign, all monolithic and freestanding, placed on base-slabs below ground. Like the Barabar caves, their quality speaks highly of the technical expertise involved:

> The pillars have a certain air of perfection; they are admirably polish-
> ed, their tapering gives them elegance, their proportions are well-
> balanced. The threefold capitals have been designed and produced with
> a quality never to be reached again by later copyists. It requires some

Fig. 10.4: Ashokan pillar at Lumbini, with the modern Maya Devi temple by its side

skill and experience to produce such pieces of art; another sort of experience is needed to transport them from the quarry to their place of erection, and it requires still further expertise to erect the pillars weighing from 8.6 (Lumbini) to 51 (Vesali) tons and finally to top them with capitals weighing a further two tons.[26]

Pillars and poles were the kind of paraphernalia constructed at festivals and religious places. However, it is unlikely that those erected in times before Ashoka were remotely like his. This combination of a tapering polished monolith topped with animals and other sacred symbols was an Ashokan innovation.[27] The pillars were fashioned out of Chunar sandstone, a high quality variety common in the Vindhya hills on the southern edge of the Gangetic plains. Transporting the monoliths from there would have been some task, even if facilitated by the proximity of the Ganga.[28] The cylindrical blocks would have had to be rolled down hills and taken from the base areas to the river. The archaeologists P.C. Pant and Vidula Jayaswal, who first drew attention to the Chunar stone quarries, noted that five stone blocks could still be seen lying partly submerged in the river. The ancient quarries also yielded several semi-finished and unfinished cylinder blocks of stone, some of which bear letters of the Kharoshthi script. However, these are unlikely to be of Ashokan lineage since their proportions (between 1.65 to 2.25 metres in length) do not match with those of the majestic Mauryan monoliths.

As for the temple, before Ashoka at least two construction phases have been unearthed which included brick pavements and a kerb. A series of postholes below these pavements and kerb defined a sacred space going back to the sixth century BCE, possibly earlier.[29] Within the open centre of this area, substantial root features were located which the excavators interpreted as representing the remnants of a tree shrine. If so, this is possibly the first tree shrine to have been identified at a Buddhist place of worship, a feature which became much more common subsequently in the form of Bodhigrihas (shrines around living trees).

Large additions were made to the temple in Mauryan times, in two stages of construction.[30] One of these saw the erection of a rectangular temple or chaitya whose foundation trench had a filling of material that is thought to be Mauryan. The superstructure was apparently of timber. After this, the circumabulatory path was enlarged with paving added on the west and north sides. The temple enlargement did not carry an Ashokan epigraph, certainly none that has survived. The pillar, however, did. The emperor inscribed on it a record of his visit.

> When king Devanampriya Priyadarsin had been anointed twenty years, he came himself and worshipped (this spot), because the Buddha Sakyamuni was born here.
>
> (He) both caused to be made a stone bearing a horse (?) and caused a stone pillar to be set up, (in order to show) that the Blessed one was born here.
>
> (He) made the village of Lummini free of taxes, and paying (only) an eighth share (of the produce).[31]

There has been quibbling over some of the terminology used in this epigraph: what did the term 'vigadabhi (ca)' mean? While the translator Hultzsch thought it a reference to a horse, two words that occur joined there, 'silavigadabhiti(ca)', have also been thought to mean 'wall made from, or decorated with stone'. The stone 'sila' has also been interpreted as a reference to the marker stone found inside.[32] Similarly, the meaning in the allusion to 'an eighth share' or 'athabhagiya' is debated. While this has usually been understood as indicating a reduction in taxes to one-eighth, a competing theory has pointed out that this would not have shown Ashoka as a particularly generous donor since the amount of tax from a village the size of Lumbini was not likely to be a princely sum.[33] An alternative explanation has been to see this as referring to a one-eighth share of the relics of the Buddha. The remains of the Buddha after he was cremated have been frequently described in Buddhist literature as having being divided into eight equal parts which went to Rajagriha, Vaishali, Kapilavastu, Allakappa, Ramagrama, Vethadipa, Pava, and Kushinagara. Two centuries or so down the line, Ashoka is supposed to have had most of the stupas at these locations reopened so as to redistribute the relics across India. One part of the remains could well have come to Lumbini, and Ashoka's edict could be read as referring to getting a share for it from one of those one-eighth portions.[34] The problem, however, is that there is no large or substantial stupa here that can be considered Mauryan, nor have any relics been recovered at Lumbini. For the moment, therefore, it seems best to see Ashoka as having made a revenue concession, even if not a generous one!

Beyond such conflicting interpretations of the royal epigraph, most striking is the way in which memorialization was combined here with an overt expression of political power. The emperor recorded his visit when he came to worship at the place where the Buddha was born. At the same time, the pillar that he put up was of such monumental dimensions that it must have more or less eclipsed the original shrine. So the shrine too was renovated and expanded via royal patronage. The emperor then used the occasion to announce a reduction in agricultural taxes for Lumbini village. This is possibly the earliest documented example in South Asia of a political patron deploying a sacred landscape to announce revenue concessions. The example is multiplied in later times: there are plenty of examples of exemptions and privileges given by kings alongside endowments to religious establishments, including on occasion tax exemptions.[35]

The inscribing of Ashoka's presence here was followed by Ripu Malla more than 1600 years later. This king of the Naga dynasty made a pilgrimage to Lumbini in 1312 CE, where a Buddhist mantra—'Om Mani Padme Hum', or 'Hail to the jewel of the lotus'—was engraved along with his name on the very Ashoka pillar recording the emperor's pilgrimage.[36]

At Gotihawa can be seen the remnants of a pillar that Ashoka put up over perhaps the same tour.[37] Unlike the grass-covered stupa, only a small portion of the pillar is now visible. It used to be known as Phuteshwar Mahadeva—an appellation which suggests it was worshipped as a broken (or 'phuta') Shivalinga. In the late nineteenth century three pillar fragments, including a portion of the bell capital base, were also to be seen in the village.[38] These fragments were called 'gutis' or broken pieces and the name Gotihawa is apparently derived from these 'gutis'.

Fig. 10.6: Gotihawa pillar remnant, once known as
Phuteshwar Mahadeva

Excavations at Gotihawa, associated with Krakuchhanda, have
revealed a very old village going back to the ninth century BCE. The
pottery and bones found here are common at such sites, as also
fragments impressed with straw and reeds that were accidentally
baked when huts at the location caught fire.[39] The third century
BCE shows a brick stupa here with a diameter of some 10 metres
and a core made of bricks of different types. On the basis of there
being North Black Polished pottery, the archetypal early historic
ware—which has been found via the paste in a couple of bricks and
in the clayey layer which constitutes the binder of the bricks—the
stupa could well have been Mauryan. The likelihood is reinforced
by all the bricks being handmade and of different sizes, suggesting
the absence of mass production.

'Mauryan' does not of course mean 'Ashokan': gaps in our
understanding of Gotihawa persist. There are no such doubts
about the other monumental element here—a pillar, or, to be more
precise, the broken portion of a pillar which stands south-west
of the stupa. Set up by Ashoka, only the lower part has survived, causing the inscription, if any, to have disappeared. Unlike a

Fig. 10.7: Nigali Sagar pillar segments

number of Ashokan pillars such as that at Lumbini and at Sarnath where the lower parts are rough (since these were meant to be embedded), the Gotihawa stump is finished from the base itself.[40] The tapering is similar to that of the one at Lumbini. The foundation slab bears a simple geometric rendering of the hill-and-crescent symbol, which is considered typically Mauryan.[41]

At Nigali Sagar Ashoka had expanded the stupa of Konakamana six years earlier: this is recorded over his subsequent visit alongside his worship at the spot and his setting up a pillar.[42] The pillar is now broken, but of the two surviving parts one bears his epigraph. The pillar capital has not survived, Xuanzang's sighting of a lion figure on top of it our only evidence of what it looked like. The emperor may have set up pillars elsewhere in the terai but they have not come to light. As it is, the surviving monoliths provide us a bird's eye view of the pilgrim circuit that then existed around the predecessors of and in relation to the Buddha.

\* \* \*

Ashoka's terai pilgrimage shows a worshipful monarch combining obeisance with a building project that modifies and expands the elements which made up the existing sacred landscape there. He appears in this respect to have been an innovator on a grand scale. The cartography of Buddhism was now subcontinental: the faith was substantially transformed from its original small base in North India. The increased or expanded monumentality of each sacred place also made the individual site much more prominent than it had been, altering regional micro-economies.

This is most evident in the religious architecture of Vaishali. Situated some 29 kms north of Hajipur on the left bank of the Ganga river in Bihar, present-day Basarh has many ruins that can be identified with the ancient city and its suburbs. Ruins and structural remains have also been found in neighbouring villages and areas like Baniya, Charamdas, Lalpura, Virpur, and Kolhua. Vaishali, as we saw, was the Vajji confederacy's bustling capital much before the third century BCE: the Buddha lived many times in it, specifically in the vicinity of Mahavana where the Kutagarshala or hall stood on the banks of the 'Monkey Pool' ('markataharadarira'); and at the monastery in the Amrapalivana, built for him by Vaishali's famous courtesan Amrapali.[43] Because of the Buddha's close association with the clan, the Lichchavis received a share of the relics collected from the pyre after he was cremated.

The cadence around the archaeological landscape of Basarh confirms these literary allusions. At the large mound known as Raja Visala ka Garh, a fortified town was revealed, whose twenty-foot wide mud rampart appears to have been constructed around the sixth century BCE.[44] The Abhisheka Pushkarni, a tank that had been used to consecrate the Lichchavi rajas, was also identified with the Kharauna Pokhar which lies less than a couple of kilometres from the garh. In this case, while a wall complex protected the tank, this was apparently a second century BCE construction. There are earlier layers too, their exact antiquity uncertain. The most striking part of the landscape of the Lichchavis is the relic stupa in which they are said to have placed their share of the Buddha's remains. Excavated out of a mound north of the Kharauna Pokhar, the stupa was built in about the fifth century BCE. Constructed of mud, it was subsequently enlarged on four different occasions with bricks. This makes it one of the oldest stupas in India. Made entirely of earth, with as many as twenty-seven mud layers, each separated from the next by a thin layer of gravel, it stood at a height of a little more than three and a half metres with about an eight metre diameter.[45] The original stupa was probably constructed around 550–450 BCE and continued to stand till the first century of the Christian era. The stupa was built on the foundations of an earlier shrine. That edifice, though, was of an entirely different order from the Buddhist monument constructed over it. Its excavated floor has yielded goat bones, which appear to be part of offerings, and for this reason it was described by the excavators as a pre-Buddhist shrine ('chaitya').[46] So, obviously, the Lichchavis used a place that they already considered sacred to create an entirely new kind of hallowed structure over it.

It is, however, the earlier phases of the stupa's construction which concern us here. The mud stupa was said to have been constructed after the Buddha's death, when relics were placed inside it. It was this relic-bearing stupa which Ashoka is believed to have changed in an altogether novel way. The Buddhist literature is full of allusions to Ashoka's ambitious programme of opening up seven of the eight original stupas containing the Buddha's relics. Remarkably, the Vaishali relic stupa confirms that this was indeed dug into. The dug-up section was not a pit. If it had been, it would have contained lots of waste material. Evidently, an intentional breach was made in the stupa to reach the relics: the relic casket was found in this breach. The breach extended beyond the relic casket to a distance of nearly a metre. Probably, more relic caskets were expected, or the original position of the casket was somewhere near the end of the present breach. In any case, when it was redeposited it came to be placed higher up in the breach, which was then filled up.[47]

Those who had dug into the stupa in the first millennium BCE had done so with the intention of reaching the relics. Their only purpose would have been to remove a large portion of these. Apparently, three-fourths of the relics were removed; the portion left contained

Fig. 10.8: The mud stupa of Vaishali is in the centre, surrounded by later brick constructions

Fig. 10.9: Relic box from the Vaishali stupa (now in the Patna Museum)

no bones but only ash mixed with earth, a punch-marked coin, two glass beads, a conch, and a tiny piece of gold.

This, of course, invites speculation on whether the event described in Buddhist texts is the one detectable at Vaishali. An intentional breach is clearly discernible but why it was made is not. Theoretically, there are many possibilities, including mischief by miscreants in unsettled times and desecration by a rival religious group. Their likelihood, though, is weakened by the casket having been reinterred inside the stupa rather than removed from it, which then raises the plausibility of the hypothesis that the breach was caused in order to remove a portion of the relics, perhaps by Ashoka as the literature asserts. If so, Ashoka was expanding not just the monumentality of these sites but also future perceptions of their degree of sacredness, an imaginative innovation towards altering the dimensions of pre-existing religiosity. The proliferation of stupas beyond North India seems to have been at least partly a result of this innovation.

Some 5 km north-west of Vaishali's relic stupa, a pillar and possibly a stupa too were also built by Ashoka. A magnificent monolith with a stone lion still standing on the capital, the Vaishali specimen is not merely the heaviest of all Ashoka's pillars but also one of the most impressive.[48] Though uninscribed (unclear why), its other characteristics show it as indisputably Ashokan. The stupa in its vicinity is contemporary with the pillar. It yielded the fragment of a stone umbrella and pieces of a relic casket, all bearing the polish typical of monuments and artefacts associated with the emperor.[49] Not all stupas attributed to Ashoka can be so easily identified. The original fabric of the Dharmarajika stupa in Taxila, for instance, has not survived, and the only tangible indication is the name Dharma-raja, linked with Ashoka as he who built dharmarajikas, i.e. stupas over relics of the Buddha. The presence of two small mullers of sandstone, of the kind used in Ashokan pillars, is considered as the clinching evidence for the excavator.[50]

Xuanzang, when describing the many structures associated with the Buddha, noted that the Vaishali stupa built by 'Ashoka-raja' had on its side a high stone pillar with a lion on top.

Oddly, Ashoka's presence in Pataliputra is much less in evidence. This is perhaps because much of ancient Pataliputra is buried under Patna and most excavations have been in the outskirts. No

Fig. 10.10: The Vaishali pillar in the vicinity of a brick stupa

inscribed Ashokan pillar or stupa ruin has appeared, the only major architectural relic that may have had something to do with Ashoka being a pillared hall at the Kumrahar locality of Patna.[51] Traces of eighty monolithic pillar bases and fragments of pillars bearing Mauryan polish were found here. Access was through a pillared porch approached by steps constructed on wooden platforms. The platforms themselves stood in the waters of a canal which brought visitors to the hall by boat. The pillared hall was possibly open on all sides (since no screen walls of any kind were found) and huge quantities of wood were possibly used in making the ceiling, a thick layer of ash at the site suggesting this.

Those who believe that Ashoka facilitated the meeting of a Buddhist council to give the final touches to sacred Buddhist texts argue that it was likely to have been held here. The *Mahavamsa* mentions this council, presided over by Moggaliputta Tissa. The pillared structure could well have been the religious assembly hall where the discussants gathered,[52] though there are no positive indications on the matter. At the same time it is worth remembering—and this feeling constantly recurs as one wades through the archaeology of sites showing Ashoka's patronage—no secular constructions such as palaces or sculptures that the emperor may have built have survived. If he had indeed invested substantial resources in such structures, it is unlikely that they would have all disappeared. His building ambitions evidently were an extension of his religious beliefs. It is thus likely that the Pataliputra pillared hall was made for religious use, even if the specifics of what transpired there remain unknown.

Ashoka as Buddhist convert, patron, and pilgrim is inseparable from Ashoka as spiritual regulator and protector of Buddhist unity. He styled himself a spiritual guide in a quite remarkable way on the hillside of Bairat, a Rajasthan town in a narrow valley surrounded by three concentric ranges of hills, some 85 km from Jaipur. The ancient settlement lies buried beneath the town. A couple of kilometres to the south-west of it, on top of a hill known as Bijak-ki-Pahari ('inscription hill'), beneath a large boulder, a stone slab with a message for the Buddhist Sangha was installed by Ashoka, who

Fig. 10.11: The circular temple at Bairat. The Ashokan inscription was found below the overhanging rock at the edge of the hill

identified himself as the 'Magadha king'. This is today described as the Calcutta-Bairat edict because the stone bearing this record was taken away, after it was discovered in the middle of the nineteenth century, to the Asiatic Society of Bengal in Calcutta.

In this edict, after a traditional Buddhist greeting the king offered advice on religious expositions. Even while acknowledging that what the Buddha had spoken was well spoken, he made it clear that he desired 'many groups of monks and (many) nuns' to repeatedly listen to and reflect on particular dhammic expositions.[53] The expositions were several and specific: the epigraph mentions *Vinaya-samukasa*, the *Aliya-vasas*, the *Anagata-bhayas*, the *Muni-gathas*, the *Moneya-suta*, the *Upatisa-pasina*, and the *Laghulovada*. There is no clarity about the exact canonical writings to which he alludes because what is recognizable today as part of the Buddhist canon is not in the form in which it figures in this epigraph. Scholars of Buddhism, though, maintain that such expositions were likely to contain all kinds of advice on how 'to conform to their discipline, be content with their lot, overcome their temptations, delight in solitude, enclose themselves in wise silence', and so on.[54] What seems remarkable is the confidence with which the emperor gives this advice to the Buddhist community: it is as though he sees himself as the Buddha's preacher-successor.

Much was also built for the Buddhist community of Bairat. Most unusual and impressive is a temple for the community on a platform on the hilltop where his advice is inscribed. This was in the form of a circular chamber with a circumabulatory passage, in turn surrounded by an encircling wall. The wall of the inner shrine was made of panels of brickwork alternating with twenty-six wooden columns.[55] The circumambulatory passage was covered by an inclined roof supported on one side by the outer brick wall and on the inner side by the wooden architraves of the pillars of the central shrine. Interestingly, the outer wall of the temple had Mauryan Brahmi on it: several bricks inscribed with one or two characters were found built into the wall. Daya Ram Sahni, the excavator, read a few ('pasam, visa, vi, kama') and considered the possibility that they could have been 'extracts from the very texts from the Buddhist

Fig.10.12: Chunar monolithic railing at Sarnath

scripture, which in the Bairat-Calcutta edict, Ashoka had exhorted his subjects to listen to and study for the furtherance of the Buddhist religion.'[56] Sahni also believed that originally Ashokan pillars had been erected here. This was what the hundred-odd polished Chunar stone pieces and several thousand small fragments that he found there seemed to suggest. The pieces included a fragment from the base and one broken from the shaft summit which preserved part of the well-cut tapering hole into which a metallic bolt slid to support the abacus of the capital that crowned the pillar. Obviously, the pillars were battered into tiny bits at some later point in time.

Fortunately, the monoliths with a specific message for the Buddhist community have survived better. The most famous one is the pillar at Sarnath with its superbly carved quadruple lion capital, the national symbol of India since Independence. Sarnath, some 5 km north of Banaras, is where Buddha preached his first sermon to his first disciples. The symbol of that first sermon, a wheel flanked by two deer, would later become the accepted emblem of the seals of many Buddhist monastic establishments across India.[57] As one who trudged every path the Buddha is supposed to have walked, Ashoka could hardly not have come to Sarnath, the pillar and stupa strongly indicating he did. The pillar was brought here along an ancient channel which connected the Ganga river to Sarnath. This is how the monolithic railing made of Chunar sandstone which was recovered from the foundation of a later Gupta period shrine here, either in an unfinished or semi-finished state was also brought here.[58] It could have been erected around the top of a stupa or may have surrounded a tree or pillar. If it was on top of a stupa, it was likely to have been the stupa that Ashoka built. Known as the Dharmarajika, this building, enlarged six times after it was built (the last being in the twelfth century CE) was largely destroyed in the latter part of the eighteenth century. However, inside its core a sandstone box with a green marble relic casket was found containing gold leaves, decayed pearls, and a few human bone pieces. Could this have been one of the stupas that Ashoka built over the relics of the Buddha that he is supposed to have exhumed? No identifying inscription has been found.

The edict inscribed on the Sarnath pillar shows a new persona— a king opposed to divisions ('samghabheda') among monks and nuns:

... the Samgha [cannot] be divided by any one.

But indeed that monk or nun who shall break up the Samgha, should be caused to put on white robes and to reside in a non-residence.

Thus this edict must be submitted both to the Samgha of monks and to the Samgha of nuns.

Thus speaks Devanampriya:

Let one copy of this (edict) remain with you deposited in (your) office; and deposit ye another copy of this very (edict) with the lay-worshippers.

These lay-worshippers may come on every fast-day (posatha) in order to be inspired with confidence in this very edict; and invariably on every fast-day, every Mahamatra (will) come to the fast-day (service) in order to be inspired with confidence in this very edict and to understand (it).

And as far as your district (extends), dispatch ye (an officer) everywhere according to the letter of this (edict).

In the same way cause (your subordinates) to dispatch (an officer) according to the letter of this (edict) in all the territories (surrounding) forts.[59]

Fig.10.13: The broken Sarnath pillar with the edict inscribed on it

Several aspects of this unusual edict are worth highlighting. A royal patron and builder speaks now not as a king with Buddhist inclinations but as a Buddhist head of government. Sarnath's epigraph takes Ashoka beyond the mere practice of supporting Buddhist Shramanas and that of enlarging and building in the holy places associated with the faith. Fighting dissension within the Sangha makes him sound for the first time papal. On doctrinal and disciplinary issues, as few as nine dissenting monks could be fissiparous, suggesting the high possibility of upheaval even during the Buddha's lifetime.[60] Ashoka seems opposed to the ease with which factional breakaways have been happening and proposes to punish dissidents by forcing them to give up their monastic robes and take on the white clothes ('avadatavasana') of householders. Whether this came to be enforced is not known; the existence of groups and sub-groups within the Buddhist faith in ancient India suggests that schisms of the kind which bothered Ashoka were common enough. What is extraordinary is that the emperor seems to have displaced senior monks and councils of monks who would normally discourage factional breaks. Ashoka wants his administration to ensure wide circulation of the proscription: a copy was to be submitted to the Sangha, the laity was to be inspired by it on every fast day (every fortnight, most likely), and maha-matras were ordered to retain a copy so that they too could be similarly inspired.

At Sarnath there was a large and influential Buddhist establish-ment, so the exhortation was logical. Shorter versions of this edict appear on monoliths at Kaushambi and Sanchi. At Kaushambi this was inscribed below after a much longer message issued twenty-six years into Ashoka's reign, making it a late work. The pillar on which the Kaushambi edict was inscribed stands today inside the Fort area of Allahabad, but since it mentions the mahamatras of Kaushambi, that may well have been its original location. Kaushambi, one of the six great cities of the Buddha's time, had several monasteries built by merchants for the Buddha.[61] Of these the Ghositarama, built by the merchant Ghosita, was identified with the structure of a big vihara in the north-eastern corner of the city. That Ashoka put up a schism edict at the city suggests that it was an important estab-lishment of the Sangha. It was also one which in the time of the Buddha was known to have witnessed monastic disputes.[62]

Can any such direct connection with the Buddha be suggested for Sanchi, where Ashoka also set up his proscription against schisms? This is unlikely since the Buddha spent his life in the middle Gangetic plains. It is, though, possible that Buddhist monks moved along the network of routes that linked such areas with the Gangetic plains and that, consequently, before the time of Ashoka, Buddhist communities existed in several places like Vidisha and Ujjayini: the importance of the former on account of his spouse Devi, we have noted already. 'Chetiyagiri', where Devi took their son Mahinda before he set out on a Buddhist mission to Sri Lanka, may well be a reference to Sanchi.[63]

If there was already a resident Buddhist community on the hill of Sanchi, Ashoka now built his presence into their lives in the way that he had done at Sarnath, by constructing a pillar and a stupa. The magnificent lustrous Sanchi stone pillar, or at least a part of it, remains *in situ*. Sanchi was one of the two places in the Central

Indian hills and plateaus to get a pillar of this kind, suggesting the location had some special place in his life. Sodanga was probably another such: it was where the elephant and lotus capital was found (the supporting pillar was missing). This was close to Ujjayini, with its close associations for Ashoka and Devi.[64]

The Sanchi pillar like the monolith at Sarnath has a capital with four lions and was constructed near a brick stupa. That the brick stupa was on the same floor level as the lion pillar near its South Gateway suggests that this too can be attributed to Ashoka.[65] The bricks themselves resemble those used in other structures of Ashoka's time, while the umbrella that crowned it was made of fine Chunar sandstone, polished in the manner typical of stone monuments attributed to the emperor. The inscription on the edict is a shorter version of the one at Sarnath. Its lettering is poor and the lines are rarely horizontal. This 'slovenly character of the engraving' was, in Marshall's opinion, because it was inscribed after the pillar had been set up.[66] It may also be that the scribe was careless in transcribing the king's message to the Sangha. The inscription is greatly damaged; what has survived suggests that, unlike at Sarnath and Kaushambi, there is no reference to officials. Provisions for the Sangha are set forth; Ashoka added a line highlighting the importance of monastic unity: 'The Samgha both of monks and of nuns is made united as long as (my) sons and great-grandsons (shall reign, and) as long as the moon and the sun (shall shine).'[67]

These edicts, focussed as they are on disciplinary punishment for dissenting monks and nuns, make the tradition of Ashoka having convened a Buddhist council at Pataliputra for suppressing heresy seem historical. Whether the council was held before or after these edicts, Ashoka appears as a figure whose power to impose discipline among the Sangha was accepted. It has been suggested that the recurrence of serious schisms made the Buddhist establishment seek the monarch's intervention of the king in imposing stronger measures against factionalism. While segregation—where the offending monk was made to dwell in 'what is not a residence' ('anavasa')—is mentioned in the Vinaya, the imposition of white robes on a lay person is not. One historian sees this as a crucial intervention:

The Sarnath–Kausambi–Sanchi edict leaves no doubt as to the firm determination of Asoka to put down all attempt at creating a schism in the Buddhist Church. The earnest, almost severe tone of the edict and the fact that copies of it are found at all places of important Buddhist monastic establishments presupposes that in his time the Buddhist Church was at least threatened with disruption, to prevent which he was straining every nerve ... The Edict was no doubt intended to arrest disruption, but that does not preclude us, it may be contended, from supposing that the Samgha had already broken up into a number of sections, and Asoka's endeavour was directed against further division.[68]

# 11

# An Ageing
# Emperor's Interventions

WHEN ASHOKA SET DOWN STRICTURES AGAINST schismatic monks and nuns, he had been reigning for some thirty years. It appears that as he reached middle age and before positioning himself as a regulator of the faith, he resumed communicating with his subjects at large in the familiar mode begun a dozen years earlier. Around 243 BCE, a set of six edicts elucidating his policies and ideas was inscribed. This compilation, like the major rock edicts, was put up in multiple places though not on natural rock: it was engraved on pillars. Speaking in the first person, Ashoka picks up from where he had left off. He appears consumed by the need to bring the people of his realm to greater virtue. The intervening years—from the time when the major rock edicts were inscribed to the engraving of these pillar edicts—had altered his perception of the endeavour to promote morality rooted in dhamma. Consequently, he tweaks his policies in line with the changed viewpoint.

The pillars are mainly across a fairly large part of North India. They were set up roughly in the north Bihar segment of the Gangetic plains—at Lauriya-Araraj, Lauriya-Nandangarh, and Rampurva. Eastwards, a pillar with a similar message stands at Allahabad, which, as noted, was possibly originally located at Kaushambi. As their positioning on the Allahabad pillar makes evident, the edicts on them may have been engraved before the king's proscription against schisms. The long pillar edicts were for his subjects as a whole, not for members of any specific religious community. Moving along the Ganga, further west, in the vicinity of Meerut, this set of six edicts (later brought to Delhi by Sultan Firuz Shah Tughlaq) was put up on a monolith; and beyond, at Topra in Haryana (also subsequently transported to Delhi by the same sultan), another pillar with the same message was erected. The Topra pillar was singular because it had an additional rescript, a seventh edict that has not been found in its entirety anywhere else. A short Aramaic inscription at Kandahar was drafted in a way suggesting that the engravers were aware of the seventh pillar edict, but, unlike at Topra, it is not there part of a set. Beyond North India is an inscribed sandstone slab (cut from a pillar), apparently from the Amaravati stupa site in the lower Krishna valley of Andhra. However, the few lines that have survived suggest that its language and terminology were similar to rock edicts rather than the expansive message put on pillars.[1] It is entirely possible that the edicts were put up elsewhere too, for inscribed pillars with messages purportedly by Ashoka were described centuries later by Chinese pilgrims. However, they have since disappeared.

The pillars carry practically identical messages. As with the rock edicts earlier, they seem consciously compiled into a kind of anthology. They include a record of various past Ashokan actions and initiatives and so have been described as 'a compilation of originally independent, isolated documents.'[2] Ashoka himself makes this evident by specifying the points in time at which particular policies had been initiated or implemented, the bulk having been in the twenty-sixth year of his anointment. The edicts could only have been disseminated as a connected group after that crucial year, the single exception being Topra, where the seventh edict was written in the twenty-seventh year.

The imprint of age and experience can be seen in the emperor's words as, for instance, in the very different way in which they were set down. The edicts that formed Ashoka's fourteen major rock epigraphs had, as we saw, been issued over some four years. When the emperor decided to carve them on rock they had, in several instances, been dispatched in batches. The six pillar edicts were not staggered, being all engraved like a single prearranged bunch from Haryana to Bihar, and all at around the same time. This is evident also from the edicts at all sites being in the same dialect, set down from a common exemplar and thus involving no translation changes. In the earlier rock edicts, a variety of dialects had been used.[3] Had adverse feedback modified the earlier way of transcribing? Had the variety of dialects suited to each region unsatisfactorily altered the meanings of the messages? Only speculation is possible on the reasons for the new singularity: by the time of the pillar edicts Ashoka seems likely to have been an impatient and imperious old sovereign who wanted his words conveying precisely what he wanted to say and be done.

\* \* \*

The places where these pillars were set up do not seem to have been in the vicinity of important provincial cities or major settlements, as was the case with many of the major rock edicts, which seems at odds with the pillar messages being non-sectarian addresses to the populace at large. Pataliputra, Hastinapur, and Mathura, all important settlements of the day, were bypassed and the monoliths put in locations entirely of a different character. At Rampurva, endowed with two Ashokan pillars, one of them inscribed, no vestiges of buildings were found in the vicinity. There does not appear to have been an ancient town at the location. A couple of mounds nearby contained no structures, only bits of potsherds, bricks, beads, and burnt ore. Practically the only structural remnants that emerged from excavations at Rampurva were around the pillars, in the form of an extensive brick floor of Mauryan times and an ancient well made of terracotta rings. These were in the trenches that had been made to remove the pillars from the sand and water morass in which they were found buried.[4]

One reason for lack of detail about the contexts of the pillar edicts may be that some were not found *in situ* or even close to their original locations. The Meerut pillar in Uttar Pradesh and the Topra pillar from Haryana were brought to Delhi in the fourteenth century CE by the medieval sultan Firuz Shah Tughlaq and set up on the Delhi Ridge and at Firoz Shah Kotla, respectively.[5] The places where they stood in Meerut and Topra have not been satisfactorily identified, leaving us in the dark about the reasons for those locations. Unlike the fourteenth-century sultan, whose chroniclers clearly described how these pillars were shifted to Delhi, Ashoka neither mentioned the places where he placed his edicts nor why he chose to position them there. Segments of Ashokan pillars were integrated into Sultanate architecture in the Lat ki Masjid at Hissar and in the Firuz Shah column of the Purana Qila at Fatehabad as well.[6] It has been suggested that the two segments were part of the same ancient column. While large parts of the original polish were removed for the Persian inscriptions, palimpsest traces of earlier writing can still be seen, though not, unfortunately, any Ashokan message, stray characters apart.

Some of these monoliths appear to have been placed close to pre-existing religious structures. Lauriya-Nandangarh, the only Ashokan column bearing these edicts which has survived in its entirety and still stands,[7] is located in the Gandak valley, not far from Bettiah in the Champaran area of Bihar. Here a series of mounds, mostly round at the base and conical on top, are also in evidence, some being pre-Ashokan burial grounds. In two of them (mounds M and N), human bones and a standing female figure imprinted on a small gold leaf were found, while at the bottom of one of them (mound N) was found the end of a fairly intact wooden post.[8] This female figure was given the appellation 'Prithvi' or earth goddess by the archaeologist Theodor Bloch, who excavated the mounds in the early years of the twentieth century. Bloch believed that that goddess was, in a hymn in the *Rig Veda*, entrusted with the care of the dead. Incidentally, this figure was also found impressed on a gold leaf at Piprahwa in Uttar Pradesh, again in a funerary mound and close to a Buddhist stupa that carried an inscription saying the relics of the Buddha were made by his brethren, the Sakyas.[9] Structural

Fig. 11.1: Ashokan pillar
at Hissar fort (the lowest
part) which was made
part of a composite pillar

Fig. 11.2: A close-up of the
Ashokan segment of the
Hissar pillar with some Brahmi
letters still intact

Fig. 11.3: Fatehabad segment of Ashokan pillar
(the bottom part)

portions of stupas have also emerged at Lauriya-Nandangarh, but
their chronology is uncertain and they are likely to be later than
Ashoka.[10] So, it appears that the early burial mounds were not
Buddhist, but as the location attracted congregations for rituals and
worship, a pillar in the neighbourhood was thought a good idea.
Traders and travellers would in their passage have seen it and thought
of halting, for it was positioned where the two principal routes leading
to the Nepal terai met. The religious significance of such routes was
evident to all, as borne out by Ashoka's pilgrimage and his building programme over the trail. The terai was fairly populous at the
time, dotted with settlements, some of them fortified. Such routes

emerge out of 'acts of consensual making', marked out by regular journeys across them over centuries, sometimes millennia.[11] Records of such journeys have enabled modern observers to make sense of objects such as ossuaries and relics along them, in this instance the objects observed being above ground in the shape of pillars.

Keeping in mind this perspective, the intersection of the pillars and communication routes in this part of Bihar was highlighted by the archaeologist N.G. Majumdar. One of the routes, he showed, connected Lauriya with the area where the modern frontier station of Bhikhna Thori, leading to Narkatiaganj, stood; the other passed along the Gandak river to reach Triveni on the borderland, at the junction of the Gandak with two other streams.[12] Along the first route lay Rampurva with two of Ashoka's pillars (one of which had the same edicts as the one at Lauriya-Nandangarh) while towards the south, at Lauriya-Araraj, was located the site of another similarly inscribed pillar. These were routes that merchants and caravans continued to use into modern times. Such commercial connections also marked the sites of the pillar edicts in the Indo-Gangetic Doab. The significance of their geographical locations in relation to routes of communication has been highlighted in Chakrabarti's work on the Ashokan inscriptions. He points out that Meerut was on the straight route towards the Siwaliks in the area of modern Najibabad, from where a road went to Pauri via Kotdwar.[13] As for Topra, it was likely to have been on the direct line between Sirsawa and Ambala. Whether the Hissar and Fatehabad pillar segments were part of a monolith that was originally in the Hissar area, which shows early historic occupation, or from an important ancient site like Rohtak or Agroha in that area, remains unclear. An arterial route, though, used to pass through this region, to go towards Multan, eventually ending up in Afghanistan. This route was used well into the medieval era. Hissar town, historically known as Hisar-i Firuza, came to be founded by Firuz Shah partly because it was located on the old Delhi–Multan route which branched to Khorasan.[14]

Another kind of archive is arrived at from the hundreds of objects at ancient places along these routes. Their distant origins help in tracking the significance of lines of communication. Lapis lazuli beads originating from north Afghanistan are found in the entire axis from the Swat valley of Pakistan till the Burdwan district of Bengal, at places like Bir Kot Ghundai, Taxila, Sravasti, Rajghat, Prahladpur, and Pandu Rajar Dhibi.[15] Similarly, artefacts made of sea shell from the eastern coast were found in the middle Gangetic and the lower Gangetic plains, at places like Rajghat, Prahladpur, Vaishali, and Bangarh. That raw materials of various kinds moved across the Gangetic plains to reach the Nepal terai is evident from, among other things, the range of beads found at the ancient town of Tilaurakot.[16] Chalcedony, carnelian, onyx, topaz, shell, garnet, amethyst, and jasper are among them. One also encounters a similar proliferation in the usage and manufacture of beads from the wide range of stones in cities and settlements of the minerally poor middle Gangetic plains. To all such imprints of commerce and craft along old tracks, Ashoka added his own in the form of epigraphs, virtually ensuring wide dissemination of his moral worldview.

* * *

The messages began in a fairly uniform way. Promoting morality to secure worldly and otherworldly happiness would continue as the core of state policy: such happiness was not possible 'without great love of morality, careful examination, great obedience, great fear (of sin) (and) great energy.'[17] Much remained to be accomplished, he added, requiring encouragement and monitoring. The king's officials were said to be practising dhamma, and now publicly recognized as being 'able to stir up fickle (persons)'; mahamatras for people on the borders were similarly charged.[18] Implicit in the enunciation seems the acknowledgement that, given an inconstant and vacillating populace, state vigilance was a perennial requirement.

In the second edict of this set, the emperor described his dhamma as marked by 'few sins, many virtuous deeds, compassion, liberality, truthfulness (and) purity.'[19] Ways to perform virtuous deeds and be compassionate were then explained in relation to what he had himself done:

The gift of spiritual insight has also been bestowed by me in many ways.

On bipeds and quadrupeds, on birds and aquatic animals various benefits have been conferred by me, (even) to the boon of life.

And many other virtuous deeds also have been performed by me.

For the following purpose was this rescript of morality caused to be written by me, (viz.) in order that (men) might conform to it, and that it might be of long duration.

And he who will act thus will perform good deeds.[20]

Each of these aspects was then amplified in separate edicts, making the pillar edict quoted from above a kind of table of contents listing the various ways in which the cause of dhamma was sought to be furthered.[21]

In order of precedence, the spiritual well-being of people appears at the top. The Third Pillar Edict encourages everyone to take responsibility for their actions, both 'virtuous deeds' and evil actions. Had he heard Shakespeare's Antony argue that 'The evil that men do lives after them/ The good is oft interred with their bones', he would have vehemently disagreed: the human tendency, he believes, is to acknowledge good deeds while suppressing the unpalatable—a peculiarly Ashokan notion elicited almost certainly by a recollection of his post-Kalinga contrition where he had publicly accepted his culpability. The harbouring of negative emotions is castigated: 'These (passions), viz. fierceness, cruelty, anger, pride, envy, are called sinful. Let me not ruin (myself) by (these) very (passions).'[22] Vincent Smith, while examining this insistence on self-responsibility, was reminded of a passage in the *Dhammapada*:

By ourselves is evil done,
By ourselves we pain endure,
By ourselves we cease from wrong,
By ourselves become we pure.

No one saves us but ourselves,
No one can and no one may,
We ourselves must tread the Path;
Buddhas only show the way.[23]

In the Separate Rock Edicts of Kalinga too, envy, anger, cruelty, hurry, want of practice, laziness, and fatigue had been specifically warned against, the difference being that in the Kalinga version the warning was intended to keep state officials on their toes.

The spiritual well-being of individuals is followed in the Fourth Edict, which takes up how the harshest punishments handed out by the administration might be mitigated. The edict is primarily concerned with making the rajukkas functionally autonomous. These officials, as noted in relation to the minor rock edicts, had been ordered to disseminate the Ashokan message in the country-side. Now in this edict their authority over rural people is re-emphasized, for they are to be 'occupied with the people, with many hundreds and thousands' of people.[24] The rajukka is a state equivalent of the nurse that parents put their faith in when caring for children: 'For, as one feels confident after having entrusted (his) child to an intelligent nurse, (thinking): "the intelligent nurse will be able to keep my child well", so that Rajukas were appointed by me for the welfare and happiness of the country-people.'[25] His faith in these officials is clear for he grants them independence in the discharge of their judicial functions: 'rewards or punishment are left to their discretion, in order that *Lajukas* perform (their) duties confidently (and) fearlessly, that they should bestow welfare and happiness on the people of the country, and that they should confer benefits (on them).'[26] Ashoka is at pains to emphasize that these are moral guardians to whom he is delegating full responsibility for the common weal.[27] The intent is, for the time, rather amazing and is described by a legal scholar as 'an extraordinarily progressive measure for its time, amounting to a guarantee of due process of law.'[28] The rajukkas were responsible for justice outside the cities, so the endeavour seems to have been to ensure consistency in the judicial process.

This also raises questions: had the king's proactive administrative measures demoralized the state machinery? Had there been a weakening in the administration now being redressed? Why was such functional autonomy being granted only to officers in charge of the countryside? The mahamatras who acted as judges in the city had in relation to Kalinga been exhorted to be more sensitive, proactive, and even-handed. The emperor had not spoken of their judicial independence: on the contrary he had in relation to them put in place a system of scrutiny. The reasons for taking a diametrically opposite view in relation to rajukkas is not clear, but the result would have been administrative decentralization.

Ashoka's views are also here spelt out on the death penalty, and in some detail; as in virtually every sphere of administration, he comes out here as the prototype of benevolence. If the *Arthashastra* is to be believed, the penalty was prescribed for a range of offences: the sale of human flesh, killing a person (even by accident), supplying murderers and thieves with counsel or nourishment, acts against the king and the kingdom, stealing weapons, and some other crimes considered heinous.[29] Ashoka is silent about the offences that the condemned prisoners alluded to in this edict are charged with, but orders that there be an interlude of three days from the time punishment is pronounced by the rajukkas to when condemned prisoners are led to the gallows. The respite was to allow the relatives of prisoners on death row to appeal against such decisions, or, as Ashoka's edict put it, so that relatives of the accused could persuade rajukkas to reconsider. Simultaneously, the interlude might ensure a more dignified death by allowing the condemned time to prepare: 'they will bestow gifts or will undergo fasts in order to (attain happiness) in the other (world). For my desire is this, that, even when the time (of respite) has expired, they should attain (happiness) in the other (world).'[30] Ashoka appears to have had very ambivalent feelings about the death sentence but did not get it removed from the state's judicial provisions. He did, however, on as many as twenty-five occasions from the time of his anointment, release prisoners, and some of these were conceivably commutations.[31]

A slew of substantive injunctions against the killing of animals, birds, and fish constitute another dimension of the emperor's exceptionally humane provisions. From the modern ecological perspective this edict is without doubt the most substantive royal public message in early India, and possibly anywhere in the ancient world, against a species hierarchy favouring *Homo sapiens* and for the protection of living beings in general. The persona of Ashoka as a guardian of animals first became evident, as noted, in his major rock edicts which outline personal and public measures for animal proto-conservation: sacrifices were proscribed, the slaughter of animals for consumption in the royal kitchen drastically reduced, veterinary hospices established, provisions made for pack animals along roads. Abstention from the slaughter of life was constantly invoked. These ideas were now being inscribed in the Gangetic heartland. An older and wiser man desires an extension in the imperium of welfare to cover every species in every area of the kingdom. Here, for the first time, an entire edict is devoted to the subject—even if the policy in mind is more pragmatic than the one in the edicts recommending vegetarianism to the Afghans. The emperor seems to have realized that blanket prohibitions on hunting and fishing will not succeed and a more calibrated policy which designates some animals inviolable while allowing others to be consumed may work. There are also other measures here concerning the protection of the habitat of such living creatures and preventing unnecessary cruelty towards them. This early environmentalism is perhaps the most remarkable aspect of Ashoka's philosophy and deserves to be seen at some length:

> (When I had been) anointed twenty-six years, the following animals were declared by me inviolable, viz. parrots, mainas, the *aruna*, ruddy geese, wild geese, the *nandimukha*, the *gelata*, bats, queen-ants, terrapins, boneless fish, the *vedaveyaka*, the *Ganga-puputaka*, skate-fish, tortoises and porcupines, squirrels (?), the *srimara*, bulls set at liberty, iguanas (?), the rhinoceros, white doves, domestic doves, (and) all the quadrupeds which are neither useful nor edible.
>
> Those (she-goats), ewes, sows (which are) either with young or in milk, are inviolable, and also those (of their) young ones (which are) less than six months old.
>
> Cocks must not be caponed.
>
> Husks containing living animals must not be burnt.
>
> Forests must not be burnt uselessly or in order to destroy (living beings).

Living animals must not be fed with (other) living animals.

Fish are inviolable, and must not be sold, on the three Chaturmasis (and) on the Tishya full-moon during three days, (viz.) the fourteenth, the fifteenth, (and) the first (*tithi*), and invariably on every fast-day.

And during these same days also no other classes of animals which are in the elephant-park (and) in the preserves of the fishermen, must be killed.

On the eighth (*tithi*) of (every) fortnight, on the fourteenth, on the fifteenth, on Tishya, on Punarvasu, on the three Chaturmasis, (and) on festivals, bulls must not be castrated, (and) he-goats, rams, boars, and whatever other (animals) are castrated (otherwise) must not be castrated (then).

On Tishya, on Punarvasu, on the Chaturmasis, (and) during the fortnight of (every) Chaturmasi, horses (and) bullocks must not be branded.[32]

The first question about this massive range of animals needing protection is whether such care is enjoined in sacred texts. For the most part, animals in the texts of ancient India are classified according to various principles such as anatomical characteristics and modes of procreation, domestication and wildness, suitability for sacrifice or not, edible or inedible.[33] In some texts (such as the *Satapatha Brahmana, Aitareya Brahmana,* and the *Manu Smriti*) beasts not worthy of sacrifice are considered unfit for human consumption.[34] Ashoka could in theory have had such injunctions in mind when compiling his don't-hit list.

The scholar K.R. Norman believes parallels are discernible between the Ashokan list and certain Jaina texts. Ashoka's list is not random but carefully organized to include two talking birds, a series of aquatic birds (the bat mentioned here being a water-haunting one), aquatic animals, reptiles (legged and legless), and three birds of the pigeon/dove family.[35] Ashoka, in Norman's opinion, is following a division of animal life enumerated in Jaina texts: sky-goers, water-goers, and land-goers, which shows the influence upon him in this respect of Jainism. Even the creature named 'palaste' in the list, which Hultzsch translates as 'rhinoceros', is read by Norman as 'paravata', which is similar to the Jaina 'parevaya' or turtle dove. But the influences and rationale of the list are difficult to conclusively establish because it includes birds like geese and doves that are likely to have been widely enjoyed in a way that queen ants and bats were not. If Hultzsch is right and the creature in Ashoka's list is a rhinoceros, a general anti-brahmanism could be detected: the *Manu Smriti* suggests that eating rhinos pleases dead ancestors, specifically enjoining that its flesh be eaten by the 'twice-born' because this satisfies 'the manes for endless times'.[36]

The zoologist Sunder Lal Hora, who specialized in fish and fisheries, points out that there are five species of fish in the list that are inedible and therefore not worth the killing. These are sharks and boneless fish ('Anathikamachhe'), eels or fish easily eluding the grasp ('Vedaveyake'), the porpoise, or a fish-like animal with a lumpy body ('Gamgapuputake'), skate or ray ('Samkujamchhe'), and globe-fish or a fish like a porcupine with the ability to feign death when in danger ('Kaphatasayake').[37] These five varieties, he says, are not consumed even in modern India, because—

> Globe-fishes and their allies are poisonous and should not be eaten. Unless properly treated, the flesh of Sharks, Rays, and Skates is bitter to taste and gritty on account of the deposition of uric acid crystals in their flesh. The Gangetic Porpoise is revered among the Hindus of the Indo-Gangetic Plain and its flesh is not eaten. With the exception of certain parts of South India, eels are not eaten on account of their strong resemblance to snakes. It would thus appear that the present-day prejudices of not eating these fishes are as old as the Asoka period.[38]

Culinary habits are culturally formed and what Hora shows as undesirable species had much to do with the traditional Hindu society of his own time. But over the same period, tribal and fishing communities may well have had more catholic tastes and not adhered to such taboos. Ashoka may well have been addressing fishing communities in which virtually anything caught was cooked.

The prohibitions required on certain days may well have been for sound environmental reasons. The days against catching fish were the fourteenth and fifteenth days of the moon, the first day after the full moon, on days of fasting and during the rainy season (the period of 'chaturmasya' being July to September). Many of these days are connected with the breeding habits of fish. Several fish breed in the rainy season beginning in July and usually lasting till September.[39] This is well recognized. What is less known is that there is also a lunar rhythm to the spawning of some freshwater fish such as carp and the 'hilsa', with new-moon and full-moon periods being most favourable.[40] On the basis of these injunctions, various calculations have been made about the number of such 'fish-prohibition' days, ranging from fifty-one to seventy-two, not a small number even if the days are spread over the whole year.

There is in the edict the combination of an extraordinary sensitivity to protecting the natural breeding patterns of living creatures while accepting that their slaughter will continue. An emperor pleading to his people to spare pregnant and lactating she-goats, ewes, and sows needs to say nothing else to appear extraordinary. The young of these animals, below the age of six months, were to be protected when their herds were culled for slaughter. Branding horses and bullocks is frowned upon, with a series of days specified when such cruelty is prohibited.

The prohibition days relating to Tishya, Punarvasu, and Chaturmasis are astrologically significant, Tishya and Punarvasu being lunar constellations which may have had some special significance for Ashoka. In the *Arthashastra* the two which were special constellations were supposed to be the birth-stars and consecration stars of kings ('raja-nakshatra' and 'desha nakshatra'). Possibly, Tishya signified Ashoka's birth-star and Punarvasu his anointment.[41] The Chaturmasis make sense in terms of the breeding season of fish, but there do not seem to be environmental reasons for forbidding the castration and branding of animals in that time slot. Basically, the provisions were instruments of control for reducing animal slaughter and cruelty. The purpose of stipulating days for such protective measures endowed moral meaning to what had, till then, been auspicious days in the calendar of kingship and ritual.

Did these measures lead to a change in the food habits of the emperor's subjects? There is no doubt that Ashoka's intent was taken seriously by his officers and governors. An epigraph at Deotek near Nagpur in Maharashtra, which recorded the command of a lord ('Sami') prohibiting the capture and slaughter of animals, is indicative, punishments being specified for those who dared disobey his command.[42] Even so, there is no way of ascertaining the impact of Ashoka's vegetarian predilection. In an archaeological calendar, processes that can be detected exist as relatively large chunks of time. Thus, within the layers of excavated cities and villages of his time, it becomes impossible to specify the archaeological levels that constitute the reign of Ashoka. If coins had been minted that bore the portrait of the king or had there been other kinds of artefacts emblematic of his time, a reasonably precise archaeological chronology for this Mauryan emperor would have been reached. So, on the question of whether the king's orders modified meat consumption, all one can do is to look for clues indicating a reduction in the early historic period (which includes but is not limited to the time of Ashoka).

Since the pillar edicts are overwhelmingly in North India, we could look at the fauna at sites excavated there. At several such, bones show the range of meat that was consumed and offer a broad picture. At some sites large quantities of bones have appeared: at Raja Nala-ka-Tila in the Sonabhadra area of Uttar Pradesh, there were nearly 1600 fragments of animal bones in Period III (the early historic North Black Polished Ware phase), suggesting there was no reduction in meat-eating over this time.[43] The overwhelming preference here was for cattle and buffalo meat, followed by that of the sheep and the goat. Wild animals and birds were eaten, including wild cattle ('gaur' and buffalo), deer, wild pigs, cranes, and peafowl. The early historic phase (North Black Polished Ware phase) at Siswania in the Basti district of Uttar Pradesh too shows various domesticated and wild animals and other fauna—cattle, sheep/goat, pig, various varieties of deer, wild boar, three species of turtles, and at least two species of fish.[44] The ancient city of Rajghat in the Varanasi district suggests a reduction in animal species over time, from the time period of 600–400 BCE to 400–200 BCE.[45] While in the first sub-period a total of fifteen species were represented, the numbers came down to about nine. Among the species present earlier but not in Mauryan times was fish (*Teleost*). The time period, though, for which the abrupt reduction in species has been suggested includes the time of Ashoka but is not limited to it. So there is no way of working out the results of Ashoka's exhortations against animal slaughter.

If this edict is read along with the measures for animal welfare in the earlier rock edicts, what stands out is the sheer comprehensiveness of Ashoka's intentions. He lists every variety of cruelty in order to express his abhorrence. The regulation of animal castration becomes an imperial obsession: this is nothing short of jaw-dropping. One does not know about methods of animal castration in ancient India, but if the crude methods followed in rural India are anything to go by, the painful crushing of testicles or the removal of testicles of animals through the 'open method' will have been practised, the pain being unimaginable.[46] Veterinary facilities too become an important part of state activity, as does the enforcing of 'closed seasons' to protect breeding. Normally, the state protects fauna when numbers decline.[47] The language and idiom of Ashoka's concern is radically different: it is a code of ahimsa, or non-violence. It was as if Ashoka's own self-image as a morally credible monarch involved laying down a humane code of conduct towards all living creatures.

* * *

Ashoka had, by this time, set down in stone all the measures that he had promulgated in that crucial twenty-sixth year. For some reason, in that same year, he also put out a kind of summarized account of his life and moral effort. Was this remembrance, where he mentions measures promulgated some fourteen years earlier, a sign that he was reaching the end of his days? We do know that this was close to the last time that he would speak in this way. Or perhaps being a preacher of sorts he knew the importance of repeating for effect the same idea in various forms.

The dominant impression remaining at the end of the pillar edicts is the unusually inclusive character of Ashoka's endeavour—

the new directions, as well as the number of humans and other species sought to be uplifted by the new directions. The emperor's self-image as a *people's* monarch emerges movingly and powerfully. No emperor in the ancient world expresses such deep and abiding concern for the underprivileged, the dispossessed, the suffering, the oppressed, both human and animal. No other emperor of the ancient world is heard saying that his principal duty ought to mean visiting people personally.[48]

With one exception, on this note the pillar edicts end. The exception is the Seventh Edict added on the Topra pillar, now in Delhi. Why it appeared only at one place is unclear. It seems unlikely that the officers at Lauriya-Araraj, Kaushambi, and Meerut did not follow the emperor's instructions, or that the instructions were not communicated properly to them. This Seventh Edict is an amplification of the Sixth. Its importance stems from the fact that it is an overtly retrospective statement, the kind of testimony that could only have come from an ageing sovereign looking back on his life's work with pride and humility. They are the last words of the emperor to have survived.

In them Ashoka explores the distinction between him and past rulers. Earlier kings too had desired that 'men might (be made to) progress by the promotion of morality; but men were not made to progress by an adequate promotion of morality.'[49] This led him to consider ways of succeeding where his predecessors had failed: namely, by issuing public proclamations and instructions, and giving muscle and teeth to his administration. He sees this innovation as being responsible for his success, and presumably desiring emulation by future rulers considers it necessary to explain how he came to evolve such a policy:

> How then might men (be made to) conform to (morality)?
>
> How might men (be made to) progress by an adequate promotion of morality?
>
> How could I elevate them by the promotion of morality?
>
> Concerning this, king Devanampriya Priyadarsin speaks thus.
>
> The following occurred to me.
>
> I shall use proclamations on morality, (and) shall order instruction in morality (to be given).

> Hearing this, men will conform to (it), will be elevated, and will (be made to) progress considerably by the proclamation of morality.
>
> For this purpose proclamations of morality were issued by me, (and) manifold instructions in morality were ordered (to be given), [in order that those agents] (of mine) too, who are occupied with many people, (and who) will exhort (them) and will explain (morality to them) in detail.[50]

A range of officials, from rajukkas to dharma-mahamatras, who figure in his earlier messages, are again mentioned; trees that he planted and wells dug on his orders also figure here—banyan trees for shade to cattle and men, and mango groves. The concern with the ordinary is extraordinary.

New also is the description of the ways in which his officials were occupied with the delivery of gifts and charities by him and his larger family. The recipients of charity were in Pataliputra and the provinces, and their 'dana' promoted morality. We know that donations were indeed made by his family, this being suggested by what is known as the Queen's Edict on the Allahabad pillar.

> At the word of Devanampriya, the Mahamatras everywhere have to be told (this).
>
> What gifts (have been made) here by the second queen, (viz.) either mango-groves, or gardens, or alms-houses, or whatever else, these (shall) be registered (in the name) of that queen.
>
> This (is) [the request] of the second queen, the mother of Tivala, the Karuvaki.[51]

The queen Karuvaki seems to have been no pushover. She wanted to be known as the giver of these gifts; the emperor informs his officers; the registration is done as she desires.

Family philanthropy is not of course sufficient, and Ashoka is at pains to point out that moral restrictions and conversion through persuasion have been his main methods for initiating change, the second of these having proved to be more meaningful: 'moral restrictions are of little consequence; by conversion, however, (morality is promoted) more considerably.'[52] Honesty and finality resonate in this last self-reflexive statement. Through much of his life and via his edicts Ashoka had tried to communicate the need to transform state governance from a system based on force to one anchored in morality. Looking back he acknowledges the futility of restrictions imposed from above and the gentler, more effective power of persuasion for the achievement of a dharmic life and empire. It was what he wanted to say in the end to his people and successors, and he hoped his views 'may last as long as (my) sons and great-grandsons (shall reign and) as long as the moon and the sun (shall shine), and in order that (men) may conform to it.'[53]

# 12

# Of Wifely Woes and the Emperor's Death

ACROSS THE PRECEDING PAGES THE HISTORICAL ASHOKA has emerged over nearly two decades of his reign in many avataras: the remorseful conqueror of Kalinga, the proactive propagandist of non-violence, the imperious king threatening violence against forest people, the pious Buddhist pilgrim at Lumbini, the supportive spouse implementing his consort's wishes. A variety of people in the India of his time have also appeared: officials, scribes, travellers, neighbouring monarchs, Hindu and Jaina vegetarians, Afghan meat-eaters, monks and nuns.

With the pillar edicts done, Ashoka's compelling voice falls silent all at once. No more messages appear on rocks and pillars addressed to administrators and the populace. The metaphors that he had used, the idiom and language of his edicts, the examples and intent to forge connections between his own life and that of his subjects—they all finish. The silence, because of its suddenness, is deafening.

Why? It is not as if Ashoka suddenly passed away. In fact if the literary chronicles in which the last years of his rulership and death figure are to be believed, he continued to rule for about a decade after promulgating the Seventh Pillar Edict till around 232 BCE. But he ceased to speak through public messages on stone. It is possible that new inscriptions will be discovered bearing regnal dates of that last decade, but as things stand our knowledge of Ashoka's dotage comes from the same old chronicles that were composed centuries after his reign and which were written often with the intention of deifying him. The story of Ashoka's life, then, is back where it began, embedded in unverifiable tradition. The historical issue remains: is there a way of making sense of Ashoka's unhappy twilight years from these sources that are for such purposes dubious?

We don't for a start know exactly how many years elapsed from the last edict in the twenty-seventh year after his coronation to the year of his death. His end is surmised as having happened less than ten years after the last edict from 'dates' mentioned in the *Mahavamsa* of Sri Lanka, a text dated to the fifth century CE. The twentieth chapter of this work provides a summary description of Ashoka's last years in the form of a kind of regnal calendar:

> In the eighteenth year (of the reign) of king Dhammasoka, the great Bodhi-tree was planted in the Mahameghavanarama. In the twelfth year afterwards died the dear consort of the king, Asamdhimitta, the faithful (believer) in the Sambuddha. In the fourth year after this the ruler of the earth Dhammasoka raised the treacherous Tissarakka to the rank of queen. In the third year thereafter this fool, in the pride of her beauty, with the thought: 'Forsooth, the king worships the great Bodhi-tree to my cost!' drawn into the power of hate and working her own harm, caused the great Bodhi-tree to perish by means of a mandu-thorn. In the fourth year after did Dhammasoka of high renown fall into the power of mortality. These make up thirty seven years.[1]

If these years are totalled, the events seem to have transpired across some forty-one years and not thirty-seven. However, Ananda Guruge points out that a later commentary on this text explains each year in its account after calculating it twice—as both the preceding and the succeeding year: thus the figure of thirty-seven years. This would mean that there was a gap of some eight years between the death of Ashoka's queen Asamdhimitta (in the twenty-ninth year from his consecration) and Ashoka's death (in the thirty-seventh year from his consecration).[2] Asamdhimitta died, it appears, in 241 BCE within a year from the time the emperor issued his Seventh Pillar Edict. If this is what happened, grief and personal preoccupations may have prevented the composing of further edicts.

While the corroboration of calendrical exactitude in the *Mahavamsa* is a difficult matter, the condensed way in which it provides the information—as a stray departure with no seeming link at all with the main story—is significant. Six short verses speak of Ashoka's end before the narrative resumes its history of Buddhism in Sri Lanka. The *Mahavamsa* is known to have derived a great deal from the *Dipavamsa* but the latter text is silent about Ashoka's last years. The only possible conclusion is that the brief account in the former is some version of the popular view about Ashoka's last years in this part of South Asia in the fifth century.

In terms of the internal logic of the *Mahavamsa*, it is not fortuitous that the account of Ashoka's later years begins in the eighteenth year of his rule, with a sapling of the Bodhi tree being brought to Sri Lanka: the chapter preceding the passage quoted primarily concerns itself with 'The coming of the Bodhi-tree' to Sri Lanka,[3] carried there from the eastern Indian port of Tamralipti by Ashoka's daughter Sanghamitra. She had become a nun and appears as the tree's primary guardian on this voyage, terrifying into submission certain serpents ('Nagas') who seemed interested in acquiring it. The sacred sapling was planted in the Mahameghavanarama, where 'the king of trees, the great Bodhi-tree, lasted a long time on the island of Lanka.'[4] This section of the text is followed almost immediately by six verses which recount the manner in which the 'great Bodhi-tree' of Mahabodhi came to be destroyed, the juxtaposition serving the purpose of underlining the different destinies of the two trees, the original in the north and its offshoot on the island. Ashoka's end, recounted immediately after the fate of the Bodhi tree, seems to indicate that even while the chronology of his twilight regnal years is not a calendar concocted by this chronicle, positioning Ashoka's death after elaborating in detail on the fate of the Bodhi tree in Sri Lanka is not incidental but deliberate. The underlying logic seems to be to decry the fate of the faith in the land of its origin while hailing its reception and long life in Lanka.

The contrast in the actions of the two women associated with Ashoka also links with the differing histories of Buddhism in the mainland and the island. Sanghamitra is the protector of the plant in Sri Lanka, Tissarakkha its destroyer back home. The chronicle remembers the last years of Ashoka in relation to the divergence in the behaviour of his queens and the differing nature of their engagement with Buddhism. Asamdhimitta, his 'dear consort', was a faithful devotee of the Buddha and her death is the beginning of Ashoka's end. Her place was taken, after an interregnum, by the beautiful but jealous Tissarakkha whose resentment of Ashoka's devotion to the Buddha results in a protracted vengeance with the emperor passing away after four years. The evil queen's ability to destroy something as sacred to the emperor as the Bodhi tree suggests that her husband was by then no longer the master of state affairs.

Ashoka's wives evidently become either good or bad here depending upon whether they supported or thwarted the emperor's engagement with the Buddha and his faith.[5] At the same time, the powerful voice of his queen in accounts of his later life supplements that of his queen Karuvaki in the epigraphs. The image of the latter there is of a self-possessed and strong-willed consort wanting an act of philanthropy recorded as specifically hers. The king's later consort as powerful figure—via the story of Tissarakkha's violence against the Bodhi tree—is in line with the motif of a king somewhat often besotted by his queens to the point of being under their thumbs. An emotional monarch, it might be inferred—if his queens can be interpreted as having been allowed so considerable a degree of control over his life and the realm's. Such an inference would be in keeping with the sentimentality of several of the edicts.

The Lady Macbeth figure in Ashoka's life is a character in the Northern Buddhist tradition as well, the villainous queen Tishyarakshita occupying substantial space in the *Ashokavadana*, which like the *Mahavamsa* narrates her animosity towards the Bodhi tree. Truth or myth, the story seems to have been widely believed across

various Buddhist traditions of the first millennium CE, from China
to Lanka. The *Ashokavadana* version is far more elaborate though
different in several of its details. It shows the jealousy of Tishyarakshita as stemming from her ignorance about who this 'Bodhi'
really was. Apparently, because Ashoka offered his most precious
jewels to Bodhi, she thought Bodhi was a woman and thus a rival.
She was incensed because 'although the king pursues his pleasure
with me, he sends all the best jewels to Bodhi's place.'[6] She paid
money to a sorceress to destroy Bodhi. The sorceress chanted 'some
mantras and tied a thread around the Bodhi tree.' The tree began
to wither and Ashoka fainted when the news reached him. Upon
regaining consciousness the heartbroken monarch said he would
die if the Bodhi tree perished. When Tishyarakshita consoled the
sorrowful Ashoka by saying that if Bodhi died she would pleasure
him, he realized how ignorant she was: 'Bodhi is not a woman', said
the king, 'but a tree; it is where the Blessed One attained unsurpass-
ed enlightenment.'[7] Realizing her mistake, the queen summoned
the sorceress to revive the tree and the dying tree was restored to
life. The queen's vengeance and violence are leitmotifs in both
accounts but the outcomes of their actions differ radically, the
moral of the story in the *Mahavamsa* being doom laden in relation
to Buddhism in India after Ashoka, while the *Ashokavadana* suggests
revival and subsequent continuity.

Tishyarakshita figures again and more powerfully some chapters
later in connection with Kunala, Ashoka's son by Queen Padmavati.
Named after a variety of avifauna called 'Kunala'—his bright and
beautiful eyes were similar to those of the bird—the infant grew
into a solitude-loving prince. During one of his meditative sojourns
Tishyarakshita is consumed by a burning desire for this handsome
prince. Finding him alone, she embraces him and declares: 'I get a
burning feeling inside as though a forest fire were consuming a dry
wood.'[8] Kunala says she is akin to his mother and spurns her 'non-
dharmic' advance, whereupon she tells him he is not destined to last
much longer. When Taxila rises in rebellion, Kunala is sent to quell it.
In the meantime Ashoka is struck by a virulent ailment: 'excrement
began to come out of his mouth, and an impure substance oozed
out of all his pores.'[9] No doctors can cure him and made desperate

by the thought of his impending end Ashoka expresses a desire to get Kunala to return and succeed him on the throne. Tishyarakshita, fearful of the consequences to her life if this transpires, is now determined to cure the emperor. She first asks Ashoka to forbid all doctors from tending to him. She next instructs his doctors to bring anyone suffering from the same disease to her; in fact, her *modus operandi* in finding a cure for Ashoka is the most compelling part of this tale:

> Tisyaraksita said to the doctors: 'If any man or woman should come to you suffering from a disease similar to that of the king, I would like to see him immediately.'
>
> Before long, it happened that a certain Abhira man was stricken with just such a disease. His wife went to see a doctor and described the illness to him. 'Bring him in', said the doctor, 'I will examine him and then prescribe some medicine.' However, as soon as the Abhira was brought to him, he took him straight to Tisyaraksita. She, in secret, had him killed, and when he was dead, she split open his belly and examined the stomach. She found inside it a large worm; when it moved, excrement would ooze out of the man's mouth, and when it went down, it would flow out down below.
>
> The queen then ground some peppercorns and gave them to the worm, but he did not die. She tried long peppers and ginger, but again with no success. Finally, she gave some onion to the worm; immediately it died and passed through the intestinal tract.
>
> She then went to Asoka and prescribed this treatment. 'My lord, eat an onion and you will recover.'
>
> 'Queen', the king objected, 'I am a ksatriya; how can I eat an onion?'
>
> 'My lord', she replied, 'this is medicine; take it for the sake of life!'
>
> Asoka then ate it; the worm died, and passed out through his intestines, and he fully recovered.[10]

Killing another woman's ill husband to cure her own is not very dharmic, but as we have seen in relation to Kunala this was not a queen to be kept at bay by minor dharmic considerations when something desperate and compelling required doing. Women of decisive action and swift intervention in the lives of monarchs are something of a rarity in ancient India, making Tishyarakshita seem admirable for her singularly surgical way of dealing with life in difficult times.

The malevolence of his intelligent queen is expanded upon at length with Ashoka's recovery, the grateful monarch granting Tishyarakshita a boon. She asks to be made the monarch for seven days, and, the wish granted, shows she has lost none of the old decisiveness by moving quickly to destroy Kunala. A letter addressed to the people of Taxila orders them to put out his eyes. After some understandable hesitation by the letter's recipients, they do as requested and gouge the eyes out. The blinded Kunala and his wife return to Pataliputra where they learn of Tishyarakshita's villainy. A furious Ashoka disowns her in a very un-Ashokan manner, threatening to tear her eyes out and 'rip open her body with sharp rakes, impale her alive on a spit, cut off her nose with a saw, cut out her tongue with a razor, and fill her with poison and kill her.'[11] Kunala's view of the matter, luckily, is less un-Buddhist than his father's and he pleads forgiveness for her. This magnanimity results in his own sight returning but does not lead to absolution for the queen. On Ashoka's orders, Tishyarakshita is burned to death in a 'lacquer house'; for good measure, we are told, he 'had the citizens of Taksasila executed as well.'[12]

There is clearly a recurrence of elements ascribed in the *Ashokavadana* to Ashoka's last years which formed part of his life as a prince. Like Kunala, he had as a young man been sent to Taxila to put down a provincial revolt, this being followed at once by his father falling very ill. Court intrigue—by ministers in Bindusara's court earlier, by the chief queen at Ashoka's end—is the calculation coming into play among power-brokers of state who seek to ensure a transition favourable to themselves. The recurrence of such a pattern of departure, illness, and intrigue to indicate the conditions of regime change is essentially a literary trope for signalling the conclusion of a monarchical tenure. But Ashoka's story does not end here.

Some last episodes of his life remain to be recounted. The blood and gore of Tishyarakshita and Taxila give way to a pleasanter, gentler tapestry of the dying days, 'dana' being the peg on which the *Ashokavadana* hangs its final tale, aptly titled 'Ashoka's Last Gift'.[13] From the time he became a Buddhist, Ashoka has been shown as regularly making all kinds of donations to the Sangha.

In this he was hoping to equal what a celebrated householder, Anathapindaka, had donated to the Buddha, namely one hundred 'kotis' of gold pieces. Ashoka's donations, as he neared his end, amounted to only ninety-six kotis. When he became ill he felt he had to make up the balance soon and had begun sending gold coins to the Kukkutarama monastery.

At this point Ashoka's heir apparent Sampadin (Kunala's son) and the state counsellers stepped in, issuing an order prohibiting such disbursement from the treasury. The emperor subverted them by finding other routes for donation, first giving away the gold dishes in which his food was served, then his silver plates, and finally the copper. His powers clipped, he is depicted as stating in the *Ashokavadana*: 'Who now could deny the saying of the Blessed One that "All fortune is the cause of misfortune?" Truth-speaking Gautama asserted that, and indeed he was right! Today, I am no longer obeyed; no matter how many commands I think of issuing, they are all countermanded just like a river that is turned back when it dashes against a mountain cliff.'

Thwarted and reduced, his sole possession now is only half an 'amalaka' (myrobalan). And yet he summons a man to take it to the monks at Kukkutarama, instructing him to say to them that this, his last offering, should be 'distributed in such a way that it is offered to and enjoyed by the whole community.' The half-fruit is mashed and put into a soup distributed to the whole community. This happens even as the Elder of the Sangha tells the monks about the nature of the emotions that come into play at the sight of an unhappy emperor shorn of all that distinguished his rule:

> A great donor, the lord of men,
> the eminent Maurya Asoka,
> has gone from being lord of Jambudvipa
> to being lord of half a myrobalan.
> Today this lord of the earth,
> his sovereignty stolen by his servants
> presents the gift of just half a myrobalan,
> as though reproving the common folk
> whose hearts are puffed up
> with a passion for enjoying great splendour.

The final embellishment given to the image of Ashoka is that of Supreme Donor. On the eve of his death, thanks to this last gift, his sovereign powers are restored to him—whereupon the dying emperor promptly proceeds to donate the whole earth to the Sangha, excluding only the state treasury (what the earth was worth minus the state treasury is conjectural). The donation of the earth to the Sangha was inscribed with his teeth. This act of using his teeth to seal a bequest asserted royal authority in the most unambiguous way. The composer of the *Ashokavadana* would no doubt have been surprised had he known that, many centuries later in England, the gift of lands to Paulyn de Rawdon was said to have been formalized in an identical way by William the Conqueror:

> I William, king, the third of my reign,
> Give to Paulyn Rawdon, Hope and Hopetowne,
> With all the bounds both up and downe,
> From heaven to yerthe, from yerthe to hel,
> For thee and thyne there to dwell.
> As truly as this kingright is mine,
> For a crossbow and an arrow.
> When I sal come to hunt on yarrow;
> And in token that this thing is sooth,
> I bit the whyt wax with my tooth,
> Before Meg, Mawd, and Margery,
> And my third son Henry.[14]

Ashoka is supposed to have died after sealing the document containing his donation. It was said that eventually a new king could only succeed Ashoka after the whole earth had been bought back by the ministers of the Maurya court, who agreed to give four kotis of gold pieces to complete Ashoka's shortfall.

The end is poignant, dramatic, and ironic all at once. His dying words emphasize that his last act was not to seek the rewards of rebirth or the glories of kingship but mastery over the mind: 'because I give it with faith, I would obtain as the fruit of this gift something that cannot be stolen, that is honoured by the aryas and safe from all agitation: sovereignty of the mind.'

With his last breath, the emperor sacrifices an entire empire—the empire that he had once so fiercely usurped.

# Epilogue

## The Emperor's Afterlife

WHEN ASHOKA'S COMMUNICATIONS TO HIS PEOPLE ceased, his historical persona, for all practical purposes, ceased as well; and some years later, around 232 BCE, he passed away. Yet in the centuries after his death his memory lived on, and in ways that go well beyond the events and drama of his life. His afterlife is in fact a configuration of diverse and fascinating threads made up of material relics and writings stretching across more than two millennia. In ancient and medieval India Ashoka was remembered in legendary accounts, court chronicles, travel tales, and epigraphs. To this one may add what more contemporary times have contributed to that memorialization: he has figured in film and fiction, on public architecture, in the lives and work of India's national heroes, and through Indian national symbols. The desire to deploy remembrances and memorializations of this emperor is practically irresistible among Indians. A consequence of this has been that in reconstructions of the life and times of Ashoka the line which divides history and memory is frequently blurred.

In attempting to recover the historical Ashoka I have tried to separate out these threads, highlighting in the early chapters the various possibilities and challenges of using later legends and chronicles which evoke him. Even as I have dipped into those accounts to reconstruct large parts of his life and times—for which there is nothing remotely contemporary—the core of my narrative revolves around Ashoka's own voice and the archaeological histories of the landscapes where it resonated. Now, I return to recall Ashoka's afterlife, or some of the meanderings that have not found a place in my narrative, through which the memory of this extraordinary emperor survived before modern scholarship discovered him.[1] While a monograph is waiting to be written on the pastiche of stories and images around him, here I look only at elements in the remembrance of things Ashokan. I do this to highlight the fact that he was a sovereign around whom a long tradition of memorialization came to be consolidated, as also to assess in broad brushstrokes what was retained of his historical life and what forgotten.

It is necessary, first, to keep in mind that, even though a great deal is not known about them, the Maurya dynasty's kings continued to rule for several decades after Ashoka's death. While narratives of Ashoka's unhappy last days are entangled within legends, historical events in the lives of the emperor's successors are not even known by such; and the dearth of contemporary chronicles and accounts of the Ashoka years persists into those of his successors. No Mauryan ruler after Ashoka set down a substantial body of epigraphs on stone. None was visited by a chronicler-ambassador from a foreign land, as Chandragupta was by Megasthenes. Even when these years find mention in traditions that were put together several centuries later, elementary information, such as the names and number of kings in the succession line of the later Mauryas, remains in dispute.

Ashoka's successors do not figure in the Pali chronicles of Sri Lanka either. Those texts lose interest in the Maurya dynastic line after the emperor's death, presumably because by then his Buddhist progeny were firmly ensconced on the island. There are, moreover, discrepancies in the list of successors that figure in texts of the Northern Buddhist tradition and the Brahmanical *Puranas*; in the *Puranas* the succession details are not uniformly similar. Much of the literature on Ashoka's successors consists of hair-splitting disputes over royal names, regnal numbers, and precise orders of succession.

The Puranic litany of names of Mauryan rulers, depending on the text, mention anything between four and seven as the number to follow Ashoka, while the variations in the Buddhist tradition about the number of monarchs after Ashoka range between two and five.[2] Evidently, those who ruled in the decades after Ashoka did not manage to emulate the long reigns of the first three emperors of the line. The *Puranas* are unanimous that Maurya dynastic suzerains ruled for some 137 years. So if the first three—Chandragupta, Bindusara, and Ashoka—account for some 85 years, the later Mauryas will have ruled for only 52. Whether there were three or seven rulers who shared this half century from *circa* 232 BCE to 180 BCE, each will have followed his predecessor far more quickly than did the big three.[3]

Still, some ancient Indian kings seem to have managed to do a great deal to be remembered by in their short reigns of eight to ten years. Pulumavi, the last king of the later Andhra Satavahana dynasty, ruled for only seven years (*c.* 226–232 CE) but is known by the coins that he struck, from inscriptions issued in his time as a shrine builder, and as a monarch who ruled over large parts of Maharashtra and Karnataka.[4] Naturally, one imagines that the kings who succeeded Ashoka made a range of interventions as they administered their patrimony. But what these interventions were or who they patronized, and whether Ashoka's legacy of humane governance was followed or jettisoned by them, are issues that don't figure in contemporaneous sources. Most of the later Mauryas remain mere names, unknown in the sources of the late centuries BCE and only rarely appearing as rounded historical subjects in later texts.

The *Ashokavadana's* list typically underlines this when the seven kings succeeding Ashoka are mentioned thus: 'Sampadin's son was Brhaspati who, in turn, had a son named Vrsasena, and Vrsasena had a son named Pusyadharman, and Pusyadharman begot Pusyamitra.'[5] Sampadin, it has been suggested, was the same as the Samprati mentioned in Jaina literature. He featured some pages ago, in the account of Ashoka's unhappy last years, as inheritor of the kingdom. In Jaina literature, on the other hand, Samprati is said to have converted to the Jaina faith and 'he did for

Jainism nearly everything that Ashoka did for Buddhism such as building temples and spreading the faith.'[6] So, different traditions provide different versions of Samprati. Strangely, the last Maurya ruler in the *Ashokavadana*, Pushyamitra, is also the name of the person who is said to have *killed* the last ruler—an event which, in effect, ended the Maurya dynastic line.[7] Pushyamitra, according to the *Puranas* and the *Harshacarita*, was a general in the army of Brhidratha, from whom he usurped the throne and founded a new dynasty—that of the Shungas.[8] So, one is not even sure of the reliability of the names that make up the Maurya line in the *Ashokavadana*. What one can gather is that this text considered the Maurya Pushyamitra anti-Buddhist. Apparently he became so on the advice of a mean-minded Brahman priest and undertook to eradicate the religion by destroying the very monasteries and killing the very monks Ashoka had so zealously nurtured. It was a Yaksha along with his future son-in-law who eventually rescued Buddhism and ensured Pushyamitra's death. With this, we are told, 'the Mauryan lineage came to an end.'[9] Is it possible that this is a jumbled up remembrance of how the Maurya line ended? That the dynasty dropped off the horizon of ancient India because its last scion unsuccessfully sought to overturn Ashoka's legacy is a wonderful story, especially for Buddhist admirers of the emperor, but its historical accuracy is impossible to determine.

One thing is certain. Of the later kings that figure in the Puranic and Buddhist traditions, there is only one Maurya, namely Dash-aratha, who appears as a historical figure in the sense that he happens to feature in a source contemporary with his reign. This Dasharatha was a grandson of Ashoka, and, following in his grand-father's footsteps, he made himself known through engravings on rock in structures that he caused to be built. Ashoka's imprint on him can in fact be seen in more ways than one. Calling himself 'Devanam-priya', Dasharatha put up dedicatory inscriptions at caves similar to those at Barabar, in the adjacent Nagarjuni hill. Like Ashoka again, Dasharatha had these caves excavated for the Ajivikas.[10] They were highly polished chambers, with names like Gopika, Vahiyaka, and Vadathika, created as rainy season shelters:

the donative epigraph on the Vahiyaka cave tells us that it 'has been given by Dasalatha, dear to the gods, to the venerable Ajivikas, immediately on his accession, to be a place of abode during the rainy season as long as the moon and sun shall endure.'

We do not know why Dasharatha chose to follow his grandfather in patronizing the Ajivikas, but his hope that the shelters would serve for them 'as long as the moon and sun endure' remained unfulfilled. Subsequently, 'Ajivikehi' was the one expression removed or defaced from Maurya epigraphs in the Barabar and Nagarjuni caves, and this selective removal very likely means that the caves were taken over by other religious groups.[11] Since those who chose to so carefully cut out the name of the Ajivikas would have been familiar with the Brahmi script, it is likely that they did so soon after the demise of the Mauryas. In the ensuing centuries, no ruler in North India is known to have provided any kind of patronage to the Ajivikas. There are no inscriptions of any king among the slew of dynasties that followed—the Shungas, Kushanas, and Guptas to name a few—alluding either to the Ajivikas or to donations to them.

On the other hand Buddhism continued to consolidate and prosper, and it was within its religious iconography and texts that parts of Ashoka's life came to be vividly imaged. The spectacular growth of the religion was visible in the construction and expansion of monumental stupas, viharas, and chaityas. Interestingly, these seem to have depended no longer on the patronage of proactive Buddhist rulers. Instead, common folk from diverse walks of life now made this possible. Sanchi in Central India was one of the places to which Ashoka had been partial, possibly because of his association with Devi: as we saw, he had had a brick stupa constructed and a sandstone pillar put up adjacent to it. This stupa saw a virtual reconstruction in the second century BCE, following the end of the Maurya dynasty. Not only did it expand visibly in size, its enlarged brick dome now came to be encased in stone and surrounded by a stone balustrade. The epigraphs on the balustrade reveal a staggering extravagance of donations by sundry people who supported the building programme here, including the pupils of particular teachers, lay worshippers, bankers, merchants, mothers, housewives, monks, and nuns. The donors came from near and far, from cities associated with the early life of Ashoka such as Vidisha and Ujjayini, and from more distant ones like Prathisthanapura and Pokhara.[12]

Around the same time there becomes visible the start of a tradition of sculptural art marked by strikingly carved Buddhist reliefs of events and individuals, real and legendary. Within this tradition we now see, for the first time, the imaging of elements of architecture and artefacts that Ashoka had set up at places of Buddhist worship. Among the earliest of these Ashoka-centred portrayals are features that Ashoka had added to the Mahabodhi sacred area—such as the throne that he had donated and the temple which he had had built. Less than a hundred years after his interventions, these additions were represented on a massive stone railing at Bharhut near Rewa in Central India. The railing surrounded a stupa and, like the Sanchi specimen, was built with donations by pilgrims from distant places like Vidisha, Kaushambi, and Pataliputra.[13] Unlike Sanchi's relatively plain railing, though, the one in Bharhut was luxuriantly carved with bas reliefs devoted to various subjects ranging from life scenes of the Buddha to Jataka stories about the Buddha's previous births.[14] Naturally, Mahabodhi, where the Buddha attained enlightenment, appears graphically represented. Ashoka's embellishments to the scene of supreme holiness thereby themselves gain concrete embellishment.

At this point in time the Great Sage was not represented in human form, his presence being indicated by a series of symbols. Several of these—a Bodhi tree, a wheel, and a stupa, for instance— were integrally associated with his enlightenment, his first sermon, and the aftermath of his demise. A symbol that now gained popularity to denote the Buddha was what Ashoka had donated at Mahabodhi—the majestic stone throne known as the vajrasana.[15] A sculptural relief on a pillar at Bharhut shows the Bodhi tree with the vajrasana in front. An identifying epigraph alludes to 'the building round the Bodhi tree of the holy Sakamuni'. The vajrasana is recognizable because of its monumental size, its slab and four supporting pilasters making it look somewhat similar to how it appears today. The relief also shows a pillar with a bell-shaped capital bearing the figure of an elephant, which could well be the sculptor's remembrance of an Ashokan specimen.[16] Similarly, the pillared religious sanctuary depicted here—the building mentioned in the inscription—was possibly the temple that Ashoka is said to have constructed at Mahabodhi.

The emperor himself is absent from the Buddhist iconography at Bharhut. This is not because rulers do not figure in such iconography. They do: rulers such as Pasenadi of Kosala and Ajatashatru of Magadha do appear, but these were monarchs who happened to be contemporaries of the Buddha.[17] It would take a couple of centuries for Ashoka to be similarly imaged. Eventually, he came to be remembered in this form in the early part of the first century CE on sculpted columns and lintels of the remarkable gateways which were set up at the four entrances to the stupas at Sanchi. There was, however, one major difference. Unlike Bharhut, where labels identify the kings, no identifying epigraphs accompany the figures depicted at Sanchi—neither those relating to incidents in the life of the Buddha nor to those of his patron Ashoka nor even to mythical characters from old tales and legends. Identifications have been subsequent, worked out on the basis of the subject matter of reliefs which follow the textual narratives of Buddhist stories. So, Ashoka's presence on them is based on correlations made between sculpture and story. Scholars centrally involved in the conservation and documentation of the wonderful narrative friezes at Sanchi had little doubt that some of Ashoka's visits to Buddhist places of pilgrimage were interwoven with the various stories carved on parts of the Sanchi monuments, and it is on their judgement that we must rely.

The southern gateway (or torana) of the great stupa, for instance, shows Ashoka's visit to the Ramagrama stupa.[18] In the *Ashokavadana* account he had travelled there to take possession of one of the original relic deposits of the Buddha. Ashoka is shown with the royal insignia—a turban, ewer, and fly whisk, the traditional umbrella being absent—on a chariot in an impressive procession including elephants and arms-bearing troops. The sculpted narrative—dominated by hooded Nagas and Nagis worshipping the stupa—also tells us that the Nagas resisted Ashoka and successfully circumvented his quest to dig out the relics. The southern gateway's western pillar shows the same royal personage, but quite differently: this time on his visit to the Bodhi tree.[19] The sacred tree was, as we saw in the *Ashokavadana's* account of the unhappy last years, dying out because of the jealous ignorance of Queen Tishyarakshita. So Ashoka is not here a king leading a regal procession but a figure of sorrow evoking sympathy. He is supported by two queens and seems about to swoon with grief (Fig. Epilogue 1). Above this, another panel shows the Bodhi tree, decorated with streamers and a crowning umbrella and surrounded by a temple—presumably the one Ashoka built. The same sort of representation, and of the same period, can be seen on another stupa at Sanchi (Stupa 2). This is halfway down the hill on which the great stupa stands, its railing adorned by many carvings. One of these is of Ashoka supported by his two queens and surrounded by attendants carrying the insignias of royalty.[20]

Other emblems associated with the emperor also figure. Wheel-bearing pillars, monoliths crowned with capitals of four lions, the vajrasana at Mahabodhi—all clearly recognizable as Ashokan—were constantly and conspicuously carved into the gateways of Sanchi. Several pillars of Shunga and Gupta times also imitated the Ashokan monoliths. The Shunga period pillar at Sanchi, with its capital of lotus leaves, and the four lions capital of the Gupta pillar there, have elements modelled on the Ashokan pillar.[21] These commemorations in stone help preserve memory of the emperor, though once Ashoka himself starts being engraved as a figure in sculptural reliefs he assumes an even clearer historical shape which then grows into his best-known avatara. Interestingly, in modern India it is the connection between the Bodhi tree and the women in Ashoka's life which continues as a popular leitmotif among artists, especially in the works of those who were part of the Indian nationalist art movement. Tishyarakshita looking at the Bodhi tree, for instance, was painted by Abanindranath Tagore, while Nandlal

Fig. Epilogue 2: Depiction of wheel-bearing pillar at Sanchi

Bose and Upendra Maharathi drew Sanghamitra carrying the Bodhi tree to Sri Lanka.

About a hundred years after the Sanchi depictions, in the second century CE a variation of their version of Ashoka came to be carved at the stupa in Kanaganahalli in Karnataka. This stupa stood, as we saw earlier, in the vicinity of the location where Ashoka's major edicts were inscribed on both faces of a stone slab. The upper drum (or Medhi) of the stupa here, unlike at Sanchi, was veneered with large sculpted panels that depicted events in the life of the Buddha and most uniquely included several portraits of royal personalities.[22] This gallery includes kings with their consorts, most often rulers of the Satavahana dynasty who happened to be the chief patrons of Kanaganahalli at this point in time.[23] Each appears with an epigraphic label designating them 'Raya Matalako', 'Raya Sundara Satakarni', and so on. It is at Ashoka, or 'Raya Asoko' as he is described here, that we need to pause.

There are two panels whose subject matter is Ashoka, with label inscriptions identifying him by name. One of these is like the Satavahana portraits. By this I mean that, unlike Sanchi, Ashoka does not feature on the panel as part of a narrative scene. Instead, his queen and he dominate the register. Apart from the queen, there are female 'chauri' bearers and a female umbrella bearer.[24] The royal couple seems to be sharing a tender moment: Ashoka's face is turned towards his queen while she looks at him with adoration. The subject matter of the second panel's lower register, also bearing the five-lettered label 'Raya Asoko', is qualitatively different from the portrait depiction. Ashoka stands to the left of the Bodhi tree with several others who are shown worshipping in a similar way. The excavator of Kanaganahalli believed one of these was Prince Mahinda and the woman behind the king his daughter Sangha-mitra.[25] Whether this was so or not, the frieze is a powerful reminder that in the imagination of ancient India the presence of the emperor was frequently evoked in relation to Mahabodhi, snapshots of which can be seen all the way from Bharhut to Kanaganahalli.

The strength of this association—between the place where the Buddha attained enlightenment and where India's Buddhist emperor built a shrine in his memory—is evident from its spread beyond the territories over which Ashoka had ruled. Bodh Gaya was an exceptionally important place for pilgrims and patrons from Myanmar.[26] The historian Upinder Singh points out that the importance attached to the Mahabodhi temple is manifest in Myanmar from epigraphs, as also from its representation in the form of temple models, and depictions on seals and plaques. The inscriptions which record Myanmarese 'repair missions' to Maha-bodhi, ranging from the medieval to the modern, are those in which Ashoka figures prominently. A thirteenth century CE epi-graph from Bodh Gaya, written in the Burmese language and script, while recording a mission for repair dispatched by a king Dhamma-raja from Burma, simultaneously remembers the building of the original temple there by Ashoka. 'When 218 years of the Buddha's dispensation had elapsed, one of the 84,000 *caityas* built by Siri Dhammasoka (i.e. the Maurya emperor Asoka), king of Jambud-vipa, at the place where the milk rice offering had been made (a clear reference to Sujata's offering of *payasa* to Siddhartha at Bodhgaya) fell into ruin due to the stress of age and time.' [27] A similar association was made more than five hundred years later when, in 1875, Mindon, king of Burma, sought permission to renovate the Mahabodhi complex: he too invoked Ashoka. Two millennia had passed since the Mauryan emperor was active there, with many phases of renovation since, and yet the Burmese king said he wanted to undertake the 'repair of the sacred chaitya built by the King Dharmasoka over the site of the Aparajita throne.'[28]

A different kind of remembrance which also stretched across a wider expanse appeared in the accounts of another group of Asian pilgrims, the Buddhist Chinese monks who travelled to India. This began in around the fifth century CE, before the Burmese endowments at Bodh Gaya, when Faxian came from Changan city in Shensi across a northern route that traversed Central Asia. He travelled extensively in India and then moved to Sri Lanka. His purpose in India was to obtain the correct rules and regulations of the *Vinaya Pitaka* texts. His travels were simultaneously a variant on anthropological fieldwork, a kind of ethnographic document-ation of what he noticed, ranging from the topography of the lands through which he passed to the sorts of clothes that people wore, the festivals and tales around places and people, the nature of shrines (Buddhist and Brahmanic) and monasteries, and a great deal else. His account highlights the fact that, some six hundred years after Ashoka's death, his memory was alive and well and had wormed its way into places stretching from the hilly ranges of north-west India to the Gangetic plains in the east. The Chinese monk mentions Gandhara as the place where Ashoka's son had governed; Sankisa as the holy place where Ashoka was reported to have 'erected a stone pillar thirty cubits high, and on the top placed the figure of a lion'; Ramagrama as the stupa site whose relics the emperor unsuccess-fully coveted; and Pataliputra as the city where he reigned.[29]

300 ASHOKA IN ANCIENT INDIA

Faxian described practically every place in relation to legends around Ashoka. Some of these he would have known from the Chinese version of the *Ashokavadana*, others would have been recounted by local people. Sometimes there is a mixture of both. This is suggested by his description of a message that he believed was encoded in Ashoka's epigraph at Pataliputra. The inscription was on a stone pillar and, in the words of Faxian, recorded that 'King Asoka presented the whole of Jambudvipa to the priests of the four quarters, and redeemed it again with money, and this he did three times.'[30] This story, as the poignant end to Ashoka's life has highlighted, figures in the *Ashokavadana* and Faxian would have been familiar with it. However, there was no allusion in that text to these deeds of the emperor being engraved on a pillar. Possibly, this tale was told to him by the local folk at Pataliputra who, like him, would have seen the surface of a pillar ascribed to Ashoka as bearing an indecipherable inscribed message. Evidently, by this time, the Brahmi script in which the Ashokan epigraphs were written, was no longer understood, allowing the writing to be 'read' in ways which satisfied the beliefs and expectations of local antiquarians and pilgrim travellers.

Local folk memory around Ashokan relics seems in this instance to have been uncommonly long lived. Some two hundred years later, such evidence of Ashoka's long afterlife in popular memory centres on a story around the Pataliputra pillar told by that other famous Chinese pilgrim, Xuanzang, who came to India in the seventh century. The principal part of the 'mutilated inscription' on the pillar, in his words, stated that 'Asoka-raja with a firm principle of faith has thrice bestowed Jambudvipa as a religious offering on Buddha, the Dharma and the assembly, and thrice he has redeemed it with his jewels and treasure; and this is the record thereof.'[31] Xuanzang had a remarkable appetite for antiquarian detail, noting such facts about many other places to which he travelled or where he halted.

He encountered Ashokan stone pillars at many places, including Sravasti, Varanasi, Niglihawa (described as the place of the Krakuchhanda Buddha), and Lumbini. Occasionally, the existing state of the pillar is also described. The Lumbini pillar was broken in the middle. This was because it fell to the ground, we are told, 'by the contrivance of a wicked dragon'.[32] The glittering veneer of an Ashokan column near Varanasi is admired, 'bright and shining as a mirror; its surface is glistening and smooth as ice.'[33]

While the memory of Ashoka having set up stone pillars persisted, what his epigraphs recorded was entirely forgotten. The pillar at Niglihawa, while recognized as Ashokan, is said to have been engraved with 'a record connected with the nirvana' of an earlier Buddha.[34] Later, even the connection of such pillars with Ashoka was forgotten. One sees, from an absence in chronicles about the fourteenth-century ruler Firuz Shah Tughlaq, that when he brought the Topra and Meerut pillars of Ashoka to Delhi their creator king's name does not feature, suggesting it was not known. The Buddhist connections of some of the pillars may have survived all the same. In Nepal, as we saw, Ripumalla, also a fourteenth-century ruler, inscribed his name and the message 'Om Mani Padme Hum'—the mantra common among Tibetan Buddhists—on the Ashokan pillars at Lumbini and Nigali Sagar. This suggests that these locations continued to be important places of pilgrimage, even among royalty. Ripumalla's decision to inscribe his message on Ashoka's pillars may well mean that he saw these monoliths as connected with an important Buddhist king of past times.

But coming back to Xuanzang: in addition to Ashokan pillars his account preserves vivid memories and graphic stories about stupas constructed by 'Ashoka Raja'. Stupas that he believes were built by Ashoka are among the shrines he documents, all the way from Gandhara to the Gangetic plains. Almost inevitably, from this pilgrim's progress through India it would seem that most stupas commemorated places relating to incidents in the Buddha's life. Nagarhara is an example of this. Here a carved stone stupa 'built by Ashoka Raja' was said to stand, marking the place where 'Sakya, when a Bodhisattva' had met the Dipankara Buddha.[35] Again, an Ashoka stupa, he tells us, stood between the 'Mo-su' sangharama and the 'Shan-ni-lo-shi' valley. In a clear reference to the Sibi Jataka, he asserts that this was where in a previous birth the future Buddha

was said to have chopped up his own body into pieces so as 'to re-
deem a dove from the power of a hawk'.[36] Then there are the stupas
that Xuanzang describes as having been opened up by Ashoka to
remove and redistribute the relics they contained. The Vaishali stupa
was one such, and to authenticate the event he cites Indian texts
which stated that 'In this stupa there was first a quantity of relics
equal to a "hoh" (ten pecks). Asoka-raja opening it, took away nine-
tenths of the whole, leaving only one-tenth behind.'[37] He tells us
that this was something only Ashoka could have done. Apparently,
after Ashoka 'there was a king of the country who wished again to
open the stupa, but at the moment when he began to do so, the
earth trembled, and he dared not proceed to open (the stupa).'[38]

Finally, there were those rare spots where Asoka appears to have
commemorated people and incidents in his own lifetime. Outside
Taxila, for instance, Xuanzang believes he built a stupa which
marked the place where Kunala was blinded on the orders of his
unprincipled stepmother; and 'when the blind pray to it (or before
it) with fervent faith, many of them recover their sight.'[39] How many
of these stupas had actually been constructed by Ashoka? Stone
stupas were unlikely to have been built on his orders, Ashokan
examples being mainly of brick. But evidently, in the seventh century these had come to be regarded by many Buddhist believers as
being of Mauryan antiquity. Interestingly, Xuanzang drew attention to the ruined condition of several such shrines. North-west of
Navadevakula, and at Prayaga, for instance, the stupas seem to have
been in ruins. The traveller has a typical way of alluding to their
state: they are described as possessing a reduced height, invariably
around 100 ft, and the reduction is thought to be a consequence of
their having sunk.[40]

Ashoka's association with many of the places to which Xuanzang
travelled persisted well into the medieval centuries. A good example of this is Sarnath. Here, in the twelfth century the queen of
Govindachandra of Kanauj was inscribed into a record about a
vihara that she had constructed at Sarnath. Kumaradevi was the
name of this queen while the gift was recorded as being made to
'Sri-Dharmachakra Jina'. More specifically, the copper plate grant
says the renovations undertaken at her instance are meant to restore

what existed in the time of Ashoka: 'This Lord of the Turning of the Wheel was restored by her in accordance with the way in which he existed in the days of Dharmasoka, the ruler of men, and even more wonderfully, and this *vihara* for that *sthavira* was elaborately erected by her, and might he, placed there, stay there as long as the moon and sun (endure).'[41] Fourteen hundred years after Ashoka's time a queen's donation chooses to evoke what he built at Sarnath. This is a powerful reminder of the stamp of the emperor having survived, especially in connection with Buddhist sacred places.

We know from Ashoka's own epigraph that he had a close association with Sarnath's monastic community; later sources like Xuanzang's account and Govindachandra's inscription show that this association was never forgotten. There are, on the other hand, a few instances of places where Ashoka's presence came to be invoked that are not specifically associated with the emperor during his lifetime. The kingdom of Kashmir is an example of this. It is described by Xuanzang in ways that strike a resonance with anyone who has visited it—surrounded by high mountains, with a 'cold and stern' climate, people 'handsome in appearance' who loved learning and were 'well instructed'.[42] It also happened to be a region which had its own history, and from this the pilgrim quotes to give Ashoka's connection with the kingdom. Ashoka is said to have built four stupas there. The Chinese visitor believes 'each of these has about a pint measure of relics of the Tathagata.'[43] Ashoka is described as a king of Magadha who 'extended his power over the world, and was honoured even by the most distant people. He deeply reverenced the three gems, and had a loving regard for all living beings.'[44] Of the priests whom the king honoured, though, was a group that became schismatic, and this group Ashoka intended to drown in the Ganga. They, 'having seen the danger threatening their lives, by exercise of their spiritual power flew away', and arriving in Kashmir concealed themselves.[45] When Ashoka-raja heard of this he repented and begged them to return. They refused. Consequently, as atonement, he built 500 monasteries for them in Kashmir.

These vignettes are revealing. It seems that in Kashmir, if Xuanzang is to be believed, there was a strong tradition linking Ashoka with the valley. Within this tradition the emperor was recognized in his political persona—as ruling a large empire; and in his religious role—as the builder of stupas and monasteries. Some five hundred years later Ashoka was again invoked, now in Kashmir's twelfth-century chronicle, the *Rajatarangini* of Kalhana. A learned Sanskrit poet, Kalhana had put together this chronicle replete with historical detail, causing it to be described by its modern translator, M.A. Stein, as a text that came 'nearest in character to the Chronicles of Mediaeval Europe and of the Muhammad[an] East.'[46] Regarding the possibility that the Chinese pilgrim used an early history of Kashmir, Stein noted that Kalhana had got the information on Ashoka in the *Rajatarangini* from an earlier author called Chavillakara.[47] In Chavillakara's list, Ashoka figures first in the king list—as he does in Xuanzang's account of Kashmir.

That said, there are similarities as well as differences in how Ashoka was remembered in the twelfth-century chronicle as against Xuanzang's account. Kalhana, like Xuanzang, drew attention to Ashoka's political prowess, clear from the statement that he reigned 'over the earth'.[48] Kalhana drew attention to his religious persona as well: this king had 'freed himself from sins' and 'embraced the doctrine of Jina'.[49] The reference to Jina is exactly how the twelfth-century Sarnath inscription of Govindachandra had referred to the Buddha. While we are uncertain about how this should be contextualized, what seems certain is that the emperor's personal metamorphosis is what the text appears to be hinting at, and this appears to be based on the memory of a reliable older tradition. Ashoka is also chronicled here as a builder. For the first time, however, we hear of him as the founder of a town, Srinagari, not far from present-day Srinagar. This is described with uncharacteristic hyperbole as 'most important on account of its ninety-six lakhs of houses resplendent with wealth.'[50] As for religious structures, there were two places where he built stupas, Suskaletra and Vitastatra; at the latter he also built a chaitya. He is even said to have built Shiva shrines at Vijayeshvara. One of these was in the form of a stone enclosure, which replaced the old enclosure there, and within it he erected two temples. They were called Ashokeshvara, evidently after the king himself.[51] It was also from the god Shiva, whom 'he had pleased by his austerities', that Ashoka obtained a son—who then exterminated the Mlecchas from Kashmir.[52]

Kalhana's account of Ashoka is followed by his description of the exploits of the son, Jalauka, who succeeded him. No such son is mentioned in any other textual source, not even in the list of kings in the *Puranas*. The family name 'Maurya', which figures in other sources that mention the dynasty, is missing too. The point which emerges from all these reminiscences is that there were genuine local traditions that kept the memory of Ashoka alive, and within these he and his son were seen as having been among Kashmir's early rulers.

The story of Ashoka's association with Kashmir does not end here. It continues into the sixteenth century because the *Rajatarangini* is mentioned in Abu'l Fazl's famous *Ain-i Akbari*. When the imperial standards were carried into Kashmir, Akbar was presented with a copy of this history of Kashmir. Abu'l Fazl says: 'a book called *Raj Tarangini* written in the Sanskrit tongue containing an account of the princes of Kashmir during a period of some four thousand years, was presented to His Majesty. It had been the custom in that country for its rulers to employ certain learned men in writing its annals. His Majesty who was desirous of extending the bounds of knowledge appointed capable interpreters in its translation which in a short time was happily accomplished.'[53] Among the kings narrated as having ruled Kashmir is Ashoka, who 'abolished the Brahmanical religion and established the Jaina faith'.[54] Probably 'Jaina' is a mistranslation of 'Jina'—the word in Kalhana's *Rajatarangini* now repeated in Abu'l Fazl's account. Two of Ashoka's descendants, Jalauka and Damodar (II), also figure here. So Ashoka would have been known in Akbar's court and possibly beyond, via texts that used the *Rajatarangini*.[55]

The several mnemonic ways in which Ashoka's religion and rule survived from his death in the third century BCE to Akbar's day about 1700 years later show that the existence of this ancient ruler was never entirely forgotten. What one may well ask at this point is whether these memories of Ashoka were based on what he had himself put in the public domain or were a kind of concoction. Throughout, my own analysis of the historical Ashoka and of how he fashioned his image has highlighted the centrality of his representation as a Buddhist. His image as royal convert via edicts, his stupas and pillars, his stern proscriptions against the schismatically inclined, his prescriptions to the Sangha—all reinforce the image of the monarch as virtually a Buddhist zealot. Surely, if this image of Ashoka as Buddhist sovereign is so obvious to us, it was also likely to have been the way in which his own subjects would have seen him. The archetypal Buddhist king that so often recurs seems clear evidence of how he had fashioned his image.

Yet there was another pivotal image, also nurtured in Ashoka's own lifetime and through his own edicts: of a compulsively communicative and accessible emperor seeking to reach out to his people, a sharer with them of his atonement for the carnage at Kalinga, a humane governor benevolently engaged with all living beings. In the Buddhist chronicles and texts there was no recollection of *this* persona, nor even the real reason for Ashoka's rethink on rulership in the wake of Kalinga. A similar amnesia marks the representations of events relating to his rulership in the art of ancient India. Storytellers and artists, instead of being attentive to the complexities and several aspects of Ashoka's own words, appear anxious to see him primarily through a Buddhist lens. Thus it was that the political genius of Ashoka faded away, just as knowledge of the scripts in which the words of the emperor were inscribed shrivelled into the dust. Ironically, even when those words came to be recovered and deciphered in the nineteenth century, artistic representations, as we saw with Tagore and Bose, continued to be anchored in Buddhist stories.

Closer to our own time, in the 1960s the artist Meera Mukherjee etched out a more nuanced historical Ashoka in the form of a massive metal sculpture. She is said to have cast Ashoka in this form as a protest against the violence of the Naxalite movement in Bengal during the 1960s.[56] The volume and size of Mukherjee's Ashoka suggests the great power of the emperor, but the sword turned down and the anguished face reflect his transformation at Kalinga (Fig. Epilogue 3).

For all we know, if knowledge of Ashoka's words had survived in all their nuances—as did the memory of Ashoka's Buddhist avatara—he may have been remembered as the founder of a unique political model of humane governance, one which would have been closer to the historical emperor. But in this respect the afterlife of Ashoka, like his real life, remains poised between legend and the truth.

# Appendix

## The Inscriptions of Ashoka

| Inscription and Type | Year of Discovery | Location | Substance |
| --- | --- | --- | --- |
| 1. Girnar—major rock edicts | 1822 | Junagadh district Gujarat | Fourteen edicts which concern diverse subjects: protection of animals from mindless sacrifice; reduction in royal meat consumption; centrality of dhamma; inauguration of dhamma yatras; Kalinga war and its atonement; denunciation of social rituals regarded as superficial; proper courtesy to all kinds of people ranging from slaves to Brahmans; cessation in killing of living beings; public culture in which every |

Appendix (*contd.*)

| Inscription and Type | Year of Discovery | Location | Substance |
|---|---|---|---|
| | | | sect honours every other; king's power to punish forest dwellers; spread of dhammic message to borders and states beyond borders; a foreign policy based on welfare measures; creation of senior officials called dharma-mahamatras. Below 13th rock edict, a surviving line which mentions a 'white elephant' bringing happiness to the world |
| 2. Allahabad-Kosam pillar edicts | 1834 | Allahabad city (could have come from Kaushambi) Uttar Pradesh | Six edicts which concern various subjects: promoting morality to secure worldly and otherworldly happiness; state vigilance in encouraging people to practice dhamma; insistence on self-responsibility for virtuous and evil deeds; granting functional autonomy to rajukkas; recording the release of prisoners and respite for death row convicts; injunctions against killing of animals, birds and fish on particular days, and |

Appendix (*contd.*)

| Inscription and Type | Year of Discovery | Location | Substance |
|---|---|---|---|
| | | | mitigating cruelty towards them |
| 3. Queen's Edict | 1834 | On Allahabad pillar | Records donation of Queen Karuvaki: mango groves, gardens, alms-houses which on her request were registered in her name |
| 4. Lauriya-Araraj pillar edicts | 1834 | Champaran district Bihar | Similar to Allahabad-Kosam edicts |
| 5. Lauriya-Nandangarh pillar edicts | 1834 | Champaran district Bihar | Similar to Allahabad-Kosam edicts |
| 6. Shahbazgarhi major rock edicts | 1836 | Mardan district Pakistan | Similar to Girnar edicts |
| 7. Dhauli-major rock edicts | 1837 | Puri district Orissa | Edicts 1 to 10 and 14 similar to Girnar edicts. Nos. 11–13 here replaced by two separate edicts specifically addressed to Tosali Mahamatras whose affective mould underlines Ashoka's attempt at building bridges with the people of Kalinga. Separate Rock Edict 2 addresses border people in a similar way and is aimed at winning their confidence |

Appendix (*contd.*)

| Inscription and Type | Year of Discovery | Location | Substance |
|---|---|---|---|
| 8. Delhi-Meerut pillar edicts | 1837 | Meerut district (original pillar brought to Delhi) Uttar Pradesh | Similar to Allahabad-Kosam edicts |
| 9. Delhi-Topra pillar edicts | 1837 | Ambala district (original pillar brought to Delhi) Haryana | Six edicts similar to Allahabad-Kosam edicts with the addition of a seventh edict, a retrospective statement where Ashoka sums up the work he had done and points out that while moral restrictions and conversion through persuasion have been his main methods for initiating change, the second of these has been more meaningful |
| 10. Hissar (and Fatehabad) pillar epigraph | 1838 | Hissar district Haryana | Fragments of a few letters that have survived, insufficient to understand message |
| 11. Sasaram-minor rock edict | 1839 | Shahbad district Bihar | Edict speaks of Ashoka becoming a Buddhist, the greater morality he created in Jambudvipa, the availability of this path for everyone, and instructions about engraving his message |
| 12. Bairat-Buddhist rock edict | 1840 | Jaipur district Rajasthan | Edict asks Buddhist community to listen and adhere to |

Appendix (*contd.*)

| Inscription and Type | Year of Discovery | Location | Substance |
|---|---|---|---|
| | | | specific dhammic expositions |
| 13. Barabar cave inscriptions | 1847 | Jahanabad district Bihar | Three epigraphs about donation of caves to ascetics, with Ajivikas mentioned by name |
| 14. Jaugada— major rock edicts | 1850 | Ganjam district Orissa | Same as Dhauli edicts (with Samapa Mahama-tras being addressed) |
| 15. Kalsi—major rock edicts | 1860 | Dehradun district Uttarakhand | Similar in content to Girnar edicts. Figure of elephant on north face of the rock has the word 'gajatame' ('the best elephant') inscribed below it |
| 16. Sanchi Schism edict | 1863 | Raisen district Madhya Pradesh | Commands against breaking the Sangha and prescribes punish-ment in case that was to happen |
| 17. Rupnath— minor rock edict | 1871 | Jabalpur district Madhya Pradesh | Similar in content to Sasaram edict |
| 18. Bairat— minor rock edict | 1872 | Jaipur district Rajasthan | Similar in content to Sasaram edict |
| 19. Jaugada— major rock edicts | 1872 | Ganjam district Orissa | Edicts 1 to 10 and 14 similar to Girnar edicts. Like Dhauli, nos 11–13 here replaced by two separate edicts |

Appendix (*contd.*)

| Inscription and Type | Year of Discovery | Location | Substance |
| --- | --- | --- | --- |
| 20. Allahabad-Kosam Schism edict | 1877 | On Allahabad pillar | Similar to Sanchi edict with the mahamatras of Kosambi mentioned (they were being commanded) |
| 21. Sopara—major rock edicts | 1882 | Thana district Maharashtra | Two fragments containing 8th and 9th edicts |
| 22. Mansehra—major rock edicts | 1888-9 | Hazara district Pakistan | Similar in content to Girnar edicts |
| 23. Brahmagiri—minor rock edicts[1] | 1892 | Chitaldrug district Karnataka | First segment similar to Sasaram. Second segment speaks about the ancient rule which must be acted upon: obedience to parents, elders, compassion to animals, importance of speaking the truth and reverence that students must show to elders and relatives |
| 24. Siddapura minor rock edicts | 1892 | Chitaldrug district Karnataka | Similar to Brahmagiri edicts |
| 25. Jatinga-Rameshwara minor rock edicts | 1892 | Chitaldrug district Karnataka | Similar to Brahmagiri edicts |
| 26. Lumbini pillar inscription | 1896 | Rupandehi district Nepal | Records Ashoka's pilgrimage to the place of the Buddha's birth |

[1] Unlike Udegolam and Nittur, the edicts here are not on separate surfaces but appear as a single message.

Appendix (*contd.*)

| Inscription and Type | Year of Discovery | Location | Substance |
|---|---|---|---|
| | | | Mentions that he set up a pillar and reduced taxes of Lumbini village |
| 27. Nigali Sagar pillar inscription | 1895 | Kapilavastu district Nepal | Records two events: enlargement of stupa of Buddha Konakamana by Ashoka and his pilgrimage there when he set up a pillar |
| 28. Rampurva pillar edicts | 1902 | Champaran district Bihar | Similar to Allahabad-Kosam edicts |
| 29. Sarnath Schism edict | 1904 | Varanasi district Uttar Pradesh | Similar to Allahabad-Kosam Schism edict, but with instructions that it was to be submitted to the sangha of monks and nuns as also those pertaining to dissemination |
| 30. Taxila stone edict | 1914–15 | Rawalpindi district Pakistan | Concerns avoidance of killing of living beings, respect for elders, parents, Brahmans, monks, and relatives |
| 31. Maski minor rock edict | 1915 | Raichur district Karnataka | Similar to Sasaram edict |
| 32. Erragudi minor rock edicts | 1928 | Kurnool district Andhra Pradesh | Similar to Brahmagiri with one major difference in that in its second segment, where it outlines the nature of the |

Appendix (*contd.*)

| Inscription and Type | Year of Discovery | Location | Substance |
|---|---|---|---|
| | | | morality to be propagated by officials, the manner in which this is to be done is outlined in an overly officious tone |
| 33. Erragudi— major rock edicts | 1929 | Kurnool district Andhra Pradesh | Similar in content to Girnar edicts |
| 34. Gavimath minor rock edict | 1931 | Raichur district Karnataka | Similar to Maski edict |
| 35. Palkigundu minor rock edict | 1931 | Raichur district Karnataka | Similar to Maski edict |
| 36. Pul-I Darunta edict | Pre-1932 | Jalalabad district Afghanistan | Aramaic edict concerned with prevention of killing living beings |
| 37. Rajula-Mandagiri minor rock edicts | 1953 | Kurnool district Andhra Pradesh | Similar to Erragudi edicts |
| 38. Gujjara minor rock edict | 1953 | Datia district Madhya Pradesh | Similar to Sasaram edict |
| 39. Shari-i-Kuna edict | 1957 | Kandahar district Afghanistan | Greek and Aramaic edict which says that the doctrine of piety, along with restraint in killing living beings, led to hunters and fishermen following suit |

Appendix (*contd.*)

| Inscription and Type | Year of Discovery | Location | Substance |
|---|---|---|---|
| 40. Ahraura rock edict | 1961 | Mirzapur district Uttar Pradesh | Similar to Sasaram edict |
| 41. Kandahar | 1963 | Kandahar district Afghanistan | Fragmentary edict which deals with parts of Rock Edicts XII and XIII |
| 42. Kandahar Aramaic stone edict | 1963 | Kandahar district Afghanistan | Aramaic-Magadhi edict about obedience to parents and teachers; respect for Brahmans and Shramanas; respect for the humble and slaves |
| 43. Bahapur minor rock edict | 1966 | East of Kailash New Delhi | Similar to Bairat edict |
| 44. Laghman I Aramaic edict | 1969 | Jalalabad district Afghanistan | Mentions the king's success in pushing out hunting and fishing |
| 45. Laghman II Aramaic edict | 1973 | Jalalabad district Afghanistan | Similar to Laghman I |
| 46. Panguraria minor rock edict | 1975 | Sehore district Madhya Pradesh | Similar to Sasaram edict with one addition: the first line mentions that the king was addressing a 'Kumara' from his march to 'Upunitha-vihara' in Manema-desha |
| 47. Nittur minor rock edicts | 1977 | Bellary district Karnataka | Two separate rocks with edicts but with the message being similar to Erragudi |

Appendix (*contd.*)

| Inscription and Type | Year of Discovery | Location | Substance |
|---|---|---|---|
| 48. Udegolam minor rock edicts | 1978 | Bellary district Karnataka | Two separate rocks with edicts similar to Nittur (Minor Rock Edict I on one of the rocks can barely be seen) |
| 49. Sannathi— major rock edicts | 1989 | Gulbarga district Karnataka | Stone with 12$^{th}$, 14$^{th}$ and two separate edicts, as at Jaugada and Dhauli |
| 50. Ratanpurwa minor rock edict | 2009 | Bhabua district Bihar | Similar to Sasaram edict |

# Notes

## Notes to Prelude

1. For a recent overview of these political units, Sarao (2014).
2. The nine monarchs of the Nanda dynasty were Mahapadma, the founder, who was followed—according to a Buddhist text, the *Mahabodhivamsa*—by Panduka, Pandugati, Bhutapala, Rashtrapala, Govinshanaka, Dassiddhaka, Kaivarta, and Dhana. The *Puranas* say that Mahapadma was succeeded by his eight sons, probably kings in succession. Raychaudhuri (1953): 208.
3. The *Dipavamsa* 12.5–6 says Ashoka sent the following message to the Lanka ruler: 'I have taken my refuge in the Buddha, the Dhamma, and the Samgha; I have avowed myself a lay pupil of the Doctrine of the Sakyaputta. Imbue your mind also with the faith in this triad, in the highest religion of the Jina, take your refuge in the Teacher.' Oldenberg (1879): 167.
4. Tambiah (1976): 5.
5. Deeg (2009): 128–9. Also see Deeg (2012): 370–1.
6. Wells (1920): 394.
7. Nehru (1946): 52. Nehru also wrote about his emotional appreciation of India through key historical figures, 'men who seemed to know life and understand it, and [who] out of their wisdom . . . had built a structure that gave India a cultural stability which lasted for a thousand years' (ibid.: 51–2). Ashoka was one of three figures he specifically mentioned, the other two being the Buddha and Akbar.

8. For a discussion of these authors, Edde (2011): 4–7.
9. For a comparison between Achaemenid and Ashokan epigraphs, Salomon (2009): 45–7.
10. An early statement on the differences between the West and Asia is a chapter on 'Characteristics of Asian Rhetoric' in Oliver (1971): 258–72.
11. This and other references have been discussed by Robert J. Connors in his work on Greek rhetoric. Connors (1986): 42–3.
12. Ibid.: 55.
13. Oliver (1971): 101.
14. Ibid.: 89.
15. Ibid.: 132.
16. Orality and memorization continue to be part of priestly culture in contemporary India. See Fuller (2001).
17. Lopez (1995): 38.
18. While there is a debate on the date of the Buddha's death—or his 'Parinibbana' as it is called in Buddhist tradition—with the dates ranging from the fifth to the fourth centuries BCE, it is *c.* 480 BCE that I accept here as the date of his death. Since he is said to have lived for about eighty years, his birth would have been around 540 BCE. For a summary of the various dates, Singh (2009): 257.
19. 'Thus have I heard' is how the *Maha-Parinibbana-Sutta* (The Book of the Great Decease), I.1, begins. See Rhys Davids (1881): 1. In the same chapter, while recounting the Buddha's interaction with bhikkhus (Buddhist monks), the Buddha is on more than one occasion shown as addressing the monks thus: 'Listen well, and attend, and I will speak.' *Maha-Parinibbana-Sutta* 1.6 and 1.7. See Rhys Davids (1881): 6–7.
20. *Arthashastra* (*AS* hereafter) 1.5.14. Kane (1972): 11. 'Itihasa', in the opinion of the text, was made up of the *Puranas, Itivrtta, Akhyayika, Udaharana, Dharmashastra,* and *Arthashastra.*
21. Fittingly, the title of Chakrabarti's (2011) book on Ashoka is *Royal Messages by the Wayside.*
22. The silver tetradrachm of Ptolemy I of Egypt, for instance, showed Alexander with an elephant headdress and the horns of the Egyptian god Ammon. For a description and photograph, Cherry (2007): 259. Allen's book contains an illustration of a silver coin issued by Alexander which bears an image of the conqueror himself, which Allen says is 'the only known image of Alexander to survive from

his lifetime.' No specific details are provided: see Allen (2012): 47. Apparently, this medallion was issued in very small numbers after the battle of the Hydaspes (the name of the Jhelum river in classical sources). Romm (2012): 216.

23. Cherry (2007): 295.

24. Historians of the ancient world, such as Plutarch and Cassius Dio Cocceianus, wrote about Cleopatra. While Plutarch saw her as manipulative, Dio's Cleopatra had insatiable passion and avarice. In the medieval world, the traveller and historian Al-Masudi introduced another version of the queen—as a philosopher and author. Among the most popular depictions has been Shakespeare's, which saw the queen as a heroine ruined by passion. For a brief overview of the afterlife of Cleopatra, Tyldesley (2008): 205–17.

25. Ibid.: 7–8. Joyce Tyldesley's very readable account of Cleopatra's life and times is upfront about the lack of primary material: 'Given these limitations of evidence it is clearly never going to be possible to write a conventional biography of Cleopatra; there are simply too many important details missing' (p. 7).

26. Cherry (2007): 7.

27. The names of prominent historical figures, ranging from Cleopatra to Mahatma Gandhi, frequently figure in the titles of books on them. The same holds true for Ashoka: scores of books carry his name on their title pages: *Asoka* (Bhandarkar, 1925), *Asoka, the Righteous: A Definitive Biography* (Guruge, 1993), *Asoka* (Mookerji, 1928), *Asoka and the Decline of the Mauryas* (Thapar, 1961), *Asoka – The King and the Man* (Thaplyal, 2012), *Ashoka* (Allen, 2012), and *Asoka as Depicted in his Edicts* (Hazra, 2007) are a few such. For a detailed bibliography on Ashoka, Falk (2006).

28. This is evident from the handful of books on them, as compared to the scores of writings on Ashoka. For Samudragupta, Gokhale (1962); for Chandragupta, Mookerji (1952); for a recent study of Didda, see the relevant chapters in Rangachari (2009).

29. Hinghausen (1966), Mookerji (1926), Devahuti (1970), Sharma (1970), S.R. Goyal (1986), and S. Goyal (2006).

30. Guha (2004): 246. Ramachandra Guha himself has written the biographies of Verrier Elwin (1999) and Mahatma Gandhi (2013), apart from essays on a range of scientists, statesmen, academics, and litterateurs.

31. The historian of Buddhism T.W. Rhys Davids describes Ashoka as one of the most striking and interesting personalities in world history because of his simple, sane, and tolerant view of conduct and life, a man who was 'free from all the superstitions that dominated so many minds, then as now, in East and West alike.' See Rhys Davids (1903): 306.

32. Among scholars Romila Thapar, more than fifty years ago, stated this with greater clarity than most. It was widely felt, she said, that 'a long political tradition beginning with Asoka, of conscious non-violence and a toleration of all beliefs political and religious, continued unbroken through the centuries culminating in the political philosophy of Gandhi'. Thapar (1961): 214.

33. For Tagore's invocation of Ashoka, see Sen (1997): 9.

34. Ananya Vajpeyi argues that Nehru may well have seen himself as 'the new Asoka'. For this and various elements which made Ashoka a major figure in Nehru's quest as a political leader, Vajpeyi (2012): 194–200.

35. For the text of the resolution moved by Nehru, see Agrawala (1964).

36. Allen (2012); Kejariwal (1988): 202–9; Chakrabarti (1988): 33–4.

37. This has been discussed at length in the epilogue of the present book.

38. Cunningham (1877).

39. By the time Hultzsch's *Corpus Inscriptionum Indicarum* was published in 1925, several minor rock edicts in Karnataka had been discovered and their texts were, thus, included in it. For a chronology of the discoveries of the edicts and inscriptions, see the appendix of the present book.

40. Indraji was also the discoverer of some of the Sopara edicts. Virchand Dharamsey's book (2012) is essential reading for an understanding of the remarkable life of this pioneering archaeologist.

41. Ibid.: 139.

42. See the appendix of the present book.

43. See Thaplyal (2009).

44. Smith (1909).

45. Ibid.: 23.

46. He is known to have said that 'the best elements in the plastic, pictorial, numismatic and dramatic arts of ancient India are of foreign, chiefly Graeco-Roman origin.' Smith (1889).

47. Smith (1909): 46, 47.

48. Bhandarkar (1925): vii.

49. Ibid.: 61.
50. Mookerji (1928).
51. Barua (1946): 329–30.
52. Thapar (1961).
53. Ibid.: 138–40.
54. Ibid.: 5.
55. Ibid.: 214–15.
56. Ibid.: 215.
57. Falk (2006): 13–54.
58. This is the reason why all the finer points pertaining to the sources which have been explored and analysed in hundreds of scholarly articles and books are not discussed in exacting detail. Where they figure, I have tried to write about such points in a way that will be intelligible to the general reader.

## Notes to Chapter 1:  An Apocryphal Early Life

1. The *Harshacarita* of Bana (IV.142) describes the birth of Harsha thus: 'At length in the month of Jyaistha, on the twelfth day of the dark fortnight, the Pleiads being in the ascendant, just after the twilight came, when the young night had begun to climb, a sudden cry of women arose in the harem. Hurriedly, issuing forth, Suyatra, daughter of Yasovati's nurse and herself dearly beloved, fell at the king's feet, crying, "Good news! your majesty, you are blessed with the birth of a second son."' Cowell and Thomas (1968): 109. Also see Devahuti (1970): 65.
2. Beveridge (1902): vol. I, 43.
3. Kosmin 2014: 57.
4. For a detailed and learned exposition of the date of Ashoka, see Eggermont (1956). This examines all sources which preserved the chronicle of Ashoka and arrives at the date, mentioned here, by comparing the data of his inscriptions with those that can be gleaned from the literary traditions.
5. For systems of dating used in the inscriptions of ancient India, see Salomon (1998): 172–6. For the chronology of Ashoka, Eggermont (1956). The chronology of the Maurya dynasty has been variously worked out and is usually based on a combination of the Buddhist sources and Puranic evidence. The dates can still differ depending

on the aspect of a particular tradition relied upon. Compare Thapar (1961): 14–16 with, for instance, Mookerji (1957): 9–10.

6. Saha (1953): 4.

7. For regnal and other 'dates' in ancient Indian inscriptions, Salomon (1998): 170–98.

8. Sarnath stone inscription of Kumaragupta II, verse 1. Chhabra and Gai (1981): 179, 321–2.

9. The historian Beni Madhab Barua had this to say about his reticence: 'Nothing is more striking and more disappointing to the students of Asoka's inscriptions than that nowhere in them he has either mentioned or referred to his father and grandfather, his mother and maternal relations, as well as relations of his queens. He has not even cared anywhere to introduce himself as a scion of the Maurya family.' Barua (1946): 5.

10. Line 2, Jayaswal and Banerji (1933): 86.

11. Rock Edict 9 makes this evident. See Girnar version in Hultzsch (1925): 16.

12. *AS* 2.10.4, Kangle (1972): pt II, 92.

13. For a bibliography on the life of the Buddha, Nakamura (1989): 16–21. For a popular account of the life of the Buddha, Strong (2000).

14. Schober (1997): 4.

15. For the *Ashokavadana*, Strong (1989). While there may have been earlier literary versions of the story of Ashoka, this is chronologically the earliest text to have survived.

16. For Avadana literature, Winternitz (1933): vol. II, 277–94.

17. Schober (1997): x.

18. For this story, aptly called 'The Gift of Dirt', Strong (1989): 200–4.

19. This section, including the quotations, is based on Strong (1989): 198–204.

20. For a discussion of this 'inaccuracy', Strong (1989): 21–2.

21. See Moore (1921): 102.

22. In the *Ashokavadana*, Ashoka's mother is not named. For the various names of Ashoka's mother, Guruge (1993): 26–9.

23. Strong (1989): 204.

24. Chakrabarti (2001): 166–7; Sinha (2000): 22–5; and Prasad (2006). This was a city marked by burnt brick structures ranging from an earthen rampart revetted with burnt bricks to wells and drains.

25. The fair, good-looking, and gracious daughter who would become Bindusara's wife and Ashoka's mother is in the *Ashokavadana* mentioned as being the daughter of a Brahman from Champa. See Strong (1989): 204.
26. *AS* 1.17.18–19. Kangle (1972): pt II, 39–41.
27. Strong (1989): 204.
28. Ibid.
29. Ibid.
30. Ibid.
31. This forms the subtitle of the book written by Basham (1951).
32. Ibid.: 3–9.
33. Ibid.: 135.
34. Ibid.
35. *Vinaya* ii.284, cited in Basham (1951): 136. Also see 'Maha Parinibbana Suttanta', *Digha Nikaya* ii.162, in Rhys Davids (1910): vol. II, 183–4. Here too, the same story, about the encounter between Maha-Kassapa with monks and an Ajivika along the high road to Pava, is mentioned.
36. Basham (1951): 140–1.
37. *Vamsatthappakasini* is cited on this point by Guruge (1993): 26
38. Law (1954): 8–9.
39. For the texts of the epigraphs, Hultzsch (1925): 181–2.
40. For a description of the Barabar caves, Gupta (1980): 189–221.
41. Strong (1989: 27), draws our attention to the presence of some Ashoka stories being represented on the second–first centuries BCE bas-reliefs of the great stupa at Sanchi.
42. Strong (1989): 174.
43. Chapter VI of the *Mahavamsa*. See Geiger (1912): 51. The text tells us that on seeing the tiger she 'bethought of the prophesy of the soothsayers which she had heard, and without fear she caressed him stroking his limbs.' Twins, a son and a daughter, were born of this union. All the following references to Geiger (1912) refer to his translation of the *Mahavamsa*.
44. Geiger (1912): 65.
45. Kane (1994): vol. V, pt I, 526.
46. VII.64. See Karambelkar (1959): 154.
47. For a summary, Hilton (1996). Also see Kargupta (2002), especially chapter 5.

48. The ones mentioned are: Jyestha or Vicrt (i.e. Mula nakshatra) or a day called tiger-like (on an evil or terrible nakshatra). Kane (1994): vol. V, pt I, 524.
49. Ibid.: 531.
50. Ibid.: 532.
51. Rowley (1956): 7–8.
52. Tottoli (2002): 22.
53. See Moore (1921): 110.
54. Kane (1994): vol. V, pt I, 527. A similar disdain is evident in a Buddhist legend aptly called *Nakkhata Jataka*. In this, a town family loses out on a country girl whom they want wedded to their son because the family's favoured ascetic maintains out of pique that the stars are not favourable on that particular day. The family of the girl, having made all the required arrangements, then marry her off to someone else. The advice of a wise man in the town at the end of the tale, sums up the story's attitude to 'lucky days' and planetary dispositions:

    'The fool may watch for "days,"
    Yet luck shall always miss;
    "'Tis luck itself is luck's own star
    What can mere stars achieve?'
    See Cowell (1990 reprint): I, 124–6.

55. *AS* I.9.9. Kangle (1972): pt II, 18.
56. 'Nalakasutta', *Sutta Nipata* 11, in Chalmers (1931): 165–73.
57. *Sutta Nipata* 11.690. See Chalmers (1931): 167.
58. Goswami (2001): 99–105.
59. Cowell and Thomas (1968): 109–10.

## Notes to Chapter 2:  Pataliputra and the Prince

1. Beal (1884): vol. III, 332–3.
2. It is surprising that Xuanzang got this basic fact wrong. One wonders if the Chinese translations of the *Ashokavadana*, with which he must have been familiar, had omitted the section on Ashoka's birth in which his conception is described in some detail.
3. Watters (1904–5): vol. II, 87.
4. Strong (1989): 8.
5. Beal (1884): vol. III, 327. This is Book VIII, which has a large section on Pataliputra and Ashoka.

6. Strong (1989): 7.
7. There were two Chinese translations of versions of the *Ashokavadana*, one going back to *c.* 300 CE and another compiled in 512 CE. See Strong (1989): 16, n.46.
8. In a seminar held in 1971, the issue of whether the designation of the North Black Polished Ware should be changed was discussed. This is because such pottery was found in western India and the Deccan, and we now know that it is found in the peninsular South as well. Moreover, there are shades other than black, ranging from golden to brown, and also because the term 'polished' can be misleading since the surface lustre was not produced through polishing. Archaeologists stayed with the existing designation because the material is found in much larger quantity in the North than elsewhere. Additionally, more than 80 per cent of the specimens of this pottery are black. As for the term 'polished', it accurately described what the pottery surface looked like and thus was taken to be a reference to the resultant effect that was created. See Sinha (1971–2): 29–33.
9. For an overview of the archaeology of Pataliputra, Sinha (2000): 88–134, and Kumar (1987). Kumar has summarized the issue of the dating of the NBP phase on the basis of the excavations of B.P. Sinha and L.A. Narain (p. 220): 'The NBP level in Pataliputra as based upon the excavations at Sadargali and Mahavirghata has been ascribed to a period ranging from 6th century BC to 2nd century AD. The NBP sherds continued right from the earliest occupation levels but in its upper level the NBP was found associated with coins of the lanky bull type of Kausambi prevalent before *circa* 100 BC. The coins were collected in fairly good number but immediately after this level the NBP sherds disappear completely, hence, the upper limit of this ware has been placed somewhere towards the end of 150 BC or later. The lower limit of the NBP ware was mainly fixed on the basis of the fragments of couchant bull and other polished stone pieces of the Mauryan period which came from the mid level of Period I. Right below the level the 5' deposit must have taken 2 or 3 centuries to set at the site. Punch-marked and cast coins generally belonging to the period between 5th century BC to 2nd century BC were also found in association with the NBP sherds. Thus the chronology of the NBP at Pataliputra has been determined taking into account the Mauryan sculptural fragments bearing typical Mauryan polish from the mid-level and the 5' deposit yielding NBP sherds continuing right below

this level upto the natural soil. This indicated an earlier time span of the NBP types at Pataliputra.' For the prediction of the Buddha, 'Maha Parinibbana Suttanta', *Digha Nikaya* ii.86, in Rhys Davids (1910): vol. 2, 92.

10. 'Maha Parinibbana Suttanta', *Digha Nikaya* ii.86, in Rhys Davids (1910): vol. 2, 92.

11. Ghosh (1989): vol. 2, 362–5.

12. It now seems that, contrary to received wisdom, Megasthenes was part of the entourage of Sibyrtius (as stated by Arrian) rather than of Seleucus. See Bosworth (1996): 117. For an alternative view, Kosmin (2014): appendix.

13. Bosworth (1996).

14. Brown (1957): 15.

15. Majumdar (1958) and (1960); Sethna (1960).

16. McCrindle (1877): 80 and 114.

17. Ibid.: 69.

18. Ibid.: 66.

19. Allchin (1995): 202.

20. This is George Erdosy's estimate on the basis of Megasthenes' account. See ibid.

21. Remnants of the palisade have been traced at Lohanipura, Bulandibagh, Bahadurpur, Kumrahar, Maharajakhand, Sevai Tank, and Gandhi Tank. Altekar and Mishra (1959): 7.

22. Allchin (1995): 202.

23. McCrindle (1877): 72–3.

24. *AS* 1.21.1 and I.21.13. Kangle (1972): pt II, 51, 53.

25. Luders (1963): 118–19.

26. Sinha (2000): 127–8.

27. Altekar and Mishra (1959): 7.

28. Page (1926–7): 135.

29. Beglar (1878): 27.

30. Waddell (1903):15.

31. Ibid.

32. For an account of how this hall was discovered, Lahiri (2005): 134–8.

33. Bose (2009): 81–2, 109. At Chirand and Senuar, sal has been found in neolithic horizons which go back to many centuries before the construction of Pataliputra's ramparts. The remains in Senuar belong to *c.* 2200–1950 BCE; in the case of Chirand these go back to

*c.* 2600 BCE. For the excavations of Chirand, Verma (2007), and Senuar, Singh (2003).

34. Dhavalikar (1977): 21.

35. Gupta (1980): 157–8.

36. Shere (1951).

37. Gupta (1980): 55–9.

38. In later sources Kautilya is sometimes known by other names: Vishnugupta and Chanakya. The *Arthashastra's* first chapter mentions towards the end that the 'shastta' was composed by Kautilya. In the colophons at the end of the various books as well, that is was composed by Kautilya is also mentioned.

39. Shamasastry cites several such sources such as the *Vishnupurana*, Kamandaka's *Nitisara*, Dandin's *Dasakumaracarita* and the *Panchatantra*. Importantly, as he pointed out, these mention the Mauryas and the nature of this text when they allude to the author of the *Arthashastra*. The *Vishupurana*, for instance, noted that '(First) Mahapadma; then his sons, only nine in number, will be the lords of the earth for a hundred years. Those Nandas Kautilya, a Brahman, will slay. On their death, the Mauryas will enjoy the earth. Kautilya himself will install Chandragupta on their throne. His son will be Bindusara, and his son Asokavardhana.' The author of the *Panchatantra* ascribed the text to the author in this way: 'Then the Dharma - sastras are those of Manu and others, the Arthasastras of Chanakya and others, the Kama Sutras of Vatsyayana and others'. See Shamasastry (1915): vii–viii.

40. See Shamasastry (1915).

41. For details, see Kangle (1969): pt I, xi–xviii.

42. The *Arthashastra* has been used for writing on different aspects of Mauryan times by Sastri (1967), Thapar (1961), and Singh (2009), among others. Even Trautmann, who has pointed out the possibility of multiple authors for different parts of the text, has no hesitation in using it as a source for his work on elephants and the Mauryas (1982). For an early discussion on the controversy, Kangle (1965): pt III, ch. 4.

43. Olivelle (2013): 9–25.

44. An example of this is the importance that Olivelle gives to allusions to coral—which he believes to be Mediterranean coral—in the *Arthashastra*. Trade with the Mediterranean, he argues, could not have been flourishing before the first century BCE, which would be

the earliest date for Kautilya to mention coral. Actually, if we look at the archaeological evidence for coral in India, it is present much before the first century BCE. Coral, in fact, has a long history of usage going back to the time of the Indus civilization when it is present, for instance, at Harappa. Again, in the second millennium BCE, coral has been found at the neolithic-chalcolithic sites of Navdatoli in Central India, Prakash in Maharashtra, and Maski in Karnataka. In early historic India, much before *c.* 200 BCE, coral beads are found at  Taxila, Rajghat, Ganwaria-Piprahwa, and Vaishali. They are also found in Nevasa and Paunar in Maharashtra, and at T. Kallupati in Tamil Nadu. This long history of usage may be one reason why it was considered sacred by Buddhists and Hindus. The references to coral form part of the data that I had compiled for my PhD thesis in the early 1990s; there is no clarity on whether these were from the Mediterranean or Indian seas. In fact, the early presence of coral from Taxila to Tamil Nadu is evidence of the possibility of the *Arthashastra's* core being Mauryan, and not later, as argued by Olivelle. See Olivelle 2013: 26–7 for the argument relating to coral. For references to coral in pre-Mauryan and Mauryan times, Lahiri (1992).

45. *AS* 2.4.6. Kangle (1972): pt II, 68.
46. *AS* 1.20.2. Kangle (1972): pt II, 48.
47. *AS* 1.20.6–8. Kangle (1972): pt II, 49.
48. For a discussion of this, Guruge (1993): 29–31.
49. *AS* 1.19.6–24. Kangle (1972): pt II, 46.
50. Tyldesley (2008): 33.
51. A prince's training has been described in the *AS* (all citations in the following footnotes pertaining to it are from Kangle (1972), pt II, *AS* 1.5.7–12). For the age of tonsure (called 'Chaula karma' in *AS* 1.5.6) and initiation (or Upanayana in *AS* 1.5.7), *Asvalayana-grhya Sutra* says that the first should be performed in the third year after birth or according to family usage, and the second according to caste, i.e. for a brahmana, kshatriya, or vaisya boy the proper ages are 8th, 11th, and 12th from conception. See Kane (1994): vol. V, pt I, 606–7.
52. *AS* 1.5.14 states that the 'Puranas, Itivrtta, Akhyayika, Udaharana, Dharmshastra and Arthshastra—these constitute Itihasa.' See Kangle (1972): pt II, 11. Puranas deal with the creation and destruction of the universe, king lists, heroes, sages, geography, and philosophy. Arthashastra is as a discipline the ancient equivalent of modern economics.

53. *AS* 1.20.12. Kangle (1972): pt II, 50. The term used is 'kumaraa-dhyaksa sthanam'.
54. *AS* 1.17.23 says that 'like a piece of wood eaten by worms, the royal family, with its princes undisciplined, would break the moment it is attacked.' See Kangle (1972): pt II, 41.
55. See *AS* 1.17. Kangle (1972): pt II, 39–43. The section's heading is 'Guarding against Princes'.
56. *AS* 1.17.42. Kangle (1972): pt II, 42.

## Notes to Chapter 3:　Mauryan Taxila

1. Strong (1989): 208.
2. Ibid.
3. Ibid.: 52–3.
4. Mukherjee (1984): 56; Dani (1986): 56. Marshall (1951): vol. I, 165, though, provided an entirely different reading. An official of Taxila, Romedote by name, he noted was mentioned here and the fact that he owed his advancement to the patronage of 'Priyadarshi'.
5. Mukherjee, for this reason, noted that the epigraph could be compared to Ashoka's rock edict IV. See Mukherjee (1984): 26.
6. For Taxila, Sir John Marshall's three-volume excavation report is the best available publication: Marshall (1951). For later excavations there, Ghosh (1948) and Sharif (1969).
7. For an excellent analysis of this disjunction in the case of ancient Greece, Snodgrass (1985).
8. On forests in the Gangetic plains, Lal (1986): 84. There were, however, areas where, much before the time of the Mauryas, land seems to have been cleared. The widely occurring 'woody' monocotyledon that has emerged out of the wood charcoal analysis of Alamgirpur suggests clearing of tracts of forest there for agricultural purposes. See Singh, *et al.* (2013): 52–3.
9. Chandra (1977): 12; Lahiri (1992): 367–77.
10. *Mahavagga* VIII. I, 5–7. Rhys Davids and Oldenberg (1882): 174–6.
11. For the distribution of lapis lazuli and other raw materials in the upper and middle Gangetic plains cities and settlements in Mauryan times, Lahiri (1992): 204–314.
12. For the Indus to the Oxus orbit, Chakrabarti (2010): 18–19.
13. Marshall (1951): vol. I, 13.

14. Arrian's account of the campaign of Alexander mentions his sojourn there. Romm (2012): 208.
15. Marshall (1951): vol. I, 20.
16. Ibid.: 3.
17. Ibid.: 93.
18. Ibid.: 88–9.
19. Ibid.: vol. 2, 477.
20. The other streets are narrower and vary between some 3 and 6 m.
21. Ibid.: vol. 1, 90.
22. Ibid.: 91.
23. The description of Mohenjodaro in Marshall (1931), especially of the city's eastern sector, is peppered with such details.
24. Marshall (1951): vol. 1, 89–90. For a graphic sense of the alignment of the streets and lanes, Plate I in ibid.: vol. 3.
25. Ibid. (1951): vol. 1, 89.
26. Ibid.: 91.
27. Ibid.: 90. The streets and lanes mentioned here all belong to the second stratum.
28. Marshall (1951): vol. 1, 90. The bin measures 2.7 m. by 1.5 m.
29. This is shown as square 29.33" in the plan.
30. Marshall (1951): vol. 1, 94. Marshall's suggestion that the well was filled up with pottery vessels so as to prevent the sides from collapsing may well be true for unlined wells. However, in this instance, the well was lined with stone to a considerable depth.
31. The pillared hall measures 17.9 x 7.3 m.
32. Marshall (1951): vol. 1, 98.
33. Ibid.: vol. 2, 449.
34. Ibid.: 447.
35. Ibid.: 450.
36. Ibid.: vol. 1, 92.
37. Ibid.: 97. Rooms 3 and 4 had a drain below and room 17 was the one which had subterranean jars.
38. Marshall (1911–12): 31.
39. Sali (1986): 98, 133–7.
40. Marshall (1951): vol. 1, 95.
41. Ibid.: 97.
42. Dani (1986): 87.
43. This is no. 6 in Marshall (1951): vol. 2, 677.
44. This is no. 41 in ibid.: 682.

45. This is no. 7 in ibid.: 677.
46. Marshall (1951): vol. 1, 109.
47. Ibid.: vol. 2, 425, 501.

## Notes to Chapter 4:  Affairs of the Heart and State

1. For South Asian discourses on love, Orsini (2007).
2. This was how the *Mahavagga* (V.13.7) described it. Rhys Davids and Oldenberg (1882): 34.
3. Singh (1996): 1.
4. Banerjee (1989): 448.
5. These reliefs bear identifying labels that mention the names of the kings—'King Pasenaji, the Kosala' and 'Ajatsatu worships the Holy one.' See Luders (1963 ): 113, 118.
6. *AS* 10.2.1–3. Kangle (1972): pt II, 435. Here, the preparations for a military march are described: 'After calculating the halts on the way in villages and in forests, in accordance with the supply of fodder, fuel and water, and (calculating) the time for camping, halting and marching, he should start on the expedition. He should cause food and equipment to be transported in double the quantity required to meet the case. Or, if unable to do so, he should assign it to the troops, or should store them at intervals on the route.' It is unlikely that similar preparations were not undertaken when a viceroy-prince travelled to take charge in a distant province.
7. Chandra (1977): 54.
8. *Mahavagga* (VIII.I.23). Rhys Davids and Oldenberg (1882b): 186.
9. *AS* 7.12.24. Kangle (1972): pt II, 360.
10. Hare (1947): 143–67.
11. *Mahavagga* (V.13.13). Rhys Davids and Oldenberg (1882b): 39.
12. For a brief description of the Ujjayini road, Banerjee (1989): 448.
13. Deloche (1993): 272.
14. For the significance of Sasaram, especially in relation to the Rajgir-Gaya-Bhabua alignment, Chakrabarti (2011): 17.
15. Chakrabarti (2005): 26. Chakrabarti points to the presence of early historic North Black Polished Ware on the mound of thirty acres at Deo Markandeya, as also Black and Red Ware which is protohistoric.
16. Ibid.
17. *The Imperial Gazetteer of India*, XXI (1908): 280.
18. Sharma and Misra (2003): 110–12.

19. A summary of the later evidence in the form of Gupta gold coins, sculptural remains, and temples is available in Chakrabarti (2005): 85.
20. For the excavations at Eran, Sharma and Mishra (2003): 102–6.
21. *Dipavamsa* VI.16. Oldenberg (1879): 147.
22. *Mahavamsa* XIII.10–11. Geiger (1912): 88–9.
23. Thapar (1973): 22–3.
24. The Sri Lankan texts, for example, do not mention the battle of Kalinga that Ashoka himself refers to at great length in Rock Edict XIII.
25. For a summary of the arguments, Guruge (1993): 44.
26. This is the argument of Thapar (1973): 23.
27. Guruge (1993): 40.
28. See Dhauli Separate Rock Edict I. Hultzsch (1925): 94 and 97.
29. Ancient Vidisha is also known as modern Besnagar. For excavations, Mishra and Sharma (2003): 90–4.
30. Marshall, Foucher, and Majumdar, *The Monuments of Sanchi* (1940): vol. I, 2.
31. See Lamotte (1988): 56.
32. *Mahavamsa* V.40. Geiger (1912): 29.
33. *Dipavamsa* VI.21–2. Oldenberg (1879): 148.
34. 'When Mahinda was ten years old, his father put his brothers to death; then he passed four years reigning over Jambudvipa. Having killed his hundred brothers, along continuing his race, Ashoka was anointed king in Mahinda's fourteenth year. *Dipavamsa* VI.21–2. Oldenberg (1879): 148.
35. Strong (1989): 208–9.
36. Ibid.: 209.
37. *Dipavamsa* VI.22. Oldenberg (1879): 148. This is unlikely to be true since, as we shall see later, Ashoka does mention the households of his siblings in his epigraphs.

## Notes to Chapter 5:  The End and the Beginning

1. Strong (1989): 210–13. The ensuing discussion and quotations are from this section of the text.
2. *AS* 1.10.3. Kangle (1972): pt II, 19.
3. This paragraph and the quotations in it are from Strong (1989): 210–11.

4. The quotations are from Strong (1989): 211–12.
5. *The Mahavamsa*, V.189–90. Geiger (1912): 42.
6. *The Dipavamsa* 6.24–28. Oldenberg (1879): 148.
7. This is what Ashoka said to his minister when asking him to bring Nigrodha to him. *The Dipavamsa* 6.45. Oldenberg (1879): 150.
8. *AS* 2.19 has provisions on the various aspects mentioned here. See Kangle (1972): pt II, 55–9.
9. The quotation about the Rod is from *AS* 1.4.11. Kangle, (1972): pt II, 10.
10. *AS* 8.2.1; Kangle (1972): 390.
11. *AS* 7.1.20; Kangle (1972): pt II, 322.
12. Bradford (2001): 53–9.
13. For the campaigns of Alexander, Romm (2012).
14. Ebrey (1996): 60.
15. Parker (1995): 2.
16. Bradford (2001): 42.
17. See Hultzsch (1925): xxxv.
18. *AS*, 9.1.37 and 9.1.45. Kangle (1972): pt II, 408–9.
19. Apparently, Chandragupta's army according to Megasthenes, had 600,00 foot-soldiers, 30,000 cavalry, and 9000 elephants. Megasthenes also provides a vivid description of the governing body which directed military affairs in the time of Chandragupta. This consisted of six divisions, with five members each: 'One division is appointed to cooperate with the admiral of the fleet, another with the superintendent of the bullock-trains which were used for transporting engines of war, food for the soldiers, provender for the cattle, and other military requisites. They supply servants who beat the drum, and others who carry gongs; grooms also for the horses, and mechanists and their assistants. To the sound of the gong they send out foragers to bring in grass, and by a system of rewards and punishments ensure the work being done with dispatch and safety. The Third division has charge of the foot-soldiers, the fourth of the horses, the fifth of the war-chariots, and the sixth of the elephants . . . The chariots are drawn on the march oxen but the horses are led along by a halter, that their legs may not be galled and inflamed, nor their spirits damped by drawing chariots. In addition to the charioteer, there are two fighting men who sit up in the chariot beside him. The war-elephant carries four men– three who shoot arrows, and the driver.' McCrindle (1877): 79–80 and 139.

20. Line B of Rock Edict XIII at Kalsi. See Hultzsch (1925): 47–8.
21. G-I and K of Rock Edict XIII, Kalsi version. Hultzsch (1925): 47.
22. Lines 6, 8, and 12 of the Hathigumpha inscription of Kharavela. Jayaswal and Banerji (1933): 87–8.
23. Line 11 of the Junagadh inscription of Rudradaman; Kielhorn (1905–6): 47.

## Notes to Chapter 6: The Emperor's Voice

1. For the location and distribution of Ashoka's edicts, Allchin and Norman (1985); Mukherjee (1997); Falk (2006).
2. The minor rock edicts are brief as compared to the more expansive major rock edicts. There is also a basic difference in the subject matter, with minor rock edict 1 being overtly Buddhist in character.
3. *AS* 2.10.38–46; Kangle (1972): pt II, 94–5.
4. *AS* 2.10.3–4; Kangle (1972): pt II, 92.
5. For an overview of writing materials and the oldest documents to have survived in those materials, Buhler (1904): 112–18.
6. These are the findings of the palaeobotanist K.S. Saraswat. See Bose (2003): 82.
7. Cartledge (2012): xv.
8. The discovery of the edicts is not something I get into as it has already been described at length in many monographs, most recently in Allen (2012). But it is worth mentioning that they were documented and discovered under very diverse circumstances. The Rajula-Mandagiri inscription, for instance, was first copied by Colin Mackenzie in the nineteenth century, although its significance was only discovered in the middle of the twentieth century. Sircar (1960): 211. The Delhi epigraph, on the other hand, was discovered in 1966 when one Sri Jang Bahadur Singh noticed the inscribed rock before it could be blasted—a residential colony was under construction at the site. See Joshi and Pande (1967): 96.
9. For the texts of these inscriptions, Sircar (1942): 79–80 and 82–3.
10. The 'Great Conqueror' ('maha-vijayo') is how Kharavela described himself. The conquests included the sack of Goradhagiri, the seige of Rajagriha, the breaking up of the confederacy of the Dramira, among various other places and kingdoms. See Jayaswal and Banerji (1933).
11. Singh (2012): 133. Also see Norman (2012): 58.
12. Hultzsch (1925):175–80.

13. Norman (2012): 49. As he has pointed out, the mahamatras at Isila had the edict inscribed as they received it, incorrectly retaining the address at the beginning.
14. Line R in Brahmagiri inscription, Hultzsch (1925): 178; Line 22 in Siddapura edict, Hultzsch (1925): 179; as for the Jatinga-Rameshwara inscription, it has not survived well, and the name is missing. There is little doubt that it was originally inscribed since the end of the last sentence—which mentions Capada and alludes to the writer, has partially survived.
15. Falk (2006): 58.
16. Sircar (1979): 4.
17. Anderson (1991): 268.
18. On orality and textuality in Europe, Ong (1984) and Connors (1986).
19. For text and translation, Hultzsch (1925): 166–9.
20. Norman (2012): 51.
21. These are Brahmagiri, Erragudi, Gavimath, Jatinga-Rameshwara, Maski, Nittur, Palkigundu, Rajula-Mandagiri, Siddapura, and Udego-lam.
22. Lamotte (1988): 76.
23. I have used association to describe Ashoka's relationship with the Sangha because it subsumes the various ways in which the term 'upagamana' has been interpreted: as an attachment to the Sangha, as a visit to it, even as a stay with the Sangha. See Sircar (2000): 64–5.
24. Lamotte (1988): 77.
25. Strong (2012): 349–57.
26. For a scholarly account of the life of the Buddha, Lamotte (1988): ch. 1. Also see Reynolds (1976).
27. Falk (2006): 55.
28. Lines N-P of Brahmagiri edict. Hultzsch (1925): 178.
29. Olivelle (2012): 172.
30. Ibid.
31. Falk (2006): 58.
32. See Line II of the Nittur version of Minor Rock Edict II, for instance. Sircar (1979):128. This paragraph is based on that version and what it says.
33. Raychaudhuri (1953): 255.
34. Thapar (1957). B.K. Thapar's excavations revealed a cultural sequence of four periods, stretching from chalcolithic times till the

medieval. Period II, the megalithic culture, as he designated it, was assigned to the last three quarters of the first millennium BCE. For this, also see Ghosh (1989): 282. Thus, it was likely to have existed in the time of Ashoka. For an earlier assessment of Maski, Gordon and Gordon (1943).

35. Thapar (1957): 103.
36. Ibid.: 21, 24.
37. Hultzsch (1925): xxvi refers to the inscriptional references to Maski. The battlefield of Musangi is referred to in the Tirumalai rock inscription of Rajendra Chola I. See Hultzsch (1907–8): 233.
38. Thapar (1957): 119.
39. This is what K. Rajan's work has revealed. His unpublished work has been extensively cited in Chakrabarti (2006): 312–13.
40. Rajan and Yatheeskumar (2010–12): 290.
41. Wheeler (1947–8): 186.
42. While Mortimer Wheeler believed that the Polished Stone Axe culture's last phase was coterminous with the time of Ashoka, much earlier dates have been suggested for it subsequently, as also for the megaliths. See Ghosh (1989): 84.
43. Falk (2006): 65.
44. Wheeler (1947–8): 186–7.
45. Hultzsch (1925): xxvii.
46. Ibid.
47. Although *Indian Archaeology—A Review* (1976–7: 60) says the inscription was in the Prakrit language and Brahmi characters of about the second century BCE, the accompanying plate (LVIII C) reveals that the Brahmi characters could well be Mauryan. The shaft and the umbrella have a Mauryan polish on them.
48. Ghurhupur/Ratanpurwa in Bhabua district (Bihar), not far from Ahraura, is the other place where an Ashokan minor rock edict has been found amidst painted rock shelters. This was reported in 2009 and published by K.K. Thaplyal. There has been some controversy about the genuineness of the edict, although archaeologists like Rakesh Tiwari (personal conversation) and Dilip Chakrabarti believe it is not a fake. See Chakrabarti (2011): 19–22.
49. Sircar (1979): 94–5.
50. Line I, ibid.: 102.
51. This is surmised by Dilip Chakrabarti: Chakrabarti (2011): 28.
52. Ibid.: 29.

## Notes to Chapter 7:  Extending the Arc of Communication to Afghanistan

1. For the geographic zones of Afghanistan, Dupree (1997): 3–31.
2. Dupree (1997): 19–21. For routes of communication, Channing (1885).
3. Lahiri (1992): 64.
4. Shaffer (1978): 172.
5. Ciarla (1981): 57. For ceramics that are commonly found in this time in the Indo-Iranian borderland, Biscione (1984).
6. Chakrabarti (2006): 147.
7. Bernard (2005): 16–17.
8. MacDowall and Taddei (1978): 188–9; also Stoneman (2010): 365.
9. Kosmin (2014): 33.
10. Ibid.
11. Channing (1885): 360.
12. Mukherjee (1984): 35–42.
13. Ibid.: 9–22.
14. Ibid.: 28–32.
15. Vogelsang (1985): 55.
16. Helms (1982): 1.
17. Vogelsang (1985): 64; also see Ball and Gardin (1982): 145.
18. Helms (1979): 4.
19. Scerrato (1958): 4.
20. Sircar and Krishnan (1957–8).
21. Izre'el and Drorp (1997): 43.
22. Oikonomides (1984): 145–7.
23. Fraser (1979): 11.
24. Diringer (1996): 255–9.
25. Carratelli and Garbini (1964): 32.
26. Bernard (2005): 19.
27. Wheeler (1968): 69.
28. See Afterword in the 2008 impression of Thapar (1961): 276. Here, she argues that the intention of using eusebeia was to introduce dhamma to the local people.
29. Sick (2007): 258.
30. This is the translation published in Mukherjee (1984):33.

31. Ibid.: 12, 14, and 30.
32. For a recent statement see Afterword in the 13th impression of Thapar (1961): 317.
33. Ibid.: 319.
34. These are mentioned by Ashoka in the thirteenth rock edict.
35. Filliozat (1961–2): 5.
36. Adrados (1984): 4. Here, the commonalities and differences between the Bishutun inscription and those of Ashoka have been dealt with at length.
37. Dupree (1997): 224–35.
38. Shaffer (1978): 74–5.
39. Ibid.: 149.

## Notes to Chapter 8:  An Expansive Imperial Articulation

1. This information about Kalinga is absent at Dhauli, Jaugada, and Sannathi and the reasons for this will be discussed in the next chapter.
2. Line B of Rock Edict XIII at Kalsi. Hultzsch (1925): 47.
3. The term dhamma occurs about 111 times in Ashoka's edicts. See Hiltebeitel (2011).
4. Line E of Rock Edict VIII at Kalsi. Hultzsch (1925): 37.
5. *Mahabharata*, Vanaparva, chapter 238, shloka 5 and shloka 20. Cited in Bose (1998): 114–15.
6. Lines 4–7 of Erragudi Rock Edict III, in Sircar (1979): 17.
7. See Lamotte (1988): 230–3 for the similarities between the advice that Ashoka gave and that of the Buddha. So, for instance, he points out: 'In the field of domestic virtues, Asoka unceasingly counselled obedience to one's father and mother, obedience to one's teachers, irreproachable courtesy towards one's friends, acquaintances, companions and family, kindness to the poor, the old and the weak as well as to slaves and servants, generosity towards brahmins and sramanas. The Buddha gave exactly the same advice to the young householder Singalaka: "How does the noble disciple protect the six regions of space? These six regions are composed as follows: father and mother are the east; teachers are the south; sons and wife are the west; friends and companions are the north; slaves and servants are the nadir; sramanas and brahmins are the zenith."'
8. Line I, Erragudi Edict IV, in Sircar (1979): 27.

9. Line III, ibid.
10. Line V, ibid.
11. Line XIV, Erragudi Rock Edict V, in Sircar (1979): 24.
12. For the various classes of people whose welfare and happiness was the concern of this class of officials, Lines X–XIII, ibid.
13. Lines II–VIII of Erragudi Edict VI, ibid.: 18–19.
14. *AS* 1.19.28. Kangle (1972): pt II, 47.
15. *AS* 1.20.22. Kangle (1972): pt II, 51.
16. *AS* 1.19.34–5. Kangle (1972): pt II, 47.
17. This is a different view from that of scholars who see the genesis of Ashoka's welfare measures in his Buddhist faith. S.J. Tambiah, for instance, argued that 'Asokan political Buddhism and social ethics committed kingship and state to the creation of welfare facilities and a prosperous society as the precondition for the support of monastic institutions, and for the escape from suffering and the realization of moral law (the *Dhamma*) in the society as a whole.' Tambiah (1973): 5.
18. For a description of the engraved rocks, Hultzsch (1925): xii.
19. Falk (2006): 111.
20. The three engraved boulders are described in Hultzsch (1925): xii–xiii.
21. For an excellent analysis of the dispatch pattern of the rock edicts, Falk (2006): 111–12.
22. In the case of the major rock edict fragments at Kandahar, it seems that these were actually on a stone slab.
23. This is the translation of Lines II–V of the first rock edict at Erragudi as provided by Sircar (1979): 14. That the sort of festive gathering— samaja—where animals were sacrificed is what Ashoka did not want held is implied here since it is an adjunct of the earlier sentence that no living being should be killed for sacrifice. See Bose (1998): 111–12.
24. Falk (2006): 111.
25. Chakrabarti (2011): 52.
26. Thomas and Joglekar (1994): 196–8.
27. Kane (1997): 781 notes this statement from Vanaparva 208.11–12 of the *Mahabharata*.
28. Ibid.: 775, quoting *Satapatha Brahmana* XI.6.1.3.
29. Lines VI to IX of Erragudi Rock Edict I, in Sircar (1979): 14.
30. Lines II, III, V, and VI of Erragudi Edict V, ibid.: 23.

31. Line XV of Erragudi Edict V, in Sircar (1979): 24.

32. K. Rajan's excavations at Kodumanal in this regard have been most crucial. The excavator and his team have obtained three AMS dates— 275 BCE, 330 BCE, and 408 BCE (all uncalibrated)—from well-stratified layers. These come from layers which have yielded a considerable number of potsherds bearing inscriptions in the Tamil-Brahmi script. Around 100 such potsherds have been found in 2012 alone, while, on the whole, the excavations have yielded 500 Tamil-Brahmi inscribed sherds. The names on these potsherds, in several instances, have affiliations with names from the North. The excavations have also yielded a couple of sherds of North Black Polished Ware which is associated with the first phase of the early historical period in North and Central India. Considering that in earlier seasons at Kodumanal silver punch-marked coins were found, there is now excellent evidence to argue that this commercial centre had well-established trade and cultural contacts with the middle Gangetic plains in the fifth century BCE. Rajan and Yatheeskumar (2010–12). Also see Rajan, Selvakumar, Ramesh, and Balamurugan (2013) for scientific dates from Porunthal.

33. Line II, Erragudi Edict IV. See Sircar (1979): 27.

34. Lines II–III, Erragudi Edict VII, ibid.: 25

35. Line XIV, Erragudi Edict V, ibid.: 24.

36. Lines III–IV, Erragudi edict IX, ibid.: 40.

37. Line VIII, ibid.

38. See Rich (2008): 166.

39. Sircar has translated the word 'samavaya' as 'restrained speech' whereas it is generally understood as 'concord'. See Hultzsch (1925): 21, and Pandeya (1965): 16, for the later interpretation.

40. Line XIV, Erragudi Edict XIII. Sircar (1979): 85.

41. *AS* 8.4.43. Kangle (1972): pt. II, 400.

42. Lines XVIII–XIX, Erragudi Edict XIII. Sircar (1979): 85.

43. While the impact of such measures in the various independent kingdoms must have depended on a variety of issues, scholars like Rhys Davids read this part of the rock edict with an element of disbelief, bordering on disdain: 'It is difficult to say how much of this is mere royal rhodomontade. It is quite likely that the Greek kings are only thrown in by way of make-weight, as it were; and that no emissaries had been actually sent there at all. Even had they been sent, there is little reason to believe that the Greek self-complacency

would have been much disturbed. Asoka's estimate of the results obtained is better evidence of his own vanity than it is of Greek docility. We may imagine the Greek amusement at the absurd idea of a "barbarian" teaching them their duty; but we can scarcely imagine them discarding their gods and their superstitions at the bidding of an alien king.' See Rhys Davids (1903): 298–9. Possibly, this disdain may have been partly a consequence of Rhys Davids being a colonial civil servant: he served as one in Sri Lanka.

44. A strong political connotation of the term 'dharmavijaya' has been suggested by Dikshitar (1944): 81–3.

45. See Norman (1997–8): 483. Norman also states, quite rightly, that the many elements of dhamma that are mentioned in this edict as forming what was presumably preached abroad cannot be considered Buddhist doctrine. Therefore, Ashoka cannot be seen in his edicts as propagating Buddhism among contemporary rulers.

46. Norman (1997–8): 483.

47. Line V of Erragudi Edict XIV, in Sircar (1979): 20.

## Notes to Chapter 9:  The Message in the Landscape

1. Tod (1839): 370–1.

2. Later, the need to understand Ashokan epigraphs as integrated wholes was underlined by Upinder Singh, who spoke of them as epigraph-monuments: Singh 1997–8: 1–3.

3. Line 8 in Kielhorn (1905–6): 47. The epigraph provides an exceptionally vivid account of the lake and bund and its destruction in 150 CE in a storm: 'the clouds pouring with rain the earth had been converted as it were into one ocean.' Consequently, the swollen floodwaters simply 'tore down hill-tops, trees, banks, turrets, upper stories, gates and raised places of shelter' (lines 5–7). The dam, built during the time of Chandragupta, suffered a huge breach and the Sudarshana lake drained out. Rudradaman's minister Suvishaka then carried out repairs, creating a dam three times larger than the original.

4. These details and those pertaining to what was added in the time of Ashoka are there in Line 8 of the epigraph.

5. Spodek (1974): 451 demonstrates this.

6. Rajyagor (1975–9): 8.

7. Tod (1839): 401.

8. Ghosh (1989): 350.
9. Spodek (1974): 450.
10. Marshall (1951): 95.
11. How this was identified is described in Jamsedjee (1890–4): 47–55.
12. Jamsedjee (1890–4): 54.
13. Lahiri (2011). A great deal mentioned here formed part of my field survey in 2011 in Junagadh and its surrounding area.
14. The bricks used for the stupa measure 45.7 x 38.1 x 7.62 cm.
15. Cousens (1891): 21.
16. Rawat (2009): 99–100.
17. Strong (1989): 219. In the words of the *Ashokavadana*: 'Asoka had eighty-four thousand boxes made of gold, silver, cat's eye, and crystal, and in them were placed the relics. Also, eighty-four thousand urns and eighty-four thousand inscription plates were prepared. All of this was given to the yaksas for distribution in the (eighty-four thousand) dharmarajikas he ordered built throughout the earth as far as the surrounding ocean, in the small, great, and middle-sized towns, and wherever there was a (population of) one hundred thousand (persons).'
18. For this and the observations that follow, Lahiri (2011).
19. Pramanaik (2004–5): 181.
20. Chhabra (1949–50): 174–5.
21. For the four surviving Ashokan edicts at Sannathi, Sarma and Rao (1993): 3–56.
22. Poonacha (2013): 1. Sannathi has also been called Sannati and Sonthi.
23. These Mauryan finds were recovered from two excavations, those conducted by the Department of Archaeology and Museums, Mysore, in 1993–5 and the Archaeological Survey excavations in 2001–2 and 2005–6. See Devraj and Talwar (1996): 9–17 and Poonacha (2013): 16–18. A stupa mound was excavated by the Society for South Asian Studies along with the Archaeological Survey of India between 1986 and 1989. However, no Mauryan remains were found in that excavation. See Howell (1995).
24. Poonacha (2013): 14.
25. Ibid.: 162.
26. Veluthat (2000): 1085.
27. For the separate rock edicts, Hultzsch (1925) and Norman (1997): 82–5.

28. Hultzsch (1925): xiii.
29. Patra (2006): 50.
30. Gupta (1980): 85.
31. Mohanty and Tripathy (1997–8): 87.
32. Chakrabarti (2011): 71.
33. Line 1 (B) of Separate Rock Edict I at Jaugada. Hultzsch (1925): 111.
34. For an analysis of the references to Tosali, Chakrabarti (2011): 67–71.
35. B.B. Lal, the excavator of Sisupalgarh, was of the view that there was only circumstantial evidence of this which could not be considered conclusive. See Lal (1949): 66. Allchin, in 1995, however, had no hesitation in identifying it with the ancient city of Tosali. Allchin (1995): 142.
36. Mohanty and Tripathy (1997–8): 88–9.
37. Ibid.: 90.
38. Chakrabarti (2011): 82.
39. Ibid. Interestingly, if at Sannathi there is a mound known as Ranamandala, it has been pointed out by Chakrabarti that between Srikakulam and Vizianagaram, there is a place called Ranasthalam which means 'the place of battle'.
40. The numbering of the Orissa edicts—Separate Rock Edicts 1 and 2—follows the arrangement that Prinsep first used in the case of Dhauli, although there is unanimity that what is called the first separate edict was actually engraved after the second separate edict. This is the case at Jaugada as well where No. 2 is actually placed above No. 1.
41. Hultzsch (1925): 113. Lines E and F of Jaugada Separate Rock Edict 2.
42. Hultzsch (1925): 118. Line J of Jaugada Separate Rock Edict 2.
43. Norman (1997): 83.
44. Gokhale (1966): 21.
45. Hultzsch (1925): 116. Line 4 (G) of Separate Rock Edict 2 of Jaugada.
46. Hultzsch (1925): 117.
47. Lines K-P of Separate Rock Edict 1. Hultzsch (1925): 96.
48. This is the reading in Norman (1997): 84.
49. Line L, Edict 6. See Hultzsch (1925): 58–9.
50. Line 9 (W and X) of Separate Rock Edict I of Jaugada and Lines 17 and 18 (V and W) of Separate Rock Edict I of Dhauli. Hultzsch (1925): 94 and 113.

51. Line Z of Separate Rock Edict I of Dhauli. Hultzsch (1925): 97.
52. Lines Z-BB of Separate Rock Edict I of Dhauli. Hultzsch (1925): 97.
53. Norman (2012): 61.

## Notes to Chapter 10:  Building Beliefs into Edifices

1. Smith (1909): 35. Ashoka himself never mentions becoming a monk in any of his edicts. Still, the links with the Buddhist Sangha were very strong and he exercised an unusually powerful influence over it.

2. Jackson (1925): 11. This contains the journal of Buchanan Hamilton which is among the most evocative accounts of the Barabar hill and its environs.

3. For the caves and their architecture, Gupta (1980): 189–92 and 202–21. For the inscriptions, Hultzsch (1925): 181–2.

4. Line 2 of First Cave Inscription. Hultzsch (1925): 181.

5. Lines 1 and 2 of Second Cave Inscription, ibid.

6. Third Cave Inscription, ibid.: 182.

7. Forster (1924): 198.

8. Falk (2008): 246.

9. See Gupta (1980): 206–9 for an excellent reconstruction of the process. The summary here presented is based on his description and my field observations.

10. Basham (1981): 135–7.

11. Poonacha (2013): 447, 466.

12. *Mahavamsa* X.96–102; Geiger (1912): 75.

13. Cunningham (1892): 4.

14. Coomaraswamy (1927): 33.

15. Sinha (2000): 9.

16. Watters (1904–5): 115.

17. Cunningham (1892): 76.

18. Bidari (2007): 83–5 cites such episodes from the life of Konakamana.

19. Xuanzang, for instance, wrote about it in the seventh century CE: 'To the north-east of the town of Krakuchchhanda Buddha, going about 30 li, we come to an old capital (or, great city) in which there is a stupa. This is to commemorate the spot where, in the Bhadra-kalpa when men lived to the age of 40,000 years, Kanakamuni Buddha was born ... Further north there is a stupa containing the relics of his bequeathed body; in front of it is a stone pillar with a lion on the top, and about 20 feet high; on this is inscribed a record of the events

connected with his *Nirvana*; this was built by Ashoka-raja.' Beal (1884): vol. III, 272.

20. Chakrabarti (2001): 191. There is a very useful section in Chakrabarti's book on the archaeological geography of this stretch.

21. Mukherji (1901): 1.

22. For a long time after Cunningham's survey, the location of Kapilavastu remained uncertain. This is why Vincent Smith, in his instructions to P.C. Mukherji—who undertook a tour of the Nepal terai—asked him to 'first try and fix the position of Kapilavastu, as a whole, accurately as possible.' Smith (1901): 1. The location of Kapilavastu, though, still remains controversial with academics divided about whether it was Tilaurakot in Nepal and Piprahwa-Ganwaria in India that was known by this name.

23. Mukherji (1901): 19.

24. The recently published results of the excavations conducted there in 2011 and 2012, by a team directed by Robin Coningham and Kosh Prasad Acharya, have provided radiocarbon dates that go back to the eight century BCE. For details, Coningham and Acharya, *et al.* (2013).

25. Tiwari (1996): 2–3. Also Rai (2010): 93–4. This marker stone and other archaeological remains were revealed in archaeological excavations conducted jointly by the Japan Buddhist Federation and Lumbini Development Trust between 1993 and 1996.

26. Falk (2006): 139.

27. For a discussion of Indradhvajas and their intrinsic difference in relation to Ashokan pillars, Gupta (1980): 318–20. Gupta also sees the pillars as an Ashokan innovation.

28. Pant and Jayaswal (1990–1): 49. Also see Jayaswal (1998).

29. Coningham and Acharya, *et al.* (2013).

30. This is based on what was reported in Tiwari (1996): 5–10.

31. Rummindei pillar inscription in Hultzsch (1925): 164–5.

32. A summary of these interpretations is available in Falk (2006): 179.

33. See Falk (2012): 206.

34. Falk believes this is a more likely explanation. In this context, he has drawn attention to an inscription from Kanaganahalli which bears an inscription which in translation reads: 'Above (you see) the stupa of Ramagrama (containing) one eighth part.' The term used for one eighth part is 'athabhaga'. Falk (2012): 206.

35. A few of the grants made to Buddhist and Hindu temple establishments in Orissa carry such exemptions. See the Mallar plates of a

Panduvamsi king to a small Buddhist monastery at Taradamshaka, as also the Santa-Bommali plates of Indravarman in Singh (1994): 253, 258.

36. Rai (2010): 96.
37. For an early description of Gotihawa, Mukherji (1901): 31.
38. Ibid.: 32.
39. Verardi and Coccia (2008): 255–6.
40. Mitra (1972): 228.
41. Verardi (2002).
42. Lines A and B of Nigali Sagar pillar inscription. Hultzsch (1925): 165.
43. The textual references to Vaishali have been cited in detail by Sarao (1990): 106–7.
44. Deva and Mishra (1961). For a summary of the 1950 excavations of Deva and Mishra, Sinha (2000): 211.
45. Sinha and Roy (1969): 21.
46. Ibid.: 23.
47. Ibid.: 22.
48. The monolith stands 14.6 m.
49. Chakrabarti (2011): 109–10.
50. Marshall (1951): vol. I, 234–5.
51. Kumrahar was excavated twice, first by D.B. Spooner as part of 'Mr Ratan Tata's excavations at Pataliputra', and then in 1951–5 by A.S. Altekar and V. Mishra. See Spooner (1912–13) and Altekar and Mishra (1959).
52. *The Mahavamsa* XII.1–2. Geiger (1912): 82.
53. Line E of Calcutta-Bairat inscription, Hultzsch (1925): 174.
54. Lamotte (1988): 236.
55. The temple and the archaeological remains on Bijak-ki-Pahari are described at length in the excavation report. See Sahni (1937): 19–38.
56. Ibid.: 31.
57. Mitra (1971): 66–7.
58. Jayaswal (2009): 14.
59. Sarnath edict in Hultzsch (1925): 162–5.
60. Lamotte (1988): 237.
61. Ghosh (1936): 25.
62. Sarao (1990): 76. Sarao mentions the *Kosambi Jataka* and the *Vinaya* as sources for this story.

63. Marshall, Foucher, and Majumdar (1940): vol. I, 14.
64. Ali, Trivedi, and Solanki (2004): 113–15.
65. Marshall, Foucher, and Majumdar (1940): vol. I, 20.
66. Ibid.: 27.
67. Line C of Sanchi pillar edict, Hultzsch (1925): 161.
68. Bhandarkar 1925: 85–6.

## Notes to Chapter 11:  An Ageing Emperor's Interventions

1. This is what Sircar (1979): 121 noted: 'the language of the inscription resembles that of the Girnar version of Asoka's Rock Edicts and also some MRE texts of the south.' MRE means Minor Rock Edict.
2. Tieken (2012): 185.
3. Norman (2012): 56.
4. Sahni (1907–8): 181–2.
5. For an evocative account of the medieval and modern histories of those ancient Ashokan pillars in Delhi, see Singh (2006): xxx–xxxii.
6. Shokoohy and Shokoohy (1988): 32, 118.
7. Chakrabarti (2011): 111.
8. Bloch (1906–7): 123.
9. This discovery was made by W.C. Peppe in the late nineteenth century. For a summary, Srivastava (1996): 5–6.
10. Majumdar (1935–6).
11. For 'acts of consensual making'—by which paths become habits of a landscape—Macfarlane (2012): 17.
12. Majumdar (1935–6): 55.
13. Chakrabarti (2011): 145–7.
14. Shokoohy and Shokoohy (1988): 6.
15. Understanding the pattern of routes on the basis of artefacts of non-local origin formed the core methodology of my PhD thesis. Specifically for lapis lazuli in early historic India, Lahiri (1992): 371.
16. For an extensive description of the beads, Mitra (1972): 123–40.
17. Line C of the 1st Delhi-Topra pillar edict, Hultzsch (1925): 120.
18. Lines E and F of the 1st Delhi-Topra pillar edict, ibid.
19. Line C of 2nd Delhi-Topra pillar edict, ibid.: 121.
20. Lines E to H of 2nd Delhi-Topra pillar edict, ibid.
21. This has been discussed by Tieken (2012): 185.
22. Line F of 3rd Delhi-Topra pillar edict. Hultzsch (1925): 122.

23. Smith (1909): 34.
24. Line C of 4th Delhi-Topra pillar edict, Hultzsch (1925): 124.
25. Line I of 4th Delhi-Topra pillar edict, ibid.
26. Line D of 4th Delhi-Topra pillar edict, ibid.
27. Line J of 4th Delhi-Topra pillar edict, ibid.
28. Rich (2008): 175.
29. See 4.11.1–26. The death penalty is also mentioned in other chapters, as for instance in 4.12.1 where a woman who has not attained puberty dies because she has been violated by a man of the same 'varna', the punishment being death. Kangle (1972): pt. II, 282–5.
30. Lines M and N of 4th Delhi-Topra pillar edict, Hultzsch (1925): 125.
31. Line L of the 5th Delhi-Topra pillar edict states that 'Until (I had been) anointed twenty-six years, in this period the release of prisoners was ordered by me twenty-five (times).' Ibid.: 128.
32. 5th Delhi-Topra pillar edict, ibid.: 127–8.
33. Smith (1991): 527–8.
34. Ibid.: 537.
35. Norman (1967): 31.
36. Bose (2014).
37. Hora (1950): 49.
38. Ibid.
39. Ibid.: 51.
40. Ibid.: 51–3.
41. Barua (1946): 132.
42. Mirashi (1960): 111.
43. Joglekar (2013): 247–51.
44. Bose (2003): 144–5.
45. Ibid.: 139.
46. For a description of these methods, *Report of the Committee for the Prevention of Cruelty to Animals* (1957): 126.
47. See 'Contests over Game', in Rangarajan (2001): 46–59.
48. Line F of 6th Delhi-Topra edict, Hultzsch (1925): 130.
49. Line B of 7th Delhi-Topra edict, ibid.: 133.
50. Lines F-M of 7th Delhi-Topra edict, ibid.: 134.
51. Hultzsch (1925): 159.
52. Line KK of 7th Delhi-Topra pillar edict, ibid.: 136.
53. Line OO of 7th Delhi-Topra edict, ibid.: 137.

## Notes to Chapter 12:  Of Wifely Woes and the Emperor's Death

1. *Mahavamsa* XX.1–6. Geiger (1912): 136. The name of this queen occurs in three forms in this chapter, depending upon the source—as Tissarakha in the *Mahavamsa*, Tishyarakshita in the *Ashokavadana*, and Tissarakshita in Abanindranath Tagore.
2. Guruge (1993): 260. He refers to the *Vamsatthappakasini*.
3. *Mahavamsa* XIX. Geiger (1912): 128–35.
4. *Mahavamsa* XIX.85, ibid.: 135.
5. For an essay on the ambiguities of Buddhist kingship as seen through the microcosm of Ashoka's wives, Strong (2002).
6. Strong (1989): 257.
7. Ibid.: 258.
8. Ibid.: 270.
9. Ibid.: 273.
10. Ibid.: 273–4.
11. Ibid.: 284.
12. Ibid.: 285.
13. This entire section is based on that chapter. See Strong (1989): 286–92.
14. Beal (1880): 86.

## Notes to Epilogue:  The Emperor's Afterlife

1. For the memory of Ashoka, see the collection of articles in Olivelle (2009), especially Deeg (2009). Also see Strong (1989) and Ray (2012). For the historical traditions of ancient India, Thapar (2013).
2. While the *Vayu Purana* and the *Brahmanda Purana* mention Kunala, Bandhupalita, Indrapalita, Devavarma, Shatadhanus, and Brhadratha, the *Matsya Purana* list is made up of four names—Dasharatha, Samprati, Shatadhanvan, and Brhadratha. A list of seven is provided in the *Vishnu Purana*—Kulala, Bandhupalita, Dashona, Dasharatha, Samprati, Shalisuka, Devadharman, Shatadhanvan, and Brhadratha. As for Buddhist texts, the *Ashokavadana's* list is made up of several names that do not figure in the *Puranas*. The five kings mentioned are Sampadi, Vrihaspati, Vrishasena, Pushyadharman, and Pushyamitra. The Tibetan scholar Taranatha, on the other hand, mentioned only Vigatashoka and Virasena.

3. Pargiter (1913): 29.
4. For the Satavahanas and their successors, Chattopadhyay (2014): 71–95.
5. Strong (1989): 292.
6. Sastri (1967): 245.
7. While the dynasty is said to have come to an end around 180 BCE, there are occasional references to later rulers related to the Mauryas. Bhandarkar, for instance, draws attention to Xuanzang's allusion to Purnavarman, a king of Magadha who ruled some time before the Chinese traveller's visit. Purnavarman is said to have restored the Bodhi tree destroyed by Sashanka, king of Karnasuvarna (Bengal). He is described by the Chinese pilgrim as the 'last of the race of Asoka-raja'. Bhandarkar (1957): 49.
8. Raychaudhuri (1953): 328.
9. Strong (1989): 294.
10. For details of the caves at Nagarjuni hill and Dasharatha's epigraphs, Basham (1951): 151–2, 154–6. The Gopika cave is a single rectangular chamber with a vaulted roof; the Vahiyaka cave is similarly shaped; the Vadathika cave is smaller and less imposing than the other two.
11. The Sudama cave and the Vishvamitra cave at Barabar, as also the Vahiyaka and Vadathika caves at Nagarjuni, show such defacement. Basham (1951): 157.
12. Pratishthanapura is modern Paithan in Maharashtra while Pokhara is Pushkar in Rajasthan. Many other place-names figure as well. See Marshall, Foucher, and Majumdar (1940): vol. 1, 297–362. There are more than 600 inscriptions on Stupa 1, of which nearly 350 are on the ground balustrade.
13. For donations where the domicile of donors is mentioned at Bharhut, Luders, Waldschmidt, and Mehendale (1963): 16–35. The railing and other surviving elements of the Bharhut stupa were dismantled on the initiative of Alexander Cunningham in the nineteenth century and brought to the Indian Museum, Calcutta where they are on display.
14. Ibid.: 66–178.
15. Ibid.: 95–6.
16. For a description of the sculptural relief and the epigraph, ibid.: 95–6.
17. An inscription mentions 'King Pasenaji, the Kosala' and another label inscription refers to Ajatashatru as he who 'worships the Holy One'. Luders, Waldschmidt and Mehendale (1963): 113, 118.

18. Marshall, Foucher, and Majumdar (1940): vol. 1, 215–16; vol. 2, Plate 11. This is on the middle lintel.
19. Ibid.: vol. 2, Plate 18.
20. Ibid.: vol. 3, Plate 79.
21. Nagar (1992): 58–9, 88–9.
22. Each panel was divided into two or three registers with as many as 32 registers in 16 panels devoted to narratives in the life of the Buddha. For the dimensions and details of the drum slabs and their subject matter, Poonacha (2011): 86–90, 262–304.
23. Their names being Chhimuka, Satkarni, Pulumavi, and Sundara Satakarni.
24. Ibid.: 293–4.
25. Ibid.: 296–7.
26. A connection most recently highlighted in all its spatial and temporal resonances in Singh (2014 forthcoming). Also see Singh (unpublished).
27. This is the purport of the relevant (from our perspective) part of the inscription as presented by Singh from the translation offered by Gordon H. Luce. For an early translation of this inscription, Sein Ko (1911–12): 119.
28. This figured in the text of the proposals sent by the foreign minister of the Government of Burma when he wrote to the governor general. Quoted in Ahir (1994): 86.
29. Beal (1884): vol. I, 17, 22–3, 30, 34–6.
30. Ibid.: 35.
31. Ibid.: vol. 3, 327.
32. Ibid.: 277.
33. Ibid.: 292.
34. Ibid.: 272.
35. Beal (1884): vol. 2, 145.
36. Ibid.: 170.
37. Ibid.: 308.
38. Ibid: 309.
39. Ibid.: 181.
40. Ibid.: 246, 251.
41. See verse 23 in Konow (1907–8): 328.
42. Beal (1884): vol. 2, 188–9.
43. Ibid.: 189.
44. Ibid.: 190.

45. Ibid.
46. Stein (1900): vol. I, 4.
47. Ibid.: 74.
48. *Rajatarangini* I.101. Ibid.: 19.
49. *Rajatarangini* I.104. Ibid.
50. *Rajatarangini* I.104. Ibid.
51. *Rajatarangini* I.105–6 for Shiva shrines. Ibid.:20.
52. *Rajatarangini* I.107. Ibid.
53. Jarrett (1896 ): vol. 2, 375–6.
54. Ibid.: 377.
55. Stein's preface states: 'As early as the seventeenth century Dr. Bernier, to whose visit to Kashmir in the summer of 1664 we owe the first European account of the Valley, and one as accurate as it is attractive, had turned his attention to the "histories of the ancient Kings of Kachemire." The Chronicle, of which he possessed a copy, and of which, as he tells us, he was preparing a French translation, was, however, not Kalhana's work, but a Persian compilation, by Haidar Malik Cadura, prepared in Jahangir's time avowedly with the help of the *Rajatarangini*. Also the summary of Kasmir rulers which Father Tieffenthaler a century later reproduced in his "Description de l'Inde" was still derived from that abridged rendering.' Stein (1900): vol. I, viii.
56. Guha-Thakurta (1996): 54.

# Bibliography

Agrawala, V.S. 1964. *The Wheel Flag of India—Chakra-Dhvaja*. Varanasi: Prithvi Prakashan.

Ahir, D.C. 1994. *Buddha Gaya through the Ages*. Delhi: Sri Satguru Publications.

Allchin, F.R. 1995. 'Early Cities and States beyond the Ganges Valley', in F.R. Allchin *The Archaeology of Early Historic South Asia—The Emergence of Cities and States*. Cambridge: Cambridge University Press, pp. 123–51.

———— and K.R. Norman. 1985. 'Guide to the Asokan Inscriptions', *South Asian Studies* 1: 43–50.

Ali, R., A. Trivedi, and D. Solanki. 2004. *Buddhist Remains of Ujjain Region—Excavation at Sodanga*. Delhi: Sharada Publishing House.

Allen, C. 2012. *Ashoka*. London: Little, Brown.

Altekar, A.S. and V.K. Mishra. 1959. *Report on Kumrahar Excavations (1951–53)*. Patna: K.P. Jayaswal Research Institute.

Anderson, P.K. 1991. 'Notes on the Engraving Procedures for the Erragudi Version of Asoka's Minor Rock Edict', *Indo Iranian Journal* 34: 267–91.

Adrados, F.R. 1984. 'Asoka's Inscriptions and Persian, Greek and Latin Epigraphy', in S.D. Joshi (ed.), *Amrtadhara Professor R.N. Dandekar Felicitation Volume*. Delhi: Ajanta Publishers, pp. 1–14.

Armstrong, K. 2000. *Buddha*. London: Phoenix.

Ball, W. and J.C. Gardin. 1982. *Archaeological Gazetteer of Afghanistan I*. Paris: Editions recerche sur les civilisations.

Banerjee, N.R. 1989. 'Ujjain', in A. Ghosh (ed.), *An Encyclopaedia of Indian Archaeology*, vol. 2. New Delhi: Munshiram Manoharlal Publishers Private Ltd., pp. 447–9.

Barua, B.M. 1946 (rpntd 1968). *Asoka and His Inscriptions*. Calcutta and New Delhi: New Age Publishers Pvt. Ltd.

Basham, A.L. 1951 (rpntd 2009). *History and Doctrine of the Ajivikas—A Vanished Indian Religion*. Delhi: Motilal Banarsidass Publishers Pvt. Ltd.

Beal, S. 1880. 'The Tooth-seal of Asoka', *The Indian Antiquary IX*: 86.

———. 1884 (rpntd 1963). *Buddhist Records of the Western Countries, Volume One*. Calcutta: Susil Gupta (India) Pvt. Ltd.

———. 1884 (rpntd 1980). *Buddhist Records of the Western Countries, Volumes Two and Three*. Delhi and Varanasi: Bharatiya Publishing House.

Beglar, J.D. 1878 (rpntd 2000). 'Archaeological Survey of India Report of a Tour in the Bengal Provinces, 1872–73', in A. Cunningham (ed.), *Archaeological Survey of India Report of a Tour through the Bengal Provinces*, vol. VIII. New Delhi: Archaeological Survey of India.

Bernard, P. 2005. 'Hellenistic Arachosia: A Greek Melting Pot in Action', *East and West* 55 (1/4): 13–34.

Beveridge, H. (trans). 1902 (rpntd 1979). *The Akbar Nama of Abu-l-Fazl, Volume I*. New Delhi: Ess Ess Publications.

Bhandarkar, D.R. 1925. *Asoka*. Calcutta: University of Calcutta.

———. 1957 (rpntd 1987). 'Asoka and his Successors', in K.A. Nilakanta Sastri (ed.), *A Comprehensive History of India—Volume Two*. New Delhi: People's Publishing House, pp. 20–49.

Bidari, B. 2007. *Kapilavastu: The World of Siddhartha*. Lumbini: The Author.

Biscione, R. 1984. 'Baluchistan's Presence in the Ceramic Assemblage of Period I at Shahr-I Sokhta', in B. Allchin (ed.), *South Asian Archaeology 1981*. Cambridge: Cambridge University Press, pp. 69–80.

Bloch, T. 1906–7 (rpntd 1990). 'Excavations at Lauriya', *Archaeological Survey of India Annual Report 1906–7*. Delhi: Swati Publications, pp. 119–26.

Bose, M.M. 1928. 'Ashoka's Rock Edicts I, VIII, IX and XI', *Indian Historical Quarterly* (IV): 110–23.

Bose, S. 2003. 'Forests and Fields in the Middle Gangetic Plains (from the Mesolithic upto *c.* 3rd century BC)', M.Phil. dissertation, University of Delhi.

———. 2009. 'Human–Plant Interactions in the Middle Gangetic Plains', in U. Singh and N. Lahiri (eds), *Ancient India—New Research*. New Delhi: Oxford University Press, pp. 71–123.

———. 2014. 'From Eminence to Near Extinction: The Saga of the Greater One-Horned Rhino', in M. Rangarajan and K. Sivaramakrishnan (eds), *Shifting Ground: People, Mobility and Animals in India's Environmental Histories*. New Delhi: Oxford University Press, pp. 65–87.

Bosworth, A.B. 1996. 'The Historical Setting of Megasthenes' *Indica*', *Classical Philology* 91: 113–27.

Bradford, A.S. 2001. *With Arrow, Sword and Spear—A History of Warfare in the Ancient World*. Westport: Praeger Publishers.

Brown, T. 1957. 'The Merits and Weaknesses of Megasthenes', *Phoenix* 11: 12–24.

Buhler, G. 1901 (rpntd 1987). *Indian Palaeography—From About B.C. 350 to About A.D. 1300*. Patna: Eastern Book House.

Carratelli, G.P. and G. Garbini. 1964. *A Bilingual Graeco-Aramaic Edict by Asoka—The First Greek Inscription Discovered in Afghanistan*. Roma: Instituto Italiano Per Il Medio Ed Estremo Oriente.

Cartledge, P. 2012. 'Introduction', in James Romm (ed.), *The Landmark Arrian—The Campaigns of Alexander*. New York: Anchor Books, pp. xiii–xxviii.

Chakrabarti, D.K. 1968. *A History of Indian Archaeology from the Beginning to 1947*. New Delhi: Munshiram Manoharlal Publishers Pvt. Ltd.

———. 2001. *Archaeological Geography of the Ganga Plain—The Lower and the Middle Ganga*. Delhi: Permanent Black.

———. 2005. *The Archaeology of the Deccan Routes—The Ancient Routes from the Ganga Plain to the Deccan*. New Delhi: Munshiram Manoharlal Publishers Pvt. Ltd.

———. 2006. *The Oxford Companion to Indian Archaeology: The Archaeological Foundations of Ancient India, Stone Age to AD 13th Century*. New Delhi: Oxford University Press.

———. 2010. *The Geopolitical Orbits of Ancient India: The Geographical Frames of the Ancient Indian Dynasties*. New Delhi: Oxford University Press.

———. 2011. *Royal Messages by the Wayside—Historical Geography of the Asokan Edicts*. New Delhi: Aryan Books International.

Chalmers, Lord. 1931 (rpntd 2000). *Buddha's Teachings, being the Sutta-Nipata or Discourse-Collection*. Delhi: Motilal Banarsidass Publishers Pvt. Ltd.

Chandra, M. 1977. *Trade and Trade Routes in Ancient India*. New Delhi: Abhinav Publications.

Channing, E. 1885. 'Roads from India to Central Asia', *Science* 5 (117): 360–2.

Chattopadhyay, R.K. 2014. 'The Satavahanas and their Successors', in D.K Chakrabarti and M. Lal (eds), *History of Ancient India Volume IV—Political History and Administration (c. 200 BC–AD 750)*. New Delhi: Vivekananda International Foundation and Aryan Books International.

Cherry, J.F. 2007 (rpntd 2009). 'The Personal and the Political—The Greek World', in S.E. Alcock and R. Osborne (eds), *Classical Archaeology*, USA, UK, Australia: Blackwell Publishing, pp. 288–306.

Chhabra, B. Ch. 1949–50. 'Intwa Clay Sealing', *Epigraphia Indica* XXVIII: 174–5.

——— and G.S. Gai. 1981. *Inscriptions of the Early Gupta Kings. Corpus Inscriptionum Indicarum Volume III*. New Delhi: Archaeological Survey of India.

Ciarla, R. 1981. 'A Preliminary Analysis of the Manufacture of Alabaster Vessels at Shahr-I Sokhta and Mundigak in the 3rd Millennium B.C.', in H. Hartel (ed.), *South Asian Archaeology 1979*. Berlin: Dietrich Reimer Verlag, pp. 45–63.

Coningham, R.A.E. and K.P. Acharya, *et al*. 2013. 'The Earliest Buddhist Shrine: Excavating the Birthplace of the Buddha, Lumbini (Nepal)', *Antiquity* 87: 1104–23.

Connors, R.J. 1986. 'Greek Rhetoric and the Transition from Orality', *Philosophy & Rhetoric* 19 (1): 38–65.

Coomaraswamy, A. 1927 (rpntd 1972). *History of Indian and Indonesian Art*. New Delhi: Munshiram Manoharlal Publishers Pvt. Ltd.

Cousens, H. 1891. 'Report on the Boria or Lakha Medi Stupa near Junagadh', *Journal of the Asiatic Society of Bengal* LX: 17–23.

Cowell, E.B. 1990 (rpntd). *The Jataka, or Stories of the Buddha's Former Births*. New Delhi: Munshiram Manoharlal Publishers Pvt. Ltd.

——— and F.W. Thomas, trans. 1968 (rpntd 1993). *The Harsa-Carita of Bana*. Delhi: Motilal Banarsidass.

Cunningham, A. 1877 (rpntd 1961). *Inscriptions of Asoka. Corpus Inscriptionum Indicarum Volume 1*. Varanasi: Indological Book House.

————. 1892 (rpntd 1998). *Mahabodhi, or the Great Buddhist Temple under the Bodhi Tree at Buddha-Gaya*. New Delhi: Munshiram Manoharlal Publishers Pvt. Ltd.

Dani, A.H. 1986. *The Historic City of Taxila*. Paris and Tokyo: The United Nations Educational Scientific and Cultural Organization and the Centre of East Asian Cultural Studies.

Deeg, M. 2009. 'From the Iron-Wheel to Bodhisattvahood: Asoka in Buddhist Culture and Memory', in P. Olivelle (ed.), *Asoka in History and Historical Memory*, Delhi: Motilal Banarsidass Publishers Pvt Ltd, pp. 109–44.

————. 2012. 'Asoka: Model Ruler without a Name?', in P. Olivelle, J. Leoshko, and H.P. Ray (eds), *Reimagining Asoka: Memory and History*, New Delhi: Oxford University Press, pp. 362–79.

Deloche, J. 1993. *Transport and Communication in India Prior to Steam Locomotion Volume 1*. New Delhi: Oxford University Press.

Deva, K. and V. Mishra. 1961. *Vaisali Excavations*. Vaisali: Vaisali Sangh.

Devahuti, D. 1970. *Harsha: A Political Study*. Oxford: Clarendon Press.

Devraj, D.V. and H.T. Talwar. 1996. *Interim Report on the Excavations at Sannati 1993–95*. Mysore: Directorate of Archaeology and Museums.

Dharamsey, V. 2012. *Bhagwanlal Indraji—The First Indian Archaeologist*. Vadodara: Darshak Itihas Nidhi.

Dhavalikar, M.K. 1977. *Masterpieces of Indian Terracottas*. Bombay: Taraporevala.

Dikshitar, V.R.R. 1944 (rpntd 1948). *War in Ancient India*. Madras, Bombay, Calcutta, London: Macmillan and Co.

Diringer, D. 1996 (rpnt). *The Alphabet—A Key to the History of Mankind*. New Delhi: Munshiram Manoharlal Publishers Pvt. Ltd.

Dupree, L. 1997. *Afghanistan*. Karachi: Oxford University Press.

Ebrey, P.B. 1996. *The Cambridge Illustrated History of China*. Cambridge: Cambridge University Press.

Edde, A.M. (trans. J.M. Todd). 2011. *Saladin*. Cambridge and London: Harvard University Press.

Eggermont, P.H.L. 1956. *The Chronology of the Reign of Asoka Moriya—A Comparison of the Data on the Asoka Inscriptions and the Data of the Tradition*. Leiden: E.J. Brill.

Falk, H. 2006. *Asokan Sites and Artefacts—A Source-Book with Bibliography*. Mainz am Rhein: Verlag Philipp von Zabern.

————. 2008. 'Barabar Reconsidered', in E.M. Raven (ed.), *South Asian Archaeology 1999*. Groningen: Egbert Forsten, pp. 245–51.

————. 2012. 'The Fate of Asoka's Donations at Lumbini', in P. Olivelle, J. Leoshko, and H.P. Ray (eds), *Reimagining Asoka—Memory and History*, New Delhi: Oxford University Press, pp. 204–16.

Filliozat, J. 1961–2. 'Graeco-Aramaic Inscription of Asoka near Kandahar', *Epigraphia Indica*, XXXIV: 1–8.

Forster, E.M. 1924 (rpntd 2005). *A Passage to India*. London: Penguin.

Fraser, P.M. 1979. 'The Son of Aristonax at Kandahar', *Afghan Studies* 2: 9–21.

Fuller, C.J. 2001. 'Orality, Literacy and Memorization: Priestly Education in Contemporary South India', *Modern Asian Studies* 35 (1): 1–32.

Geiger, W. 1912 (rpntd 1964). *The Mahavamsa or the Great Chronicle of Ceylon*. London: Pali Text Society and Luzac & Company, Ltd.

Ghosh, A. 1948. 'Taxila (Sirkap), 1944–5', *Ancient India* 4: 41–84.

————. 1989. *An Encyclopaedia of Indian Archaeology*. New Delhi: Munshiram Manoharlal Publishers Pvt. Ltd.

Ghosh, N.N. 1936 (rpntd 1985). *Early History of Kausambi (from the Sixth Century BC to the Eleventh Century AD)*. Delhi: Durga Publications.

Gokhale, B.G. 1962. *Samudra Gupta—Life and Times*. Bombay: Asia Publishing House.

————. 1966. 'Early Buddhist Kingship', *Journal of Asian Studies* 26 (1): 15–22.

Gordon, D.H. and M.E. Gordon. 1943. 'The Cultures of Maski and Madhavpur', *Journal of the Royal Asiatic Society of Bengal. Letters* IX: 83–98.

Goswami, B. 2001. *Lalitavistara—English Translation with Notes*. Kolkata: The Asiatic Society.

Goyal, S. 2006. *Harsha: A Multidisciplinary Political Study*. Jodhpur: Kusumanjali Book World.

Goyal, S.R. 1986. *Bharat ke Mahan Naresh Granthmala—Harsha Shiladitya*. Meerut: Kusumanjali.

Guha, R. 1999. *Savaging the Civilized: Verrier Elwin, His Tribals and India*. Chicago, London: University of Chicago Press.

————. 2004. *The Last Liberal and Other Essays*. New Delhi: Permanent Black.

————. 2013. *Gandhi Before India*. New Delhi: Penguin India.

Guha-Thakurta, T. 1996. 'Meera Mukherjee: Recasting the Folk Form', in G. Sinha (ed.), *Expressions & Evocations—Contemporary Women Artists of India*. Bombay: Marg Publications, pp. 48–59.

Gupta, S.P. 1980. *The Roots of Indian Art* (*A Detailed Study of the Formative Period of Indian Art and Architecture: Third and Second Centuries BC— Mauryan and Late Mauryan*). Delhi: B.R. Publishing Corporation.

Guruge, A.W.P. 1993. *Asoka, the Righteous: A Definitive Biography.* Colombo: The Central Cultural Fund.

Hare, E.M. 1947. *Woven Cadences of Early Buddhists* (*Sutta Nipata*). London: Geoffrey Cumberlege.

Hazra, K.L. 2007. *Asoka as Depicted in His Edicts.* New Delhi: Munshiram Manoharlal Publishers Pvt. Ltd.

Helms, S.W. 1979. 'Old Kandahar Excavations 1976: Preliminary Report', *Afghan Studies* 2: 1–9.

———. 1982. 'Excavations at the City and the Famous Fortress of Kandahar, the Foremost Place in all of Asia', *Afghan Studies* 3–4: 1–24.

Hiltebeitel, A. 2011. *Dharma: Its Early History in Law, Religion and Narrative.* Oxford: Oxford University Press.

Hilton, J. 1996. 'The Good, the Bad and the Ugly: Birds, Animals and Omens in Ancient Indian Literature', in S.D. Singh (ed.), *Culture through the Ages.* Delhi: Agam Kala Prakashan, pp. 59–83.

Hinghausen, M.L. 1966. *Harsa Vardhana Empereur et Poete.* Londres, Paris, Louvain: Lusac & Co, Ernest Leroux, and J.B. Istas.

Hora, S.L. 1950. 'Knowledge of the Ancient Hindus concerning Fish and Fisheries of India—Fishery Legislation in Asoka's Pillar Edict V', *Journal of the Royal Asiatic Society of Bengal: Letters*, XVI (1): 43–56.

Holt, F. 2012. *Lost World of the Golden King—In Search of Ancient Afghanistan.* Berkeley and Los Angeles: University of California Press.

Howell, J.R. 1995. *Excavations at Sannathi 1986–89.* Memoirs of the Archaeological Survey of India No. 93. New Delhi: Archaeological Survey of India.

Hultzsch, E. 1907–8. 'Tirumalai Rock Inscription of Rajendra-Chola I', *Epigraphia Indica* IX: 229–33.

———. 1925 (rpntd 1991). *Corpus Inscriptionum Indicarum Vol. I: Inscriptions of Asoka.* New Delhi: Archaeological Survey of India.

*Imperial Gazetteer of India, Vol. XXI.* 1908 (rpntd, n.d.). New Delhi: Today and Tomorrow's Printers and Publishers.

Izre'el, S. and R. Drorp. 1997. *Language and Culture in the Near East.* Leiden: Brill.

Jackson, V.H. 1925. *Journal of Francis Buchanan (afterwards Hamilton), Kept during the Survey of the Districts of Patna and Gaya in 1811–1812.* Patna: Superintendent, Government Printing, Bihar and Orissa.

Jamsedjee, A. 1890–4. 'The Sudarshana or Lake Beautiful of the Girnar Inscriptions, B.C. 300–A.D. 450, with an Introduction by O. Codrington', *Journal of the Bombay Branch of the Royal Asiatic Society*, XVIII: 47–55.

Jarrett, H.S. (corrected and annotated by J. Sarkar). 1949 (1978). *The Ain-i Akbari by Abu'l Fazl Allami*. Volume II. New Delhi: Oriental Books Reprint Corporation.

Jayaswal, K.P. and R.D. Banerji. 1933. 'The Hathigumpha Inscription of Kharavela', *Epigraphia Indica* XX (1929–30): 71–89.

Jayaswal, V. 1998. *From Stone Quarry to Sculpturing Workshop—A Report on the Archaeological Investigations around Chunar Varanasi & Sarnath*. Delhi: Agam Kala Prakashan.

———. 2009. *Ancient Varanasi: An Archaeological Perspective (Excavations at Aktha)*. New Delhi: Aryan Books International.

Joglekar, P.P. 2008. 'A Fresh Appraisal of the Animal-based Subsistence and Domestic Animals in the Ganga Valley', *Pragdhara* (18): 309–21.

———. 2013. 'Faunal Remains from Raja-Nala-ka-Tila, District Sonabhadra, Uttar Pradesh', *Pragdhara* (21–2): 227–77.

———, V. Tripathi, and P. Upadhyay. 2012. 'Faunal Diversity at Agiabir, District Mirzapur, a Multi-Cultural Site in Uttar Pradesh', *Pragdhara* (20): 43–59.

Joshi, M.C. and B.M. Pande. 1967. 'A Newly Discovered Inscription of Asoka at Bahapur, Delhi', *Journal of the Royal Asiatic Society*, 1967: 96–8.

Kane, P.V. 1994 (rpntd). *History of Dharmasastra (Ancient and Medieval Religious and Civil Law)*. Poona: Bhandarkar Oriental Research Institute.

———. 1997 (rpntd). *History of Dharmasastra (Ancient and Medieval Religious and Civil Law)*, II (ii). Poona: Bhandarkar Oriental Research Institute.

Kangle, R.P. 1965 (rpntd 2000). *The Kautilya Arthasastra. Part III*. Delhi: Motilal Banarsidass Publishers Private Limited.

———. 1972 (rpntd 2000). *The Kautilya Arthasastra. Part II*. Delhi: Motilal Banarsidass Publishers Pvt. Ltd.

Karambelkar, V.W. 1959. *The Atharvavedic Civilization: Its Place in the Indo-Aryan Culture*. Nagpur: University of Nagpur.

Kargupta, S. 2002. *Understanding the Prophetic—The History and Philosophy of Prognostication in Ancient India*. Kolkata: The Asiatic Society.

Kejariwal, O.P. 1988. *The Asiatic Society of Bengal and the Discovery of India's Past*. Delhi: Oxford University Press.

Kielhorn, F. 1905–6. 'Junagadh Rock Inscription of Rudradaman; The Year 72', *Epigraphia Indica* VIII: 36–49.

Konow, S. 1907–8. 'Sarnath Inscription of Kumaradevi', *Epigraphia Indica* 9: 319–28.

Kosmin, P.J. 2014. *The Land of the Elephant Kings: Space, Territory and Ideology in the Seleucid Empire*. Cambridge and London: Harvard University Press.

Kumar, B. 1987. *Archaeology of Pataliputra and Nalanda*. Delhi: Ramanand Vidya Bhawan.

Lahiri, N. 1992. *The Archaeology of Indian Trade Routes Upto c. 200 BC— Resource Use, Resource Access and Lines of Communication*. Delhi: Oxford University Press.

———. 2005 (rpntd 2011). *Finding Forgotten Cities: How the Indus Civilization was Discovered*. Gurgaon and Delhi: Hachette India and Black Kite/Permanent Black.

———. 2011. 'Revisiting the Cultural Landscape of Junagadh in the Time of the Mauryas', *Puratattva* 41: 114–30.

Lal, B.B. 1949. 'Sisupalgarh 1948: An Early Historical Fort in Eastern India', *Ancient India* 5: 62–105.

Lal, M. 1986. 'Iron Tools, Forest Clearance and Urbanisation in the Gangetic Plains', *Man and Environment*, X: 83–90.

Lamotte, E. 1988. *History of Indian Buddhism—From the Origins to the Saka Era*. Louvain-Paris: Peeters Press.

Law, B.C. 1954 (rpntd 1984). *Historical Geography of Ancient India*. New Delhi: Oriental Books Reprint Corporation.

Lopez, D.S. 1995. *Religions of India in Practice*. Princeton: Princeton University Press.

Luders, H.E. Waldschmidt and M.A. Mehendale. 1963. *Bharhut Inscriptions—Corpus Inscriptionum Indicarum, II (ii)*. Ootacamund: Government Epigraphist for India.

MacDowall, D.W. and M. Taddei. 1978. 'The Early Historic Period: Achaemenids and Greeks', in F.R. Allchin and N. Hammond (eds), *The Archaeology of Afghanistan—From Prehistoric Times to the Timurid Period*. London, New York, San Francisco: Academic Press, pp. 187–232.

Macfarlane, R. 2012. *The Old Ways—A Journey on Foot*. New York: Viking.

Majumdar, N.G. 1935–6. 'Explorations at Lauriya-Nandangarh', *Annual Report of the Archaeological Survey of India 1935–36*, pp. 56–66.

Majumdar, R.C. 1958. 'The Indika of Megasthenes', *Journal of the American Oriental Society* 78 (4): 273–6.

———. 1960. *The Classical Accounts of India*. Calcutta: Firma K.L. Mukhopadhyay.

Marshall, J. 1911–12. 'Excavations at Bhita', *Archaeological Survey of India Annual Report 1911-12*, pp. 29–94.

——— (ed.). 1931 (rpntd). *Mohenjodaro and the Indus Civilization* (3 vols). Delhi: Swati Publications.

———. 1951 (rpntd 1975). *Taxila—An Illustrated Account of Archaeological Excavations carried out At Taxila under the Orders of the Government of India between the Years 1913 and 1934*. Delhi, Varanasi and Patna: Motilal Banarsidass.

———, A. Foucher, and N.G. Majumdar. 1940 (rpntd 1983). *The Monuments of Sanchi*. Delhi: Swati Publications.

McCrindle, J.W. 1877. *Ancient India as Described by Megasthenes and Arrian*. Calcutta and Bombay: Trubner & Co.

Mirashi, V.V. 1960. 'New Light on Deotek Inscriptions', in V.V. Mirashi (ed.), *Studies in Indology Volume I*. Nagpur: Vidarbha Samshodhana Mandal.

Mitra, D. 1971 (rpntd 1980). *Buddhist Monuments*. Calcutta: Sahitya Samsad.

———. 1972. *Excavations at Tilaurakot and Kodan and Explorations in the Nepalese Terai*. Kathmandu: The Department of Archaeology.

Mohanty, P. and B. Tripathy. 1997–8. 'The Prehistoric, Protohistoric and the Early Historic Cultures of Orissa', *Pragdhara* 8: 69–98.

Mookerji, R. 1926 (rpntd 1965). *Harsha*. Delhi, Varanasi, Patna: Motilal Banarsidass.

———. 1928 (rpntd 2007). *Asoka*. Delhi: Motilal Banarsidass.

———. 1952 (rpntd 1960). *Chandragupta Maurya—Emperor of Northern India*. Delhi: Motilal Banarsidass.

———. 1957. 'The Foundation of the Mauryan Empire', in K.A. Nilakanta Sastri (ed.), *A Comprehensive History of India Volume 2: The Mauryas & Satavahanas 325 BC—AD 300*. New Delhi: People's Publishing House, pp. 1–19.

Moore, C.H. 1921. 'Prophecy in the Ancient Epic', *Harvard Studies in Classical Philology* 32: 99–175.

Mukherjee, B.N. 1984. *Studies in the Aramaic Edicts of Asoka*. Calcutta: Indian Museum.

———. 1997. 'Locations of the Asokan Edicts', in H.B. Chowdhury (ed.), *Asoka 2300—Jagajjyoti: Asoka Commemoration Volume 1997*. Calcutta: Bauddha Dharmankur Sabha.

Mukherji, P.C. 1901 (1969 rpntd). *A Report on a Tour of Exploration of the Antiquities in the Tarai, Nepal the Region of Kapilavastu; During February and March 1899*. Varanasi: Indological Book House.

Nagar, S.L 1992. *Indian Monoliths*. New Delhi: Intellectual Publishing House.

Nakamura, H. 1987 (rpntd 2007). *Indian Buddhism: A Survey with Bibliographical Notes*. Delhi: Motilal Banarsidass Publishers Pvt. Ltd.

Nehru, J. 1946 (1990 rpntd). *The Discovery of India*. New Delhi: Oxford University Press.

Norman, K.R. 1967. 'Notes on Asoka's Fifth Pillar Edict', *Journal of the Royal Asiatic Society of Great Britain and Ireland*: 26–32.

———. 1997. 'Asoka's Debt to His People', in H.B. Chowdhury (ed.), *Asoka 2300—Jagajjyoti: Asoka Commemoration Volume*. Calcutta: Bauddha Dharmankur Sabha, pp. 81–97.

———. 1997–8. 'Asoka's Thirteenth Rock Edict', *Indological Taurinensia* (23–4): 459–84.

———. 2012. 'The Languages of the Composition and Transmission of the Ashokan Inscriptions', in P. Olivelle, J. Leoshko, and H.P. Ray (eds), *Reimagining Asoka—Memory and History*. New Delhi: Oxford University Press, pp. 38–62.

Oikonomides, Al. N. 1984. 'The [Teuevoc] of Alexander the Great at Alexandria in Arachosia (Old Kandahar)', *Zeitschrift fur Papyrologie und Epigraphik* 56: 145–7.

Oldenberg, H. 1879 (rpntd 1982). *The Dipavamsa: An Ancient Buddhist Historical Record*. New Delhi: Asian Educational Services.

Olivelle, P. 2009. *Asoka in History and Historical Memory*. Delhi: Motilal Banarsidass Publishers.

———. 2012. 'Asoka's Inscriptions as Text and Ideology', in P. Olivelle, J. Leoshko, and H.P. Ray (eds), *Reimagining Asoka—Memory and History*, New Delhi: Oxford University Press, pp. 157–83.

———. 2013 (rpntd 2014). *King, Governance, and Law in Ancient India—Kautilya's Arthashastra*. New Delhi: Oxford University Press.

Oliver, R.T. 1971. *Communication and Culture in Ancient India and China*. Syracuse: Syracuse University Press.

Ong, W.T. 1984. 'Orality, Literacy and Medieval Textualization', *New Literary History* 16 (1): 1–12.

Orsini, F. (ed.). 2007. *Love in South Asia—A Cultural History*. New Delhi: Cambridge University Press India Pvt. Ltd.

Page, J.A. 1926–7 (rpntd 1990). 'Bulandi Bagh, near Patna', in *Annual Report of the Archaeological Survey of India 1926–27*. Delhi: Swati Publications.

Pandeya, R. 1965. *Ashoka ke abhilekha*. Varanasi: Gyanmandal Ltd.

Pant, P.C. and V. Jayaswal. 1990–1. 'Ancient Stone Quarries of Chunar: An Appraisal', *Pragdhara* 1: 49–52.

Pargiter. F.E. 1913 (rpntd 1962). *The Purana Text on the Dynasties of the Kali Age*. Varanasi: The Chowkhamba Sanskrit Series Office.

Parker, G. (ed.). 1995. *The Cambridge Illustrated History of Warfare—The Triumph of the West*. Cambridge: Cambridge University Press.

Patra, B. 2006. 'Dhauli: An Early Historic Urban Centre of Orissa', *Orissa Review*: 49–53.

Poonacha, K.P. 2013. *Excavations at Kanaganahalli (Sannati) Taluk Chitapur, Dist. Gulbarga, Karnataka*. Memoirs of the Archaeological Survey of India No. 106. New Delhi: Archaeological Survey of India.

Pramanaik, S. 2004–5. 'Significant Discoveries around Sudarshan Lake, Junagadh', *Puratattva* 35: 179–81.

Prasad, A.K. 2006. 'Champa, an Ancient Urban Centre of Bihar—A Case Study', in B.R. Mani and S.C. Saran (eds), *Purabharati Studies in Early Historical Archaeology and Buddhism (Commemoration Volume in Respect of Prof. B.P. Sinha)*. Delhi: Sharada Publishing House, pp. 48–50.

Rai, H.D. 2010. *Lumbini: The Supreme Pilgrimage*. Kathmandu: Holy Ashoka Tours & Travels Pvt. Ltd.

Rajan, K. and V.P Yatheeskumar. 2010–12. 'New Evidences on Scientific Dates for Brahmi Script as Revealed from Porunthal and Kodumanal Excavations', *Pragdhara* 21–2: 279–95.

———, S. Selvakumar, R. Ramesh, and P. Balamurugan. 2013. 'Archaeological Excavations at Porunthal, District Dindugul, Tamil Nadu', *Man and Environment* XXXVIII (2): 62–85.

Rajyagor, S.B. 1975. *Gujarat State Gazetteers, Junagadh District*. Ahmedabad: Government of Gujarat.

Rangachari, D. 2009. *Invisible Women, Visible Histories: Gender, Society and Polity in Northern India (Seventh to Twelfth Century AD)*. New Delhi: Manohar.

Rangarajan, M. 2001. *India's Wildlife History—An Introduction*. Delhi: Permanent Black and Ranthambhore Foundation.

Rawat, Y.S. 2009. 'Hill Fort of Anarta: Discovery of a Unique Early Historical Fort with Cave Dwellings, Buddhist Idols and Remains at Taranga in North Gujarat', *Purattatva* 39: 96–106.

Ray, H.P. 2006. 'Archaeology and Asoka: Defining the Empire', in P. Olivelle, J. Leoshko, and H.P. Ray (eds), *Reimagining Asoka—Memory and History*. New Delhi: Oxford University Press, pp. 17–37.

Raychaudhuri, H. 1953 (1972 edition). *Political History of Ancient India—From the Accession of Parikshit to the Extinction of the Gupta Dynasty*. Calcutta: University of Calcutta.

*Report of the Committee for the Prevention of Cruelty to Animals*. 1957. New Delhi: Government of India.

Reynolds, F.E. 1976. 'The Many Lives of Buddha: A Study of Sacred Biography and Theravada Tradition', in F.E. Reynolds and D. Capps (eds), *The Biographical Process—Studies in the History and Psychology of Religion*. The Hague and Paris: Mouton & Co., pp. 37–61.

Rhys Davids, T.W. (trans.) 1881 (rpntd 1965). *Sutta Pitaka. Sacred Books of the East XI*. New Delhi: Motilal Banarsidass Publishers Pvt. Ltd.

———. 1903 (rpntd 1971). *Buddhist India*. Delhi, Patna, Varanasi: Motilal Banarsidass Publishers Pvt. Ltd.

——— (trans.) 1910 (rpntd 2001). *Dialogues of the Buddha. Translated from the Pali of the Digha Nikaya*. Delhi: Low Price Publications.

——— and H. Oldenberg (trans). 1882 (rpntd 1968). *Vinaya Texts Part I and II. Sacred Books of the East XVII*. New Delhi: Motilal Banarsidass.

Rich, B. 2008. *To Uphold the World—The Message of Ashoka & Kautilya for the 21st Century*. New Delhi: Viking.

Romm, J. (ed.). 2012 (trans. P. Mensch). *The Landmark Arrian: The Campaigns of Alexander—Anabasis Alexandrou*. New York: Anchor Books.

Rowley, H.H. 1956. *Prophecy and Religion in Ancient China and Israel*. New York: Harper & Brothers.

Saha, M.N. 1953. 'Different Methods of Date-recording in Ancient and Medieval India, and the Origin of the Saka Era, *Journal of the Asiatic Society: Letters*, XIX (1): 1–24.

Sahni, D.R. 1907–8 (rpntd 1990). 'Excavations at Rampurva', *Archaeological Survey of India Annual Report 1907–8*. Delhi: Swati Publications, pp. 181–8.

———. 1928–9 (rpntd 1990). 'The Yerragudi Rock Edicts of Asoka',

*Annual Report of the Archaeological Survey of India 1928–29*. Delhi: Swati Publications.

———. 1937. *Archaeological Remains and Excavations at Bairat.* Jaipur: Department of Archaeology & Historical Research, Jaipur State.

Sali, S.A. 1986. *Daimabad 1976–79.* New Delhi: Archaeological Survey of India.

Salomon, R. 1998. *Indian Epigraphy—A Guide to the Study of Inscriptions in Sanskrit, Prakrit, and the other Indo-Aryan Languages.* New Delhi: Munshiram Manoharlal Publishers Pvt. Ltd.

———. 2009. 'Asoka and the "Epigraphic Habit" in India', in P. Olivelle (ed.), *Ashoka in History and Historical Memory,* Delhi: Motilal Banarsidass Publishers Pvt. Ltd, pp. 45–52.

Sarao, K.T.S. 1990 (rpntd 2010). *Urban Centres and Urbanisation—As Reflected in the Pali Vinaya and Sutta Pitakas.* New Delhi: Munshiram Manoharlal Publishers Pvt. Ltd.

———. 2014. 'Janapadas, Mahajanapadas, Kingdoms, and Republics', in D.K. Chakrabarti and M. Lal (eds), *History of Ancient India, Volume III: The Texts, Political History and Administration till c. 200 BC,* New Delhi: Vivekananda International Foundation and Aryan Books International, pp. 183–204.

Sarma, I.K. and J.V. Rao. 1993. *Early Brahmi Inscriptions from Sannati.* New Delhi: Harman Publishing House.

Sastri, K.A.N. 1967. *Age of the Nandas and Mauryas.* Delhi: Motilal Banarsidass.

Scerrato, U. 1958. 'An Inscription of Asoka Discovered in Afghanistan: The Bilingual Greek-Aramaic of Kandahar', *East and West* 9 (1/2): 406.

Schoeber, J. 1997. 'Trajectories in Buddhist Sacred Biography', in J. Schoeber (ed.), *Sacred Biography in the Buddhist Traditions of South and Southeast Asia,* Honolulu: University of Hawai'i Press, pp. 1–15.

Sein Ko, T. 1911–12.'Burmese Inscription at Bodh-Gaya', *Epigraphia Indica* XI: 118–20.

Sen, P. 1997 'Asoka: The Great Emperor—Rabindranath Tagore', in H.B. Chowdhury (ed.), *Asoka 2300—Jagajjyoti: Asoka Commemoration Volume.* Calcutta: Bauddha Dharmankur Sabha, pp. 9–10.

Sethna, K.D. 1960. 'Note on R.C. Majumdar's Objections against Megasthenes and Schwanbeck', *Journal of the American Oriental Society* 80: 243–50.

Shaffer, J. 1978. 'The Later Prehistoric Periods', in F.R. Allchin and N. Hammond (eds), *The Archaeology of Afghanistan—From Earliest*

*Times to the Timurid Period.* London, New York, San Francisco: Academic Press, pp. 71–186.

Shamasastry, R. (trans). 1915 (rpntd 1960). *Kautilya's Arthasastra.* Mysore: Mysore Printing and Publishing House.

Sharif, S.M. 1969. 'Excavations at Bhir Mound, Taxila', *Pakistan Archaeology* 6: 7–99.

Sharma, B.N. 1970. *Harsa and His Times.* Varanasi: Sushma Prakashan.

Sharma, R.K. and O.P. Misra. 2003. *Archaeological Excavations in Central India (Madhya Pradesh and Chattisgarh).* New Delhi: Mittal Publications.

Shere, S.A. 1951. 'Stone Discs of Murtaziganj 1951', *Journal of the Bihar Research Society* XXXVII: 178–90.

Shokoohy, M. and N.H. Shokoohy. 1988. *Hisar-i Firuza—Sultanate and Early Mughal Architecture in the District of Hisar, India.* London: Monographs on Art Archaeology and Architecture.

Sick, D. 2007. 'When Socrates Met the Buddha: Greek and Indian Dialectic in Hellenistic Bactria and India', *Journal of the Royal Asiatic Society* 17 (3): 253–78.

Singh, B.P. 2003. *Early Farming Communities of Kaimur: Excavations at Senuar.* Jaipur: Publication Scheme.

Singh, V.L. 1998. *Ujjayini: A Numismatic and Epigraphic Study.* New Delhi: Khama Publishers.

Singh, R.N., C.A. Petrie, P.P Joglekar, S. Neogi, C. Lacelotti, A.K. Pandey, and A. Pathak. 2013. 'Recent Excavation at Alamgirpur, Meerut District: A Preliminary Report', *Man and Environment* XXXVIII (1): 32–54.

Singh, U. 1994. *Kings, Brahmanas and Temples in Orissa—An Epigraphic Study AD 300–1147.* New Delhi: Munshiram Manoharlal Publishers Pvt. Ltd.

———. 1997–8. 'Texts on Stone: Understanding Asoka's Epigraph-Monuments and their Changing Contexts', *Indian Historical Review* 24 (1–2): 1–19.

———. 2006. *Ancient Delhi.* New Delhi: Oxford University Press.

———. 2009. *A History of Ancient and Early Medieval India: From the Stone Age to the 12th Century.* Delhi: Pearson Longman.

———. 2012. 'Governing the State and the Self: Political Philosophy and Practice in the Edicts of Asoka', *South Asian Studies* 28 (2): 131–45.

———. 2014. 'Gifts from Other Lands: Southeast Asian Religious Endowments in India', in U. Singh and P.P. Dhar (eds), *Asian Encounters: Exploring Connected Histories.* Delhi: Oxford University Press.

————. Unpublished. 'Bodhgaya: The View from Myanmar'. Paper presented at the conference on 'Bodh Gaya through the Centuries' at Bihar Heritage Development Society, 7–9 March 2014.

Sinha, B.P. 2000. *Directory of Bihar Archaeology Silver Jubilee Year Publication*. Patna: Bihar Puravid Parishad.

———— and S.R. Roy. 1969. *Vaisali Excavations 1958–1962*. Patna: Directorate of Archaeology and Museums.

Sinha, K.K. 1971–2. 'Remarks', *Purattatva*, 5: 29–33.

Sircar, D.C. 1942 (rpnt 1993). *Select Inscriptions Bearing on Indian History and Civilization*, vol. I. Delhi: V.K. Publishing House.

————. 1960. 'Rajula–Mandagiri Inscription of Asoka', *Epigraphia Indica* XXXI (1955–6): 211–18.

————. 1979 (rpnt 2000). *Asokan Studies*. Calcutta: Indian Museum.

———— and K.G. Krishnan. 1957–8. 'Bhubaneswar Inscription of Ganga Narasimha', *Epigraphia Indica* XXXII: 229–38.

Smith, B.K. 1991. 'Classifying Animals and Humans in Ancient India', *Man* (New Series), 26 (3): 527–48.

Smith, V.A. 1889. 'Graeco-Roman Influence on the Civilization of India', *Journal of the Asiatic Society of Bengal* 58: 107–98.

————. 1901 (rpnt 1969). 'Prefatory Note', in P.C. Mukherji, *A Report on a Tour of Exploration of the Antiquities in the Tarai, Nepal the Region of Kapilavastu; During February and March 1899*. Varanasi: Indological Book House, pp. 1–22.

————. 1909 (rpnt 1957). *Asoka The Buddhist Emperor of India*. Delhi, Lucknow and Jullunder: S. Chand & Co.

Snodgrass, A.M. 1985. 'Greek Archeology and Greek History', *Classical Antiquity*, 4 (2): 193–207.

Spodek, H. 1974. 'Rulers, Merchants and Other Groups in the City-States of Saurashtra, India around 1800', *Comparative Studies in Society and History*, 16 (4): 448–70.

Spooner, D.B. 1912–13 (rpnt 1990). 'Mr Ratan Tata's Excavations at Pataliputra', *Archaeological Survey of India Annual Report 1912–13*. Delhi: Swati Publications, pp. 53–86.

Srivastava, K.M. 1996. *Excavations at Piprahwa and Ganwaria*. New Delhi: Director General, Archaeological Survey of India.

Stein, M.A. 1900 (1989 rpnt). *Kalhana's Rajatarangini—A Chronicle of the Kings of Kasmir*, vol. I. Delhi: Motilal Banarsidass Publishers.

Stoneman, R. 2010 (rpnt 2012). 'The Persian Empire and Alexander', in J. Romm (ed.), *The Landmark Arrian—The Campaigns of Alexander Anabasis Alexandrou*, New York: Anchor Books, pp. 361–6.

Strong, J.S. 2002. 'Asoka's Wives and the Ambiguities of Buddhist Kingship', *Cahiers d'Extreme-Asie* 3: 35–54.

———. 1989 (rpntd 2008). *The Legend of King Asoka: A Study and Translation of the Asokavadana*. Delhi: Motilal Banarsidass.

———. 2012. 'The Commingling of Gods and Humans, the Unveiling of the World, and the Descent from Trayastrimsa Heaven—An Exegetical Exploration of Minor Rock Edict I', in P. Olivelle, J. Leoshko, and H.P. Ray (eds), *Reimagining Asoka—Memory and History*. New Delhi: Oxford University Press, pp. 348–61.

Tambiah, S.J. 1973. 'Buddhism and This-worldly Activity', *Modern Asian Studies* 7 (1): 1–20.

———. 1976. *World Conqueror and World Renouncer: A Study of Buddhism and Polity in Thailand against a Historical Background*. Cambridge: Cambridge University Press.

Thapar, B.K. 1957. 'Maski 1954: A Chalcolithic Site of the Southern Deccan', *Ancient India* 13: 4–142.

Thapar, R. 1961 (second edition 1997). *Asoka and the Decline of the Mauryas*. New Delhi: Oxford University Press.

———. 2013. *The Past Before Us: Historical Traditions of Early North India*. Ranikhet: Permanent Black.

Thaplyal, K.K. 2009. *A New Asokan Inscription from Ratanpurwa*. Varanasi: Jnana Pravaha.

———. 2012. *Asoka—The King and the Man*. New Delhi: Aryan Books International.

Thomas, P.K. and P.P. Joglekar. 1994. 'Holocene Faunal Studies in India', *Man and Environment* XIX (1–2): 179–203.

Tieken, H. 2012. 'The Composition of Asoka's Pillar Edict Series', in P. Olivelle, J. Leoshko, and H.P. Ray (eds), *Reimagining Asoka: Memory and History*, New Delhi: Oxford University Press, pp. 184–94.

Tiwari, S.R. 1996. 'Recent Discoveries and its Implications on History of Building at Lumbini', *Tribhuvan University Journal* XIX: 1–14.

Tod, J. 1839 (rpntd 1971). *Travels in Western India Embracing a Visit to the Sacred Mounts of the Jains and the Most Celebrated Shrines of Hindu Faith between Rajpootana and the Indus; with an Account of the Ancient City of Nehrawala*. Delhi: Oriental Publishers.

Tottoli, R. 2002. *Biblical Prophets in the Qu'ran and Muslim Literature*. Surrey: Curzon.

Trautmann, T.R. 1982. 'Elephants and the Mauryas', in S.N. Mukherjee (ed.), *India: History and Thought*. Calcutta: Subarnarekha, pp. 254–81.

Tyldesley, J. 2008. *Cleopatra: Last Queen of Egypt*. New York: Basic Books.

Vajpeyi, A. 2012. *Righteous Republic—The Political Foundation of Modern India*. Cambridge and London: Harvard University Press.

Veluthat, K. 2000. 'The Sannathi Inscriptions and the Questions they Raise', *Proceedings of the Indian History Congress*. Golden Jubilee Session 1999, Calicut, pp. 1081–6.

Verardi, G. 2002. *Excavations at Gotihawa and a Territorial Survey in Kapilavastu District of Nepal*. Lumbini: Lumbini International Research Institute.

———— and S. Coccia. 2008. 'Further Excavations at Gotihawa (1998–99)', in E.M. Raven, *South Asian Archaeology 1999*. Groningen: Egbert Forsten, pp. 254–63.

Verma, B.S. 2007. *Chirand Excavations Report 1961–64 and 1967–1970*. Patna: Directorate of Archaeology, Dept. of Youth, Art and Culture (Govt of Bihar).

Vogelsang, W. 1985. 'Early Historical Arachosia in South-East Afghanistan: Meeting-place between East and West', *Iranica Antiqua* XX: 55–99.

Waddell, L.A. 1903 (rpntd 1975). *Report on the Excavations at Pataliputra (Patna), The Palibothra of the Greeks*. Delhi: Sanskaran Prakashak.

Watters, T. 1904–5 (rpntd 2012). *On Yuan Chwang's Travels in India AD 529–645*. New Delhi: Munshiram Manoharlal Publishers Pvt. Ltd.

Wells, H.G. 1927. *The Outline of History: Being a Plain History of Life and Mankind*. London: Macmillan.

Wheeler, R.E.M. 1947–8. 'Brahmagiri and Chandravalli 1947: Megalithic and Other Cultures in the Chitaldrug District, Mysore State', *Ancient India* 4: 180–310.

————. 1968. *Flames over Persepolis*. New York: Reynal.

Winternitz, M. 1933 (rpntd 1972). *A History of Indian Literature Volume II. Buddhist Literature and Jaina Literature*. New Delhi: Oriental Books Reprint Corporation.

# Index

*Note*: 'n' stands for notes; 'f' for figures